It's the only way! And it's a pleasure with Sophie Leavitt—at the check-out counter, in the kitchen . . . and especially at the dinner table.

You won't believe you're cutting costs as you dine on savory treats such as "leftover" *Chicken Soufflé, Old Fashioned Roast Chicken,* or succulent *Breast of Lamb* with *Melt in Your Mouth Biscuits.* There are make-ahead party-time favorites such as *Chicken Breasts Italian Style,* fast and fabulous desserts such as *Homemade Pineapple Upside Down Cake, Handy Dandy Chocolate Pudding, Quickie Mix Apricot Cobbler.* Plus hundreds more recipes that will save your time and your money.

With Sophie Leavitt in your kitchen, the only left-overs will be the extra dollars in your pocket.

All New Sophie Leavitt's Penny Pincher's Cookbook

ALL NEW SOPHIE LEAVITT'S PENNY PINCHER'S COOKBOOK
A Bantam Book / published by arrangement with the author
Bantam edition / September 1980

ISBN 0-553-13329-2

Published simultaneously in the United States and Canada

Bantam Books are published by Bantam Books, Inc. Its trademark, consisting of the words "Bantam Books" and the portrayal of a bantam, is Registered in U.S. Patent and Trademark Office and in other countries. Marca Registrada. Bantam Books, Inc., 666 Fifth Avenue, New York, New York 10103.

PRINTED IN THE UNITED STATES OF AMERICA

0 9 8 7 6 5 4 3 2 1

CONTENTS

A MESSAGE TO MY FRIENDS

How far I have traveled from my first book, "Dining Out At Home," to this, my third "Penny Pincher." I have changed; you have changed; and our world has changed. Now, more than ever with so many women working, many men willingly or unwillingly are lending a hand and finding the kitchen a fine place. Our children, too—hopefully—are sharing.

Oh yes, times have changed, and we are again turning back to more nutritious foods. Is this wishful thinking? We have no money to waste; we have no time to waste; and for our health's sake we want to know and to cook the best, the healthiest foods and—being Americans—we are forever in a hurry. So my dear, dear friends—and there are so many of you—I want to share with you the abundance of good food and, hopefully, recipes that will be helpful, good tasting, penny pinching and what you need to make your lives and your family's lives happy, healthy and long.

This is the time of our lives when the new Penny Pincher comes from my heart to your hand as one friend to another.

With all my love,

Sophie Leavitt

HOW TO READ A RECIPE

You can read?!
All you need
Read it right
Read it right.
Pay attention!
Let me mention
Read it right!
Make it right!
Eat it? right!

SHOPPING TIPS

Listen to radio; read the newspapers and watch supermarket advertisements for best buys. USDA reports best buys in produce, eggs, poultry, beef and dairy products.

Read columns written by nutritionists and columnists on food articles.

Make a shopping list carefully based on your weekly meal plan and the newspaper's specials. Choose nutritional foods when making your list.

Shop early in the day if you can. Never shop when hungry. Take your list and stick to it except when there are specials when it is an advantage to change. If possible, shop without the children.

Check the cost of the store brand item against the advertised brand, as it is usually cheaper. Compare prices and quality.

Read the labels. What's in it. Read the dates. Buy the freshest!

Save coupons if it is for what you really need.

Remember, a food sale bargain is no bargain if it winds up in the garbage can!

Watch for meat and chicken sales. Look for the USDA label.

When a supermarket advertises a certain meat at cheaper prices, if you don't see it in the case, ask for it. Try buying less marbled meats. Don't pay for "fatty" meats—you pay twice—once in wealth and again in health. Fat is not protein, and you want to buy protein.

For stews and pot roasts and ground beef, buy the "Good Grade." "Good Grade" needs slow cooking, is less expensive.

When meats are too high, buy smaller amounts and add other proteins, such as less expensive eggs, beans, split peas, lentils, liver and chicken.

Buy whole chickens, and cut them up yourself. They are cheaper this way.

Don't be ashamed to buy day old bread; it's plenty fresh, and you save money.

Bread is cheaper than rolls. Be sure to buy enriched bread.

Buy cereals that you can cook. They're cheaper and healthier, because most don't have sugar. Don't buy the too sweet cereals and cookies and candies.

Buy fruits and vegetables in season. Frozen vegetables many times are "specials," so don't miss these bargains.

Watch for sales for canned fruits and vegetables. Be smart. Buy foods in the least expensive form; for instance, you get more sliced peaches in a can than peach halves.

Check prices of different cans to see which is a better buy. Check the amount of the contents in the can. Compare sizes of cans; sometimes a small can or container is less expensive than the larger ones.

Don't hesitate to return dented cans or no good dairy products that have gone bad in their wrapping.

Nonfat dry milk is a real bargain. You can bake with it and cook with it. It's a true "penny pincher."

"Know" your supermarket. Know how it is laid out and make your shopping list accordingly. Start with the household items; and end up with perishable foods and frozen foods last. For prompt, efficient service, go to your supermarket at "off peak" hours.

Try not to shop often—even just every other week if you can. You will save money if you do.

Finally, shop where you get the best bargains!

EQUIVALENTS

1 tablespoon	=3 teaspoons
1 teaspoon	=2 half teaspoons
1 teaspoon	=4 quarter teaspoons
⅓ tablespoon	=1 teaspoon
⅔ tablespoon	=2 teaspoons
1 cup	=16 tablespoons
½ cup	=8 tablespoons
¼ cup	=4 tablespoons
⅓ cup	=5 tablespoons and 1 teaspoon
⅓ cup	=16 teaspoons
⅔ cup	=½ cup plus 3 tablespoons
⅔ cup	=10 tablespoons plus 2 teaspoons
2 cups	=1 pint
2 pints	=1 quart
2 tablespoons baking powder	=1 ounce
4 teaspoons salt	=1 ounce
4 tablespoons flour	=1 ounce
4 cups flour	=1 pound
1 tablespoon dry milk	=¼ cup liquid milk
2 tablespoons dry milk	=½ cup liquid milk
4 tablespoons dry milk	=1 cup liquid milk
¼ cup dry milk	=1 cup liquid milk
½ cup dry milk	=2 cups liquid milk
8 tablespoons dry milk	=2 cups liquid milk
1 cup buttermilk	=1 cup sweet milk plus 1 tablespoon vinegar; let stand 5 minutes
1 cup whipping cream	=2 cups or more whipped cream
2 large eggs	=3 small eggs
1 cup macaroni	=2¼ cups cooked macaroni
½ pound cooked macaroni	=5 cups
⅔ cup granulated sugar	=9 tablespoons plus 2¾ teaspoons; or a scant 10 tablespoons

¾ cup granulated sugar	=12 tablespoons
1 pound granulated sugar	=2 cups sugar
6 ounces brown sugar	=1 cup packed
1 pound brown sugar	=2¼ to 2½ cups packed
1 pound 10X sugar	=3½ cups, sifted
1 tablespoon quick cooking tapioca	=1 tablespoon cornstarch; or 1⅓ to 1½ tablespoons flour
¼ stick margarine or butter	=2 tablespoons or 1 ounce
½ stick margarine or butter	=¼ cup or 4 tablespoons
1 stick margarine or butter	=½ cup or ¼ pound
2 sticks margarine or butter	=1 cup or ½ pound
4 sticks margarine or butter	=2 cups or 1 pound
1 pound shortening	=2½ cups
1 lemon	=2½ to 3 tablespoons strained lemon juice
7 ounce can tuna fish	=1⅓ cups flaked
olives, stuffed (6 ounces)	=1 cup chopped
grated orange rind (1 ounce)	=¼ cup (about)
fresh peaches (1 pound)	=2 cups sliced
potatoes (1 pound) cooked	=2¾ cups diced
spaghetti (1 pound) cooked	=8 cups cooked
fresh spinach (cooked) 1 pound	=1½ cups
6 hard cooked eggs	=2 cups chopped
mayonnaise (½ pound)	=1 cup (about)
molasses (12 ounces)	=1 cup
nuts (4 ounces)	=1 cup chopped
apples (1 pound) sliced	=3½ cups sliced
bananas, mashed (1 pound)	=2 cups
bananas (6 ounces)	=1 cup
carrots, shredded (½ pound)	=2 cups
carrots, diced (1 pound)	=3½ cups
cabbage, shredded (8 ounces)	=2 cups
cabbage, chopped fine (1 pound)	=2 cups
American cheese, grated (½ pound)	=2 cups (about)

SUBSTITUTIONS

IF YOU DON'T HAVE THIS	*SUBSTITUTE THIS*
1 teaspoon baking powder	1 teaspoon cream of tartar plus ½ teaspoon soda
1½ teaspoons cornstarch, potato starch, arrowroot starch	1 tablespoon flour
1 tablespoon cornstarch, potato starch, arrowroot starch	2 tablespoons flour
1 square (1 ounce) chocolate	3 tablespoons cocoa plus 1 tablespoon fat
2 squares (2 ounces) chocolate	6 tablespoons cocoa plus 2 tablespoons fat
3 squares (3 ounces) chocolate	9 tablespoons cocoa plus 3 tablespoons fat
1 cup cake flour	1 cup flour less 2 tablespoons
¼ cup cinnamon sugar	¼ cup granulated sugar plus 1 teaspoon cinnamon
1 cup honey	1¼ (cups sugar plus ¼ cup liquid
1 cup sour milk or buttermilk	1 cup sweet milk plus 1 tablespoon vinegar
1 cup fresh whole milk	1 cup nonfat milk plus 2 tablespoons fat
1 whole egg	2 egg yolks plus 1 tablespoon water
1 cup beef broth	¾ cup canned bouillon broth plus ¼ cup water; or 1 beef bouillon powder or cube mixed with 1 cup water
1 cup chicken broth	1 chicken bouillon powder or cube mixed with 1 cup water or 1 cup canned chicken broth
1 cup chopped, fresh tomatoes	¾ cup canned tomatoes

1 cup canned tomatoes	about 1⅓ cups cut up fresh tomatoes cooked 10 minutes
1 teaspoon oregano	½ teaspoon basil
dash of red pepper or cayenne	few drops of Tabasco
½ pound fresh mushrooms	4 ounce can mushrooms

1. MIXES

A few words about this chapter on Penny Pinching mixes. I have worked hard and long making and testing my mixes until I have perfected them. I thought it important enough to devote an entire chapter to these mixes and have included tasty, tempting recipes using them.

It is my hope that you will enjoy using them.

A Homemade Cake Mix

it's easy to make, easy to use, easy to see it's a true Penny Pincher and nutritious . . . you have enough "Mix" to make 5 different 8 × 8 inch cakes, each cake is enough for 8 portions . . . the cakes are unusually light textured, too

Put into a large container (a rubber dishpan is fine) *5 cups flour, 2 tablespoons and 2 teaspoons baking powder, 2½ teaspoons salt, 2½ cups sugar, ½ cup and 2 tablespoons non-fat dry milk, 1¼ cups oil.*

With a pastry blender mix until fine.

Store in an airtight container or a plastic bag and use within a month. Keep in the refrigerator.

Homemade Cake Mix
Vanilla Cake

good and easy

Heat oven 350°.

Grease an 8 × 8 inch square cake pan with vegetable shortening or margarine. Flour. Shake excess flour out.

Put into a large bowl *2 cups Homemade Cake Mix.*

Separate *2 large eggs.* Put the yolks in a medium bowl and the whites in a medium or large bowl. Measure *¼ cup sugar.* Set aside.

Stir the yolks with a fork, then stir in *⅓ cup and 2 tablespoons cold tap water* and *1 or 2 teaspoons vanilla.*

Add to the mix and mix until smooth.

With an electric hand beater or a rotary beater, beat the whites until foamy. Add a *pinch of salt* and *¼ teaspoon cream of tartar.* Beat until soft peak forms when you lift the beaters out. Gradually add the ¼ cup sugar. Continue to beat until you can feel no grains of sugar when you taste. Stir ¼ of the meringue into the batter. Fold, fold the rest of the meringue in.

Pour into the cake pan. Bake in the preheated 350° oven about 30 to 35 minutes until done.

Remove to a rack to cool 5 minutes. Loosen the edges of the cake with a spatula or dull knife. Turn out onto the rack. Turn over face up and let get cold.

Good, isn't it?

You can ice it if you wish, see our recipes index. Tastes good with a lemon or chocolate sauce, ice cream, or fresh strawberries are perfect with it.

Homemade Cake Mix

Orange Cake

the orange rind gives it a true orange taste

Heat oven 350°.

Grease an 8 × 8 inch square cake pan with vegetable shortening or margarine. Flour lightly. Shake excess flour out.

Separate *2 large eggs*. Put the yolks in a medium bowl and the whites in a medium or large bowl. Measure *¼ cup sugar*. Set aside. Grate *3 tablespoons orange rind*. Set aside.

Put into a large bowl *2 cups Homemade Cake Mix*. Add the grated orange rind.

Stir the yolks with a fork, then stir in *⅓ cup and 2 tablespoons cold tap water*. Add this to the cake mix and mix until smooth.

With an electric hand beater or a rotary beater, beat the whites until foamy. Add a *pinch of salt* and *¼ teaspoon cream of tartar*. Continue to beat until a soft peak forms when you lift the beaters out. Gradually add the ¼ cup sugar. Continue to beat until you feel no grains of sugar when you taste. Stir ¼ of this "meringue" into the batter to lighten it. Fold, fold the rest of the meringue in.

Pour into the cake pan. Bake in the preheated 350° oven about 30 to 35 minutes until done.

Remove to a rack. Cool 5 minutes. Loosen the edges of the cake with a spatula or a dull knife. Turn out onto the rack. Turn over face up and let get cold.

A touch of orange makes all the difference, and this is truly Penny Pinching using the rind of the orange.

Homemade Cake Mix

Marble Cake

a two tone cake that looks pretty and tastes good

Heat oven 350°.

Grease an 8 × 8 inch square cake pan with vegetable shortening or margarine. Flour lightly. Shake out excess flour.

Separate *2 large eggs.* Put the yolks in one bowl and the whites in a large bowl. Mix together *3 tablespoons sugar* with *2 tablespoons cocoa.* Set aside. Set aside *¼ cup sugar.*

Put into a large bowl *2 cups Homemade Cake Mix.*

Stir the yolks with a fork, then stir in *⅓ cup and 2 tablespoons cold tap water* and *1 teaspoon vanilla.*

Add to the mix and mix until smooth.

With an electric hand beater or a rotary beater, beat the whites until foamy. Add a *pinch of salt* and *¼ teaspoon cream of tartar.* Beat until a soft peak forms when you lift the beaters out. Gradually add the ¼ cup sugar. Continue to beat until you can feel no grains of sugar when you taste. Stir ¼ of this meringue into the batter. Fold, fold the rest of the meringue in.

Remove ¼ of the batter to a bowl. Stir in the cocoa/sugar mixture.

Pour the rest of the batter into the cake pan.

Spoon the cocoa batter on. Don't smooth it. With a dull knife swirl it into the batter. Don't over mix.

Place in 350° oven. Bake about 30 to 35 minutes.

Remove to a rack. Let stand 5 minutes. Loosen the edges with a dull knife or spatula. Turn out onto the rack. Turn over, face up and let get cold.

Pretty? yes! good? yes.

Homemade Cake Mix
Spice Cake

the spices really spice up this cake

Heat oven 350°.

Grease an 8 × 8 inch square cake pan with vegetable shortening or margarine. Flour lightly. Shake out excess flour.

Separate *2 large eggs*. Put the yolks in one bowl and the whites in a large bowl. Set aside *¼ cup sugar.*

Stir the yolks with a fork, then stir in *⅓ cup and 2 tablespoons cold tap water* and *1 teaspoon vanilla.*

Put *2 cups Homemade Cake Mix* into a large bowl. Add *½ teaspoon cinnamon, ¼ teaspoon nutmeg, ⅛ teaspoon ground cloves*. Mix with a pastry blender.

Add the yolk mixture. Mix until smooth.

With an electric hand beater or a rotary beater, beat the whites until foamy. Add a *pinch of salt* and *¼ teaspoon cream of tartar*. Continue to beat until a soft peak forms when you lift the beaters out. Gradually add the ¼ cup sugar. Continue to beat until you feel no grains of sugar when you taste. Stir ¼ of this meringue into the batter to lighten it. Fold, fold the rest of the meringue in.

Pour into the cake pan. Bake in the preheated 350° oven about 30 to 35 minutes.

Remove to a rack. Cool 5 minutes. Loosen the edges of the cake with a spatula or a dull knife. Turn out onto the rack. Turn over face up and let get cold.

Chocolate Cake From Our Homemade Cake Mix

tender and tasty, easy to make, easy to bake, easy to eat!

Heat oven 350°.

Grease and flour 1 8-inch round cake pan. Shake excess flour out.

Put into the large bowl of your electric mixer or into a large bowl and use your hand beaters, *1¾ cups Our Homemade Cake Mix, ¼ cup and 2 tablespoons sugar, ¼ cup unsweetened cocoa, 3 tablespoons vegetable shortening.*

Put *1 large egg* into a cup. Mix with a fork. Stir in *½ cup and 2 tablespoons cold tap water.*

Add to the rest of the ingredients.

Turn the mixer to low just to combine, then to highest speed and mix 2 minutes. Use a rubber spatula to get the batter into the beaters.

Pour the batter into the baking pan.

Place in the preheated 350° oven. Bake about 35 minutes. Test to see if done. Remove from oven. Let stand on rack 10 minutes. Loosen the edges. Turn out onto a rack. Turn right side up. Let cool on a rack.

Homemade Pineapple Upside Down Cake

Heat oven 350°.

Melt *⅓ cup margarine* in an 8″ × 8″ cake pan.

Sprinkle *½ cup brown sugar (packed)* evenly over the margarine.

Arrange *drained pineapple slices* on top. (Save the juice.)

Put into a large bowl *2 cups Homemade Cake Mix.*

Separate *2 large eggs.* Put whites into a large bowl and yolks into a small bowl.

Measure *¼ cup sugar.* Set aside.

Stir the yolks with a fork. Stir in *⅓ cup and 2 tablespoons pineapple juice* and *1 teaspoon vanilla.* Add to the cake mix and mix until smooth.

With an electric hand beater or a rotary beater, beat the whites until foamy. Add a *pinch of salt* and *¼ teaspoon cream of tartar.* Beat until soft peaks form when you lift the beaters out.

Gradually add the ¼ cup sugar; continue to beat until you can feel no grains of sugar when you taste it.

Stir ¼ of this meringue into the batter. Fold the rest of the meringue in. Pour into the cake pan.

Bake in preheated 350° oven about 30 to 35 minutes until done.

Remove to a rack to cool 5 minutes. Loosen the edges of the cake with a spatula or a dull knife. Turn out onto a plate. Let get cool.

Sophie's Cookie Mix

you can make all kinds of cookies from this mix without making a mess every time and it's so easy to use . . . you don't even have to run out to get milk, as it's in the mix too . . . hooray!

You need a large container. We use our faithful "Rubber Maid" round dishpan (no noise and so easy to clean) and our pastry blender to mix.

Put into the large container *8 cups flour, 10 teaspoons baking powder, 2 teaspoons salt, 3 cups sugar, 2 cups dried milk*. Mix well with a pastry blender.

Add *2 cups vegetable shortening*. Mix well until it looks very fine, almost like flour.

You can keep this one month without refrigeration and 3 months in the refrigerator or freezer.

You can make Drop Cookies from this mix and also Freezer Cookies (not Icebox).

You can make the following cookies: Vanilla, Raisin, Nut, Spice, Nutmeg, Fig, Date, Peanut Butter, Oatmeal, Chocolate Chip, Carrot or Pumpkin.

Basic Drop Cookies
From Sophie's Cookie Mix

from this basic recipe you can make these cookies: Vanilla, Raisin, Nut, Nutmeg, Spice, Fig, Date, Chocolate Chip, Orange and Cinnamon Butterscotch Cookies

Heat oven 400°.

Put *2½ cups Sophie's Cookie Mix* into a bowl.

Add *1 tablespoon grated orange rind* if you wish.

Mix *1 egg* with a fork. Stir in *¼ cup water;* and if you don't use the orange rind, add 1 teaspoon vanilla.

Stir into the "Cookie Mix."

Drop by teaspoonfuls on a preferably Teflon lined cookie sheet.

Bake in 400° oven about 8 to 10 minutes.

To make these cookies from our "Basic" recipe:

1. Vanilla: Add 1 teaspoon vanilla.

2. Nutmeg: Add ½ teaspoon nutmeg.
3. Spice: Add 1 teaspoon cinnamon, ½ teaspoon nutmeg, ¼ teaspoon ground cloves and ½ teaspoon ginger.
4. Orange: Add 2 tablespoons grated orange rind.
5. Raisin: Add ½ cup raisins, and you can add 1 tablespoon grated orange rind.
6. Nut: Add ¼ to ½ cup finely chopped nuts.
7. Date, Nut: Add ½ cup chopped dates and ¼ cup chopped nuts.
8. Fig, Nut: Add ¼ cup cut small figs and ¼ cup nuts, chopped.
9. Chocolate Chip: Add ½ cup chocolate chips.
10. Cinnamon, Butterscotch: Add ½ teaspoon to ¾ teaspoon cinnamon and ¼ cup butterscotch chips.

Basic Freezer Cookies

you can make from this basic cookie recipe: Vanilla, Nut, Spice, Peanut Butter, Nutmeg, Chocolate Chip and Orange Cookies

Heat oven 400°.

Put *2½ cups Sophie's Cookie Mix* into a bowl.

Mix *1 egg*. With your clean hands mix together. Shape into 1 roll.

Wrap in wax paper. Put in freezer overnight or until firm enough to cut.

Bake in 400° oven about 8 minutes.

To make these cookies from our "Basic" recipe:

1. Vanilla: Add 1 teaspoon vanilla.
2. Nutmeg: Add ½ teaspoon nutmeg.
3. Spice: Add ½ teaspoon cinnamon, ½ teaspoon nutmeg, ¼ teaspoon ground cloves.
4. Orange: Add 2 tablespoons grated orange rind.
5. Nut: Add ½ cup finely chopped nuts.
6. Chocolate Chip: Add ½ cup chocolate chips cut into smaller pieces.

Sophie's Cookie Mix

Peanut Butter Freezer Cookies

these are not only good, tasty cookies but also nutritious . . . when you cut back on your meat protein for the day, it's nice to have the protein in the peanut butter cookies

Heat oven 400°.

Put into a large bowl *2½ cups Sophie's Cookie Mix.*

Put *½ cup peanut butter* in a bowl.

Mix *1 egg* with a fork. Gradually, a little at a time, stir the egg into the peanut butter.

Stir in *2 tablespoons cold tap water* and *1 tablespoon oil.*

Mix well with your clean hands.

Divide in half. Mix and shape each half into a roll about 6 inches long. Cut into slices about ¼ inch thick.

You can cut these at once and bake them; or put in the freezer, then slice and bake.

Bake in preheated 400° oven about 9 to 10 minutes.

Remove the cookies to a rack to cool.

Tip: These are a little touchy. Handle carefully with a spatula when you have baked them and put on the rack to cool, or they may crumble.

Pastry Mix

With Vegetable Shortening

with vegetable shortening . . . it's a breeze to make . . . it makes excellent pies and you can use it whenever you need a pastry dough . . . it's there waiting for you to use

In a large bowl put *6½ cups flour* and *½ cup wheat germ.*

Add *2 teaspoons salt* and *1 teaspoon sugar.* Mix with a pastry blender.

Add *2⅓ cups vegetable shortening* and mix with pastry blender into large crumbs.

Put ½ of this mix to one side of the bowl, and mix the other half into fine crumbs. Combine the two crumbs. This is what helps to make crusts flaky.

Store this mix in a plastic bag in the refrigerator for 1 month or in the freezer for 3 months.

To make a 9 inch crust:
Put *1 cup Pastry Mix* into a bowl.
Add *2 tablespoons* and *2 teaspoons iced water.*
Mix into a soft ball with a fork or your hands. Over a clean surface throw from one hand to the other 20 times.
Sprinkle a little flour lightly over a clean surface.
Roll out the dough to fit an 8 or 9 inch pie plate or whatever you intend to use it for.
To make a two crust pie, double the above recipe and add water gradually as you may need less.

The Healthy Pie Crust Mix With Oil

all you have to do is add water when you are ready to make a crust

In a large bowl put *9½ cups flour, ½ cup wheat germ, 5 tablespoons dry milk, 1 tablespoon salt* and *1 teaspoon sugar.* Mix together with a pastry blender.
Add *2 cups and 2 tablespoons oil.*
Mix with the pastry blender until fine crumbs but not as fine as cornmeal.
Store in a plastic bag in the refrigerator for one month or in the freezer 3 months.

To make 1 pie crust:
Put *1 cup Pie Crust Mix* into a bowl.
Add about *2 tablespoons plus 1½ teaspoons iced water.*
Start stirring with a fork and immediately use your hands to make into a soft ball.
Over a clean surface, throw from one hand to the other.
Roll out between 2 pieces of waxed paper.
To use, lift one sheet off the crust. Pick up the dough on the wax paper and turn it over onto the pie plate. Lift off the top piece of wax paper.
Don't stretch the dough, but fit the dough into the pie plate.
For a top crust do the same, only put the dough on top of the filling; then remove the wax paper.
To pre-bake a crust, crimp 1 inch foil around the edges of the crust. Prick the crust all over with a fork to keep the

crust from ballooning up when baking. Preheat the oven 425° and bake 10 to 12 or 13 minutes.

When baking a 2 crust pie, crimp the edges of the 2 crusts together and crimp 1 inch foil over the edges and bake.

Sophie's 6 Pack Freezer Pastry Dough

you can make it once, store them in the freezer and each dough is ready to be rolled into a crust . . . these are fine crusts, easy as can be to make

Put enough water in a bowl with ice to make *1 cup icy cold water.*

With a pastry blender mix together in a large container *5 cups and 5 teaspoons flour, 7 teaspoons wheat germ, 1½ teaspoons salt* and *¼ teaspoon sugar.*

Add *1¾ cups vegetable shortening*. Mix with the pastry blender until it looks like fine crumbs (like cornmeal).

Add *¼ cup and 2 tablespoons vegetable shortening* and mix with the pastry blender to look like large crumbs. (The combination of fine and large crumbs makes for tender crusts.)

Pour 1 cup of the icy cold water into a measuring cup.

Push ⅓ of the flour mixture away from the rest.

Pour about ⅓ cup water over this ⅓ mixture and mix lightly with your hands to form a rough, soft ball. Do the same with another third; then add as much to the last ⅓ cup water over the last ⅓ flour mixture as you need to make a soft ball. Sometimes you use all the water; sometimes a little less.

Divide the 3 doughs into 6 pieces. They should be soft.

Throw one ball at a time, from one hand to the other hand, about 25 times. This trick I learned from a French woman, Yolande, who lives in Strasbourg, Alsace, and when I said, I never saw anything like that, she haughtily said, "Every French woman knows that!"

Wrap each piece of pastry dough in Saran Wrap, then in foil and freeze.

When ready to use, defrost; then roll out as usual.

Of course, you can use one or two, or whatever, without freezing them, but isn't it nice not to have to make a mess every time you want to make a pie?

Sophie's 6 Pack Freezer Dough

how to make a single or double crust . . . easy as easy can be!

Defrost one or two pie doughs, takes about 30 to 60 minutes.

Roll out as usual and make the pie you wish to make, or see Index for recipes under "H" How to Make a One Crust or a Two Crust Pie. (I didn't write the recipes here, because those of you who make the Freezer Dough have made enough pies to know how to make a pie. What you and I needed was the convenience of the recipe, which I made and is on a separate page. See Index recipe under "S"—Sophie's 6 Pack Freezer Pie Dough.)

Sophie's 6 Pack Freezer Pie Dough will be a blessing for "in a hurry pie" with no messy measuring and clean ups. It waits for you.

"Make And Bake" Mix

for Oven Fried Chicken or for any food you need "flavored crumbs" . . . and! . . . you know exactly what's in it, and there's absolutely no artificial flavor or color! . . . and you will save money—"Penny Pinch" at the same time and it's so easy to make

Mix together with a pastry blender, *1 cup bread crumbs, ½ cup flour, 1 teaspoon cornstarch, 1¾ teaspoons onion powder, 1¾ teaspoons garlic powder, 1¾ teaspoons poultry seasoning, 1 teaspoon paprika, 1¼ teaspoons salt and 1 teaspoon sugar.*

Add *1 tablespoon and 2 teaspoons vegetable oil.*

With your clean fingers mix until well combined. You will feel no oil—just crumbs.

Store in a screw-top jar.

Can be kept in the refrigerator or freezer.

To save time and work make the Mix as follows: use 3 bowls.

Put in each bowl all the ingredients as above.

Mix each separately and store in a separate plastic bag. Use as needed.

White Sauce Mix

Mix together with a pastry blender 1 cup flour, 1 cup oil or margarine, 4 cups plus 5 tablespoons dry milk. You can store this in a plastic bag in the refrigerator or freezer for 3 months and use as needed.

To make the following white sauces you cook:
½ cup Mix plus 1 cup water or broth = 1 cup thin sauce
¾ cup Mix plus 1 cup water or broth = 1 cup medium sauce
1 cup Mix plus 1 cup water or broth = 1 cup thick sauce

Tuna Souffle

made with our White Sauce Mix it's easier than ever to make

Heat oven 400°.

Grease with margarine a 2 quart heatproof glass casserole. Sprinkle some *grated cheese or seasoned crumbs* over it. Shake out excess.

Set aside 2 large bowls.

Drain *1 can (7½ ounces) tuna fish*. Shred with a pastry blender or two forks.

Chop fine *1 medium onion* and *¼ cup celery*. Cook, stir in heated skillet with *2 tablespoons oil*. Put a lid on. Turn heat to low. Cook about 10 minutes until onions are soft and clear.

Drain, add the onions and celery to the tuna fish. Mix gently and set aside.

Separate *4 eggs*. Put yolks in a small bowl. Put the 4 whites and *1 extra white* (5 whites) into a large bowl.

Put into a saucepan the 1 cup of the white sauce mix. Stir in *1 cup water*. Place on medium heat. Cook, stir, take off and on heat until it gets thick. Be sure to stir so there are no lumps. Takes about 5 to 10 minutes. Take off heat. Add *salt and pepper* to taste.

Pour into a large bowl. Stir in 1 yolk; then 1 at a time stir in the other 3 yolks. Stir in the tuna mixture.

With an electric hand beater or a rotary beater, beat the 5 whites until foamy. Add a *pinch of salt* and *¼ teaspoon cream of tartar*. Beat until stiff (when you lift the beaters out, the whites in the bowl will form a stiff straight peak).

Take about ¼ of the whites and mix into the other mixture to lighten it. Fold the rest of the whites into the mixture quickly so as not to deflate it.

Quickly spoon into the casserole. Place immediately in the 400° oven. Turn heat to 375° immediately. Bake 30 minutes until done. Serve at once.

Brush On Browning Sauce Mix

wonderful to broil lamb chops or steaks . . . keep it on hand in the refrigerator

Mix together *1 tablespoon and 1 teaspoon onion powder, 1 tablespoon and 1 teaspoon garlic powder, 1 tablespoon and 1 teaspoon paprika, ½ teaspoon dry mustard, 2 tablespoons soy sauce, 3 tablespoons and 1 teaspoon Worcestershire Sauce, 2 tablespoons oil, 1 tablespoon and 1 teaspoon cold tap water* and *1 teaspoon sugar.*

Sophie's Homemade Dried Onion Mix

to make delicious onion soups and to use as a flavoring in many dishes, also as a dip . . . this is something like Lipton's Dried Onion Soup Mix, only we don't use any artificial flavors

If you have not "toasted" your dried onions, do this:

Put *3 tablespoons minced, dried onions* into a small skillet.

On medium heat, cook, stir about 3 minutes without burning. (A tip is to lift the skillet off and on the heat while you cook, stir.)

Cool.

This is called "toasted dried minced onions."

Dried Onion Soup Mix

Mix together in a large bowl *2 Instant Onion Broth Powders, 2 Instant Beef Broth Powders, ¼ teaspoon sugar, ¼ teaspoon celery salt, ½ teaspoon oil* and the *3 tablespoons "toasted dried minced onions."*

This is our "Homemade Dried Onion Soup Mix."

It makes a delightful, easy soup, too. (See Index for recipe.)

It is also nice with baked chicken or beef, or in chicken or beef casserole dishes.

To make a large amount of this Mix, repeat each ingredient in 4 separate bowls; then store in 4 separate plastic bags in refrigerator.

How to Make "Toasted Instant Minced Onions"

makes an ordinary taste into a "something special" taste, or to transfer Cinderella into a Princess

Put your *jar or can of instant minced onion* in a large skillet (4.25 ounces).

Cook, stir with a wooden spoon, first on high heat, then turn to next heat, medium high, taking the skillet off and on the heat, so the onions do not burn or brown. Take off and on heat about 5 minutes until the onions turn to a golden brown color. Beautiful! And the flavor is enhanced!

Be careful; don't burn. Keep taking the skillet off and on the heat. Also, when golden brown, turn immediately onto a large plate to cool.

When cold, put back in container it came in. Check, we did, and bought the largest size we could find because we saved money, and this is a good, flavorsome product, which we use often. And to you fresh onion lovers, we use fresh onions most of the time, of course, but sometimes these toasted dried onions "hit the spot" for taste, too!

"Handy Dandy" Pudding Mix

you have it handy to make vanilla pudding, chocolate pudding, pumpkin pudding, butterscotch pudding and peanut butter pudding . . . this is a "handy dandy" mix if there are children around as well as the "over sixty" crowd

With a pastry blender mix together well *1½ cups sugar, 1½ cups cornstarch, 1½ teaspoons salt* and *8 cups nonfat dry milk.*

Put into a plastic bag. Keep in a cool place. If you have room, keep in the refrigerator.

Use in one month if kept in refrigerator, or freezer three months.

Handy Dandy Peanut Butter Pudding

from our "Handy Dandy" Pudding Mix

Put into a saucepan *1½ cups "Handy Dandy" Pudding Mix.*

Stir in *2½ cups cold tap water.*

Gradually stir in *¼ cup peanut butter.* If necessary, strain so there are no pieces.

Cook, stir on medium high heat until it comes to a simmer and gets thick, takes about 10 minutes. Cook, stir 2 minutes.

Take off heat. Stir in *1 tablespoon margarine.*

Stir in *1 teaspoon vanilla.*

Pour or spoon into 4 or 5 custard cups. Put a small piece of Saran Wrap right on top of each pudding to keep a skin from forming.

Place in refrigerator.

Handy Dandy Vanilla Pudding

it's just what it says

Put into a saucepan *1½ cups "Handy Dandy" Pudding Mix.*

Stir in *2½ cups cold tap water.*

Cook, stir on medium high heat until it comes to a simmer and gets thick, takes about 10 minutes. Cook, stir 2 minutes.

Take off heat. Stir in *1 tablespoon margarine.*

Stir in *1 teaspoon vanilla.*

Pour or spoon into 4 or 5 custard cups. Put a small piece of Saran Wrap right on top of each pudding to keep a skin from forming.

Place in refrigerator.

Handy Dandy Chocolate Pudding

from our "Handy Dandy" Pudding Mix

Put into a saucepan *1½ cups "Handy Dandy" Pudding Mix.*

Stir in *⅓ cup cocoa* and *¼ cup sugar.*

Slowly stir in *2½ cups water.*

On medium high heat, cook, stir; take off and on heat until it comes to a simmer and thickens, takes about 10 minutes.

Cook, stir slowly about 2 minutes.

Take off heat. Stir in *1 tablespoon margarine.*

Stir in *1 teaspoon vanilla.*

Pour or spoon into 4 or 5 custard cups. Put a piece of Saran Wrap right on top of each pudding to keep a skin from forming.

Place in refrigerator.

Handy Dandy Butterscotch Pudding

from our homemade "Handy Dandy" Pudding Mix

Put into a saucepan *1½ cups "Handy Dandy" Pudding Mix.*

Stir in *2½ cups cold tap water.*

Cook, stir on medium heat until it comes to a simmer and thickens, takes about 10 minutes. Cook, stir 2 minutes.

Take off heat. Stir in *1 tablespoon margarine.*

Stir in *½ teaspoon "Imitation Maple Flavoring."*

Pour or spoon into 4 or 5 custard cups. Put a small piece of Saran Wrap right on top of each pudding to keep a skin from forming.

Place in refrigerator.

Handy Dandy Pumpkin Pudding

from our "Handy Dandy" Pudding Mix

Put into a saucepan *1½ cups "Handy Dandy" Pudding Mix.*

Stir in *½ teaspoon ground ginger, 1 teaspoon cinnamon, ½ teaspoon nutmeg, ¼ teaspoon ground cloves.*

Stir in *2½ cups cold tap water.*

Gradually stir in *1 cup canned or fresh pumpkin.*

Cook, stir on medium high heat until it comes to a simmer and thickens, takes about 10 minutes. Cook, stir 2 minutes.

Remove from heat. Stir in *1 tablespoon margarine.*

Pour or spoon into 4 or 5 custard cups. Put a small piece of Saran Wrap right on top of each pudding to keep a skin from forming.

Place in refrigerator.

Our Chocolate Syrup Mix

make it so you have it on hand when you need it

Mix together *1 cup cocoa* with *2½ cups sugar* and a *pinch of salt.*

Stir in *2 cups water.* Boil 3 minutes.

Stir in *2 teaspoons vanilla.* Cool.

Refrigerate.

One Cup Chocolate Milk

Stir *3 tablespoons of "Our Chocolate Syrup"* into *1 cup milk* to make 1 cup of cocoa.

Instant Cocoa Mix

want a hot cup of cocoa? . . . just reach into your jar of cocoa mix and add hot water

Cocoa Mix

Put into a large bowl *1 pound instant nonfat dry milk or 5 packages (3.2 ounces each), ¾ cup cocoa, 1 cup sugar.*

Mix together well with a pastry blender or push through a strainer and mix well.

That's all there is to it! Store in a jar with a tight lid.

How to Make 1 Cup Cocoa from Cocoa Mix

Put *⅓ cup Cocoa Mix* into a cup. Stir in *a little cold water* to make a paste.

Carefully fill the cup with *boiling water.* Stir slowly and drink.

To Make 4 Cups of Cocoa

Put *1⅓ cups Cocoa Mix* in a saucepan or whatever.
Stir in a *little cold water* to make a paste.
Stir in *1 quart boiling water.*
Tip: Why did I say use a saucepan? Because a saucepan has a handle which makes it easier to hold and pour. You might use a heat-proof pitcher, like a Pyrex one, if you have it. To me it's safer to make 1 cup at a time. How about that?

Chocolate Sauce Mix

Mix together *1 cup cocoa* with *2 cups sugar* and a *pinch of salt.*
Stir in *3 tablespoons vegetable oil or margarine.*
Stir in *2 cups water.* Cook, stir 6 minutes.
Cool.
Refrigerate.
Use on plain cakes, ice cream or whenever you need a chocolate sauce.

Maple Syrup Mix

Bring to a boil *¾ cup water* with *1½ cups corn syrup.*
Add *½ teaspoon "Maple Flavoring" or "Mapeline."*
Stir well. Cool.
This will make a pint of "Maple Flavored Syrup" at little cost.

Brown Sugar Syrup Mix

you "know" what's in your syrup if you make it yourself

Stir in *2 cups water* to *2 cups brown sugar* in a saucepan.
Bring to a boil.
Cook, stir until the sugar is melted completely and there are no lumps of sugar in the syrup.

Store in a bottle in the refrigerator.

Use with pancakes, waffles, French toast, or whenever you want some dark syrup.

Golden Caramel Syrup Mix

a good taste and a good way to save money

In a saucepan put *1 box (1 pound, which is about 2¾ cups) light brown sugar* and *2⅔ cups water.*

Cook, stir and bring to a boil, takes about 10 minutes.

Turn heat to medium low or low, depending on your stove, and cook, stir about 10 minutes to form a liquid syrup.

Cool, store in refrigerator.

We keep a plastic squeeze bottle filled with this syrup in the refrigerator ready to use on pancakes, waffles and French toast or whenever we want a caramel syrup. The squeeze bottle puts the syrup on the pancake, not the plate, saves waste and is easy to wash.

Tip: If you have used your brown sugar to make cookies or whatever and are left with some that has become hard as a brick, make some syrup of it by mixing altogether 1 cup water and 1 cup hard lumps of brown sugar. Cook, stir until it comes to a boil. Turn heat to low. Cook, stir now and then about 10 minutes to form a liquid syrup. Remove from heat. Cool. Store in refrigerator.

Snick Snacks

Put in a large soup kettle or other large container: *3 cups Kix, 3 cups Cheerios, 3 cups puffed rice, 3 cups thin pretzel sticks* (broken in thirds), *1 jar (7¼ ounces) dry roasted sunflower seeds, 1 jar (1 pound) dry roasted unsalted peanuts, 1 jar (8 ounces) dry, roasted soy nuts, 3½ teaspoons garlic powder, 3 teaspoons onion powder, 2 teaspoons celery seeds* and *1½ to 2 teaspoons salt.*

With a rotary beater mix well *2 cups oil* with *¼ cup Worcestershire Sauce.* Sprinkle over the cereal mixture. Mix with 2 large spoons.

With a rotary beater mix *½ cup oil* with 1½ tablespoons Worcestershire Sauce.

Put *2 cups spoon size shredded wheat* in a large bowl.

Sprinkle this oil mix over it, mixing with 2 spoons to impregnate the shredded wheat.

Add to the cereal mixture and mix together.

Put into 2 shallow roasting pans in a 200° oven. You can put 1 in at a time if you only have 1 oven.

Let bake 2 hours, mixing 6 times at least.

Let get cold.

Store in refrigerator or in freezer for a longer time.

The New "Pancake Mix"

because we wanted you not only to have the "convenience" and good taste of our "Quickie Mix" in our last Penny Pincher, we added "oil" the unsaturated fat, rather than vegetable shortening . . . now we again change our recipe to get more nutrition and yet the same good taste and good texture . . . we have added Wheat Germ . . . please, make this "Pancake Mix" and keep it on hand, "easy and ready to use" when you want to make pancakes . . . and it's nutritious . . . no additives, no preservatives . . . just plain good taste for good health!

Mix with a pastry blender in a large container, *7½ cups flour, ½ cup wheat germ, 3 cups instant nonfat dry milk, 5 tablespoons baking powder, 1 tablespoon salt* and *¼ cup sugar* until well blended.

Cut in *1½ cups vegetable oil* with the pastry blender, 2 knives, or your clean fingers. Mixture will look crumbly.

Store in a tightly covered container. We use 2 plastic pitchers that have a wide opening and an easy to close top and are very easy to hold and a breeze to wash. Also, they last forever . . . we've had ours for years and years.

It is necessary to refrigerate this Pancake Mix. Use within a month in the refrigerator; or in the freezer it will keep 3 months.

Tip: We use a "Rubber Maid" round dishpan, which is inexpensive, easy to clean, makes no noise and will last and last.

Pancake Mix Pancakes

Measure *2 cups Pancake Mix* into a bowl.

Put *2 eggs* into another bowl. Stir eggs with a fork; then

stir in *1 cup water*. Add to the Pancake Mix; mix just to combine. Let stand 10 minutes.

For those who have an electric stove, heat the griddle or skillet hot on medium heat. This takes about 8 to 10 minutes or 3 to 4 minutes on a gas stove. You don't need to grease the skillet. Tip: Don't overheat or underheat the skillet or griddle, as pancakes will then stick. You can tell whether the skillet or griddle is hot enough by dropping a few drops of water on, and if they skitter around . . . it's ready. This sounds hard, once you do it, you will see how easy it is. It's easier to do than to read all of this!

Spoon or pour the batter onto the heated skillet or griddle. When bubbles appear, turn the pancakes over and bake.

Serve the pancakes hot with syrup or jelly. If the jelly is your homemade strawberry preserves, you can proudly serve it to the President of the United States, or, better still, to that nice husband of yours.

Tip: As soon as the children are old enough, let them make the Pancake Mix . . . and the pancakes. Your husband? . . . that depends! If he has other virtues, don't push him!

Buttermilk Pancakes

Substitute *buttermilk* for the water and add *¼ teaspoon soda.* The rest is the same as our pancake recipe.

Pancake Mix Waffles

Put *2 cups Pancake Mix* into a bowl.

With a fork mix *2 eggs*. Stir in *1 cup water.*

Mix into the Pancake Mix just to combine. That's all there is to it!

Heat the waffle iron hot.

Pour in enough batter but not so much it will run over. The batter always spreads a little while it cooks. It's messy to clean an electric waffle iron.

Serve the waffle hot with syrup or jelly.

Our waffles are especially tasty and nutritious.

2. QUICKIE MIX AND RECIPES

The Original "Quickie Mix"

to make biscuits, muffins, pancakes, cakes, coffee cakes, quick breads

Mix with a pastry blender or strain *8 cups enriched flour, 3 cups instant nonfat dry milk, 5 tablespoons baking powder, 1 tablespoon salt, ¼ cup sugar* until well blended.

Cut in *2 cups vegetable shortening or 1½ cups vegetable oil* with a pastry blender, 2 knives or your fingers.

Mix will look crumbly.

Store in a tightly covered container. It is not necessary to refrigerate, but keep in a cool place. Use within a month. You can keep it in refrigerator if you have room.

Makes 11 cups.

We have included this recipe just in case someone, for whatever reason, does not want to use wheat germ.

Quickie Mix Pancakes

there's only one trouble with these . . . they keep asking for more!

Measure *2 cups Quickie Mix* into a bowl.

Put *2 eggs* into another bowl. Stir eggs with a fork; then stir in *1 cup water.* Add to the Quickie Mix; mix just to combine. Let stand 10 minutes.

For those who have an electric stove, heat the griddle or skillet hot on medium heat. This takes about 8 to 10 minutes or 3 to 4 minutes on a gas stove. You don't need to grease the skillet. Tip: Don't overheat or underheat the skillet or griddle, as pancakes will then stick. You can tell whether the skillet or griddle is hot enough by dropping a few drops of water on, and if they skitter around . . . it's ready.

Spoon or pour the batter onto the heated skillet or griddle. When bubbles appear, turn the pancakes over and bake.

Serve the pancakes hot with syrup or jelly.

Buttermilk Pancakes

Substitute buttermilk for the water and add ¼ teaspoon soda. The rest is the same as our pancake recipe.

Quickie Mix Waffles

a "Weekend Special" or what's better for a Sunday morning breakfast?

Put *2 cups Quickie Mix* into a bowl.

With a fork mix *2 eggs*. Stir in *1 cup water*.

Mix into the Quickie Mix just to combine. That's all there is to it!

Heat the waffle iron hot.

Pour in enough batter but not so much it will run over. The batter always spreads a little while it cooks. It's messy to clean an electric waffle iron.

Serve the waffle hot with syrup or jelly.

Our waffles are especially tasty and nutritious.

Biscuits From Quickie Mix

they're delicious and so easy to make

Heat oven 450°.

Put into a large bowl *2 cups Quickie Mix*.

Gradually, a little at a time, with a fork, stir in as much of *½ cup water* as you need to make a dough that is soft but not sticky.

Sprinkle a *little flour* on a surface or board.

Lightly shape the dough smooth.

Roll or pat ½ or ¾ inch thick.

Cut with a floured biscuit cutter or a glass, and don't wiggle it; or cut into squares with a dull knife.

Place the biscuits on an ungreased baking sheet.

Bake in preheated 450° oven about 10 to 15 minutes, depending on the size of your biscuits.

Remove from oven.

Biscuits taste delicious eaten hot.

Tip: If you wiggle the cutter, the biscuits will look like the "leaning tower of Pisa"!

Quickie Mix Drop Biscuits

when you're in a hurry this is it!

Heat oven 450°.
Put into a large bowl *2 cups Quickie Mix*. With a fork, stir in *½ cup water.*
Drop by spoonfuls on a cookie sheet.
Bake in 450° oven about 10 or more minutes until lightly browned and done.
Serve hot.

Ring Around Biscuits

looks pretty, tastes good

Heat oven 450°.
Open *1 can (15½ ounces) Libby's Sloppy Joe* and *1 can (15 ounces) dried black-eye peas.* Place the peas in a strainer and shake to remove the liquid. Add the peas to the Sloppy Joe and mix together gently. Cook *½ cup diced onions* in *2 tablespoons oil* until soft and clear. Add to the Sloppy Joe and mix.
Make biscuits with *1 cup Quickie Mix.* With a fork stir as much of *⅓ cup milk* as needed to make a soft, but not sticky, dough. Shape into a ball. Roll out. Cut with a small biscuit cutter.
Cook, stir the Sloppy Joe mixture until it comes to a boil.
Pour into a deep, fireproof dish.
Arrange a ring of biscuits on top.
Sprinkle a little paprika on top.
Bake in 450° oven about 10 to 12 minutes until biscuits are browned nicely. Eat while hot.

Crazy Cheese Biscuits

they look like something out of Mars but taste heavenly ...

Heat oven 450°.
Cut into very small pieces *½ cup Velveeta Cheese.*
Add to *3 cups Quickie Mix.*
Stir in *½ cup and 2 tablespoons water.*
It will be sticky. Let stand 3 minutes.

With a spoon and a rubber spatula put the dough onto a clean well-floured surface.

Flour your clean hands well and shape into a ball. Throw ball hard from one hand to the other 25 times.

Pat or roll out into a "round."

Cut with a biscuit cutter or a glass ½ or ¾ inch thick.

Put on ungreased cookie sheet.

Bake in the preheated 450° oven about 10 minutes, more if needed, depending on the thickness of your biscuits. Biscuits should be a golden color, not browned hard. The cheese runs out and tastes very good.

Quickie Mix Biscuits With Bran

these are super nutritious and just as easy to make as they're easy to eat . . . they already have wheat germ in them

Heat oven 450°.

Put oven rack on second shelf from the top heat in electric stove. (This browns the top of the biscuits better in my stoves, as heat rises to the top.)

Put *1 cup Quickie Mix* into a large bowl.

Add *2 tablespoons bran* and mix together.

Pour *¼ cup water* in. Mix together with a spoon. Let stand 3 minutes.

Sprinkle a clean surface with *flour.*

Spoon or scoop with your hands the sticky dough onto the flour. Sprinkle a little flour on top of the dough so you can handle it. Mix with your hands to make into a ball. Throw the ball hard from one hand to the other about 25 times. Smooth in your hands.

Place on the floured surface and smooth the ball of dough into a "round" the thickness you wish your biscuits to be. We usually have them about ¼ inch high or ½. You can even let them be 1 inch if you wish.

Cut with a biscuit cutter. We usually have a 2-inch biscuit cutter or a glass. If we want larger biscuits, we usually double this recipe. Cut the biscuits without wiggling the cutter.

Place on a cookie sheet. Don't grease. Bake in 450° oven about 8 to 10 minutes. The smaller ones bake in 8 minutes. Stoves vary in their degree of heat, so once you bake them, you'll know which heat and how long to bake.

All this talk is for the beginner cook, whether going to school, college, boy, girl, man or woman—or young bride. The rest of you can just make the biscuits and let the "talk" go.

Rich Quickie Mix Muffins

leaves a wonderful taste in your mouth

Heat oven 400° (hot oven).

Grease muffin pans with *margarine* or use paper baking cups. (We use 2 paper cups for each muffin and place on a cookie sheet.)

With a pastry blender mix together quickly *2½ cups Quickie Mix* with *1 tablespoon sugar* and *3 tablespoons margarine*. Don't overmix. Margarine should be size of large crumbs.

Mix *1 egg* with a fork. Stir in *½ cup water*. Add to Quickie Mix. Using fork, barely mix, just until flour is moistened. Batter will be lumpy. (This makes tender muffins.)

For easy filling use ¼ measuring cup or spoon to fill muffin cups ¾ full.

Bake in 400° oven about 20 to 25 minutes. (In our oven we bake 20 minutes.)

Remove from oven to rack. Let stand 5 minutes before removing from paper cups. If using muffin pans, to prevent muffins from getting soggy, loosen muffins immediately from pans, tilt or remove.

The best way to eat muffins is while hot or warm.

Muffins freeze well.

Muffins reheat well. Wrap in foil. Reheat in 400° oven 5 to 10 minutes, 5 for defrosted muffins, 10 for frozen ones.

Raisin Muffins

the good tasting way to get some needed iron

Heat oven 400° (hot oven).

Grease muffin pans with margarine or use paper baking cups.

With a pastry blender mix together quickly *2½ cups Quickie Mix* with *1 tablespoon sugar* and *2 tablespoons mar-*

garine until margarine is size of large crumbs. Gently mix in *½ cup raisins.*

Mix *1 egg* with a fork. Stir in *½ cup water.* Add to Quickie Mix. Using fork, barely mix—just until flour is moistened. Batter will be lumpy. (This makes tender muffins.)

For easy filling use ¼ measuring cup to fill greased muffin pans about ¾ full. (If using paper baking cups, put on a cookie sheet.)

Bake in 400° oven about 20 to 25 minutes.

Remove from oven to rack. Let stand 5 minutes before removing from paper cups. If using muffin pans, to prevent muffins from getting soggy, loosen muffins immediately from pans, tilt or remove.

The best way to eat muffins is while hot or warm.

Muffins freeze well.

Muffins reheat well. Wrap in foil. Reheat in 400° oven 5 to 10 minutes, 5 for defrosted muffins, 10 for frozen ones.

Blueberry Muffins

to wake up to "Blueberry Muffins" is like waking up to Spring . . . these are made with your "Quickie Mix"

Heat oven 400° (hot oven).

Grease muffin pans with *margarine;* or use paper baking cups. (We prefer these.)

Drain well *1 cup wild blueberries, canned or frozen, or fresh blueberries.*

With a pastry blender mix together quickly *2½ cups Quickie Mix* with *2 tablespoons sugar, 2 tablespoons margarine* just until margarine is the size of large crumbs.

With a spoon gently fold in the blueberries.

Mix *1 egg* with a fork. Stir in *½ cup water.* Add to Quickie Mix. Using fork, barely mix—just until flour is moistened. Batter will be lumpy.

Fill each cup ¾ full. (If using paper baking cups, put on a cookie sheet.)

Bake in 400° oven about 20 to 25 minutes.

Remove from oven. Let stand 5 minutes before removing if using paper cups. If you use muffin pans, to prevent muffins from getting soggy, loosen muffins immediately from pan, tilt or remove.

Muffins freeze well.

Muffins reheat well. Wrap in foil. Reheat in 400° oven 10 minutes for frozen and 5 minutes for defrosted.

Tip: We have found it is better to use 2 paper baking cups instead of 1 for each muffin—keeps the bottom from browning too much.

Herbed Cheese Bread

made with Quickie Mix, it is so good I had to add it

Grease and flour an 8-inch square or round cake pan.

Preheat oven 400°.

Mix *2 cups Quickie Mix with 1 tablespoon sugar, 1 tablespoon instant dry onions, ¼ teaspoon dried dill, ¼ teaspoon dried basil leaves.*

Mix *1 egg* with a fork. Stir in *¼ cup oil* and *¾ cup cold tap water.*

Add to the Quickie Mixture. Don't stir, just mix together to combine.

Spoon into the cake pan. Sprinkle *½ cup shredded or grated aged (for a better taste, stronger taste) Cheddar cheese* over the top.

Bake in the preheated 400° oven about 25 minutes.

The cheese topping will be beautifully brown and crusty.

Serve warm.

Batter Bread

different and delicious . . . goes lovely with casseroled chicken dishes; in fact, any kind of chicken

Heat oven 425°.

Grease a 9-inch, deep pie dish well with *margarine.*

Put into a bowl *1 cup Quickie Mix.*

Separate *2 eggs.*

Mix the egg yolks with a fork; then stir in *½ cup cold water.*

Mix into the Quickie Mix; don't overmix.

With a rotary beater, beat the 2 egg whites until stiff.

Fold the egg whites into the batter.

Pour the batter into the greased, deep pie dish.

Bake in 425° oven about 15 minutes until the Batter Bread is golden brown and done.

Carefully loosen the Batter Bread from the baking dish, but do not take out.

Cut into slices and serve with your chicken dishes while hot.

Batter Bread is always welcome!

Date Nut Dessert Bread

with some Philadelphia Cream Cheese, this is a "want more" dessert . . . you will never miss the sugar we didn't put in

Grease and flour a 9 × 5 inch loaf pan.

Preheat oven 400°.

Cut with scissors or chop *¾ cup dates.*

Chop *½ cup nuts.*

Put into a bowl *2 cups Quickie Mix, ¼ cup sugar, ½ cup chopped nuts, ¾ cups chopped dates.* Mix with a pastry blender.

Mix *1 egg* with a fork. Stir in *½ cup water.*

Stir into the Quickie Mixture to blend.

Pour into the loaf pan.

Bake in 400° oven about 30 minutes.

Remove to a rack to cool 3 minutes, then remove from pan to the rack to cool.

Tip: To make something special for a "special somebody," soak the chopped dates in Sherry or Brandy for a day or two before using.

Pumpkin Spice, Raisin Dessert Bread

this is not just for Halloween or Thanksgiving . . . you can give thanks you made it anytime

Preheat oven 400°.

Grease and flour a 9½ × 5½ inch loaf pan.

Put into a bowl *2 cups Quickie Mix, ½ cup sugar, 1 teaspoon cinnamon, ½ teaspoon nutmeg, ½ teaspoon ground cloves* and *½ cup raisins.* Mix with a pastry blender.

Mix *1 egg* with a fork. Stir in *1 cup fresh cooked or canned pumpkin.*

Add to the Quickie Mixture. Mix about one minute.

Pour into the loaf pan.
Bake in 400° oven about 30 minutes.
Remove to a rack to cool 3 minutes, then remove it from the pan to a rack to cool.

Corn Bread

with Quickie Mix, which is ready "quick"

Heat oven 425°.
Mix *1 cup Quickie Mix* with *¼ teaspoon salt* and *1 cup cornmeal.*
Mix *2 eggs* with a fork. Stir in *1 cup milk.*
Add to the Quickie Mix mixture. Mix just to combine. It will look lumpy.
Spoon into an 8-inch baking pan. Bake in preheated 425° oven about 20 minutes.
Remove to a rack to cool.
We like this served hot.

Quickie Mix Egg Dumplings

these are light and fluffy

Put *1 cup Quickie Mix* into a bowl.
Mix *1 egg* with a fork. Stir in *1 tablespoon and 1½ teaspoons cold tap water.* Add to the Quickie Mix, barely mix just to moisten.
Bring the soup or stew on low heat to a slow boil (not fast) just so it steams.
Drop the dumplings in by spoonfuls, dipping the spoon in the hot liquid first. Cover.
Let steam without removing the lid 12 minutes.
The dumplings will be light and fluffy.

Chicken and Dumplings

everybody likes chicken and dumplings . . . this is a "quickie" recipe because the dumplings are "Quickie Mix" dumplings

You can do this part the day before or right before, if you wish.

Cut up a *3 or 3½ pound fryer*. Put into a deep casserole that has a lid.

Add *4 or 5 cups cold water, 1 medium onion,* a *bunch of celery tops or 1 stalk celery, 1 carrot* cut into thirds and *1 teaspoon salt.*

Bring to a simmer. Cover. Turn heat to low. Simmer about 45 minutes or until chicken is tender but not overcooked.

Remove chicken and vegetables to a plate. Put a paper towel in a strainer over a large bowl and strain the broth. It will be clear. Remove the fat from the broth.

Taste to see if any more salt is needed.

Put 4 cups broth back into the cleaned casserole.

Remove the skin and bones from the chicken. Cut the chicken into pieces with a sharp scissors. Put the chicken and the vegetables back into the broth. Heat until hot and bubbling.

The Dumplings: Put 1 cup *Quickie Mix* into a bowl.

Mix *1 egg* with a fork. Stir in *¼ and 2 tablespoons water.* Add to the Quickie Mix and barely mix.

Dip a tablespoon into the boiling broth; then dip the spoon into the batter. (The batter will not stick to the spoon.)

Drop by spoonfuls into the boiling chicken stew until all are added. Cover; turn heat to low; cook 12 minutes.

Don't remove cover until 12 minutes are up.

When you serve the chicken and dumplings, sprinkle some finely minced parsley on top. Good eating!

Sesame Tiny Quickie Mix

Bread Sticks

nice to nibble on or fine as a snack . . . children and "you know who" love them . . . especially to eat with chicken

Heat oven 425°.

Put *1 cup Quickie Mix* into a bowl.

Spread *1 teaspoon sesame seeds* over a large plate.

Make this "Egg Wash" if you want a shiny look: Put *1 egg yolk* into a saucer. With a fork stir in *2 teaspoons cold water.*

Spread 3 sheets of foil over a cookie sheet.

Put *1 teaspoon margarine* on a plate.

With a fork stir *3 tablespoons cold tap water* into the Quickie Mix. Make into a ball that cleans the bowl. Throw hard from one hand to the other 25 times. Make into a smooth ball. Cut in half. Continue to cut each half into halves until you have 32 pieces. With your clean hands roll each piece into a stick, being careful not to have it thicker in the middle. These sticks are about 2 inches long.

If you don't want to use the "Egg Wash," do this; it's very good, too.

Lightly smear your hands with a little of *1 teaspoon margarine.* Lightly roll each stick in your margarined hands, then lightly into the sesame seeds. Place on the foiled cookie sheet. Continue until all are done.

Put into preheated 425° oven. Bake about 15 minutes. You can check at 12 minutes if you wish.

Tip: For a glossy look, instead of using the margarine, dip the sticks, one at a time, into the Egg Wash, then into the sesame seeds.

Place on the foiled cookie sheets.

Place in preheated 425° oven. Bake about 8 or more minutes, depending on your stove. Remove to a rack to cool.

Homemade Baked Roll Stuffed With Beef

this is a wonderful way to use your "Ready Cooked" or "Ready Roasted" beef . . . it's a spectacular dish to serve at a buffet dinner . . . served with hot soup, such as a vegetable soup, you don't have to cook any extra vegetables . . . or you can have a bowl of mushroom sauce to serve with the baked rolls . . . let's begin!

Put *enough of your "Ready Cooked" beef* through the grinder to make *3 cups.* Put into a bowl. Add *4 tablespoons chopped parsley, 1 jar (2 ounces) chopped pimentos,* drained, *½ teaspoon salt* to taste, *1 teaspoon onion powder, 6 tablespoons Hellman's Mayonnaise* and *pepper* to taste. Mix together well.

Put *4 cups Quickie Mix* into a bowl.

Add *1 can (10¾ ounces) Cream of Mushroom Soup* and mix. Let stand 5 minutes.

With your floured clean hands, make the dough into a soft ball.

Throw the dough ball from one hand to the other hand 25 times.

Put on a clean floured surface. Roll into a rectangle 15 × 11 inches.

Smear a *little margarine* over the dough.

Spoon the seasoned meat over the dough.

Starting at the long end, roll up. Put on a cookie sheet. Curve the roll into a half moon shape. With your sharp scissors, cut the dough from the outside at 1 inch intervals, turning the dough over a little. This makes it look pretty after it is baked.

Make an Egg Wash by stirring *1 teaspoon water* into an *egg yolk*. Brush the dough with the Egg Wash. This will make it bake into a beautiful shiny brown color.

Bake about 45 minutes in 375° oven.

Crescent Ham Roll

baked in a crust . . . it's even perfect for a party, and it's a true "penny pincher"

Heat oven 375°.

Saute *1 large chopped onion or ½ bag (6 ounces) frozen chopped onions* in *2 tablespoons oil* until soft and clear, takes about 10 to 12 minutes. If using frozen onions, place in ungreased skillet on medium high heat and cook and stir to get out the water before sauteing with the oil. Cool.

Grind in a meat grinder, alternately, the onions with *1 can (1 pound) ham,* gelatin removed and ham sliced into pieces so it can be ground.

Stir in *3 tablespoons unsweetened mayonnaise* and *pepper* to taste.

Put *2 cups Quickie Mix* into a bowl.

Add as much of *⅓ cup milk* as you need.

Stir with a fork until it forms a soft, but not sticky, dough.

Place on a heavily floured surface.

Knead and smooth into a ball.

Roll with a rolling pin to make a rectangle about 11″ × 13″.

Brush with your hand *soft or melted margarine* over it.

With your hands pat the ham stuffing over the dough, being careful to leave a good inch edge without the stuffing.

Sprinkle *2 tablespoons dried parsley* over the ham stuffing.

Roll, wide side up; place on a baking sheet, seam side down, shaping the roll into a half moon.

Make an Egg Wash by mixing with a fork the *yolk with 1 teaspoon water.*

With a pastry brush, brush the Egg Wash over the roll. Cut 1 inch cuts on the outside of the roll leaving the inside attached. Separate gently on its side so as not to tear each cut, so that the roll can bake better. Bake in 375° oven 30 minutes until roll is baked and a beautiful brown. You can double the recipe for a party and bake about 50 minutes.

Quickie Mix Mini Pizzas

use Quickie Mix and water, they're easy to make and they bake quicker than the large ones and they're not apt to get soggy either

Heat oven 425°.

You will have 8 pizzas.

Put into a large bowl *3 cups Quickie Mix*. And *¼ cup plus 2 tablespoons cold tap water*. Mix with a fork into a ball.

Put on a cutting board and cut into halves then quarters then again into halves to make eight pieces. Shape into 8 balls.

One at a time, throw hard from one hand to the other 25 times.

Roll each ball into a 6-inch circle. Put each one onto a cookie sheet shaping the edges of each one into a rim. Spoon your favorite pizza or spaghetti sauce over it. Cut mozzarella, muenster, cheddar or Harvarti cheese into small strips and decorate with them. If you wish you can sprinkle some grated Parmesan or Romano cheese over it.

Bake in preheated 425° oven about 15 or 20 minutes.

For a fancy pizza you can choose from any of the following: Ham, or other meat; canned fish; sausage; little bits of tomatoes; little bits of onion; luncheon meat; little pieces of anchovies; or whatever you like.

You can freeze the pizza dough rolled out, if you wish, as they freeze well and fill as you wish before baking them. You can also make cheese pizzas or other filled pizzas and freeze them and then all you have to do is bake them.

We like the "mini" pizzas because we don't have soggy "middles" with them.

Pizza Fancy

Mix *2 cups Quickie Mix* with *⅓ to ½ cup water* to make a soft but not sticky dough.

Make into a ball. Let rest 10 minutes.

Roll out to make pizza the size or sizes you prefer about ⅛ inch thick. You can make 2 9-inch size ones or individual small ones.

Place on a baking sheet or in cake pans.

Roll up the edges with your hands to make a slight rim.

Brush the pizza, not the rim, with *1 tablespoon oil.*

Make the sauce or spoon your favorite sauce on.

The Sauce:

Mix *1 can (16 ounces) Progresso Pizza Sauce* with *½ teaspoon dried basil, ½ teaspoon dried oregano* and *½ teaspoon dried garlic powder.*

Put in a saucepan. On medium heat, cook and stir 3 minutes.

Add *1 teaspoon vegetable oil.* Cook and stir 1 minute. Take off heat. Cool.

This makes enough sauce for 3 medium size pizzas.

When cold, spoon as much of the sauce on the pizzas as you prefer.

Arrange *pieces of mozzarella cheese* on the sauce.

Choose from these: pieces of *salami, sausage, frankfurters, baloney* or *luncheon meat.*

You can add *mushrooms,* canned or cooked, cut up.

You can add *olives,* either black or green, cut up.

You can add *salty anchovies* for an anchovy pizza. Choose whatever you like.

Be sure to sprinkle *½ cup grated Parmesan cheese* on top.

Bake in 425° oven about 15 or more minutes, longer time according to size. Eat while hot.

Quickie Mix Orange Raisin Coffee Cake

this is not only delicious but so easy and "quick" to make . . . when you're in a hurry and want something extra special good, this is it!

Preheat oven 375°.

Grease an 8-inch square baking pan; sprinkle flour over. Shake off excess.

Make the topping:

Mix together *¼ cup sugar, 2 teaspoons cinnamon, ¼ cup flour*. Add *2 tablespoons margarine.*

Crumble together with your fingers. The mixture must be moist.

The Coffee Cake:

With a pastry blender mix *2 cups Quickie Mix* with *⅓ cup sugar, 3 tablespoons grated orange rind, ½ cup to 1 cup raisins* and *½ cup chopped nuts.*

Add *2 tablespoons margarine.* Mix with the pastry blender. It will look crumbly. Don't overmix.

Mix *1 egg* with a fork. Stir in *½ cup cold tap water.*

Stir into the Quickie Mixture just to combine.

Spoon the batter into the greased baking pan.

Sprinkle the topping over it. Don't push down.

Bake in 375° oven about 25 minutes.

You can eat it warm for a special treat.

Raisin Or Nut Or Chocolate Chip Or Date Coffee Cakes

these will become your favorite desserts . . . everyone loves them and you can "dress" them up with whatever your heart desires . . . raisins, nuts, chocolate chips, dates, spices . . . each will taste different and each will be delicious! . . . and each is so easy and quick to make . . . when you have your nutritious, delicious "homemade" Quickie Mix, you know what's in it

Preheat oven 375°.

Grease and flour an 8-inch square baking pan. Shake out any excess flour.

Make the topping: Mix together *¼ cup sugar, 1½ teaspoons cinnamon, ¼ cup flour.* Add *2 tablespoons margarine or butter.* Crumble with your fingers.

Grate *3 tablespoons orange rind.* If using grated orange rind that you have frozen, defrost it. Wipe carefully to get any juice out.

The Coffee Cake: We usually add 3 tablespoons grated orange rind to all of our coffee cakes. It's the secret ingredient that makes each one so especially good.

Put into a large bowl *2 cups Quickie Mix, ⅓ cup sugar, 3 tablespoons grated rind*. Mix with a pastry blender.

Add *2 tablespoons margarine*. Mix with the pastry blender just until crumbly. Don't overmix. Add *½ cup or 1 cup* of the *raisins, or nuts, or dates or chocolate chips*.

Mix *1 egg* with a fork. Stir in *½ cup cold tap water*.

Add to the Quickie mixture and just stir to combine; don't overmix.

Spoon the batter into the greased baking pan. Don't smooth it.

Sprinkle the topping over it but don't push it down.

Bake in 375° oven about 25 minutes.

You can use 1 teaspoon vanilla instead of the orange rind.

You can even eat this warm for a special treat.

Tip: It's the "don'ts" which make this coffee cake so easy to make and so easy to eat.

"Swirly" Coffee Cakes

how about a peanut butter, chocolate, an orange or apricot marmalade "swirling" through your coffee cake? . . . try it . . . it's different than our other coffee cakes and like the rest . . . it's "good eating!"

Preheat oven 375°.

Grease and flour an 8-inch square baking pan. Shake out any excess flour.

Make the topping of your choice. See recipe index under T-Toppings and Glazes.

Grate *3 tablespoons orange rind*. Tip: If using grated orange rind that you have frozen to have on hand, which we do, defrost it, then dry it with a paper towel until it is dry.

We usually add the orange rind to all our coffee cakes because we love its delicate flavor. Of course, you can use vanilla flavoring instead.

Put into a large bowl *2 cups Quickie Mix, ⅓ cup sugar, 3 tablespoons grated orange rind*. Mix with a pastry blender.

Mix in *2 tablespoons margarine* with the pastry blender just until crumbly. Don't overmix.

Mix *1 egg* with a fork. Stir in *½ cup cold tap water*. Add to the Quickie Mixture and stir just to combine—don't overmix!

For a peanut butter swirl—Have ½ cup peanut butter get to room temperature so it is soft enough to use. Stir in 1 tablespoon sugar.

Swirl the peanut butter, but don't swirl too much, into the batter.

Spoon into the baking pan. Bake in 375° oven about 25 minutes.

Cool on a rack.

To make the chocolate swirl—Mix together 2 tablespoons cocoa with 2 tablespoons sugar and 2 tablespoons oil. Swirl it through the dough but don't overwork the dough.

To make the marmalade swirl—Soften the marmalade by just mixing with a spoon until manageable, but by no means "runny," and swirl through the batter.

Fresh Fruit, Chopped, Coffee Cakes

something different and believe me there's something fresh fruits do to a coffee cake that makes you glad . . . you can use fresh apples, blueberries, peaches, plums, apricots

Grease and flour an 8″ × 8″ square baking pan. Shake out any excess flour.

Preheat oven 375°.

Make the topping: Mix together *¼ cup sugar, 2 teaspoons cinnamon, ¼ cup flour, 2 tablespoons margarine.* Mix with your fingers into moist crumbs.

Wash, peel, cut into small pieces *1 cup, apples, peaches or apricots.*

Put into a large bowl *2 cups Quickie Mix, ½ cup sugar, 3 tablespoons grated orange rind.* Mix with a pastry blender. Add *2 tablespoons margarine.* Mix with the pastry blender just until crumbly, don't overmix.

Add the fruit of your choice, mixing gently so as not to crush.

Mix *1 egg* with a fork. Stir in *½ cup cold tap water.* Add to the Quickie mixture. Mix just to combine. Don't overmix.

Spoon the batter into the greased baking pan, don't smooth it. Sprinkle the topping over it and don't push down.

Bake in preheated 375° oven about 25 minutes.

Chopped Apple, Raisin Coffee Cake

smells heavenly . . . it's a Quickie Mix recipe

Grease and flour an 8″ × 8″ square baking pan.

Preheat oven 375°.

Make the topping: Mix together *¼ cup granulated sugar* with *¾ teaspoon cinnamon* and *2 tablespoons flour*. Add *2 tablespoons margarine*. With your clean fingers or a pastry blender crumble into crumbs.

Make the coffee cake: With a pastry blender, mix *2 cups Quickie Mix* with *⅓ cup sugar* and *2 tablespoons margarine.*

Add *1 cup chopped apples* and *½ cup raisins* and mix in with a spoon.

Mix *1 egg* with a fork. Stir in *½ cup cold tap water.*

Add to the Quickie Mix mixture and mix just to combine.

Spoon into the greased baking pan.

Sprinkle the topping over the coffee cake.

Place in the 375° oven. Bake about 25 minutes.

Remove from oven. Serve warm. It's good cold, too.

Delicious Canned Fruit Coffee Cakes

the canners . . . bless them . . . have "cooked" the fruit for us! take your choice from a can of Wild Blueberries, Cherries, Peaches, Apples, Plums, Apricots, or did I miss one?

Grease and flour an 8-inch square baking pan. Shake out excess flour.

Preheat oven 375°.

Strain well *1 cup of any of the canned fruit* you have chosen and cut into pieces, such as canned peaches, apples, plums or apricots.

Measure *½ cup fruit juice;* remove *2 tablespoons.*

Grate *3 tablespoons orange rind.* (If you use your frozen, grated rind, defrost. When defrosted, dry carefully and well.)

Make the topping: Mix together *¼ cup sugar, 2 teaspoons cinnamon* and *¼ cup flour.* Add *2 tablespoons margarine.* Mix with your fingers into crumbs—some loose, some not.

Put into a large bowl *2 cups Quickie Mix, ½ cup sugar, 3*

tablespoons grated orange rind. Mix with a pastry blender. Add *2 tablespoons margarine.* Mix with the pastry blender until just crumbly, don't overmix.

Add the strained fruit to the Quickie Mixture, mixing through gently, not to crush.

Mix *1 egg* with a fork. Stir in the ½ cup fruit juice less 2 tablespoons. Add to the Quickie Mixture. Mix just to combine; don't overmix.

Spoon the batter into the greased baking pan, don't smooth it. Sprinkle the topping over it, but don't push it down.

Bake in preheated 375° oven about 25 minutes.

You can use vanilla instead of the orange rind, putting it in with the fruit juice. You can also use another topping.

You can eat this warmish. It's delicious cold, too. Of course, eating it the day it is baked is best.

Fresh Sliced Fruit Coffee Cake With Quickie Mix

what will you have? apples? peaches? prune plums? blueberries? apricots? . . . these are "different" but equally as delicious as the rest of our coffee cakes, in fact . . . it's our favorite

Grease and flour an 8″ × 8″ square baking pan. Shake out any excess flour. We do this over the sink.

Preheat oven 375°.

Wash, peel, slice the fresh fruit of your choice, enough to cover in one layer, overlapping, on top of the dough.

Grate *3 tablespoons orange rind.* If you have some you made and froze, defrost the 3 tablespoons orange rind and be sure to dry it well. Make the topping of your choice—see recipe index under T-Toppings, or mix together *¼ cup sugar, 2 teaspoons cinnamon, ¼ cup flour.* Add *2 tablespoons plus 1 teaspoon margarine.* Crumble with your fingers.

Put into a large bowl *2 cups Quickie Mix, ⅓ cup sugar, 3 tablespoons grated orange rind.* Mix with a pastry blender.

Add *2 tablespoons margarine.* Mix with a pastry blender, blending just until crumbly. Don't overmix. Mix *1 egg* with a fork. Stir in *½ cup cold tap water.*

Add to the Quickie Mixture and just stir enough to combine. Don't overmix.

Spoon the batter into the greased baking dish.

Arrange the fruit in one layer; make a pretty pattern if you wish, on top.

Sprinkle the topping over the apples.

Bake in 375° oven about 25 minutes.

Tastes very good served warm.

Tip: You can glaze the apples instead of using this topping by glazing with apricot or orange marmalade.

Quickie Mix Cinnamon Raisin Lattice Apple Coffee Cake

made with Quickie Mix and apples

Chop *3 large apples or 4 medium ones.*

Mix together *1 tablespoon butter, ¼ cup sugar, ¼ teaspoon cinnamon, 1 tablespoon lemon juice, 1 teaspoon flour.* Add *½ cup raisins* and mix with the apples.

Mix together *2 cups Quickie Mix* with *1 tablespoon butter or margarine* and *1 tablespoon sugar.*

Stir together *2 tablespoons milk* and *1 egg.*

Add to the Quickie Mix mixture.

Mix with a fork, then your hands, to make a dough that cleans the bowl and forms a ball.

Hold in your hands and smooth into a ball.

Break off a piece the size of a golf ball.

Put the rest of the dough into the baking pan.

Push until it covers the bottom and comes about ½ inch up the sides.

Spoon the apple mixture over the batter.

Divide the ball of dough into 6 pieces.

Roll each piece in your hands to fit the pan.

Make a lattice of these strips on top of the apples.

Bake in preheated 375° oven about 20 to 35 minutes.

Quickie Mix Sticky Buns

don't hesitate to make these, they will become everyone's favorite

Heat oven 375°.

Cut *¼ cup pecans* into pieces. Set aside.

Grease an 8-inch round cake pan with a little *margarine*. Sprinkle *¼ cup dark brown sugar* packed over the greased cake pan. Pour over *¼ cup clear corn syrup* and dot with *¼ cup margarine*. Set aside.

Prepare the buns:

Put into a large bowl *3 cups Quickie Mix*. With a fork, stir in *¾ cup cold tap water* and make into a ball. Let stand 5 minutes.

Remove to a floured surface. If necessary, flour your hands lightly. Throw the ball hard from one hand to the other 25 times; then smooth into a smooth ball. Roll out the dough into a rectangle about 10 × 16 inches.

Smear *2 tablespoons margarine* over the dough.

Mix together *1 tablespoon sugar* and *½ teaspoon cinnamon*. Sprinkle this over the dough, then sprinkle *½ cup raisins* on top. Put a piece of wax paper on top and roll over with a rolling pin so the raisins stick and won't fall out. Remove the wax paper.

Roll the dough tightly, starting at the wide side until a roll like a jelly roll. Cut into 12 pieces.

Put the cake pan and its mixture into the 375° oven for 10 minutes. When done sprinkle the chopped nuts on top of the syrup mixture. Arrange the 12 pieces of dough on top.

Place in the preheated 375° oven. Bake about 30 minutes.

Place on a rack for 10 minutes, then turn over *onto a plate*. If a little of the "sticky" topping clings to the pan, use a knife and stick it back on, it's too good to waste.

Quickie Mix Apricot Cobbler

Preheat oven to 450°.

Put *1 can Apricot Pie Filling* into a saucepan.

Stir in *2 tablespoons lemon juice* and *2 teaspoons sugar* to your taste.

Place on medium heat.

Cook and stir until bubbling hot.

Pour into *1½ quart casserole*.

Place in 450° oven.

To make the batter:

Put *1 cup Quickie Mix* into a bowl.

Add *2 tablespoons soft margarine*.

With a pastry blender mix into large crumbs.

With a spoon stir in, just to mix, *¼ cup cold water.*
Drop by spoonfuls onto the hot fruit mixture.
Bake 15 minutes.
You can make blueberry, peach, apple or cherry cobbler by substituting these for the apricot pie filling. Taste to see if the amount of sugar you added is to your taste.

Quickie Mix Chocolate Cake

what a breeze! . . . you just measure in your mixer and whiz! quick! . . . it's ready to bake

Heat oven 350°.
Grease and flour an 8-inch square pan.
Put in the large bowl of electric mixer *1½ cups Quickie Mix, 1 cup sugar, 3 tablespoons soft margarine, ¼ cup cocoa, ¾ cup water, 1 egg* and *1 teaspoon vanilla.*
Mix on highest speed 2 minutes.
Pour into baking pan.
Place in 350° oven. Bake 35 to 40 minutes.

Pineapple Upside Down Cake

made with Quickie Mix

Heat oven 350° (medium heat).
Melt *2 tablespoons margarine* in a 9-inch square pan on low heat.
Sprinkle *¼ cup (packed) brown sugar* over the margarine.
Drain *4 slices pineapple* in a strainer. Measure the *juice* and add *enough water to make ½ cup.* Set aside.
Arrange the 4 slices pineapple over the brown sugar.
Into a bowl put *1½ cups Quickie Mix.*
Stir *½ cup sugar* into the Quickie Mix.
Separate *1 egg.* Into the yolk stir the ½ cup pineapple juice mixture and *1 teaspoon vanilla.*
Pour into the Quickie Mix mixture. Beat 2 minutes.
Whip the egg white until stiff; then fold into the batter.
Carefully pour batter over the top of the pineapple.
Bake in 350° oven about 40 minutes.
Remove, loosen edges and turn upside down on a plate.

Let stand a few seconds; then lift the cake pan off.
Tastes mighty good!

Quickie Mix Vanilla Cake

Heat oven 350°.
Cut wax paper to fit an 8-inch square pan. Grease with *margarine.*
Put in large bowl of electric mixer *1¾ cups Quickie Mix, ¾ cup sugar, 3 tablespoons soft margarine, ¾ cup water, 1 large egg* and *1 teaspoon vanilla.*
Mix; then beat 2 minutes on highest speed.
Pour into the greased pan.
Bake in 350° oven 35 to 40 minutes. (I bake 35 minutes.)

A Quickie Mix Two Layer Chocolate Cake

it's so good you don't even need an icing, but for chocolate lovers we give you a chocolate icing

Grease and flour 2 8-inch cake pans and heat oven 350°.
Put into the large bowl of your electric mixer or a large bowl *3 cups Quickie Mix, 1¼ cups sugar, ½ cup cocoa, 6 tablespoons vegetable shortening, butter or margarine.* Mix with a pastry blender.
Add *1¼ cups cold tap water, 2 eggs, 1 teaspoon vanilla.*
Mix by hand or on low speed just until combined, then turn to highest speed and beat 2 minutes.
Divide between the 2 pans. Bake in the 350° oven about 30 to 35 minutes.
Remove from oven. Let stand 10 minutes, then remove to racks to cool.

Chocolate Icing

Put into a bowl *2 cups 10X Confectioners sugar, 6 tablespoons soft margarine, ½ cup unsweetened cocoa, a pinch of salt, 1 teaspoon vanilla, ¼ cup milk.*
Mix together until smooth and creamy.

Quickie Mix Brownies

if you didn't know you could make brownies with Quickie Mix . . . just try these!

Grease a 9 × 9 inch baking pan.
Heat oven 350°.
Chop *1 cup walnuts.*
With a pastry blender mix together *¾ cup Quickie Mix, 1 cup brown sugar, 6 tablespoons cocoa* and *1 cup chopped walnuts.*
Mix *2 eggs* with a fork. Stir in *5 tablespoons oil.*
Add to the Quickie Mixture and mix.
Spoon into the 9 × 9 inch pan.
Bake in 350° oven about 30 minutes to 35 minutes.
Remove pan to a rack. Cut the brownies while warm, not hot, right in the pan. Has a nice chocolatey flavor.

Raisin Cookies

everyone loves raisin cookies!

Heat the oven 375°.
Put *¼ cup soft margarine* in a large bowl.
Add *¾ cup sugar, 1 egg, 2 tablespoons water* and *2 teaspoons vanilla.* With a wooden spoon mix well.
Add *2 cups Quickie Mix* and *1 cup raisins.* Stir together.
Use 2 teaspoons to drop the batter onto a baking sheet. Don't crowd, as the cookies will spread.
Place in 375° oven.
Bake about 8 to 10 minutes, longer if necessary.
Remove from the oven. With a spatula remove right away from the baking sheet to a rack to cool.
These cookies freeze well. You can freeze them in plastic bags.

Quickie Mix Chocolate Drop Cookies

for chocolate lovers and who isn't?

Heat oven 350°.
Grease a baking sheet or use a Teflon one.

Mix together *3 cups Quickie Mix* with *1 cup sugar, ⅓ cup cocoa.*

Beat *1 egg* with a fork. Stir in *½ cup nonfat skim milk, 1 teaspoon vanilla.*

Stir into the Quickie Mixture.

Drop by teaspoonfuls onto the cookie sheet.

Bake in 350° oven about 10 to 12 minutes.

Remove to a rack to cool.

Peanut Butter Cookies

Preheat oven 375°.

Put *¼ cup soft margarine* in a bowl.

Add *1 cup peanut butter, 1 cup sugar* and *1 egg.* Mix well with a wooden spoon.

Stir in *1½ cups Quickie Mix.* Mix until smooth.

Pinch off small balls the size of marbles.

Put on a baking sheet.

Press the back prongs of a fork on each ball. Criss-cross to flatten it and make a design.

Bake in 375° oven about 8 minutes or more if necessary.

Remove from oven. Remove the cookies to a rack to cool.

To keep, place in a cookie jar or in plastic bags and freeze.

These freeze beautifully.

Quickie Mix Ginger Snaps

they're so good . . . everyone will snap them right up

Heat oven 375°.

Grease 2 cookie sheets; or use Teflon ones ungreased.

Into a large bowl put *2¼ cups Quickie Mix, ¾ cup brown sugar,* packed down, and *1 teaspoon ground ginger.* Mix together well.

Mix *1 egg* with a fork. Stir in *¼ cup Mother's Molasses.* Add to the Quickie Mix mixture. Mix with your clean hands until well combined and make into a ball.

Put about *½ cup 10X sugar* over a large plate. Sprinkle some 10X sugar on your hands. Throw dough hard from one hand to the other 20 times. Dip a knife into the 10X sugar and cut the dough into 5 or 6 strips. Using the 10X sugar as necessary, cut one strip at a time into ½ inch pieces. Make each into a ball; place on the cookie sheet leaving space between each ball. Cut a piece of wax paper 4″ × 5″; dip into the 10X sugar; put over each ball and flatten with the palm of your hand into a thin cookie.

Bake in 375° oven about 10 minutes on the rack second from the top of the oven.

Remove immediately with a metal spatula to a rack to cool and become crisp.

Continue until all are done.

It is best to keep these Ginger Snaps in a can lined with wax paper and closed with a lid.

Children love to make these, and mothers, fathers—everyone—love to eat them!

Quickie Mix Raisin Nut Porcupine Balls

the nuts give you extra protein and the raisins iron and altogether it's fun to eat

Heat oven 375°.

Chop fine ⅓ *cup pecans, walnuts* or *peanuts.*

Mix ½ *cup brown sugar,* not packed down, with ½ *teaspoon cinnamon.*

Mix with the nuts.

Mix together *2 cups Quickie Mix, 2 tablespoons sugar* and ½ *teaspoon nutmeg.*

Add ¼ *cup plus 1 tablespoon cold tap water* and mix with a fork into a dough that cleans the bowl.

Take in your hands and smooth the dough and work it into a ball for about 1 or 2 minutes; or knead it in your hands.

Add ½ *cup raisins* and make it into a ball.

Cut the dough into halves, then quarters, then divide again and once more to have 16 pieces.

Shape each piece into a ball by working in your hands.

Melt ¼ *cup butter or margarine.*

Dip the balls in the butter, then into the nut/sugar mixture, coating each ball well.

Place on a Teflon cookie sheet, or greased cookie sheet. Bake in 375° oven about 15 to 20 minutes.

They do look like porcupines—sorta.

Wintertime Quickie Mix
Strawberry Shortcakes

so easy to make and so good to eat . . . you can make it anytime

Open *1 box (16 ounces) frozen, sliced, sweetened strawberries* and defrost in a bowl. Read the label on the box to see how long it will take to defrost.

The Shortcake:

Put *2 cups Quickie Mix* into a large bowl.

Stir in *as much as you need of ½ cup milk or water to* make a soft but not sticky dough.

Spread *1 tablespoon flour* on a surface.

Roll out the dough to make 4 thick biscuits.

Cut with a 3 inch biscuit cutter or glass to make the 4 biscuits.

Place on ungreased baking sheet. Bake in 450° oven about 10 minutes. Let cool.

When ready to eat, cut the biscuits across. Spoon some strawberries and juice over the open shortcakes.

Top with the other half.

Now it's ready.

Some people like to pour some milk over it; while others put some whipped cream on. We like it just with the good strawberry taste.

You can use fresh strawberries. Wash and slice them. Put sugar to taste. Let stand a while so the sugar melts. You can use these when strawberries are in season.

Coconut Blender Pie

it's magic . . . makes its own crust while baking and you've never made a pie so easy . . . just dump everything into the blender . . . it makes the pie for you

Heat oven 350°.

Put into the blender *½ cup Quickie Mix, ¼ cup margarine, 2 cups milk, 4 eggs, 1 teaspoon vanilla, 1 cup sugar* and *1 cup coconut.*

Blend in blender 3 minutes.

Pour into 10 inch pie plate.

Bake in preheated 350° oven 50 to 55 minutes.

This pie has to be kept in refrigerator when cold.

Custard Pumpkin Blender Pie

just whiz it in the blender, put it in the oven, and you've got it made . . . couldn't be easier

Heat oven 350°.

Put into the blender *½ cup Quickie Mix, ¼ cup margarine, 2 cups milk, 4 eggs, 1 teaspoon vanilla, ¾ cup sugar, 1 cup canned pumpkin* and *¼ teaspoon salt.*

Blend in blender 3 minutes.

Pour into 10 inch pie plate.

Bake in preheated 350° oven 50 to 55 minutes.

Keep this pie in the refrigerator when cold.

3. WHOLE WHEAT QUICKIE MIX AND RECIPES

Whole Wheat Quickie Mix

this is a brand new recipe and has the most nutrition . . . our other Quickie Mix and is nutritious, too, but I thought you might want the convenience and the choice of using "whole wheat," so here it is . . . I am pleased to report I was amazed, and so pleased, to see what light, delicious pancakes this makes and all you have to add is fresh eggs and water . . . what could be easier?

Measure into a large container *8 cups whole wheat flour, 3 cups instant nonfat dry milk, 6 tablespoons baking powder, 1 tablespoon salt* and *¼ cup sugar.*

Mix with a pastry blender until well blended.

Add *2½ cups vegetable shortening.* Mix with the pastry blender. Mixture will look sort of like crumbs, but my husband says it looks like sand on the beach.

Store in a tightly closed container. It will keep 1 month in the refrigerator and 3 months in the freezer.

This Quickie Mix is so good, it never lasts that long.

Whole Wheat Quickie Mix Pancakes

they're as delicious and light as they are nutritious! . . . and easy as easy can be to make

Put *2 cups Whole Wheat Quickie Mix* into a mixing bowl.

Mix *2 eggs* with a fork. Stir in *1 cup cold tap water.* Add to the Quickie Mix. Mix just to combine.

Heat your griddle or your skillet until hot on medium heat. Test by dropping a drop or so of water on; and if it skitters around, the skillet is ready. Don't overheat, or the pancakes will burn and shrivel. On the other hand, if not hot enough, the pancakes will stick.

Without crowding, drop by tablespoonfuls onto the hot skillet. When bubbles start to appear on the batter, check to see if the bottoms are light brown. Don't let get too dark. Turn; brown the other side.

Tip: For the best taste, heat your plates for serving the

pancakes on the lowest heat in your oven. Use a hot pad to remove them.

Another tip: Serve the pancakes "one order" at a time for the best taste. Pancakes don't like to be kept waiting.

I hope you will have enough batter for the "cook" to get to taste these.

Whole Wheat Quickie Mix Waffles

they're always a treat

Heat plates in the oven on lowest heat to have ready for the waffles.

Put *2 cups Whole Wheat Quickie Mix* into a mixing bowl.

Mix *2 eggs* with a fork. Stir in *¾ cup plus 2 tablespoons cold tap water.*

Add to the Quickie Mix. Mix just to combine.

Heat the waffle iron hot.

Pour in about ½ cup batter. Bake until the waffle is as you like it, soft or crisp.

Serve immediately on the heated plates.

These are good served with syrup or the juice from jelly.

You can serve these waffles topped with creamed chicken or tuna fish.

You can thin 1 can Cream of Mushroom Soup with ½ cup chicken broth or half chicken broth and half milk, and bring to a boil. Add bite size pieces of chicken and cook, stir until piping hot and serve over the waffles for dinner. You might also want to add some peas or fresh or canned mushrooms; or stir in some drained pimento for a change.

A crisp waffle makes a good base for leftovers, which we call "ready cooked" foods—the little bits of this and that, that we wonder what in the world to do with!

Whole Wheat Quickie Mix Raisin Coffee Cake

and if you have some nuts, why not add some for a change?

Heat oven 375°.

Grease and flour an 8 inch square baking pan. Shake out excess flour.

Make the topping:

Mix together *½ cup brown sugar, 1½ teaspoons cinnamon* and *¼ cup flour.* Add *2 tablespoons soft margarine* and crumble together into crumbs. Set aside.

Put into a mixing bowl *2 cups Whole Wheat Quickie Mix, ⅓ cup sugar* and *2 tablespoons soft margarine.* Mix with a pastry blender. Add *½ to 1 cup raisins* and mix.

Mix *1 egg* with a fork. Stir in *½ cup cold tap water.*

Add to the Quickie Mixture. Mix together just to combine.

Spoon into the baking pan.

Sprinkle the topping over the coffee cake.

Place in 375° oven. Bake about 25 minutes until done.

Remove from oven. Cool on a rack.

This is doubly delicious served fresh but tastes mighty good, too, the next day. Freezes well, too, so why not bake two while you're at it?

Whole Wheat Quickie Mix Muffins

make them plain or add raisins, blueberries or "whatever" . . . they're good, good!

Preheat oven 400°.

Grease your muffin pan or use paper baking cups and put on a cookie sheet.

Put *2 cups Whole Wheat Quickie Mix* into a large bowl.

Mix in *2 tablespoons sugar* with a pastry blender.

Mix *1 egg* with a fork. Stir in *½ cup cold tap water.*

Add to the Quickie Mix. Barely mix, just until flour is moistened. Batter will be lumpy, which makes for tender muffins.

Fill cups ⅔ full.

Bake in 400° oven 15 to 25 minutes depending on size of the muffins.

If using metal muffin pans, loosen or remove immediately. If using paper baking cups, let stand 5 minutes before removing.

Muffins taste best served warm.

You can reheat muffins by wrapping in foil and reheating in 400° oven about 5 minutes.

For a change, make blueberry muffins by making recipe above but adding 3 or 4 tablespoons sugar and 1 cup fresh blueberries or 1 cup drained wild blueberries.

4. QUICK BREADS

American Pancakes

the old fashioned kind that are so easy to make from scratch and you know what's in it and you know it's nutritious! . . . and they taste good!

Into a large bowl put 2 *cups flour, 1 tablespoon wheat germ, 1 tablespoon baking powder, ½ teaspoon salt, 1½ teaspoons sugar, ⅓ cup instant nonfat dry milk.* Mix with a pastry blender.

In a medium bowl put *2 eggs.* Mix with a fork. Stir in *¼ cup vegetable oil;* then stir in *1½ cups cold tap water.*

Stir this mixture into the flour mixture. Don't overmix—it will be light but lumpy.

On an electric stove, heat the griddle or skillet on third heat until hot. Test by dropping some drops of water, and if they skitter around, the griddle or skillet is ready. If you don't overheat or underheat your griddle or skillet, you will need no fat, and the pancakes will not stick.

Pour by tablespoons onto the griddle or skillet.

When brown on one side, turn and brown the other side. These are puffy pancakes.

Tip: Before you start to mix your pancakes, put the plates to serve the pancakes on in the oven set at its lowest heat. Turn oven off when you start to bake the pancakes.

Another tip: If you have any batter left, put it in the refrigerator. The next day, add a little milk to thin it and bake as usual. These make a sort of "Swedish" pancakes, thin and delicious. You don't have to buy expensive lingonberries to serve with these—use any of your own preserves. Once you try these, you might want to make a whole recipe of them, they're that good!

Still another tip: If you double your recipe and use half, you can freeze the rest. Defrost when needed. Don't mix. Bake. This will keep a month in the refrigerator.

Buttermilk Pancakes

with buttermilk and oil you have delicious pancakes and also healthy ones

With a pastry blender, mix together *2 cups flour, 2*

teaspoons wheat germ, 1 teaspoon soda, 1 tablespoon sugar, ½ teaspoon salt.

Put *2 eggs* into a medium bowl.

Mix with a fork. Stir in *¼ cup vegetable oil* and *2 cups buttermilk.*

Add to the flour mixture. Mix together but don't over-mix—the batter will be lumpy.

Heat the griddle or skillet until hot.

Drop by tablespoonfuls onto the hot griddle.

Brown on one side, then the other. Serve hot. Continue until all are baked and served.

Whole Wheat Pancakes

they're every bit as "light" as our other pancakes which was a big surprise to me and they are more nutritious, so please try them

Put into a large bowl *2 cups whole wheat flour, 4 teaspoons baking powder, ¾ teaspoon salt, ¾ teaspoon sugar, ½ cup nonfat dry milk.*

Mix with a pastry blender.

In a 4-glass measuring cup or a bowl mix *2 eggs* with a fork. Stir in *¼ cup and 2 tablespoons oil (or 6 tablespoons oil),* then stir in *1¾ cups cold tap water.*

Add to the flour mixture. Mix together. Let stand 5 to 10 minutes, or you can use at once.

Heat the griddle or the skillet until hot. We do not grease them, but be careful not to heat too hot. Drop a few drops of water on, and if they skitter around, the griddle or skillet is ready. On an electric stove we heat on the second highest heat.

Watch as you "bake" them because they seem to cook faster (and burn) quicker than the white flour pancakes.

These pancakes are light and have an earthy taste that is very satisfying.

Sunday Morning Waffles

always a treat

Into a large bowl put *2 cups flour, 1 tablespoon wheat germ, 1 tablespoon baking powder, ½ teaspoon salt, ½ table-*

spoon sugar and *½ cup instant nonfat dry milk.* Mix with a pastry blender.

Break *2 eggs* into a medium bowl.

Stir with a fork. Gradually stir in *½ cup oil;* then stir in *1¼ cups cold tap water.*

Add to the flour mixture and mix just to combine.

The batter is ready.

Preheat the waffle iron. Don't overheat. Pour or spoon the batter onto the heated waffle iron, being careful not to pour too much, as it will run out and it will be a "mess" to clean the waffle iron.

Bake as you like it, soft or crisp—soft for less time, crisp a little longer.

A tip: If you have a 4 cup Pyrex glass measuring cup . . . beat the 2 eggs in it (it comes up to the "4" mark). Then add oil so that it comes up to the "8" mark, then add cold water to come up to the "18" mark.

Shall I explain? The 2 eggs are ½ cup, the ½ cup oil then comes to the "8" mark and 1¼ cups water comes up to the "18" mark.

You wash one glass this way instead of a bowl and 2 or 3 measuring cups. Of course, if you don't have the 4 cup glass measuring cup, use what you have!

Old Fashioned Biscuits

with wheat germ added for old fashioned nutrition and old fashioned good taste!

Preheat oven 450°.

You need a cookie sheet, a cookie cutter or a glass, and a pastry blender.

Into a bowl put *2 cups flour, 2 teaspoons wheat germ, 3 teaspoons baking powder, ¾ teaspoon salt, ¼ cup nonfat dry milk* and *¾ teaspoon sugar.*

Add *⅓ cup oil.* Mix with the pastry blender. Mix into large crumbs. Mix ¾ of this into fine crumbs. Mix together.

Add *½ cup cold tap water.* With a fork, mix just until it forms a somewhat sticky ball. Let stand 5 minutes.

Sprinkle a *little flour* over it, and also flour your hands lightly. Remove the dough and throw hard from one hand to the other 25 times.

Roll out with a rolling pin about ½ inch thick.

Place on an ungreased cookie sheet. Bake 8 to 10 minutes or more if your biscuits are large. We use a 2-inch biscuit cutter.

The biscuits should be a light golden color and flaky, so don't overbake. These reheat well, too.

Tasty Biscuits With Vegetable Shortening

made with vegetable shortening and wheat germ . . . it tastes good and is easy to make

Preheat oven 450°.

Put into a large bowl *2 cups flour, 3 teaspoons wheat germ, 1 tablespoon baking powder, ½ teaspoon salt, ½ teaspoon sugar.* Mix together with a pastry blender.

Add *½ cup vegetable shortening.* Mix with the pastry blender into fine crumbs.

Add *½ cup plus 3 tablespoons nonfat milk.* With a fork, then your hands, stir until the flour mixture forms a ball that cleans the bowl.

Throw the ball hard from one hand to the other over a clean surface 25 times.

Roll out on a piece of wax paper or between 2 sheets of wax paper, as thick or thin as you wish, from ¼ inch to 1 inch thick. Remove the top sheet if using 2 sheets. Of course, you can roll the biscuits on a clean, lightly floured surface.

Cut with a biscuit cutter. Place on ungreased cookie sheet. Bake 8 to 14 minutes until done.

Remove to a rack to cool. Serve hot if you wish.

Drop Biscuits

when you're in a hurry

Preheat oven 450°.

Put into a large bowl *2 cups flour.* Add *3 teaspoons wheat germ, 3 teaspoons baking powder, ½ teaspoon salt,* and *½ teaspoon sugar.* Mix with a pastry blender.

Add *¼ cup plus 2 tablespoons oil.* Mix with the pastry blender until it looks like small crumbs.

Add *1 cup nonfat milk.*

Drop by tablespoonfuls onto a "Teflon preferred" cookie sheet.

Bake in preheated 450° oven about 10 to 12 minutes.

Remove to a rack to cool.

Egg Dumplings

old fashioned but still good . . . makes a plain dish fancy

Have the lid ready.

Heat the stew or broth while you make the dumplings.

Mix *1 cup flour* with *1½ teaspoons baking powder, 1 teaspoon wheat germ* and *½ teaspoon salt.*

Beat *1 egg* with a fork. Stir in *1½ tablespoons oil* and *¼ cup plus 2 tablespoons nonfat milk.*

Pour into the flour mixture. Barely mix, just to combine.

Dip a tablespoon into the boiling stew or broth; then dip the spoon into the batter. Tip: The batter will not stick to the spoon if you do this.

Drop by spoonfuls into the boiling broth.

Continue until all have been added.

Cover immediately. Turn heat to low. It should bubble slowly. If not, turn heat to medium low. Cook 12 minutes. Do not remove cover while it cooks.

This makes about 10 dumplings.

Never Fail Egg Dumplings

Heat the stew or broth while you make the dumplings:

Mix *1 cup flour* with *1½ teaspoons baking powder* and *½ teaspoon salt.*

With a fork or a pastry blender, cut in *1½ tablespoons vegetable shortening* until mixture looks flaky or crumbly.

Beat *1 egg* with a fork. Add to *½ cup milk.* Pour into flour mixture. Barely mix, just to moisten.

Dip a tablespoon into boiling broth or stew; then with this spoon, dip into dumpling batter and drop by spoonfuls into the boiling broth. (Batter will not stick to spoon.)

Continue doing the same each time, until you have dropped by spoonfuls all the dumplings into the boiling broth or stew.

Cover immediately, turn heat to low, and cook 12 minutes. Do not remove cover while it cooks.

This makes about 10 dumplings, and it never fails to be good.

You can vary this by adding 1 teaspoon poultry seasoning or chopped onions, green pepper or parsley to the dry ingredients.

Remember the good trick of putting your spoon first into the boiling broth or stew before dipping it into the batter, so it won't stick.

Heavenly Light Corn Muffins

if you're Southern, use less sugar . . . if Northern, increase the sugar to ¼ cup

Heat oven 350°.

You need paper baking cups and a cookie sheet to put them on.

With a pastry blender mix together *1 cup flour, ½ cup yellow or white cornmeal, 2 tablespoons sugar, 2 teaspoons baking powder, ¼ teaspoon salt, 1 tablespoon nonfat dry milk.*

Beat *2 eggs* well with a fork. Stir in *½ cup oil,* then *¼ cup cold tap water.*

Add to the flour mixture.

Spoon ¾ full into each baking cup.

Place in preheated 350° oven. Bake about 15 minutes.

Light, Easy To Eat Muffins

there is one trouble with muffins, when you start you can't stop! . . . our muffins are not too sweet so they can be eaten at breakfast, or dinner, too

Preheat oven 400°.

Grease a muffin pan or use heat proof paper cups. Put on a cookie sheet.

Mix *1¾ cups flour* with *2 teaspoons wheat germ, 3 teaspoons baking powder, ½ teaspoon salt, 2 tablespoons sugar, ½ cup nonfat dry milk.*

Beat *1 egg* with a fork. Stir in *¼ cup vegetable oil* and *1 cup cold tap water.*

Add to the flour mixture. Mix just until flour is moistened. Batter will be lumpy.

Fill the baking cups ⅔ full.

Bake about 20 to 25 minutes in preheated 400° oven.

Loosen immediately from pan so muffins won't steam.

If using paper baking cups, let stand about 5 to 10 minutes before removing; otherwise, the muffins will stick.

Raisin Muffins

These are, if anything, more delicious if you add ½ to 1 cup raisins to the flour mixture.

Blueberry Muffins

Add 1 cup drained canned wild blueberries or 1 cup fresh blueberries to the flour mixture. Again, don't beat . . . just combine! Follow the rest of the muffin recipe except add ¼ cup sugar.

Ever Ready Muffins

you bake one batch and keep the other batch in the freezer until you are ready to use it . . . it keeps up to 1 month . . . our muffins are not too sweet so they can be eaten at breakfast, lunch or dinner, too

Mix together with a pastry blender *3½ cups flour, 4 teaspoons wheat germ, 2 tablespoons baking powder, 1 teaspoon salt, 2 tablespoons sugar* and *1 cup nonfat dry milk.*

Beat *2 eggs* with a fork. Stir in *½ cup vegetable oil* and *2 cups cold tap water.*

Add to the flour mixture; mix just until flour is moistened. Batter will be lumpy.

Divide this batter in half. Put ½ into a container that closes tightly. We use a glass or plastic container with a tight lid. Freeze until needed. When ready to use, defrost. Do not stir; just spoon into muffin cups and bake.

Bake in 400° oven about 20 minutes.

Bran Muffins

this is a very nice way to eat your bran

Preheat oven 400°.

Grease baking cups or use foil baking cups.

With a pastry blender, mix together *1 cup flour, 1 cup natural bran, ½ teaspoon soda, 1 teaspoon baking powder, 2 tablespoons sugar, 2 teaspoons wheat germ* and *½ cup nonfat dry milk.*

Mix *1 egg* with a fork. Stir in *¼ cup vegetable oil;* then stir in *1 cup cold tap water.*

Add to the flour mixture and mix just to combine. The batter will be lumpy.

Fill the cups ⅔ full.

Bake in the 400° preheated oven about 20 minutes.

Remove to a rack to cool. If using a muffin pan, tilt the muffins in the pan so they don't sweat. If using foil cups or paper baking cups, let stand 10 minutes before removing them so they won't stick to the paper.

Tip: Raisins added are most welcome.

Old Fashioned Whole Wheat Raisin Nut Muffins

these are "old fashioned" goodness that has become "new fashioned" delights

Heat oven 400°; or in slow oven, preheat 425°.

With a pastry blender mix together *2 cups whole wheat flour, ¾ teaspoon salt, 1 teaspoon soda, 1½ teaspoons baking powder, ¼ cup brown sugar* and *½ cup nonfat dry milk.*

Mix in *½ cup nuts* and *½ cup raisins.*

Beat *1 egg* with a fork. Stir in *¼ cup oil* and *1 cup plus 2 tablespoons cold tap water.*

Add to the flour mixture. Barely mix just to combine.

Spoon into paper baking cups or into a cup cake pan.

Bake in 400° oven about 17 to 20 minutes.

Remove from oven. Cool.

Makes 12 muffins.

Popovers

Heat oven 425°.

Grease 6 glass Pyrex baking cups with vegetable shortening well. Place on a cookie sheet.

Put *1 cup flour* into a bowl with *½ teaspoon salt.* Mix with a pastry blender.

Beat *3 large eggs.*

Stir in *1 cup milk* and *1 tablespoon oil.*

Add to the flour mixture.

Beat with rotary beater, just until smooth.

Spoon into greased cups.

Place in 425° preheated oven.

Bake 25 minutes.

Reduce heat to 350°. Bake 15 minutes.

Remove from cups immediately.

Whole Wheat "Mini" Breads

these are as good as they are nutritious with nuts and raisins . . . you will want to keep them on hand . . . they freeze beautifully too

Chop *½ cup nuts.*

Steam *½ cup raisins.*

Grease 3 foil pans 6 × 3½ inches.

Preheat oven 350°.

Mix with pastry blender *1¼ cups white flour, 1¼ cups whole wheat, ½ teaspoon salt, 1 tablespoon baking powder, ¼ teaspoon soda, ⅓ cup dry milk, ¼ cup sugar, ½ cup chopped nuts.*

Beat *1 egg* with a fork. Stir in *¼ cup oil* and *¾ cup plus 2 tablespoons water.*

Stir into the flour mixture.

Spoon into the "mini" pans.

Let stand 20 minutes.

Bake in preheated 350° oven about 30 minutes.

Three Mini Whole Wheat Raisin Nut Breads

these are wholesome, tasty, easy to make, breads to have on hand or in your freezer

Grease 3 foil (6″ × 3½″) bread pans.
Heat oven 375°.
With a pastry blender mix together *2 cups whole wheat flour, ½ teaspoon salt, 3 tablespoons grated orange rind (optional), ½ cup nonfat dry milk, 1¼ teaspoons soda, 1 teaspoon baking powder.*
Add *½ cup nuts* and *1 cup raisins.* Mix together.
Mix *1 egg* with a fork. Stir in *¼ cup oil, 2 tablespoons brown sugar* and *¼ cup cold tap water.*
Add to the flour mixture. Mix well.
Spoon into the pans.
Bake in 375° oven about 25 minutes.

Three Whole Wheat Pumpkin Mini Breads

you've got "good eating" with two good foods, whole wheat and pumpkin

Heat oven 375°.
Grease and flour 3 foil mini loaf pans (6 × 3½ inches).
With a pastry blender mix together *2 cups whole wheat flour, 1 teaspoon soda, 1½ teaspoons baking powder, ½ teaspoon salt, ½ cup nonfat dry milk, ½ teaspoon ground cinnamon* and *½ teaspoon ground nutmeg.*
Add *1 cup raisins* and *½ cup nuts.* Mix with the pastry blender.
Mix *1 egg* with a fork. Stir in *¼ cup oil, 1 cup canned pumpkin* and *¼ cup brown sugar.* Then stir in *¾ cup water.*
Pour into the flour mixture. Barely mix just to combine.
Spoon into the 3 mini loaf pans. Bake in 375° oven about 25 minutes.
Remove to a rack; turn out and cool.

Banana Date Whole Wheat Mini Breads

as delicious as they are nutritious with a touch of lemon and a sprinkle of nuts

Heat oven to 375°.

Grease 3 foil (6½ × 3 inch) loaf pans.

Mash *enough ripe bananas* in a blender or push through a strainer *to make 1¼ cups liquid bananas.* Stir in *1 full teaspoon lemon juice.*

Grate *3 tablespoons orange rind.*

Chop *½ cup dates* and *½ cup pecan nuts.*

With a pastry blender mix together *2 cups whole wheat flour, 1 teaspoon soda, 1½ teaspoons baking powder, ½ teaspoon salt, ½ cup instant nonfat dry milk* and *3 tablespoons grated orange rind.*

Add *½ cup chopped nuts* and *½ cup chopped dates.* Mix together.

Mix *1 egg* with a fork. Stir in *¼ cup oil* and *1¼ cups mashed bananas, ¼ cup brown sugar.* Then stir in *½ cup and 2 tablespoons cold tap water.*

Pour into the flour mixture. Barely mix just to combine.

Spoon into the 3 mini loaf pans.

Bake in 375° oven about 25 minutes.

Remove to a rack, turn out and cool immediately.

A Super Corn Bread

this is a "so good" corn bread and so nutritious, which makes for a good marriage

Preheat oven 425°.

Put *1 tablespoon bran* and *1 tablespoon wheat germ* into a one-cup measure. *Fill the rest of the cup with flour* and put into a large bowl. Add *1 cup cornmeal, 2 teaspoons baking powder, ¼ teaspoon soda, 1 tablespoon sugar, ½ teaspoon salt, ½ cup nonfat dry milk.* Mix with a pastry blender until well combined.

Mix *1 egg* with a fork. Stir in *¼ cup oil* and *1 cup cold tap water.*

Add to the flour mixture. Stir with a fork just to combine. It will be a little lumpy, but that is OK.

Bake in 425° preheated oven 20 to 25 minutes.

Remove the cornbread to a rack to cool.

Tip: The cornbread is usually done at 20 minutes, so test. Don't overbake, as you will have cornbread that is too dry.

PS: Some people might like a little more salt, but remember, "you know who" says cut back on the salt and sugar!

Sliced Tea Cakes

good with coffee too . . . has a taste that says "more"

Heat oven 375° or 400° depending on oven.

Mix together *3¼ cups flour, 3 teaspoons baking powder, 1 teaspoon soda, 1 cup plus ¼ cup sugar, 1 teaspoon salt, ¼ teaspoon mace* and *¼ teaspoon cardamon.*

With a pastry blender or 2 knives, work in *2 tablespoons grated lemon rind* and *¾ cup plus 2 tablespoons soft margarine* until it looks like crumbs.

Mix *1 egg* with *3 tablespoons rum, ¼ teaspoon almond extract, 1 teaspoon vanilla* and *¼ cup plain yogurt.*

Add *½ cup golden raisins* and *½ cup slivered almonds.*

Mix together with a fork until the dough forms a ball that cleans the bowl.

Work with your hands to form a smooth ball.

If necessary, sprinkle a little flour on a clean surface. With a sharp knife cut the ball in half, then in half again.

Roll one ball at a time into a round loaf 11 × 3 inches. Place on an ungreased Teflon pan.

Bake at 375° if your oven is a hot oven for 20 to 25 minutes; or in a slow oven bake at 425° for 20 to 25 minutes.

Remove to a rack to cool.

When ready to eat, cut into slices as you use them. Freeze the "bread cakes" whole and slice them as you use them, too.

Banana Oat Crisp

easy to make and easy to eat

Heat oven 375°.

Sprinkle *juice of 1 lime* over *4 bananas.*

Mix together *3 tablespoons sugar* and *½ teaspoon cinnamon* and sprinkle over bananas.

Dot with *1½ tablespoons margarine.*

Mix together with a pastry blender or your fingers: *½ cup flour, 1 cup rolled oats, ½ cup brown sugar, ½ teaspoon salt* and *⅓ cup margarine.*

Sprinkle over the bananas.

Bake 30 to 35 minutes.

The bananas give this a "Down South" taste!

Apple Crisp

old fashioned and still delicious today

Heat oven 375°.

Core and slice *5 apples.*

Sprinkle *1 tablespoon lemon juice* over them to keep them from darkening.

Arrange in an 8″ × 8″ square baking dish.

Mix together *¼ cup sugar, ½ teaspoon cinnamon, ¼ teaspoon nutmeg.* Sprinkle over the apples.

Dot with *1½ tablespoons margarine.*

Mix together with a pastry blender or your fingers *½ cup flour, 1 cup rolled oats or rolled wheat, ½ cup brown or white sugar, ½ teaspoon salt* and *⅓ cup margarine.*

Spread over the apples.

Bake in 375° oven about 30 to 35 minutes.

Tastes mighty good warm.

Rich Baking Powder Dough

this is a dough you can use for many baked recipes . . . it's almost as rich as our pastry dough . . . it's easy to handle

Put into a large bowl *2 cups flour, 3 teaspoons wheat germ, 1 tablespoon baking powder, ½ teaspoon salt, 1 tablespoon sugar.* Mix together with a pastry blender.

Add *½ cup vegetable shortening.* Mix with the pastry blender into fine crumbs.

Put *1 egg* in a medium bowl. Mix the egg with a fork.

Stir in *¼ cup plus 3 tablespoons nonfat milk.*

With a fork, then your clean hands, stir until the flour mixture forms a ball and cleans the bowl.

Throw the ball hard from one hand to the other over a clean surface 25 times.

Now it is ready to be used as needed. Wrap in Saran Wrap to keep from drying out.

Fresh Peach Squares

when peaches are in season these are a special taste treat!

Preheat oven 450°.

Put the oven rack on the second shelf from the top nearest the heat.

The Filling: Wash, peel, stone, and cut into cubes *enough peaches to make 2½ cups.* Stir in *2 tablespoons lemon juice* and *½ cup and 4 teaspoons sugar* and mix well. Let this stand while you make the dough.

The Rich Baking Powder Dough:

Put into a large bowl *2 cups flour.* Add *2 tablespoons wheat germ, 3 teaspoons baking powder, ¾ teaspoon salt* and *½ teaspoon sugar.* Mix with a pastry blender.

Add *½ cup oil.* Mix with the pastry blender until it looks like small crumbs (more the size of wheat germ, not as fine as cornmeal).

Add *½ cup nonfat milk.* Mix with your clean hands to form a sticky ball. Let stand 3 minutes. It will not be sticky and will be easy to handle. Throw each one hard from one hand to the other over a clean surface 25 times.

Flour a clean surface. Cut the dough into 4 pieces. Roll out one piece at a time 11″ × 4½″. Smear with margarine down the middle. Strain the peaches. Set aside the juice. You can make our Peach drink from it, or you can make a sauce with it. Sprinkle lightly with sugar. Divide into 4 portions. Arrange one portion of the peach mixture down the middle of the dough lengthwise. Sprinkle a little sugar over the peaches. Fold one side over the peaches then the other to enclose the peaches. Pinch the ends closed. Cut into 4 pieces.

Put on a cookie sheet one next to the other to look like a roll. Do the same with the rest of the three pieces of dough and filling.

Make an egg wash with *1 egg yolk* mixed with *2 teaspoons cold tap water.* Brush each roll with this egg wash. Sprinkle a little sugar on. Do the same to the rest.

Place in the preheated 450° oven. Bake about 20 minutes.

Make some sauce if you wish. Add *enough water* to the *juice* to make *1 cup.*

Mix 2 *tablespoons* of this mixture with 2 *teaspoons cornstarch.*

Bring the rest of the juice mixture to a boil.

Stir the cornstarch mixture in. Cook, stir until the juice mixture thickens and turns clear. Cook 2 minutes. You can serve this sauce either hot or cold with the peach roll.

Old Fashioned Fresh Apple Rolls Or Squares

baked in our Rich Baking Powder Dough and served with our Lemon Sauce, you've got it made!

Preheat oven 450°.

The Filling: Wash, peel and core *enough apples to make 2 cups.*

Mix together in a bowl *½ cup sugar, 2 teaspoons cinnamon.* Stir in *1 tablespoon lemon juice.* Mix with the apples. Let stand.

Make the Rich Baking Dough. See recipe on page 67.

Cut the dough into half, then each into halves to make 4 pieces. Throw hard from one hand to the other 25 times. Roll out one at a time. Put Saran Wrap on the rest so they won't dry out while you roll out one at a time.

Roll out into an 11″ × 4½″ rectangle. Smear a little margarine down the middle of the dough but not the edges. Sprinkle a little sugar on.

Drain the apples. Save the juice to make a sauce.

Arrange ¼ of the apples down the middle. Dot with margarine. Work fast so it doesn't melt.

Fold over one side at a time lengthwise to enclose it. Pinch the ends closed together.

Cut each into four portions. Place on a cookie sheet close together to make a roll.

Brush with egg wash made by mixing 1 egg yolk with 2 teaspoons cold tap water.

Sprinkle a little sugar on top. Cut into four pieces. Place on a cookie sheet close together.

Place on the second shelf from the heat in electric oven in 450° preheated oven about 20 minutes.

Sauce for those who like a sauce:

To the juice left from soaking the apples, *add 1 can (5½*

ounces) apple juice and *1 teaspoon cornstarch.* Cook, stir until it comes to a boil. Cook, stir until it clears and thickens a little, takes about 2 or 3 minutes to cook.

Tip: This is delicious served hot with the hot sauce served with it. Some of us like the apple rolls "as is" without the sauce. . . . It's all a matter of what you like!

Tender Peach Squares In A Peachy Sauce

you can make this in winter because we use canned peaches

Preheat oven 450°.

Put the oven rack on the second shelf from the top nearest the heat.

The Filling: Strain *1 can (1 pound 2¾ ounces) Peach Halves* (halves are firmer than slices); then slice and cut into cubes. You will have a little more than 1 cup juice.

In a saucepan mix together *3 tablespoons lemon juice, 3 tablespoons sugar, 1 tablespoon flour.* Cook, stir until it thickens. Mix with the peaches.

The Sauce: To the canned peach juice add *3 tablespoons lemon juice, 2 tablespoons sugar* (or more if needed). In a screw top jar put ½ cup of this juice. Add *½ teaspoon flour.* Shake well to combine and see that there are no lumps. (Tip: if there are lumps, strain.) Stir this flour mixture into the rest of the juice.

Make our Rich Baking Powder Dough Recipe. See recipe on page 67.

Cut the dough into half, then each into halves making four equal pieces.

One at a time roll out the dough into a rectangle 11 × 4½ inches. Smear with a little soft margarine down the center but not on the edges. Arrange one portion peaches down the center lengthwise, but don't cover the edges. Fold the dough one side at a time lengthwise over the fruit. Press it to close and pinch the two ends to close.

Brush the top with soft margarine and sprinkle a little sugar on.

Cut into five pieces. Continue until all are done this way.

Arrange in a 12″ × 7½″ × 1¾″ baking dish.

We use a glass baking dish and serve from it.

Bring the sauce to a boil. Spoon it quickly around the fruit rolls.

Place in the preheated 450° oven. Bake about 20 to 25 minutes.

We like this served hot, but hot or cold . . . it's good.

Home Baked Fresh Prune Plum Squares

when the trees are laden with prune plums treat your family to this delicious dessert

Preheat oven 450°.

The Filling: Wash, seed and cut into small cubes *enough prune plums to make 2 cups.*

Mix together *1 tablespoon flour* and *½ cup sugar.* Stir into the prunes.

Stir in *1 tablespoon lemon juice.*

Cook, stir until it comes to a boil. Cook and stir 5 minutes. Spoon onto a large plate to get cold.

See the recipe for Rich Baking Powder Dough on page 67, and make it.

Divide the dough into four equal pieces.

Roll out one at a time 11″ × 4½″. Smear with some soft margarine. Sprinkle lightly with sugar. Spoon ½ cup of the filling down the middle of the dough lengthwise. Fold one side over the filling. Fold the other over to enclose the filling. Cut into four pieces. Remove to a cookie sheet, one piece next to the other.

Do the same with the rest of the dough.

Make an egg wash by mixing with a fork *1 egg yolk* with *2 teaspoons cold tap water.*

Brush the egg wash over the rolls. Place in the preheated 450° oven. Bake about 20 to 25 minutes.

Peach Prune Plum Squares

tastes like real "down home" country baking

Preheat oven 450°.

Wash, seed and cut into small cubes *enough prune plums to make 1 cup and 1 cup peaches.* Stir in *2 tablespoons lemon juice* and *½ cup sugar plus 2 tablespoons.*

Cook, stir until it comes to a boil. Cook, stir 5 minutes. Strain in a strainer over a bowl. Spoon the fruit onto a large plate to cool quickly. Save the juice to make a sauce if you wish, or use another time.

Make our Rich Baking Powder Dough; see page 67.

Divide the dough into four pieces. Roll out one at a time 11″ × 4½″.

Smear with soft (not melted) margarine. Sprinkle lightly with sugar. Spoon ½ cup of the filling down the middle of the dough. Fold one side over the filling; then fold the other side over to enclose the filling.

Cut into four pieces. Remove to a cookie sheet, one piece next to the other.

Do the same to the others.

Make an egg wash with *1 egg yolk* mixed with *2 teaspoons water*. Brush on the rolls. Place in the preheated 450° oven.

Bake about 20 to 25 minutes.

This freezes fine and is good defrosted to room temperature and also reheats well enclosed in foil and put on a rack to reheat at 400°.

For singles or doubles, if you have a "Toaster Oven" use it.

Tip: Be sure and put it on a little rack which you can buy at either—"good kitchen ware" department stores, supermarkets, hardware stores, or "cut rate" stores.

Tip: A 6-inch round rack is "handy" to have for singles and doubles to use in Toaster Ovens for reheating "baked goods" such as rolls, biscuits and whatever you don't want to burn on the bottom.

Baking Powder Dough Biscuits And A "Melt In Your Mouth" Fruit Roll

this is a 2 in 1 recipe . . . you have biscuits and a "fruit roll" baked in a sauce when you make the dough

Preheat oven 450°. Put the oven rack on the 2nd shelf from the top heat.

The Filling: Strain *1 can (1 pound) of Peach Halves* or

your favorite fruit. Cut the fruit into bite size pieces. Add *3 tablespoons sugar* and mix gently. Let stand.

The Sauce: You will have about *1 cup or a little less canned fruit juice.* Stir in *1 tablespoon lemon juice, 2 tablespoons sugar.* Put into a screw top jar ½ cup of the juice and add *1 teaspoon flour.* Shake well to combine. Stir into the rest of the juice. Let stand.

Make the recipe for our Rich Baking Dough; see page 67.

Cut the dough in half. Make biscuits out of ½ and the fruit rolls as follows—Cut the ½ piece dough in half. Roll each half one at a time into 11″ × 4½″ rectangle. Smear with a little margarine down the center but not on the edges.

Arrange the fruit lengthwise down the middle but not the edges.

Fold the dough one side at a time, lengthwise, over the fruit to enclose. Pinch the ends together to close. Brush the top with soft margarine and sprinkle a little sugar on. Cut into 5 pieces. Arrange in a 12″ × 7½″ × 1¾″ baking dish.

We use a glass baking dish.

Bring the sauce to a boil. Spoon it quickly around the fruit rolls.

Place in the preheated 450° oven. Bake about 20 to 25 minutes.

We like this served hot.

Tasty Fillings

for Hors D'Oeuvres, Tidbits or Large Half Moons or small crescents made with Rich Baking Powder Dough

UNSWEETENED FILLINGS:

1. Deviled ham
2. Bacon bits and mayonnaise
3. Ready Cooked chicken, chopped or ground and seasonings
4. Ready Cooked meat, chopped or ground and seasonings
5. Tuna fish
6. Canned salmon
7. Sardines; plain, with mustard, with tomato sauce.

SWEETENED FILLINGS (combine sugar, margarine, raisins, nuts):

1. Chopped dates or chopped dates and nuts and sugar, margarine.

2. Raisins and nuts or just raisins, or just nuts, sugar and cinnamon and margarine.
3. Fresh chopped apples and lemon juice and sugar and margarine.
4. Grated orange rind, sugar, margarine and raisins.
5. Fresh chopped apples, nuts, cinnamon and sugar, margarine.
6. Figs, nuts, orange rind and sugar.
7. Thick preserves, nuts

TOPPINGS:

1. 10X sugar mixed with milk
2. 1 whole egg wash. 1 egg mixed with fork with 1 teaspoon water. Put on dough before baking and again after it is half baked.
3. 1 egg yolk mixed with 2 teaspoons cold tap water—brush on just before putting in oven.
4. Orange 10X icing. Mix ½ cup 10X sugar, 1 tablespoon grated orange rind and 1 tablespoon orange juice.
5. Cranberry topping—mix together ½ cup of a can of cranberry, orange mixed with 2 tablespoons sugar. Spoon on dough.
6. Mix together with pastry blender ¼ cup sugar, ¼ cup flour. Add 2 tablespoons margarine and mix with pastry blender until crumb-like.

SHAPES:

1. Roll out dough, spread with filling, roll up, slice, bake.
2. Roll out dough, spread with filling, roll up, shape into "Half Moons," cut 1 inch intervals from outside, turn out to show fillings, glaze.
3. Roll out dough, cut into sizes you wish, fill, shape into turnovers.
4. Roll out dough, fill, roll like jelly roll, cut into slices, bake.
5. Roll out dough into round shape, cut into wedges, roll up starting at wide end.
6. Fruit Filled Coffee Cake—spread filling on rolled dough. Put on baking sheet. Spread filling lengthwise in center of dough. Make cuts about 2 inches at 1 inch intervals on both sides; then fold the strips over the filling. After baking, pour or drizzle 10X icing over the dough (10X sugar mixed with water or milk . . . just enough to drizzle).

Apple Lattice Coffee Cake Pie

it's not a pie nor a cake . . . it's a cake pie . . . it doesn't taste like a cake . . . it doesn't taste like a pie . . . but . . . it's delicious . . . serve it hot . . . serve it cold . . . make it . . . it only takes about 20 minutes to bake . . . and it's EASY!

If you have a slow oven, heat it 425°; if not heat it 400°.

Grease a 9-inch glass baking dish.

You need *1 jar (14½ ounces) "Lucky Leaf Dutch Baked Apples"* or *another canned, sliced apples.* If you're using another canned, sliced apples and they have no seasoning, add cinnamon and sugar.

With a pastry blender in a large bowl mix together *1½ cups flour, ¼ cup dry milk, 2 teaspoons baking powder, 1 teaspoon sugar* and *¾ teaspoon salt.*

Add *⅓ cup margarine.* Cut in with the pastry blender until the mixture looks like fine crumbs, but not too fine.

Mix 1 egg with a fork. Stir in *4 tablespoons water.*

Add to the flour mixture. Mix with a fork until the dough cleans the bowl and forms a ball.

Put a little flour lightly on a surface and dust your hands with a little flour.

Take the dough in your hands and shape and smooth it. Cut one piece a little larger than the other. Flatten the larger piece, or roll out, to fit the pie plate. Cover the bottom with the dough about half way up the sides.

Spoon in the jar of apples. Roll the other piece of dough about the size of the top of the pie. Cut into 6 strips. Arrange 3 across one way and 3 strips on top the other way. Place in preheated oven. Bake about 20 minutes.

Isn't it good! And easy!

Chopped Apple Raisin Coffee Cake

the perfume of the apples baking invites everyone into the kitchen

Grease and flour an 8″ × 8″ square baking pan.

Preheat oven 375°.

The Topping: Mix with a pastry blender or your fingers ¼

cup flour, ¼ cup sugar, 1 teaspoon cinnamon and *2 tablespoons margarine* into crumbs. Set aside.

Peel and chop *1 cup apples.*

With a pastry blender, mix together *1½ cups* and *3 tablespoons flour, 1 tablespoon wheat germ, 3 teaspoons baking powder, ½ teaspoon salt, ½ cup sugar* and *2 tablespoons grated orange rind.*

Add *½ cup margarine.* With the pastry blender, mix into a crumb-like mixture. Add the chopped apples and mix together gently.

Mix *1 egg* with a fork. Stir in *½ cup nonfat milk* and *1 teaspoon vanilla* and add to the flour mixture. Mix just to combine.

Spoon into the baking pan.

Sprinkle the topping over the coffee cake.

Place in the preheated 375° oven. Bake about 25 to 30 minutes.

Serve warm; or, of course, you can serve it cold too.

Fresh Sliced Peach Or Apple Coffee Cake

both are so good I'm sure you will be making each when in season!

Grease and flour an 8″ × 8″ square baking pan. Shake out any excess flour.

Preheat oven 375°.

Grate *3 tablespoons orange rind* (Tip: it's wonderful to have orange rind grated and frozen; and if so, be sure to dry it well).

The Topping: Mix together *¼ cup sugar, 2 teaspoons cinnamon, ¼ cup flour.* Add *2 tablespoons and 1 teaspoon margarine.*

Crumble with your fingers.

Wash, peel, slice *enough fruit:* apples, peaches, pears, nectarines, plums or apricots (cut in halves). Use apricots if you grow them yourself . . . the "store bought" ones have no flavor.

Mix together with a pastry blender, *1½ cups and 3 tablespoons flour, 1 tablespoon wheat germ, 3 teaspoons baking powder, ½ teaspoon salt, ½ cup sugar* and *3 tablespoons orange rind.* Add *½ cup margarine.*

With the pastry blender, mix into a crumb-like mixture.

Mix *1 egg* with a fork. Stir in *½ cup nonfat milk*. Add to the flour mixture and mix just to combine. Don't overmix.

Spoon into the baking pan.

Arrange the sliced fruit on top in a pretty design overlapping the slices.

Sprinkle the topping on top.

Place in the preheated 375° oven. Bake about 25 to 30 minutes.

Serve warm if you can.

Chocolate Swirl Coffee Cake

this coffee cake teases your taste buds with two tastes

Heat oven 375°. Grease and flour an 8″ × 8″ square pan. Shake out excess flour.

Chocolate batter: With a mixing spoon mix together *2 tablespoons cocoa, 2 tablespoons sugar* and *2 tablespoons oil.* Set aside.

Topping: Mix with a pastry blender *¼ cup flour, ¼ cup sugar, 1 teaspoon cinnamon* and *2 tablespoons margarine* into crumbs. Set aside.

With a pastry blender mix together *1¾ cups plus 3 tablespoons flour, 2 teaspoons wheat germ, 3 teaspoons baking powder, ½ teaspoon salt, ½ cup sugar* and *¼ cup nonfat dry milk.*

Add *½ cup margarine* and with the pastry blender mix into crumb-like mixture.

Beat *1 egg* with a fork. Stir in *¾ cup plus 2 tablespoons cold tap water* and *1 teaspoon vanilla.* Add to the flour mixture and just mix to combine.

Spoon the batter into the baking dish.

Spoon the chocolate batter onto the cake batter.

With a knife swirl the chocolate batter through the cake batter in spiral fashion, which gives a marbled effect. Don't smooth; let it look rough.

Sprinkle the topping over the batter.

Bake in 375° oven about 30 minutes until done.

Tip: If you don't want to use the topping, don't. We prefer this coffee cake without the topping.

Peanut Butter Swirl Coffee Cake

Children aren't the only ones who love this cake! You follow the Chocolate Swirl recipe and substitute ½ cup room temperature peanut butter instead of the chocolate. Stir the peanut butter with 1 tablespoon sugar until it is soft enough to use. The rest of the recipe is the same. Delicious, isn't it?

Blueberry, Huckleberry, Raspberry Brickle

one is as delicious as the other, so you choose which berry you like best, or have raised, or can buy . . . what's a brickle? . . . to us, it's a coffee cake

When fresh blueberries are in season, but in season or not . . . they can always be found in cans in the supermarkets, try the canned wild blueberries, they're delicious.

We make Blueberry Brickle with canned wild blueberries as follows:

Heat oven 375°.

Grease an 8″ × 8″ baking pan and sprinkle flour over. Shake excess flour off.

Drain *1 can (15 ounces) wild blueberries.*

Mix together this topping:

¼ cup sugar, ¼ cup flour, 1½ teaspoons cinnamon, then add *2 tablespoons margarine.* Mix until crumbly; set aside.

With a pastry blender, mix together *1¾ cups flour* and *2 teaspoons wheat germ, 3 teaspoons baking powder, ½ teaspoon salt* and *½ cup sugar* and *¼ cup nonfat dry milk.*

Add *½ cup margarine* and mix with the pastry blender. It will look crumbly.

Mix *1 egg* with a fork. Stir in *¾ cup cold tap water* and *1 teaspoon vanilla.*

Add to the flour mixture and just mix to combine.

Spoon into the greased 8″ × 8″ baking pan.

Spoon the blueberries over the batter.

Sprinkle the topping over the blueberries.

Bake in 375° oven about 35 minutes until done.

Remove from oven and cool.

If you wish to use fresh milk, omit the dry milk and water and substitute 3/4 cup skim milk or nonfat milk.

Orange Coffee Cake

this is the kind of coffee cake you can make spring, summer, fall and winter, because oranges in our USA are always available

Grease and flour an 8″ × 8″ baking pan. Heat oven 375°.

Grate *enough orange rind to make 3 tablespoons.*

With a pastry blender, mix together *1 3/4 cups flour* and *2 teaspoons wheat germ, 3 teaspoons baking powder, 1/2 teaspoon salt, 1/2 cup sugar* and the *3 tablespoons grated orange rind* and *1/4 cup instant nonfat dry milk.*

Add *1/2 cup margarine* from the refrigerator and mix with the pastry blender. It will look crumbly.

Mix *1 egg* with a fork. Stir in *3/4 cup plus 2 tablespoons cold tap water* and *1 teaspoon vanilla.*

Add to the flour mixture, and just mix to combine.

Topping: Mix together with a pastry blender, *1/4 cup sugar, 1/4 cup flour, 1 1/2 teaspoons cinnamon* and *2 tablespoons margarine* until crumbly—the crumbs should not be too small.

Spoon the batter into the greased and floured 8″ × 8″ baking dish.

Drop *1/3 cup thick orange marmalade* by teaspoonfuls onto the batter. Swirl through the batter. Sprinkle the topping on top.

Bake in 375° oven about 35 to 40 minutes until done.

Big tip: Don't let the margarine get to room temperature. Take it from the refrigerator when ready to use in the recipe.

Another tip: We use the tub margarine, because it has more oil than the sticks and is thus less saturated.

Another tip: Before you measure flour, take a mixing spoon and lift the flour. This makes it lighter, and you don't have to sift the flour. We don't sift flour, as the flour mill people have already done so.

Raisin Coffee Cake

and what these raisins do to this coffee cake will make you very happy

Heat oven 375°.
Grease and flour an 8″ × 8″ baking pan.
Steam *1 cup raisins* to soften. Wipe.
The Topping: With a pastry blender, mix *¼ cup sugar* with *1½ teaspoons cinnamon, 2 tablespoons margarine* and *¼ cup flour.*
With a pastry blender mix together *1¾ cups flour, ¼ cup nonfat dry milk, 2 teaspoons wheat germ, 3 teaspoons baking powder, ½ teaspoon salt* and *½ cup sugar.*
Add *½ cup margarine* and mix with the pastry blender. It will look crumbly. Do not make it fine.
Add the *1 cup raisins* and mix together.
Mix with a fork *1 egg.* Stir in *¾ cup plus 2 tablespoons cold tap water* and *1 teaspoon vanilla.*
Add to the flour mixture and just mix to combine.
Spoon into the baking pan.
Spoon the topping on top.
Bake in preheated 375° oven 35 minutes until done.
Remove from oven to cool.
If you wish to use liquid nonfat or skim milk, use ¾ cup milk and 2 tablespoons instead of the water and omit the dry milk. Remember that the dry milk is a good Penny Pincher saver, and the coffee cake tastes just as good with it as the liquid milk.

Glazed Apple Kuchen

it tastes as good as it looks

Grease 11½″ × 8″ glass baking pan with margarine.
Heat oven 350°.
Peel, core and cut *4 apples* into quarters, then into ⅛ inch slices. Sprinkle *lemon juice* over.
With the pastry blender mix together *2 cups flour, 2 teaspoons wheat germ, ¼ cup plus 2 tablespoons sugar, 1 teaspoon baking powder.*
With the pastry blender mix in *¼ cup plus 2 tablespoons margarine.*

Mix *3 eggs* with a fork and stir into the flour mixture. Let stand 5 minutes.

With your clean, floured hands press the dough into the pan over the bottom.

Arrange the apple slices on top, overlapping to make a pretty design.

Cook, stir *¾ jar, or more if needed, apricot preserves* until melted. With a spoon glaze the apples.

Bake in 350° oven for about 45 minutes.

The glaze really makes this dish beautiful, and it certainly adds to the flavor of the apples, too.

German Apple Kuchen

that's taking in a lot of territory but it's the best I've ever eaten! This recipe years and years ago crossed the ocean from Russia to the United States. My wonderful little mother-in-law learned it from the cook on her grandfather's farm in Lithuania. The wheat germ is my touch to her recipe.

Heat oven 375°.

You need a heat proof glass baking dish 12″ × 7½″ × 2″ so you can serve in it too.

The Topping: Mix together *½ cup sugar* with *2 teaspoons cinnamon*.

Wash, peel *5 or 6 Golden Delicious or Stayman Winesap apples*. Cut into quarters, core, then slice into thin slices but not paper thin to make about 6 cups. Sprinkle with *¼ cup lemon juice*. Mix and let stand.

Put into a large bowl *1¼ cups and 2 tablespoons flour, 1 teaspoon wheat germ, 1½ teaspoons baking powder, ¼ cup sugar, ¼ teaspoon salt*. Mix with a pastry blender.

Add *3 tablespoons margarine* and mix with the pastry blender until it has largish crumbs.

Put *¼ cup thick sour cream* into a bowl. Don't use any of the watery sour cream.

Mix *1 egg* with a fork. Slowly and gently stir the egg into the sour cream so it remains thick.

Add the sour cream mixture to the flour mixture. With a fork, mix until it forms a ball of dough that cleans the bowl.

Flour your hands, throw the ball hard from one hand to the other 20 times.

Divide the dough into 4 equal pieces. Wrap each one in plastic wrap so that it doesn't dry out.

Put some flour on a clean surface.

Unwrap one piece of dough and roll out to fit one half of the baking dish. If necessary to keep from sticking, lift the dough and flour the surface lightly. Fit the dough into the pan. If it should tear it's easy to patch. Repeat with another piece of dough and put into the pan. Now you have the bottom crust.

Shake off the lemon juice from each slice of apple as you arrange them in rows overlapping on the dough. Sprinkle 3 tablespoons of the topping over the apples. Make another layer of the apples on top as you did before. Sprinkle 3 more tablespoons of the topping over the apples.

Melt *2 tablespoons margarine*. Spoon it over the apples.

One at a time, roll out the other 2 pieces of dough and fit on top of the apples.

Mix *1 egg yolk* with a fork. Add *2 teaspoons cold tap water* and mix just to combine. Using a soft bristle brush, brush this *egg wash* over the dough. Sprinkle 1 tablespoon cinnamon sugar mixture on top.

Place in preheated 375° oven. Bake about 25 minutes until done and a beautiful brown color.

To serve, cut in the pan.

To reheat, put a piece of foil over the top and reheat in a 350° oven.

Homemade Sticky Buns

in Germany they call them "Schnecken" and in any language they're delicious . . . these are not runny . . . just sticky

Heat oven 375°.

Have handy a pastry blender or fork.

Cut *¼ cup pecans* into pieces. Set aside.

Grease an 8-inch round cake pan with a little margarine.

Sprinkle *¼ cup dark brown sugar* packed down over the greased cake pan. Pour over *¼ cup clear corn syrup* and dot with *¼ cup margarine*. Set aside.

Prepare the buns:

Put into a large bowl *1¾ cups flour, 2 tablespoons wheat germ, 3 teaspoons baking powder, ¼ teaspoon salt, ½ teaspoon sugar*. Mix with the pastry blender. Add *6 table-*

spoons margarine. Mix with the pastry blender just until the mixture looks as coarse as wheat germ.

Measure *½ cup nonfat milk.* Set aside. Measure *½ cup raisins.* Set aside. Then mix together *1 tablespoon sugar* and *¼ teaspoon cinnamon* and set this aside.

Put the cake pan and its mixture into the 375° oven for 10 minutes. When done sprinkle the chopped nuts on top.

Make the buns:

Immediately add *½ cup milk* to the flour mixture. With a fork stir just until the dough cleans the bowl and is soft but not sticky. Sprinkle about 3 tablespoons flour over a clean surface. Roll out the dough into a rectangle about 10 × 16 inches.

Smear *2 tablespoons margarine* over the dough. Sprinkle the sugar, cinnamon mixture over it, then sprinkle *½ cup raisins* on top. Put a piece of wax paper on top and roll over with a rolling pin so the raisins stick and don't fall out. Remove the wax paper.

Roll the dough tightly, starting at the wide side, into a roll like a jelly roll. Cut into 12 pieces.

Be sure to check whether you added the nuts to the syrup; and if you forgot, do it now.

Arrange the buns on top of the syrup/nut mixture.

Place in the preheated 375° oven. Bake about 30 minutes.

Place on a rack for 10 minutes, then turn over onto a plate. If a little of the "sticky" topping clings to the pan, use a knife and stick it back on . . . it's too good to waste.

Baked Topping

Baked Chocolate Nut Topping

Grate *enough Semi-Sweet Chocolate to make 1 cup.*

Chop *½ cup walnuts.*

Sprinkle chocolate and walnuts over the cake batter and bake the cake as directed.

Baked Meringue Nut Topping

Chop coarsely *½ cup walnuts or pecans.*

Beat *2 egg whites* stiff. Gradually add *1 cup sugar* and

continue to beat until you feel no grains of sugar when you taste.

Spread on the cake batter. Sprinkle the nuts on. Bake cake as directed.

Creamy Butter Frosting

Cream *½ cup butter*. Add gradually about *1 pound (3½ cups) sifted 10X sugar,* stirring until well blended. Add a few grains salt.

Stir in liquid a little at a time, adding just enough to give a good spreading consistency, beating until fluffy (4 to 5 tablespoons cream, milk or hot water). Add *1½ teaspoons vanilla* or other flavoring. Makes enough for 3 8-inch or 2 9-inch cakes or 2 dozen cup cakes.

Glazes And Toppings For Baked Doughs

Roll Glaze

Mix together *1½ tablespoons warm water* with *1 cup strained 10X Confectioner's sugar.*

Cool rolls, rings or crescents a little.

Spoon the glaze on top.

Butter Sugar Topping

Mix together until creamy *½ cup butter* at room temperature with *1 cup 10X sugar* put through a strainer to remove any lumps.

Lemon, Coconut Topping

Mix together *½ cup strained 10X sugar* with *2 tablespoons lemon juice.* Stir in *1 cup grated coconut.* You can substitute chopped nuts if you wish.

Orange Glaze or Lemon Glaze

Mix together in a saucepan ½ *cup sugar,* ¼ *cup clear corn syrup,* ¼ *cup water.* Bring to a simmer. Simmer about 10 minutes. Add the *grated peel of 1 orange or 1 lemon.* Cool just a little before glazing, as it will thicken a little. Also, have the rolls or baked doughs warm when you glaze.

A Dark Glaze

Mix together ⅓ *cup dark corn syrup, 2 tablespoons melted butter or margarine* and *1 teaspoon vanilla* or ½ *teaspoon almond flavor.* This gives the dough flavor and a nice shine.

Heavy Topping

Mix together ½ *cup sugar,* ½ *cup flour, 1 teaspoon cinnamon* and ¼ *cup margarine* with a pastry blender until crumbly.

Light Topping

Mix together with a pastry blender ¼ *cup sugar,* ¼ *cup flour, 1 teaspoon cinnamon* and *2 tablespoons margarine* until crumbly.

Another Topping

Mix together ¼ *cup sugar, 2 tablespoons flour,* and *1 teaspoon cinnamon.* Add *2 tablespoons margarine.* Crumble into crumbs.

Streusel Topping

Mix together ½ *cup sugar,* ½ *cup flour, 1 teaspoon cinnamon.* Rub in ⅓ *cup melted butter* or use pastry blender.

A Second Streusel Topping

Mix together *½ cup sugar, 1 cup flour, 1 tablespoon grated orange rind.* Add *⅓ cup melted butter or margarine.* Rub together into large crumbs.

A Third Streusel Topping

Mix together *½ cup sugar, ½ cup flour, 2 teaspoons grated lemon rind.* Rub in *⅓ cup melted butter or margarine* and *½ teaspoon vanilla.* You can add *⅓ cup ground almonds.*

Raisin Nut Topping

Mix together *½ cup sugar, 1 teaspoon cinnamon, ¼ cup melted butter.* Add *½ cup chopped nuts, ½ cup or 1 cup raisins.*

Chocolate Nut Topping

Mix *¼ cup cocoa* with *½ cup sugar.* Melt *¼ cup butter or margarine.* Mix with the cocoa mixture. Add *½ cup raisins* and *¼ cup chopped nuts* as you wish.

Luscious Fillings

we give you a choice . . . one very quick, the other you cook . . . both are very good . . . to tell the truth, most of the time we do the "Easy One"

Apricot Filling Number 1

Soak *1 cup dried apricots* in *1¼ cups water* overnight or at least 5 hours, or you can cook them without soaking but they will take much longer.

Cook, stir the soaked apricots and the water 10 to 15 minutes until soft. Push through a food mill or strainer. Put back into the saucepan with *¾ cup sugar* to your taste and *1 tablespoon lemon juice*. Cook, stir 5 minutes.

Apricot Filling Number 2
The Easy Way "No Cooking!"

Stir into *1 cup apricot preserves, 2 teaspoons butter, 1 teaspoon lemon juice to taste* and *½ cup chopped walnuts.* The walnuts are optional but they taste good and add some protein.

Orange Filling Number 1

can also be used as a glaze

Mix together *1 cup 10X sugar* (Confectioner's sugar) with *2 teaspoons "soft" butter, 2 tablespoons defrosted orange juice concentrate and 1 tablespoon lemon juice,* and *½ cup walnuts or pecans* chopped.

Orange Filling Number 2

Mix together *1 cup Crosse and Blackwell sweet* or *Seville Orange Marmalade,* or your favorite with *2 teaspoons soft butter* and *½ cup chopped walnuts.*

Cheese Filling

Mix together *1 package (8 ounces) well drained cottage cheese* with *1 tablespoon melted butter or margarine, 1 egg yolk, 3 tablespoons sugar* and *salt* if needed. Add *½ cup raisins.* For an extra special taste add *¼ teaspoon cinnamon* to the sugar.

Tip: When using cottage cheese you might need to add 2 tablespoons bread crumbs or cookie crumbs or Graham cracker crumbs to keep from running.

Apricot Filling or Orange Marmalade Filling

Tip: Krafts, Polaner and some store label apricot jam is good. Crosse and Blackwell have a good orange marmalade.

Mix together *1 tablespoon butter or margarine* with *⅓ cup apricot jam or orange marmalade, 1 tablespoon sugar* to taste and *¼ teaspoon cinnamon.* Add *⅓ cup chopped nuts* and *⅓ cup raisins.*

Date Filling

Mix together in a saucepan *1 (8 ounce) package of dates* which you chop or cut with a scissors and *1 cup chopped pecans, ¼ cup sugar, ¾ cup water, 1 tablespoon lemon juice* and *1 tablespoon lemon rind or orange rind.* Cook, stir until it is thick and spreadable. Cool before using. Makes 2 cups.

Tips

Never let the rind of oranges go to waste. Always wash the oranges, wipe, then grate the rind fine. Measure it in 1 tablespoon proportions. Wrap each in foil separately. Put them in a plastic bag. Freeze. You will have them on hand whenever you need them. We have found that they flavor cakes, coffee cakes, cookies and "whatever" much better than orange juice. Why throw away such a necessary, wonderful ingredient? Grate your orange rinds. You will be glad!

When we say margarine we mean the soft tub margarine, it has less saturated fat in it. We also have switched to the tub margarine that is unsalted. You have to be careful that it's fresh, as it doesn't keep as well as the salted ones.

Margarine freezes well.

How To Knead

This is the easiest way to knead. Other people may knead differently, which is OK, but we have found this is the easiest way.

Here are the directions: You knead the whole piece of dough each time. Fold the dough over itself halfway. Push the dough lightly with the palm of the hand. Make a quarter turn; repeat. You keep doing this, and you will get the rhythm of it. Don't bear down heavy. Do the procedure lightly. You won't get tired, and the "bread will like it." That's all there is to it.

The Finger Test

This is how to test whether the bread has risen enough.

Push your middle finger into the risen dough. If the indentation stays, the bread has risen enough.

How To Shape A Loaf Of Bread

Grease your clean hands.

Smooth and shape the dough into an oval loaf, rolling it in your hands to get it the length of the bread pan.

Tuck the ends under.

Put into the greased baking pan.

Egg Wash

to brush on rolls, or other baked breads, coffee rings, etc. . . . browns them beautifully

Mix *1 egg yolk* with a fork.
Stir in 2 *teaspoons cold water.*

Just stir, don't beat, *1 teaspoon cold water* into *1 egg white.*

Whole Wheat Batter Bread

Mix together for about 1 minute with electric mixer on #1 speed, or with a pastry blender or mixing spoon *3⅓ cups whole wheat flour, ½ cup whole bran, 2 tablespoons wheat germ, ¼ cup dry milk, 1½ teaspoons salt, 2 tablespoons brown sugar,* and *2 packages dry yeast.*

Mix in on #1 speed or with pastry blender or spoon *2 tablespoons oil* for a few seconds.

From the tap add *1 cup plus ¼ cup plus 2 tablespoons warm water* (not lukewarm). Be sure the water is good and warm, but not hot. Start at #1 speed, then turn slowly to #4 speed and mix 2 minutes; or beat with the mixing spoon. The dough will be sticky and some will cling to the sides.

With a rubber spatula push this dough to the dough in the center. The dough may be clinging to the beaters. Use a rubber spatula to remove. Remove the bowl to a warm spot in the kitchen where there are no drafts. Cover loosely with a light kitchen towel.

Let rise until almost double, takes about 1 hour or more.

Stir dough down.

Beat vigorously with a wooden spoon about 1 minute.

Place in a 9-inch greased with margarine bread pan or a Teflon lined pan.

Flour your hands lightly to push the dough into the corners and even the top of the bread.

Cover with the towel again lightly. Let rise just to the top of the pan, not over, takes about 45 minutes. Peep in 30 minutes.

Bake in 375° oven 45 minutes. Lay a piece of foil lightly over the top. Bake 10 minutes more to brown the bottom.

Sophie's White Health Bread

made with wheat germ and bran, it not only tastes good, but it's nutritious!

We use our Kitchen Aid Electric Mixer, Model K-45, with the flat beater, not the dough hook. You can use any "strong" electric mixer or a wooden spoon and a strong arm as we do sometimes.

Grease with *margarine* an 8¾" × 4¾" × 2½" bread

pan. (These are outside measurements, and please don't use a larger pan.)

Mix together for about 1 minute on #1 speed, or with a pastry blender, *3 cups plus 6 tablespoons white flour, ½ cup whole bran (Quaker Unprocessed Bran or Health Food Store's brand), 2 tablespoons wheat germ, ¼ cup dry milk, 1½ teaspoons salt, 2 tablespoons brown sugar* and *2 packages dry yeast.* (We use Red Star Dry Yeast.)

Turn the faucet to almost hot water. Put *1¼ cups and 2 tablespoons of this very "warm" water* into a bowl. Test with your clean finger to see that the water is warm, almost hot, not lukewarm. Add this water to the flour mixture.

Start at #1 speed; then turn slowly to #4 speed, and beat 2 minutes; or beat vigorously by hand 4 minutes. The dough will be sticky and some will cling to the sides.

With a plastic spatula, push the dough down from the sides. The dough may also stick to the beaters. Use the plastic spatula to remove. With the spatula, smooth the top lightly.

Remove the bowl to a warm spot in the kitchen where there are no drafts. Cover loosely with a light kitchen towel. Let rise almost double, takes about 1 hour in the summertime, up to 1¼ hours in the winter.

Flour your hands, and punch the dough down.

Gather into your hands and work the dough, turning the ends under. That smooths the dough. Sometimes you may have to flour your hands again lightly to do this, because the dough might be a little sticky.

Place in the greased baking pan. Flour your hands lightly and push the dough into the corners and also smooth the top lightly. Cover with the towel again lightly.

Preheat the oven 375°.

Let the dough rise just to the top of the pan, *not over,* takes about 45 minutes.

Put in oven and bake about 45 minutes.

Lay a piece of foil lightly over the top. Bake 10 minutes to brown the bottom more.

Turn the bread over and tap it. It should sound hollow. This means the bread is done.

Remove the bread to a rack to cool, turning the bread right side up.

Let cool before eating.

A Round Earthy Whole Wheat Loaf

it's real wholesome good eating!

You use whole wheat flour only in this recipe.

Put 3 sheets of foil on a cookie sheet.

Put into a large bowl *4 cups whole wheat flour.*

Put into another large bowl *1½ cups warm (almost hot) water.* Stir in *2 packages instant dry yeast.* Immediately add *2 tablespoons sugar* and *1½ teaspoons salt* and mix.

Add *2 cups whole wheat flour.* Beat until smooth, about 2 minutes. Gradually add a little flour at a time, mixing until the dough leaves the sides of the bowl. Let rest 10 minutes.

Flour a clean surface lightly, using some of the whole wheat flour in the bowl. Flour your hands, too.

Scoop the dough out and knead, adding whole wheat flour as required to knead.

Knead about 5 minutes. Put back in the bowl to rise. Place a light kitchen towel on top. The bowl should be put in a warm place in the kitchen without any drafts. Let rise 1 hour.

Punch it down. On the clean floured surface knead the dough about 2 minutes.

Shape into a round loaf. Put on the cookie sheet. Cover with the light kitchen towel. Let rise until double, about 1 hour.

Put into preheated 375° oven. Bake about 30 minutes. Turn the bread over. Thump it. It should sound hollow.

Place on a rack to cool.

This is a heavy, earthy, wonderful tasting loaf. It sticks to the ribs.

Mrs. Fry's Whole Wheat Loaf

who's Mrs. Fry? . . . she is a home economics teacher who is "really teaching" teenagers how to cook the kind of food that is nutritious and tastes good . . . she's the kind of teacher every school in the USA should have!

I must confess I gave this loaf a "Sophie" touch. In fact, I came up with two different breads, one an American type bread that my son likes, and the other a good "earthy" type bread my husband likes. Here are both: see which you like.

Grease with *vegetable shortening* a 9½" × 5½" × 2¾" bread pan.

Put into a large bowl or other container *4 cups whole wheat flour.* Open *2 packages instant dry yeast.* Measure *1½ tablespoons vegetable shortening.*

Measure *1½ cups warm* (almost hot) *water.* Instantly put it in another large bowl. Sprinkle the 2 packages instant dry yeast in, and stir. Add *2 tablespoons sugar, 1½ teaspoons salt* and *1½ tablespoons vegetable shortening.* Mix.

Add 2 cups of the whole wheat flour. Beat until smooth, about 2 minutes.

Gradually, adding a little flour at a time, mix in enough flour, about 1 cup and 1 tablespoon, until the dough leaves the sides of the bowl when you mix it. Let rest 10 minutes.

Now you are ready to start kneading. Flour a clean surface lightly with some of the flour in the bowl; also flour your hands, as the dough will be sticky. Pick up the dough and place it on the floured surface. Start kneading, adding a little flour at a time as required to knead. Only add as much flour as you need. This is the trick that makes a lighter whole wheat loaf. Use about ¼ cup flour. Knead 10 minutes. Shape into a ball.

Put back into the bowl. Cover with a light kitchen towel.

Put in a warm spot in the kitchen where there are no drafts. Let rise 1 hour.

Punch dough down. Knead again 3 minutes, adding about 2 teaspoons whole wheat flour.

Shape and smooth the dough to fit the bread pan. Cover with the *light* kitchen towel. Let rise about an hour or until the dough rises *above* the pan, about 2 inches. This is important. (The reason we said *light* kitchen towel is because the bread needs to rise *above* the pan.)

Preheat oven 375° while the bread is rising. When the bread has risen as directed, put in the center of the oven. Bake 35 minutes.

Take out of oven. Turn the bread over. Thump it. It should have a hollow sound, which means it is done. If it doesn't, bake 5 minutes longer, and test again. Usually it is done in 35 minutes.

Place the bread on a rack to cool.

The bread should be a beautiful high loaf. If it isn't, it is because you added too much flour either in its "leaving the bowl" or when kneading it.

Tip: Usually we have about ¾ cup flour left when we make this bread.

Delicious Egg Bread

as delicious as it looks . . . that's how it tastes

Close all doors in your kitchen.

Put *3 tablespoons wheat germ into a cup and fill with flour.* Put into the large bowl of your mixer.

Add *2 cups flour, ¾ teaspoon salt, 1½ teaspoons sugar, ¾ cup nonfat dry milk.* Mix on low speed just to combine.

Add *2 tablespoons oil* and *2 large eggs.* Mix.

Make a well in the center. Put in *2 packages dry yeast.* Add *¾ cup warm (not lukewarm) water.*

Mix on #4 speed for Kitchen Aid or #6 speed in Sunbeam Mixmaster for 4 minutes.

Flour your hands and lightly flour a surface; then remove the ball of dough from the mixer. Take dough in your hand and shape into a smooth ball by quickly smoothing and folding the sides under, takes about a minute or two.

Put into a clean bowl. Put a little oil in a saucer and dip a piece of Saran Wrap in it and smear all over the dough ball.

Cover the bowl with a cloth towel. Put in a warm spot in the kitchen. Let stand 30 or 35 minutes to almost double.

Put *½ cup flour* into a small bowl to use to flour your hands. Scoop the sticky dough with your hands out of the bowl and put onto the floured surface.

Dip a sharp knife into the flour. Cut the dough into thirds. You can weigh the dough, so you have equal amounts.

Roll each, one at a time, between your hands to make a thick rope 14 inches long. Braid the 3 ropes together closing well the 2 ends.

Heat oven 375°.

Put on a Teflon cookie sheet. Cover lightly with a towel. Let rise about 30 minutes.

Test to see if it has risen enough by pushing your finger into the dough. If the indentation remains, the dough has risen enough.

Put *1 egg yolk* into a saucer. Stir in *1 teaspoon cold tap water.* This is called "egg wash."

With a soft brush, brush the bread all over, being careful to brush the creases.

Place in 375° oven. Bake 30 minutes.

Test whether done by tapping on the bottom, and if it sounds hollow, the bread is done. Remove the bread to a rack to cool.

Isn't it a large, beautiful colored loaf of bread?

But wait till you taste it! It's beautiful, too. This is one time you can smear your slice of bread with butter! They deserve each other, and so do you!

Two Yeast Egg Loaves

made from our "Basic Yeast Egg Dough" . . . tastes as good as the "Twist" even if they are not so spectacular

Follow the "Basic Yeast Egg Dough" recipe.

Cut the dough into halves.

Put each half into a Teflon-lined or greased loaf pan 8½" × 4½" × 2½".

Cover with a light cloth towel. Let rise in a warm spot in the kitchen away from drafts until it doubles in size, takes about 30 minutes.

Test with the finger test by pushing a finger into the dough; if the indentation stays, the dough has risen enough. Tip: Don't let over-rise; or it will fall when baking.

While the dough is rising, preheat the oven 375°.

Put the "risen" dough into the preheated 375° oven. Bake 30 minutes.

Remove from pans and cool.

You can eat one and freeze one. This bread freezes well.

If you are a small family and can't use a whole loaf quickly, slice the loaf, then freeze. You can then remove as few or as many slices as you can use, and the bread won't get stale.

Basic Yeast Roll Recipe

with that fly-right-in-your-mouth taste to make Crescents, Parkerhouse, Snails, Clover Leaf, Pan Rolls, or Bow Knot Rolls

Into a large bowl put *2 cups flour*. Remove *2 tablespoons*. Add *2 tablespoons wheat germ, 1½ teaspoons sugar, ¾ teaspoon salt* and *¾ cup nonfat dry milk.* Mix with a pastry blender or a large spoon.

Add *6 tablespoons oil.* Mix with the pastry blender until it looks like coarse meal.

Make a well in this mixture. Put in *2 packages active dry yeast.* Pour *¾ cup "warm" water (not lukewarm)* over the yeast. Mix; then beat 4 minutes with a wooden spoon or a large mixing spoon. Put a light towel over the bowl. Place in a warm spot in the kitchen away from drafts. Let stand 30 minutes until doubled.

Put *½ cup flour* in a bowl. Sprinkle about ¼ cup of this flour on a clean surface. Flour your hands with some of the flour from the bowl.

Scoop the sticky dough with your floured hands out of the bowl onto the floured surface shaping it into a ball.

Now continue to make the rolls of your choice: Crescents, Clover Leaf, Snails, Parkerhouse, Pan Rolls or Bow Knots.

Bow Knot Rolls

Make our "Basic Yeast Roll Recipe." (See recipe on page 95.)

Put *½ cup flour* in a bowl.

Sprinkle about *¼ cup flour* over a clean surface or large board. Flour your hands with flour in the bowl.

Scoop the sticky dough with your hands out of the bowl onto the floured surface or board.

Dip a sharp knife into the flour. Cut the dough into halves, then quarters, then cut again to make 8 pieces, then again to make 16 pieces.

Dip the cut sticky sides into the flour so you can handle them. One at a time, roll between your hands to make a thick rope about 7 inches long.

Make into a bow knot. Place on a Teflon cookie sheet. Continue until all are made.

Put a towel lightly on top. Let stand 30 minutes.

When you put the towel on top, preheat the oven 400°.

After 30 minutes, test to see if the rolls have risen enough with the finger test as follows: push a finger into one of the rolls, making an indentation. If the indentation remains the rolls are ready to be brushed with Egg Wash. Make Egg Wash by mixing *1 egg yolk* with a fork with *2 teaspoons cold tap water.*

With a soft brush, brush the Egg Wash on each roll. This makes them brown beautifully when baked.

Place the rolls in the 400° preheated oven. Bake 12 minutes.

These are delicious served hot, cold or reheated. To reheat, wrap in foil. Put on a rack on a cookie sheet. Bake about 7 minutes in 400° oven. The rack keeps the bottoms from browning too much.

Crescents Or Butterhorns

Make our "Basic Yeast Roll Recipe." (See recipe on page 95.)

Roll out ½ of the dough into a 12-inch circle. Repeat with the other half.

Brush with *soft butter.*

With a knife cut each circle into 16 sections like the spokes of a wheel.

Start at the wide end, and roll up. Place on a baking sheet with the point end down, each roll about 2 inches apart. Curve the ends of each roll to make the crescent shapes.

Glaze with Egg Wash.

Bake in 450° preheated oven about 12 minutes.

Clover Leaf

Make our "Basic Yeast Roll Recipe." (See recipe on page 95.)

Pinch off enough dough for 1 inch balls.

Shape with your fingers and make smooth by tucking edges under until smooth.

Put 3 balls in each greased muffin cup.

Do this until all have been used up.

Place in 450° preheated oven and bake about 12 minutes.

Snails

Make our "Basic Yeast Roll Recipe." (See recipe on page 95.)

Roll dough into a rectangle 10 inches long and about ½ inch thick.

Cut into strips ½ inch wide. Roll each into a rope. Starting at one end, wind the strip around and around. Tuck the outside end firmly underneath.

Brush with Egg Wash.

Bake in 450° preheated oven about 12 minutes.

Parkerhouse

Make our "Basic Yeast Roll Recipe." (See recipe on page 95.)

Roll the dough about ¼ inch thick. Cut 2½ inch circles.

Use the dull edge of a knife to make a strong crease just off the center.

Brush with softened butter or margarine, and fold the large part over the small part. Press the folded edge firmly down.

Brush with Egg Wash.

Place in 450° preheated oven and bake about 12 minutes.

Pan Rolls

Make our "Basic Yeast Roll Recipe." (See recipe on page 95.)

Shape the dough into balls. Dip in melted butter or margarine.

Place in a greased round layer cake pan.

Let the balls touch one another.

Brush with Egg Wash. Make Egg Wash by mixing 1 egg yolk with 2 teaspoons cold tap water; or for a lighter color you can brush with the egg white.

Place in 450° preheated oven and bake about 8 or 9 minutes.

To Reheat Rolls Or Bread

frozen or stale

Enclose each roll in a piece of foil.

To keep the bottom of the rolls from getting too brown (or burned), if you are using a Toaster Oven, put on a small rack.

For frozen rolls turn heat to 425° and reheat 10 minutes, but remember to also enclose in foil and put on a rack.

For defrosted or stale rolls heat oven 425° and enclose in foil. Put on rack on tray, and reheat 5 minutes.

Tip: Don't use a 400° oven; use 425° oven. We could hardly believe it, but the 425° oven made the inside light, and the 400° oven made it doughy.

Homemade Crisp French Roll Cheese Pizza

these are cheaper than the "supermarket" ones and probably healthier, too, and—they taste just the way you like them—because you make them

We use Pepperidge Farms French Rolls.

Cut lengthwise *2* of the *4 rolls.* Toast lightly.

Mix together in a bowl *1 can (6 ounces) Progresso,* or other, *tomato sauce* with *2 teaspoons dried onions, 1/8 teaspoon garlic powder, 1/2 teaspoon dried basil* and *1/4 teaspoon dried oregano.*

Spoon this sauce over the cut rolls.

Cut *mozzarella, muenster or Danish Halvarti cheese* in strips and arrange on top.

Sprinkle some grated *Parmesan or Romano cheese* on top.

You can use your Toaster Oven on "Top Brown" turning the toaster knob to "9." If it isn't ready, then turn it again until it is ready. Eat while hot.

Or you can put on a baking dish in your oven. Turn to "broil" and broil on the middle rack, or lower, according to your stove, until the cheese is melted and the roll hot, takes only a few minutes, so don't go away. Watch that it melts but doesn't burn!

Matzo (Crackers) Pizza

a quickie . . . takes minutes . . . looks pretty . . . tastes good, no soggy crust . . . this is for one person . . . and it's different, no tomato sauce!

You need *1 whole large matzo,* preferably one with wheat germ added.

Cut thin slice of *mozzarella, Halvarti or muenster cheese,* and arrange so it covers the matzo.

You can now decorate with *as many or as few of these as you wish:* thin, small pieces of salami, baloney, ham, franks, Swift's Frozen Italian Style Sausages defrosted, luncheon meat, or any tasty cooked meat, tuna fish, sardines, salmon, anchovies, thin sliced tomatoes, canned or cooked mushrooms, thin pieces onion, canned pimentos, Progresso Caponate (which is eggplant appetizer), olives, canned Jalapena peppers, cut up, and dots of other kinds of cheese AND anything you can think of that tastes good.

"Sub" Sandwich

Split and open *sub roll.*

Put on bottom *4 very thin slices luncheon meat or pepper loaf.*

Then put on top *1 thin slice salami or baloney or sausage.*

Then put on top *2 thin slices American cheese.*

Then put on top *3 thin slices of tomatoes.*

Then put on *3 paper thin slices of onion.*

Then put on *2 tablespoons chopped, crisp lettuce.*

On top put *2 tablespoons shredded cabbage.*

Close roll.

How To Make
Homemade Melba Toast

Buy *"Very Thin Sliced White Bread by Pepperidge Farms."*

Roll each piece thin and flat with a rolling pin.

Put on a cookie sheet or a tray if using a toaster oven. Put a rack on top to keep the bread flat.

Place in 400° oven about 4 minutes to brown. Watch to see that it doesn't burn.

Remove from oven. Let stand as is on the rack with the rack still on top to keep it flat until it gets cold.

To make small bite-size Melba Toast, cut into size you wish and bake as above. These will take about 4 minutes to bake.

Homemade Melba Toast may cost the same or even a little more, but the taste is far superior when you use the Pepperidge Farms Bread.

Heat varies in different stoves, so watch carefully when you first make these to see how long it actually takes in your stove.

We have also made our Melba Toast in a 325° oven, which took about 12 minutes for a slice to brown nicely and 8 minutes for the slice cut into 4 pieces, which didn't brown. Both slices became crisp, but they didn't brown, so try both ways and see which way you like best.

High Rise Omelette

you bake it in the oven and you'll be glad you did!

Grease an 8-inch round cake pan.
Heat oven 350°.
Separate *4 eggs.*
Stir in *2 tablespoons flour* into the 4 yolks.
Add *2 tablespoons cold tap water* and *½ teaspoon salt* to the 4 whites.
Beat the whites until stiff but not dry.
Mix 1 tablespoon whites into the yolk mixture.
Fold the rest of the whites in.
Spoon into the greased cake pan.
Place in 350° oven 15 minutes. It will be a golden color.
For a special treat serve with your favorite preserves or your own Homemade Strawberry Preserves—the kind made in the summer when strawberries are in season. Follow our recipe. See index, and do as we do. Freeze the preserves so that they keep their lovely luscious red color, their marvelous perfume and their heavenly taste. PS—our strawberry preserves are easy to make.
Some people like a cheese sauce with this, so here it is. Make the sauce while the omelette is baking or before you make it.
Melt 2 tablespoons margarine in a saucepan. Take off heat. Stir in 2 tablespoons flour. Stir in 1 cup milk.
Cook, stir until it gets thick and smooth, takes about 8 to 10 minutes.
Add salt to taste.
Stir in 1 cup grated American or Cheddar or Velveeta cheese or other cheese of your choice.

Bacon Bits, Eggs And Tomato Omelette

perfect for a supper, lunch or dinner for 2 . . . for more . . . just multiply

Heat oven 400°.
Put 2 *tablespoons oil* in a heated skillet.

Cook 1/4 *cup each chopped celery, onions* and *green pepper* until onions are soft and clear.

Remove to a plate.

Leave fat in pan.

Beat *4 egg yolks* with a fork. Stir in *2 tablespoons water.*

Add the *vegetables* and *bacon bits* to the egg yolk mixture.

Beat *4 whites* with a *pinch of salt* until stiff.

Fold the egg whites into the yolk mixture.

Pour into the heated skillet with its oil.

When the omelette starts cooking, turn heat to low, cook until eggs are browned lightly on bottom.

Place in 400° oven.

Bake about 7 minutes until top is browned.

If your skillet handle isn't oven-proof, wrap some foil over the handle to protect it. It won't burn but hold it with a hot pad in case it gets hot.

Eggs Over Lightly

yes, you flip it over . . . but lightly, please!

Break *1 egg* into a saucer.

Heat the skillet on medium high heat until hot.

Brush the skillet with *1 tablespoon margarine.*

Add the egg.

Cook until bottom of egg is done. Turn over lightly with a spatula, and cook until yolk is as you like it. Cook a minute or so for a covered but runny yolk.

That's how I like it. How do you like it? Cook it the way you like it.

Fried Egg Basted

Open *1 egg* into a saucer.

Heat a skillet on medium heat until hot.

Put in 1/2 *teaspoon margarine.*

Add the egg.

Put *1 tablespoon water* over the egg.

Put the lid on the skillet.

Cook 1 minute.

Lift the lid. See if a white film has formed over the yolk. If it has, take the skillet off the heat.

With a spatula remove the egg to a small plate. If a film has not formed, put the lid back on the skillet and cook another minute or two until it does.

This is a good way to fry a non-greasy egg.

Scrambled Eggs

Open *2 eggs,* one at a time, into a saucer, then put into a bowl.

Mix well with a fork.

Heat the skillet on medium heat until hot. Test by dropping a little water on the skillet. If the drops "skitter" around fast and evaporate, the skillet is hot enough.

Put in *1 tablespoon margarine.* With a dull knife, move it around to cover the skillet.

Add the eggs.

As soon as they start to cook, start scrambling them with a fork.

Turn heat down. Scramble them as you like them.

Be careful not to cook too long, as the eggs continue to cook after you take them off the heat.

The best way is to remove them a little undercooked and let them finish cooking by the time you put them on your plate.

Hard Cooked Eggs

some people call them hard boiled eggs

Remove *4 eggs* from the refrigerator to get to room temperature so they won't crack when you cook them.

Place the eggs in a deep saucepan.

Add *cold tap water to cover the eggs;* then add *enough water so that the water comes about 2 inches over the eggs.*

On high heat or medium high heat bring to a boil, takes about 10 minutes.

Remove from the heat. Cover. Let stand 20 minutes.

Place under running cold water until cold.

Eggs Foo Yeung

a lovely way to use your "leftovers"

Empty your refrigerator of "leftovers," or rather your "ready cooked" bits and pieces. Drain any that have liquid—vegetables, chicken, beef, pork, ham. Cut any large piece or pieces into small cubes.

Chop *½ cup onions, ¼ cup scallions* and *½ cup celery* on the slant. Drain *1 jar (2 ounces) cut pimentos.*

If you do not have enough leftover bits and pieces of vegetables, defrost *1 package (10 ounces) Frozen Mixed Chinese Vegetables;* or drain *1 can Chinese Mixed Vegetables.*

Open *8 eggs* into a bowl. Mix well with a fork adding *salt* to taste; set aside.

Preheat your oven broiler.

Heat a large skillet with *4 tablespoons oil* and *1 tablespoon margarine or butter.* Add the onions, scallions, celery and the defrosted Chinese vegetables. Cook, stir 2 minutes. Turn heat to low. Cover. Simmer about 10 minutes until onions are soft and clear and the Chinese vegetables cooked.

Add the "ready cooked" bits and pieces and the pimentos.

If you are using a can of Chinese vegetables, instead of the frozen vegetables, add them now.

Cook, stir, adding *salt and pepper* to taste.

Turn heat to medium. Pour the beaten eggs over the vegetables, lifting the edges to let the runny eggs run under and cook. Do this until the eggs have run under all around and under the omelette and are cooked. When the bottom is browned, put under the broiler until the top is cooked and a golden brown.

Tip: If your skillet has a handle of wood or plastic and will burn in the oven or broiler, wrap the handle all over in foil so it won't burn. Use a hot pad to hold the handle, as the foil gets hot when you remove the skillet from the broiler.

Serve the "Foo Yeung" while hot; and remember, some people like some soy sauce with their omelette, so have a bottle of "Kikoman Soy Sauce" on hand.

TO FREEZE EGG WHITES, BROTHS OR ICE CUBES, the best way is to use a plastic tray with *removable* plastic containers. You freeze in these, then remove to a plastic bag to store in freezer.

Never Fail Cheese Soufflé

if you think soufflés are hard to make, just try this one and you will realize how easy they are to make.

Heat oven 400°.

Grate enough *Swiss cheese to make ½ cup* and enough *Parmesan to make ¼ cup*. Mix the two together. Set aside.

Grate *enough Parmesan cheese to coat lightly a 2-quart glass, heat-proof casserole* that has been greased with butter or margarine. Sometimes we use a French Charlotte Mold. The Pyrex 2-quart casserole is fine, and most people have one.

Grease the 2-quart casserole all over with *butter or margarine*. Sprinkle the grated Parmesan cheese over it. Set aside.

Set aside 2 large mixing bowls, a deep saucer, a saucepan, a wooden spoon, a rubber spatula, a cup and an electric hand beater or a rotary beater; also, *5 large eggs, 1 cup nonfat milk, ½ teaspoon salt,* a *pinch of cayenne pepper* and a *pinch of nutmeg* and *¼ teaspoon cream of tartar.*

Separate 4 of the large eggs. Put the 4 yolks in a cup and the 4 whites into one of the large bowls. Add 1 more egg white to the whites in the bowl. Do not use the fifth egg yolk, but put into the refrigerator to use another time.

Into the saucepan measure *3 tablespoons margarine or butter*. On medium heat melt the fat. Take off heat, stir in *3 tablespoons flour*. Off heat stir in 1 cup nonfat milk.

Put on medium high heat. Cook, stir, taking off and on heat, until it gets thick. Be sure to stir so there are no lumps.

Put into the empty bowl. Use a rubber spatula to get it all in. Wash the spatula and dry well; set aside. With the wooden spoon stir in, one at a time, the 4 egg yolks; then mix in the grated cheese, the ½ teaspoon salt, a pinch of cayenne pepper and a pinch of nutmeg.

Beat the egg whites until foamy. Add a pinch of salt and continue to beat, adding ¼ teaspoon cream of tartar. Beat the whites until a straight, not droopy, peak forms in the egg whites when you lift the beaters out.

Take about ¼ of the whites and mix into the yolk mixture to lighten it.

With a rubber spatula, put the rest of the whites on top of the yolk mixture. Fold, don't mix, the whites in quickly, so they do not deflate.

With the spatula put into the casserole.

With your clean finger make a ring one inch from the edge of the casserole, so when the soufflé bakes, this forms a crown.

Place immediately in the oven. Turn heat to 375°. Bake about 30 minutes. It should be beautifully browned and high.

Eat at once.

Tip: If any is left over, eat it as a pudding. It's quite good.

Ham Soufflé

a very tasty soufflé and a welcome way to use up a small amount of "leftover" cooked ham

Preheat oven 400°.

Set 2 large bowls on your working space.

Grease with *margarine* a 2-quart heat-proof, glass casserole. Sprinkle with *plain crumbs or grated cheese;* shake out excess.

Grind *enough ham to make ¾ cup ham.* Mix in *½ teaspoon onion powder,* a good *grind of pepper, 2 tablespoons chopped parsley or 1 tablespoon dried parsley.* Set aside.

Separate *4 eggs.* Put the yolks in a small saucer or bowl and the whites in a large bowl. Add *1 more white* to the whites, so you have 5 whites and 4 yolks.

In a medium saucepan melt, don't burn, *3 tablespoons margarine.* Take off heat. Stir in *3 tablespoons flour,* then stir in *1 cup nonfat or skim milk.* (We make ours out of ¼ cup dry milk mixed with 1 cup cold tap water.)

Place on medium high heat. With a wooden spoon, cook, stir, taking off and on heat so it doesn't burn on the bottom, until it gets thick, takes about 3 minutes. Turn heat to low, cook, stir 2 minutes. You can cook this on low heat which takes about 10 minutes to cook. The secret of fast cooking is our method of "cook, stir, taking off and on heat."

With a rubber spatula, put this white sauce into the large empty bowl. Wash and dry the rubber spatula. Set aside. With wooden spoon stir in, one at a time, the egg yolks. Mix in the ham mixture.

With electric hand beaters or a rotary beater, beat the whites until frothy. Add a *pinch of salt* and *¼ teaspoon cream of tartar.* Continue to heat until the whites hold a straight, not droopy, peak when you lift the beaters out.

Quickly take about ¼ of the beaten whites and stir into the white sauce mixture to lighten it.

Quickly, so the whites won't deflate, *fold, fold* the rest of the whites in with the rubber spatula.

Immediately, using the spatula, put into the baking dish.

With your finger make a ring one inch from the edge, so when the soufflé bakes, this forms a crown.

Immediately put into the oven. Immediately turn heat to 375°.

Bake about 30 minutes. Test with a cake tester. Ours is usually done. Eat immediately.

A soufflé waits for no one, so we have to wait for it.

One thing nice about a soufflé, you know how long it will take to bake, so you can time accordingly.

Our soufflés are so light that even after they fall after they are cooked, they still taste delicious. You can eat our soufflé cold or reheat it, but at this time we haven't found a way to make them rise again.

Chicken Soufflé

what a nice way to "use up" your "Ready Cooked" (leftover) chicken!

Heat oven 400°.

Grease with *margarine* a 2-quart heat-proof, glass casserole.

Sprinkle *seasoned crumbs* over it. Shake out excess.

Set aside 2 large bowls.

Grind *¾ cup of your "Ready Cooked" chicken.*

Drain *1 can (2 ounces) chopped mushrooms.* Drain *1 jar (2 ounces) cut up pimentos.* Add *½ to 1 teaspoon onion powder* to taste and *3 tablespoons chopped parsley.*

Separate *4 eggs.* Put yolks in a small bowl. Put the 4 whites and *1 extra white (5 whites)* into a large bowl. We do not use the fifth yolk.

In a saucepan melt (don't burn) *3 tablespoons margarine.* Take off heat. Stir in *4 tablespoons flour;* then stir in *1 cup nonfat milk.* On medium high heat, cook, stir, taking off and on heat until the sauce gets thick, takes about 3 to 5 minutes.

Take off heat. Add *salt and pepper to taste* and a *pinch of nutmeg* if you wish. Pour into a large bowl.

Stir in 1 yolk. Then one at a time stir in the other 3 yolks. Stir in the chicken mixture.

With an electric hand beater or a rotary beater beat the 5 whites until foamy. Add a *pinch of salt* and *¼ teaspoon cream of tartar*. Beat until stiff. When you lift the beaters out, the whites in the bowl will form a stiff "straight" peak.

Take about ¼ of the whites and mix into the yolk mixture to lighten it.

"Fold" the rest of the whites into the mixture quickly so as not to deflate it.

Quickly spoon into the casserole.

With your finger make a ring one inch from the edge, so when the soufflé bakes, this forms a crown.

Immediately put into the oven. Immediately turn heat to 375°.

Bake about 30 minutes. Test with a cake tester. Ours is usually done. Eat immediately.

Salmon Soufflé

you can use canned salmon, and you don't have to apologize, because it tastes so good.

Heat oven 400°.

Drain well *1 can (7¾ ounces) salmon*. Mix with a pastry blender until light and flaky.

Add *1 teaspoon onion powder* and *2 tablespoons chopped parsley*.

Grease a 2-quart heat-proof, glass casserole. Sprinkle the greased casserole with *seasoned crumbs*. Shake out excess.

Separate *4 eggs*. Put yolks in a small bowl and the whites in a large bowl. Add *1 more white* to the whites. (Save the extra yolk to use another time.)

In a saucepan melt (don't burn) *3 tablespoons margarine*. Take off heat. Stir in *4 tablespoons flour*. Then stir in *1 cup nonfat milk*. Cook, stir, taking off and on heat on medium high heat until thick. Put into a large bowl. Taste. Add *salt and pepper to taste*.

One at a time, stir in the 4 egg yolks.

Mix in the salmon mixture.

With an electric hand beater or a rotary beater whip the whites until frothy. Add a *pinch of salt* and continue to beat. Add *¼ teaspoon cream of tartar*. Beat until the whites in the bowl hold a straight peak when you lift the beaters out.

Take about ¼ of the whites and mix into the yolk mixture to lighten it.

With a rubber spatula, put the rest of the whites on top of the yolk mixture. Fold, don't mix, the whites in quickly, so they do not deflate.

With the spatula put into the casserole.

With your clean finger make a ring one inch from the edge of the casserole, so when the soufflé bakes, this forms a crown.

Place immediately in the oven. Turn heat to 375°. Bake about 30 minutes. It should be beautifully browned and high.

Eat at once.

To make a "Tuna Soufflé" do the same as above only drain 1 can (7¾ ounces) tuna fish and mix with a pastry blender until flaky. Add ½ teaspoon onion powder to taste and ½ teaspoon celery seed.

Fake Soufflé

but nothing fake about the taste . . . it's delicious . . . this is a nice luncheon or supper dish

Heat oven 350°.

You can prepare this the night before, leave in the refrigerator overnight, and bake the next day, or leave in refrigerator at least 1 hour, then bake.

You need an 8-inch square glass baking dish. (You can serve it in this.)

Cut off the crusts from *8 pieces white bread.*

Make 4 sandwiches with this by spreading in between *1 can (4½ ounces) James River Smithfield Meat Spread* topped with thin *slices of sweet pickles* or thin *slices of tomato.* You can grind baloney or salami or ready cooked ham or chicken and use it. If you use chicken, flavor it with sauteed onions and/or ground poultry seasoning or tarragon, or "Italian Dried Herbs" or "French Dried Herbs" to your taste. For a change you can fill with a tuna fish salad or canned salmon mixed with mayonnaise and spiked with capers.

Mix well *4 large eggs* with a fork and *¼ teaspoon salt.*

Stir in *2½ cups milk.* Strain. Pour over the sandwiches.

Bake in 350° oven about 1 hour or 1 hour and 10 minutes.

Serve right from the oven just like a soufflé.

Sophie's Different Eggs Benedict

it's different, easy, and just as good without the work of making Hollandaise Sauce

Preheat the broiler. Put the rack on the second rung from the heat.

Split or cut *2 English muffins* across. This is enough for four. Toast. Put each into a small fireproof dish that fits. A deep foil saucer is fine.

Spread a *little mayonnaise* (the unsweetened kind) on the muffins. Sprinkle a little *"Bacon Bits"* on each; *or* put a *slice of cooked ham* on each.

Cut some *Muenster Cheese* into small pieces, leaving a hole (well) in the center for an egg. Break an egg in the center of each. (The whites may run over, but that is OK.)

Melt enough *butter or margarine* to spoon over each egg, and do so.

Stir a little of your favorite *mustard* to your taste into *¼ cup of mayonnaise*. Divide this among the four putting some in small spoonfuls on the cheese.

Place the pans on a cookie sheet with sides. Put under broiler. Broil, cook, watch, takes about 5 minutes.

Serve hot.

We use Gulden's Mustard to mix with the mayonnaise.

This makes a nice luncheon or supper dish served with some cold, canned or fresh asparagus on a bed of lettuce or thinly sliced cucumbers or radishes. Spark it with salad dressing or seasoned mayonnaise.

7. CHICKEN

The Easy Way To Tie A Chicken

You need 1 piece of soft string (not the thin kind) about 24 inches to 36 inches—depending on the size of the chicken.

Place the chicken on its back, breast towards you, legs away from you.

Push the drumsticks up against the breast, which raises the breast.

Put string under the ends of the drumsticks and tie.

Pull the string between the legs and breast and turn the chicken over; the tail should face you.

Bring the string up into the V of the wings and tie in the middle of the back, first tucking in the neck skin if there is any.

Turn the wings akimbo; push the tail in the vent.

The chicken will be compact and there will be no string marks on the breast or thighs.

It is easier to CUT RAW CHICKEN if it is half or three quarters frozen.

An Old Fashioned Roast Chicken

with an extra bonus of gravy as well as a crisp, tasty chicken

Heat oven 475°.

Wipe dry a *2½ to 3½ pound fryer.*

Smear with *2 teaspoons soft margarine* all over. Put *1 teaspoon margarine* mixed with *¼ teaspoon dry thyme* into the fryer, rubbing it all over the inside of the fryer. Also, put in a *small onion.*

Salt lightly all over. Let stand 15 minutes.

Place the chicken, breast side up, on a rack in a shallow roasting pan. Pour *water* in the roasting pan, being careful that the water is an inch below the rack. (It should never touch the chicken.)

Put the chicken in the oven; turn heat to 450°. Roast 20 minutes.

Turn the chicken breast down; roast 15 minutes.

Turn heat to 325°. Check the water; add more, if necessary. This will turn into good tasting broth, so don't let get dry. Add boiling water, if necessary.

Roast a 2½ pound chicken 45 more minutes and test, a 3 pound chicken 55 or more minutes, as needed, and a 3½ pound chicken 60 minutes or more, as needed.

This chicken is never dry. It is beautifully browned and has a fine chicken taste.

Strain the broth in a strainer lined with a paper towel into a bowl. This clears it beautifully. Let cool. Remove the fat. We usually place this in the refrigerator for the fat to harden. Then remove it, heat and use the broth as a gravy, adding *salt*, if necessary. This gravy is fine over rice, too.

Party Chicken

one of the best chicken dishes there is . . . you can make it ahead as it reheats beautifully . . . we have made it even two days ahead, refrigerated it and when it was served everyone raved over it . . . instead of rich expensive cream we used our special thickening and spent our Penny Pincher money on fresh mushrooms and this will blow your mind . . . a bottle of Champagne which we drink and steal a few teaspoons for our chicken dish . . . also, confession is good for the soul, we use 3 tablespoons dry sherry (Christian Brothers Sherry) . . . and lest you get wrong ideas . . . my sherry, hidden back in a cupboard of the kitchen and used only in cooking, has lasted me a whole year! . . . a tip: never buy cooking sherry or any other cooking wine . . . buy regular sherry that one drinks or other wine, white or red, that one drinks and use for cooking . . . the party can be "you and him" or the family or a Good Friends Dinner Party . . . this recipe like most of my recipes are for four and can be doubled, tripled or whatever

Cut *2 skinned and boned chicken breasts* into 1 inch pieces to make 2 cups. Set aside.

Remove fat and strain *1 can (10½ ounces) onion soup,* makes about ⅔ cup, and *1 can (10¾ ounces) chicken broth* or use your own chicken broth.

Mix *1 package Vegetable Bouillon Broth* with *1 cup cold tap water* and *¼ teaspoon onion powder.*

Melt *5 tablespoons margarine or butter*. Take off heat. Stir in *5 tablespoons flour*. Then stir in *½ cup nonfat "dry" milk.* Gradually, slowly stir in the liquids.

Cook, stir until it comes to a boil. Turn heat to medium. Cook, stir 5 minutes. Set aside.

Put some flour in a large plate.

Heat a large skillet hot. Add *3 tablespoons oil.*

Dip ½ of the chicken pieces in the flour and put in the skillet. Cook, stir just until golden. Remove to a plate and flour the remaining chicken pieces. Cook, stir and put with the rest.

Leave the good brownings in the skillet but wipe up any fat.

Stir the sauce into the brownings and cook, stir to get the brownings up. Add the mushrooms, the chicken pieces and bring to a boil.

Stir in *3 tablespoons dry Sherry.* Remove from the heat. You can cool, put in the refrigerator until ready to use. When ready to use, reheat. When hot, add *2 to 4 tablespoons Champagne* to taste. Bring to a boil. Serve immediately. Do not let this dish continue to cook and do not keep on a burner to keep warm. Serve at once.

The potatoes or rice should have been cooked and ready to serve and so should the carrots.

Crusty French and Italian Bread goes nicely with this dish, or if you have in your freezer our "homemade twisted rolls" heat them for a perfect "go with." The dessert can be fresh fruit in season and some good cheese which is a no work dessert and always welcome. Don't forget to toast each other with the lovely champagne.

Smothered Chicken And Rice

delicious easy dish

Wipe a *2½ or 3 pound chicken* with a paper towel. Cut into 8 pieces; remove as much fat as possible. Sprinkle *1 teaspoon salt* over the chicken pieces. Let stand 10 minutes.

Smear *1 teaspoon soft margarine* over the bottom of the casserole.

Arrange as many of the chicken pieces, skin side down, as you can in one layer and brown.

Turn browned side up and dot with *1 tablespoon margarine.*

Slice *4 large onions* ¼ inch thick.

Put a layer of onion slices on top of the chicken. Dot with *1 tablespoon margarine.*

Repeat with another layer of chicken pieces. Dot with *1 ta-*

blespoon soft margarine. Put a layer of onions on top. Dot with *1 tablespoon margarine*.

Put lid on. Place the casserole on high heat. When the steam comes out, turn heat to low so the chicken simmers slowly.

Cook about 2 to 2½ hours to develop a rich, lovely chicken flavor.

While the chicken is simmering, cook the *rice*. (See Index for recipe under "R" Brown Rice, Cooked or White Rice, Cooked.)

When the chicken pieces are cooked, serve it with the cooked rice.

Spoon the onions and gravy over the rice.

This is a very tasty combination and it will become one of your favorite chicken dishes.

Haitian Chicken

this is good enough to serve at a party, and it always makes the dinner a party when served to the family

Cut a *3 or 3½ pound fryer* into serving size pieces; be sure to separate the thighs from the drumsticks.

Wipe the chicken pieces. Rub each piece with a cut *piece of lime or lemon and squeeze the juice over*. (We prefer lime. We love our key lime tree that keeps producing all the time. If you live in a warm climate, get yourself a key lime tree.)

Heat a medium skillet with *1 tablespoon oil* and *1 tablespoon soft margarine*.

Brown the chicken pieces quickly until a lovely golden color and don't crowd. Remove to a plate. Add *more fat* and brown the rest; or you can brush the chicken with a little margarine and put, meaty side up, under the broiler to brown quickly. Do not brown the other side, it's not necessary.

Mix together *⅛ teaspoon ground cloves, ½ teaspoon garlic powder, ½ teaspoon onion powder, ½ teaspoon dried thyme, ½ teaspoon dried tarragon* and *½ teaspoon salt*. Rub over the chicken pieces.

Slice thin *3 medium onions* and *3 cloves garlic*. Mix with the chicken pieces. Let stand ½ hour to season.

Make a sauce of *2 cans (16 ounces) stewed tomatoes, 2*

cans water, and *1 can (8 ounces) Progresso or your favorite Tomato Sauce.*

Bring to a boil. Add a *drop or two of Tabasco.*

Put in the thighs and drumsticks and their flavoring. Cover. Cook 10 minutes on medium low heat.

Add the breasts and wings. Cover and cook 25 to 30 minutes until tender but not so that the chicken falls apart.

Add *1 cup dry French vermouth* and *¼ teaspoon basil.* Cook 5 minutes.

Mix *3 tablespoons cornstarch* with *¼ cup water,* and stir into the chicken sauce. Cook, stir until the sauce is clear and is thickened just to have "body," takes about 1 minute.

Serve with some fluffy rice, which you can cook while the chicken cooks.

Tip: You can eat this at once, or you can cook early and reheat. If you do this, be sure to remove to a cold bowl and put in the refrigerator, as you do not want the chicken to continue to cook. Also, do the same if you plan to freeze it.

This is a good recipe to double, as it freezes and reheats with no loss of flavors.

Senegalese Chicken With A Curry Flavor

sounds like it will be lots of work . . . no, it's easy as easy can be

Heat oven 400°.

Remove the skin and fat from *4 chicken breasts.*

Brown the breasts in *2 tablespoons oil* and *1 tablespoon margarine.*

Stir *½ teaspoon curry powder* into *either 1 can Crosse and Blackwell Senegalese Soup or Campbell's Chicken Gumbo Soup.*

Bring to a boil.

Put the browned chicken breasts, meaty side up, in a heat-proof, shallow, baking dish that fits.

Pour the soup over the breasts. Cover with foil.

Bake in 400° oven 15 minutes. Uncover, bake 15 minutes more until the chicken is tender and the sauce has improved the chicken and the chicken has improved the sauce.

How about some crusty French or Italian bread "to go with"? Or, have a loaf of our "Homemade Whole Wheat" bread in your freezer? Remove it the night before you make this dish, so it will be ready when you're ready.

Chicken In Pastry Shells With Mushroom Sauce

fancy tasting and easy to make

The Shells:

Bake *6 Pepperidge Farms Frozen Shells* according to directions on box. These can be made early and reheated when the sauce is ready to eat.

The Cream of Mushroom Sauce:

This sauce can be made ahead and reheated when ready to eat.

Stir *½ cup nonfat milk* into *1 can Campbell's Cream of Mushroom Soup.*

Stir in *3 tablespoons chicken broth.*

Stir in *1 (2½ ounces) jar sliced or pieces mushrooms with its juice.*

Heat until hot and serve this separately.

The Chicken Filling:

Chop or cut into small pieces *enough "ready cooked" chicken to make 2 cups.*

Chop *4 tablespoons onions* and *4 tablespoons celery.* Saute in *2 tablespoons oil or margarine* until onions are soft and clear. Add to the chicken.

Add *salt to taste* and grate or use *¼ teaspoon ginger.*

Stir in *2 teaspoons Dijon type mustard* mixed with *1 tablespoon unsweetened mayonnaise.*

Add a *grind or a pinch of nutmeg* and *¼ teaspoon tarragon* crushed with your hands. Set this filling aside until ready to use.

This makes 6 portions for 4 people. There is always one or two who want more.

When ready to eat, heat the "chicken filling" and spoon it, without pressing down, into the six hot baked shells.

Both the filling and the shells can be made ahead, kept in the refrigerator separately, then heated separately—the shells in the oven—the stuffing on top of the stove. Then fill the hot shells with the hot chicken mixture.

Serve with the hot, hot sauce in a pitcher or gravy boat.

Tip: Do not try to put the cold chicken mixture in the cold baked shells, as this does not work. It gets soggy when baked together.

Barbecued Chicken

this is a welcome change from the usual barbecued chicken and it almost cooks by itself

Preheat oven 350°.

Cut a *2½ pound chicken* into 8 pieces. Sprinkle *½ teaspoon salt* over the chicken pieces. Let stand 10 minutes.

Heat a skillet with *3 tablespoons oil.*

Flour the chicken pieces. Shake off excess.

Brown, meaty side down, in the skillet. When browned, arrange in 1 layer in a heat- and fire-proof, shallow baking dish.

Seed and slice *1 large green pepper,* and slice *1 large onion.*

Put these on top of the chicken pieces. Pour *1 bottle (16 ounces) Heinz Barbecue Sauce* over the vegetables and chicken.

Bring to a boil on top of the stove. Place in the preheated oven. Bake 1 hour, basting now and then.

Very, very tasty!

Chicken Breasts Italian Style

they're easy to make and quick and they are so flavorful, you'll love to make them . . . and, there's not a bit of tomato here for a change

This is for 2 people. Double for 4 or more, depending on eaters.

Line a baking pan with foil.

Heat oven 400°.

Cut *1 chicken breast* from a 3 or 3½ pound chicken in half lengthwise.

Dip in *1 tablespoon white wine or lemon juice.* Let stand 15 minutes.

Sprinkle *salt and pepper* over lightly.

Dip each breast in *1 tablespoon mayonnaise.*

Roll in *1 tablespoon each grated Parmesan cheese* rather thickly.

Roll in *1 tablespoon Italian Seasoned Bread Crumbs* mixed with a *teaspoon of chopped parsley.*

Bake in 400° oven about 30 minutes.

This is a nice dinner party dish as well as a good buffet dish. It is also good cold.

It can be baked, frozen and reheated.

It can also be prepared ahead and frozen and then baked when ready to use.

This recipe is very easy to multiply for as many people as you wish.

Chicken Pies

they're wonderful to have on hand, especially since they freeze so well

To make these pies easy, you can use a two-step cooking method.

In a pot that fits, bring to a boil *1 cut-up 3 or 3½ pound chicken* with *water to cover,* about 4 cups.

Add *1 carrot, 1 medium onion, some celery leaves* and *1¼ teaspoons salt.* Bring back to a boil. Turn heat to low. Cover.

Cook until done but not too soft, takes about 30 minutes. Remove to a bowl.

Let chicken stay in broth about 20 minutes until it cools. This makes for a juicy, better tasting chicken.

Remove chicken. Put chicken in refrigerator. Put a piece of paper towel in a large strainer in a bowl. Strain the broth. Throw away the paper towel. The broth is beautifully clear.

Cover, let stay in refrigerator. You can remove fat from the broth, but it is easier to put broth in refrigerator overnight for the fat to congeal on top.

Defrost *2 cups frozen mixed vegetables* in refrigerator overnight.

When ready to make the pies, lift off the fat from the broth. Heat the broth just until it is not congealed. Cool.

Remove the skin and bones from the chicken and make a little extra broth with the skin and bones.

Cut the chicken with a scissors in ½ inch pieces. You need 2 cups cubed chicken.

Put the 2 cups defrosted vegetables in a large bowl. Mix in about *¼ teaspoon salt*. Gently mix in the chicken.

Bring *2 cups of the chicken broth* to a boil.

In a screw-top jar put *¼ cup cold chicken broth or water* and *2 tablespoons flour*. Shake well. (Always put broth or water in jar first.)

Stir into the boiling chicken broth. Bring back to a boil. Turn heat to low. Cook, stir 5 minutes.

Pour over the chicken and vegetables.

Let get cold. Taste; add *salt and pepper* to taste.

Spoon into 4 individual foil baking pans 5″ × 1″ deep.

Make the crust toppings. See Index for recipe under "P," "Pastry Crust, Tender and Fool Proof."

Divide the pastry ball into 4 pieces. Roll out, one at a time, to fit the top of the baking dishes.

Place on top. With a fork, crimp the edges closed.

Cut a small hole in the center and 4 very small slits around it.

Cover the edges with a little foil.

When ready to bake, brush each crust with *milk* for better browning.

Place on a cookie sheet. For easier cleaning, cover with foil. Bake in preheated 425° oven about 45 minutes to 1 hour.

If frozen, bake in 425° oven 45 minutes, then remove foil and bake until done—about 15 minutes.

Polynesian Chicken

you need 4 chicken thighs or enough chicken pieces for 2 or multiply for 4 eaters

Wash the chicken pieces, then dry them well. Set aside.

Make this large amount of sauce, as it keeps in the refrigerator 3 weeks, or you can freeze it so you really prepare once for more times: *1 bottle Wishbone Russian Dressing (8 ounces);* add *5 tablespoons orange marmalade,* and make a recipe of our "Homemade Onion Soup Mix," as follows (or use Lipton's Onion Soup Mix).

Put *3 tablespoons minced dried onions* into a small skillet on medium high heat. Cook and stir the onions, taking the skillet off and on the heat so the onions don't burn but turn a golden brown color. This takes about 3 minutes. Cool immediately by spreading out on a piece of wax paper or on a large plate.

Put into a large bowl *2 Instant Onion Broth powders, 2 Instant Beef Broth powders, ¼ teaspoon sugar, ¼ teaspoon celery salt, ½ teaspoon oil* and the *3 tablespoons Toasted Dried Onion Mix.*

Mix together with your hands or a large spoon and add to the sauce.

Cover a cookie sheet with foil.

Dip chicken pieces into the sauce—both sides, getting skin covered, too. Roll around to get sauce on.

Place on the foil lined cookie sheet.

Bake 40 minutes in 350° oven. Put under broiler to brown.

Can be frozen and reheated.

A tasty chicken.

Chicken Stroganoff

Stroganoff is such a good dish that even if the original recipe is made of beef steaks, we love to make it with chicken . . . you can use either the breasts of chicken or the dark meat and since it cooks so fast this is a fine way to use the dark chicken pieces . . . you can multiply this recipe if you wish

Cook *1 cup rice.*

Cut enough *chicken* into strips 1½ inches long by ¼ inch wide for four.

Strain *1 can onion soup,* remove the fat from *1 cup, canned or fresh, chicken broth.* Mix *1 cup cold tap water* with *1 Vegetable Bouillon powder or cube.*

Heat a skillet hot with *2 tablespoons oil.* Add *1 tablespoon margarine.* Without crowding, brown the chicken strips quickly and remove to a plate.

With a paper towel gently mop up the fat in the skillet but leave the good brownings in.

Add *3 tablespoons margarine* to the skillet. Cook, stir. Take off heat and stir in *4 tablespoons flour.* Gradually stir in all the broths. Cook, stir on medium heat until it comes to a boil. Stir in *1 tablespoon and 1 teaspoon A-1 sauce* and *1 tablespoon Worcestershire Sauce.* Cook, stir 5 minutes.

Add *1 can (4 ounces) sliced mushrooms and its juice.* Cook 10 minutes. Add salt if necessary and pepper to taste.

Add the chicken strips. Cook, stir just until very hot. You can serve as is or do as the Russians do. Take off the heat and very slowly a little at a time stir in about ¼ to ½ cup sour cream, being careful not to let it curdle. Put back on the heat, do not let it boil, but let get hot and serve at once with the rice on the side.

Pennsylvania Dutch Chicken Pot Pie

the Pennsylvania Dutch know "what good is!"

Buy a *3 or 3½ pound chicken.* Cut into breast, 2 drumsticks, 2 thighs, 2 wings with wing tip, and the back (or 8 pieces).

Bring to a boil with *5 cups cold water, 1½ teaspoons salt, 1 medium onion, 1 carrot* and *a branch of celery leaves.*

Turn heat to low. Simmer about 30 minutes. Remove from heat. Let the chicken stand in the broth about 30 minutes. Remove from broth.

For a clear chicken broth, strain the broth in a strainer lined with a piece of paper towel. We use Bounty towels. This is a wonderful "work saver," no washing of "messy cheese cloth!" Then spoon off as much fat as you can and remove the rest with pieces of paper towels.

To make the Chicken Pot Pie remove the skin and bones from the chicken. Cut the chicken with a scissors into bite size pieces.

Peel and dice *2 cups potatoes,* and chop *1 small onion.*

Drop half of these into the chicken broth with half of the chicken pieces.

Make the Noodle Dumplings, or buy the square noodles at the supermarket:

Noodle Dumplings: Mix with a fork *1 egg, 1 teaspoon cold tap water, ¼ teaspoon salt* in a medium size bowl.

Measure *¾ cup flour.* With your hands, mix a little flour at a time into the egg, about ½ cup, enough to make a dough that is sticky but you can handle.

Sprinkle some of the rest of the flour over the dough as you work it in your hands or knead it until it is hardly sticky.

Use as little flour as possible so that you can handle the dough.

Cut the dough in half.

Sprinkle some *flour* over a clean surface and also over the piece of dough as necessary. Start rolling and roll *adding flour to the board,* only as necessary, as you roll. Keep stretching as you roll. Roll as thin as possible. Tip: The thinner, the better we like these square noodles.

Cut into 1 inch squares.

Roll out and cut the other half dough the same way.

Bring the broth, the chicken, the potatoes and chopped onion to a rolling boil.

Drop ½ of the square cut noodles, one at a time, into the boiling broth. Be sure the broth boils.

When half the noodles have been dropped in, and the broth is boiling again, add the other half of the potatoes and onions. Bring back to a boil and drop in, one at a time, the rest of the noodles.

Bring back to a boil. Turn heat to low. Put lid on.

Cook about 20 minutes.

Your Pennsylvania Dutch Chicken Pot Pie is ready.

Tip: Once you make this you'll realize how easy it is to do!

Chicken Wings

Get as many *chicken wings and backs* as you need. Add *water to cover.*

Bring to a boil.

Add *1 onion chopped* and *2 carrots scraped and chopped.*

Bring back to a boil; turn heat to low.

Put lid on, simmer.

Add some *salt* after you have cooked the wings and backs about 15 minutes. Don't add much, as you can add more later, so you won't make them too salty.

Cook about 30 to 35 minutes until tender. Add a little more salt, if necessary. Add some pepper.

Drop your *homemade noodle* squares in and cook about 8 to 12 minutes. These thicken up the wings and you have a most tasty dish.

Of course, if you're working, don't make the noodle squares, buy them.

Paella

a Spanish chicken dish with vegetables and other goodies . . . you choose the "trimmings" according to whether your pocketbook is flat this week or not

Preheat oven 350°.

You need about *1 dozen or more smallest size clams in their shells* and about *1 dozen fresh shrimp.*

Cut a *3 or 3½ pound chicken* into portion size pieces. *Salt* lightly. *Flour* lightly.

Heat a large skillet that will hold all the chicken pieces in one layer with *3 tablespoons oil* and *1 tablespoon soft margarine.*

Brown the chicken pieces, meaty side down, lightly and quickly, takes about 10 minutes or so. Remove to a plate.

Put into the skillet *1 cup rice, 1 small chopped onion, ¼ teaspoon garlic powder or 2 cloves fresh garlic* and *½ teaspoon saffron.*

Stir in *2 cups chicken broth,* fresh, canned or bouillon broth, made with 3 chicken bouillon powders. Cook, stir 3 to 5 minutes.

In the meantime in another skillet, stir, fry *6 to 8 Swift's Frozen Italian Sausages* about 5 minutes to get as much fat out as possible.

Drain and wipe the sausages with a paper towel. Set aside.

Arrange the chicken pieces on top of the rice mixture. Bring to a boil. Cover with foil and a lid.

Bake in 350° preheated oven until the chicken is done, about 25 to 30 minutes.

Arrange the sausages around and also the smallest size clams in their shells (they're not tough). Arrange nicely 1 dozen shrimp on.

Bake until the shrimp are pink and the clams open.

Sprinkle some *chopped parsley* over and serve piping hot.

Shepherd's Pie

here's a chance to use your "ready cooked" chicken . . . this makes 4 individual pies

Cut *enough "ready cooked" chicken* into large cubed pieces *to make 2 cups.*

Bring *4 large Idaho potatoes,* peeled and cut into quarters, in *water to cover* with *1 teaspoon salt* to a boil.

Put lid on. Turn heat to medium. Cook until done, takes about 30 minutes.

Make the rest of the pie while the potatoes are cooking.

Bring *2 cups chicken broth,* fresh, canned or bouillon broth, to a boil. Add *1 cup frozen mixed vegetables, ¼ cup fresh or frozen dehydrated onions* and *¼ teaspoon salt.* Bring to a boil. Cook 5 minutes.

Combine with the cut up cooked chicken.

Drain the cooked potatoes. Shake in the saucepan over low heat to dry. Don't scorch. Push the potatoes through a ricer into a large bowl, or mash.

Heat about *⅓ cup milk* until hot; don't burn. In the meantime, put *3 tablespoons soft margarine* on the potatoes and mix well. Add the hot milk. Beat with a large mixing spoon until fluffy.

Stir about ½ cup of this whipped potatoes into the chicken mixture to thicken it.

Smear 4 glass baking dishes (10 ounces) with *margarine;* or use 4 small foil pans.

Spoon the vegetable-chicken mixture into the 4 baking dishes.

Top with the whipped potatoes. Sprinkle lightly with *paprika.*

When ready to eat, heat in 400° oven until hot and topping is browned nicely.

You can freeze these for later use as they freeze and reheat beautifully.

Make And Bake Oven Fried Chicken

not greasy, just about the best tasting Oven Fried Chicken you'll ever eat

Heat the oven 400°, medium heat.

Cut *1 fryer chicken, 2½ pounds,* into serving pieces.

Separate the drumsticks from the thighs. Cut the breasts in half. Cut the wings and wing tip off. (You can buy your favorite chicken pieces cut up, but it costs more.)

Sprinkle *salt* lightly on both sides of the chicken pieces; let stand.

Put ⅓ *cup oil or melted margarine* in a deep dish that fits the chicken pieces.

Put some *"Make and Bake"* on a plate. As you need more, you will add more.

Roll each piece of chicken, first in oil or margarine, then in the "Make and Bake," and put on a plate. Do this until all the chicken pieces have been done.

Place the chicken, skin side up, in a shallow baking dish. You can line the dish with foil to make it easy to wash.

Put into 400° oven. Cover the pan with foil.

Bake about ½ hour. Remove the foil; bake ½ hour. You do not have to turn the chicken.

Isn't this easy? You'll love the taste!

Make And Bake

for Oven Fried Chicken and any time you need "flavored crumbs"

YOU NEED:

1 cup bread crumbs
½ cup flour
1 teaspoon cornstarch
1¾ teaspoons onion powder
1¾ teaspoons garlic powder
1¾ teaspoons poultry seasoning
1 teaspoon paprika
1¼ teaspoons salt
1 teaspoon sugar
1 tablespoon and 2 teaspoons oil

With a pastry blender mix together everything except the oil. Add the oil and with your fingers mix until well combined. You will feel no oil—just crumbs. Store in screw-top jar.

Can be kept in the refrigerator or in the freezer.

Chicken Foldovers

makes a meal when served with a plate of vegetable soup

Heat oven 425°.

Drain *2 cans (5 ounces) boned breast of chicken;* or use your own *"ready cooked" chicken,* which we usually do.

Cut with a scissors into small pieces.

Chop *¼ cup each of onions and celery*. Saute these in *1 tablespoon oil* until onions are soft and clear. Drain.

Mix the onion mixture with *2 tablespoons mayonnaise*, the chicken and a *good grind of pepper*. Set this filling aside while you make the dough.

Remove 2 tablespoons flour from 1 cup flour.

With a pastry blender mix in *¼ teaspoon salt* and a *pinch of sugar*.

Measure *⅓ cup vegetable shortening*. Divide in half.

Put ½ into the flour mixture. With the pastry blender mix until the flour looks like fine cornmeal.

Add the rest of the vegetable shortening. With the pastry blender mix only into large crumbs.

Divide the flour mixture into thirds.

Put some ice cubes into a small bowl of water. When ice cold, measure *3 tablespoons water* into a cup. A little at a time, sprinkle 1 tablespoon water over ⅓ of the flour mixture. Use a fork or your fingers to mix it together.

Do the same with another third. Combine these thirds with as much of the dry third as will make into a ball.

To the rest of the flour, add as much of the third tablespoon of water as is needed to make a soft, but not sticky, ball of dough.

Combine into 1 large ball.

Throw the ball 20 times from one hand to the other.

For experienced pie crust makers, sprinkle as much of the 3 tablespoons ice water over the flour mixture as you need to make a soft, but not sticky, ball of dough.

Pinch off 6 small balls as big as a walnut. Roll each ball into a 5 inch circle. Place a small amount of the filling on one side of each round. Fold each one over. Close tightly by edging with the prongs of a fork. Make a slit on each top crust to let the steam escape.

Glaze by brushing on a *little milk or egg glaze*.

Mix *1 tablespoon milk* into *1 slightly beaten egg* to make this egg glaze.

Bake the Foldovers in a 425° preheated oven about 25 minutes.

The boned, canned breast of chicken tastes surprisingly good made this way and helps to make this a "quickie." Yes, your "ready cooked" homemade chicken tastes even better. It all depends on your time!

Baked Chicken In A Paper Bag

many people say this is "the best" . . . and I add, "it's the easiest" . . . what do you say? . . . this is for electric stoves, not gas stoves

Preheat oven 425°. This is for people with electric stoves.
Rub *1½ tablespoons fat* over a *3 pound, cleaned, wiped dry fryer chicken.*
Smear *½ tablespoon margarine or butter* inside the chicken.
Cross the chicken legs and tie.
Turn the wings akimbo, so they won't flop.
Salt the chicken with *1 teaspoon salt* and put some inside, too.
Sprinkle a *little paprika* on the back of the chicken.
Open a paper bag, one from the supermarket large enough to balloon around the chicken. Slip a piece of wax paper on the bottom of the bag, not on the sides, please. Place the bag on a rack in a shallow roasting pan.
Sprinkle a little paprika on the breast of the chicken.
Breast side up, slip the chicken into the bag onto the wax paper. Balloon the bag so it doesn't hug the chicken. Tie the bag shut.
Bake 1 hour. Reduce the heat to 400°; bake 45 minutes.
Remove to a plate by cutting open the paper bag. Be careful not to spill the good, good gravy.
Cut the chicken into quarters. Enjoy yourselves!
Easy, easy, easy and mighty "easy" to eat!
Here is a table with baking times:

3½ pound chicken—2 hours
3 pound chicken—1 hour, 45 minutes
2½ pound chicken—1 hour, 30 minutes

Tip: We like this better than using a plastic bag. Our supermarket is glad to "give" us a bag.

A Southern Chef's Fried Chicken

it's not greasy and you can do most of the preparation ahead of time . . . it's our favorite fried chicken!

Line a cookie sheet with paper towels.

Cut a *2½ pound fryer* into 10 pieces; separate the thighs from the drumsticks; cut the breast in half lengthwise, the back in 2 pieces and the two wing tips and their wings off, makes for easier eating.

Sprinkle lightly with *salt.*

Put a *cup or more as needed flour* and a *light sprinkle of salt* into a paper bag.

Mix *2 eggs* with a fork. Stir in *½ cup nonfat milk.*

Heat a large skillet with *enough oil to come 1½ inches deep* in the skillet until hot. Test with a small piece of bread. If it starts to rise instantly and begins browning, remove it; the fat is ready. Put immediately a large tablespoon margarine into the fat. This gives the chicken a beautiful golden color.

Dip a few pieces of the chicken at a time into the egg mixture. Then shake in the bag and put immediately, meaty side down, into the fat. Do not fry the chicken, just brown it on both sides, as it will cook later. As the chicken pieces brown, remove with a pair of tongs to the paper toweled cookie sheet to drain any fat off. Continue until all have been browned.

You can finish the chicken right away or let cool and finish later.

Place the chicken pieces in a shallow roasting pan. Cover it with foil.

Heat oven 325°.

Put chicken in the preheated 325° oven. Bake about 45 minutes until cooked. Remove the foil. Turn the heat to 400°. Let crisp about 5 to 10 minutes.

Serve at once.

Chicken And Dumplings

everybody likes chicken and dumplings

Cut up a *3 or 3½ pound fryer.*

Put into a deep casserole that has a lid.

Add *4 or 5 cups cold water, 1 teaspoon salt, 1 medium onion, a bunch of celery tops or 1 stalk celery* and *1 carrot* cut into thirds.

Bring to a simmer. Cover. Turn heat to low. Simmer about 45 minutes or until chicken is tender but not overcooked.

Remove chicken and vegetables to a plate. Put a piece of paper towel in a strainer over a large bowl. Strain the broth.

It will be nice and clear. Remove the fat from the broth. Taste to see if any more *salt* is needed.

Put 4 cups broth back into the casserole.

Remove the bones and skin from the chicken pieces and cut the chicken into pieces with a sharp scissors.

Put chicken back into the broth and the vegetables.

Heat until hot and bubbling.

The Dumplings:

Mix *½ cup flour* with *¾ teaspoon baking powder, ¼ teaspoon salt,* and *1 tablespoon finely chopped parsley.*

With a pastry blender or 2 knives mix *2 teaspoons margarine or butter* in the flour mixture until it looks somewhat crumbly, takes a minute.

Mix *1 egg* with a fork. Stir in *¼ cup and 1 tablespoon milk.* Pour into the flour mixture. Barely mix.

Dip a tablespoon into the boiling broth; then dip the spoon into the batter. (The batter will not stick to the spoon.)

Drop by spoonfuls into the boiling broth. Continue until all have been dropped in.

Cover immediately. Turn heat to medium low or low, cook 12 minutes without removing cover. This makes 10 dumplings.

You can eat your dinner in a soup plate.

Tip: Instead of the liquid milk you can add 1 tablespoon instant dry milk to the flour mixture and add ¼ cup plus 2 tablespoons water as the liquid. Whichever is easier for you to do.

Stir Fried Chicken With Sauce And Vegetables

a quickie super-quick dinner American style . . . wonderful to make when it's hot in the summertime!

Remove the skin and bones of dark meat from a 3 pound chicken.

Cut enough of the *dark meat* into strips *to make about 1 pound,* which is enough for 4. (We will add more protein.)

Cook *1 cup rice* as usual, takes about 20 minutes to cook. (See Index for recipe.) Let stand until ready to use.

Open *1 can (1 pound) stewed tomatoes.* Remove 2 tablespoons of the tomato juice. Stir *1 tablespoon cornstarch* into the 2 tablespoons tomato juice. Set aside.

Mince *2 tablespoons onions.*

Open *1 can (1 pound) chick peas;* drain.

Put in a bowl *½ teaspoon salt, ½ teaspoon garlic powder, 4 tablespoons brandy or white wine or chicken broth,* and *¼ teaspoon sugar.*

Stir in the strips of chicken. Let marinate 15 minutes.

Put *1½ tablespoons oil* in a saucer and the 2 tablespoons minced onion. Set aside.

Mix *2 tablespoons water* and *2 tablespoons cornstarch.* Set aside in a saucer.

Heat a large skillet on high heat. Add the oil.

Put in the chicken strips. Save the marinade.

With 2 wooden spoons, cook and stir quickly about 2 minutes until the strips are lightly browned.

Remove to a large plate.

Heat the skillet until hot.

Add the 1½ tablespoons oil and the onions. Cook and stir about 10 minutes.

When hot, add the drained chick peas. Cook and stir about 2 minutes.

Stir in the stewed tomatoes and the marinade. Cook, stir until hot.

Stir in the cornstarch mixture. Cook and stir until everything is hot and the sauce has thickened.

Add a few drops of *Tabasco or hot red pepper.*

Add the fried strips of chicken. Cook and stir a minute. Serve with the rice on the side, or pour over the rice, whichever way you like best.

American Chow Mein

we make this from scratch . . . we use our trusty big chopping knife to chop our vegetables and our wonderful, sharp Wiss scissors, which we have used in our kitchen for 20 years . . . the secret is that we wash and dry it immediately after using

You need to cook *1 cup rice* as usual.

You need *3 cups "Ready Cooked chicken"* (see our recipe "Bonus Chicken" which means when you cook one chicken, cook two so you have the "Bonus Chicken" to make all kinds of chicken dishes including our Chow Mein recipe) and *4 cups chicken broth.*

Cut the chicken with a scissors into bite size pieces.

Chop or cut *3/4 cup green pepper or 1 small one, 1/3 cup scallions, 1 cup celery on the slant* and *1 cup onions.*

Open and run under cold water, then drain, *1 can (8 ounces) water chestnuts* and *1 can (8 1/2 ounces) bamboo shoots.* Cut the water chestnuts into quarters or slices.

Mix together *4 tablespoons cornstarch* and *4 tablespoons cold water.* . .

In a very large skillet or a large saucepan, bring the chicken broth to a boil.

Stir in the cornstarch mixture. Cook, stir until thickened.

Add the chopped onions. Cook, stir 5 minutes.

Add the scallions, green pepper and celery. Bring to a boil, cook 5 minutes.

Add the water chestnuts and the bamboo shoots.

Taste the Chow Mein to see if it needs a little *salt.* . .

Serve with cooked rice and sprinkle with Chow Mein Noodles. We sometimes use the ones that come in a can. The ones in good Chinese restaurants that are made by the chef are much better, but who has the time to make and deep fry them? We do. See our recipe "Deep Fried" noodle.

The soy sauce we use, which can be found in any supermarket, is Kikoman Soy Sauce.

Tip: If you have some real fresh peas, add them for a good taste; and if you have some *fresh* snow peas or, as our Pennsylvania Dutch call them, sugar peas, then you've got something very special! Also, if you have raised a crop of alfalfa sprouts or bean sprouts, add them, and is that a dish!—and if you can afford some fresh mushrooms cut into slices through the stems (or use canned), mushrooms are very good in Chow Mein.

Tip: This Chow Mein freezes beautifully.

Tip: The difference between an excellent Chow Mein and the other kind is the chicken broth. You need a strong chicken broth. Sometimes you might have to add a chicken bouillon powder to your chicken broth to strengthen it!

Chicken Breasts With Mushrooms And Onions

a real chickeny taste

Use *1 chicken breast for 2—or 2 chicken breasts, depending on your eaters.*

Slice *1 small onion thin, or a little larger one if you are using two breasts.*

Wash and slice *¼ pound mushrooms;* or use *1 jar (2½ ounces) sliced mushrooms, drained.* (Use 2 jars for 2 breasts.)

Heat skillet with *2 tablespoons oil* until hot, then add *1 tablespoon margarine*. Don't burn.

Add the mushrooms to the onions. Cook and stir a few minutes to combine flavors.

Strain the onions and mushrooms from the fat. Set aside. Put fat back in the skillet.

Wash chicken breasts. Soak in *salted water* (about ¼ teaspoon salt) about 5 minutes. Drain. Wipe chicken breasts.

Pat both sides of breasts lightly with *seasoned bread crumbs,* don't use too much.

Heat the skillet with the fat.

Put chicken, meaty side down, on medium low heat in the skillet and brown lightly, about 15 or 20 minutes.

Take *2 tablespoons flour*. Stir in *3 tablespoons or a little more water*. Shake in a screw top jar.

Take the chicken off heat and put onto the onion plate.

Stir *1 cup water* into hot skillet. Keep 1 extra cup water in reserve. Add *½ cup more water plus 1 chicken bouillon powder*.

Cook, stir in the flour mixture so there are no lumps.

Add the onion mixture back in. Add the chicken breasts.

Bring to a simmer. (Don't touch heat; use the medium low heat you had.)

Put lid on and tilt. Let cook until it comes to a simmer. Turn heat to low. Let simmer 10 to 15 minutes more.

For a change add a little sherry to the gravy. Can be reheated in gravy. Serve with rice or noodles.

Rolled Chicken Breasts

for two . . . takes minutes to cook . . . the work is in the preparation . . . sorta "Chinese style—Americanized"

Defrost *½ of 12 ounce package frozen corn.*

Defrost *½ of 12 ounce package frozen Fordhook Lima Beans.*

Defrost *6 Swift's Frozen Sausage* (Italian or Smoked).

Slice *1 chicken breast* into 6 slices.

Sprinkle *salt* on.

Flatten the breast slices between 2 sheets of wax paper. . . . I use a 4 cup glass measuring cup, as it is heavy.

Cook, stir the sausages and prick with a fork in a hot skillet with 1 tablespoon water until the fat has run out and the sausages are browned lightly.

Fill each slice breast with 1 sausage.

Mix together *½ cup crumbs* with *½ cup wheat germ.*

Roll the filled chicken slices in the crumbs lightly.

Heat the skillet with *½ cup Chicken Bouillon Broth.*

Stir in the defrosted lima beans and the corn.

Bring to a boil. Put lid on. Cook about 10 minutes until done, but not overdone. There should be no broth left. Add *salt* and *pepper* to taste.

Remove to a plate. Wipe the skillet. Heat it until hot with *2 tablespoons oil* and *1 tablespoon margarine.*

Add the rolled, filled breasts of chicken.

Cook, stir the breasts about 2 or 3 minutes until done. Add the vegetables on one side of the skillet. Heat, and eat at once.

American Style Stir Fried Chicken For Two

easy cooking, quick cooking, good eating!

Cook *½ cup rice.*

You need *Swift's Premium "Brown N Serve Sausage."* No nitrite in them!

Skin, bone and cut *2 chicken thighs and drumsticks or 1 chicken breast* into ¼ inch thick and 1½ inches long strips.

Put the chicken into a bowl with *1 teaspoon cornstarch, ⅛ teaspoon ground ginger, ¼ teaspoon garlic powder, ½ teaspoon salt* and *2 tablespoons dry sherry,* and mix together with your fingers.

Let marinate 15 minutes to ½ hour.

Steam or cook *enough pole beans or green beans for 2 portions* just until tender, but crisp, not soft or soggy. These can be steamed early in the day or even the day before when we then call them "ready cooked" beans.

Put 4 or 5 frozen sausages into a small skillet with about *2 tablespoons water* on medium high heat until the water is evaporated and fat has cooked out of the sausages. With 2 forks keep turning the sausages as they brown, takes about 5 minutes only. Brown, don't dry the sausages out. When browned, put on a paper towel and wipe off any fat.

Make ½ *cup Chicken Bouillon Broth* by mixing ½ package Chicken Bouillon Powder or cubes with ½ cup water or use ½ cup fresh or canned chicken broth.

Put 2 large plates in the oven on lowest heat to get hot.

Heat a large skillet until hot. Add *2 tablespoons oil.* Add the strips of chicken. Cook, stir, until the chicken is done, takes about 2 minutes only. Put on a plate.

Put the chicken broth or Bouillon Broth into the skillet. Bring to a boil. Add the beans. Cook, stir until the beans are hot and done but still crisp. Push to one side of the skillet.

Return the chicken to the skillet with the sausage. Cook, stir until hot. Taste to see if any salt is needed. Grind a *little pepper* over the chicken.

Place the chicken on top of the rice and the beans on the other side and serve.

Children like this dish, too, especially the vegetable, as it retains its texture and color, and the broth gives it an extra good taste.

This is a true "Quick Trick" dish.

PS: You can do "all the work" ahead, too. Of course for variety you can substitute noodles for the rice, or spaghetti, groats or macaroni, or even alphabet pasta for the children.

You can "stretch" the chicken by using canned, dried (cooked) beans—kidney, Great Northern, black beans or black eyed peas. You can change your Vitamin A vegetable with carrots or the #1 nutrition bargain—broccoli, or peas, or one of the squash family. You can use strips of round steak for a change. You can substitute the Chicken Bouillon Powder or Beef Bouillon Powder or use Campbell's Beef Broth, not consomme, for lots of flavor.

This is a "magic" dish because you can make many "different" dishes from it.

The "Bonus" Chicken

you get delicious broth and a juicy chicken

Put a *3½ pound chicken* into a pot that fits (but not too large).

Add *5 cups cold water* and *1¼ teaspoons salt, 1 carrot* cut into 4 pieces, *1 large onion* cut in halves and *1 branch celery leaves* or *1 large stalk* cut into 4 pieces.

Bring to a boil. Turn heat to low. Cover. Simmer about 45 minutes until done. Don't overcook.

Remove the chicken and the vegetables to a plate.

Put a medium or large strainer over a large bowl. Put a piece of paper towel into the strainer. Slowly, pour the broth through the paper towel.

Put the chicken back in the broth for 15 minutes. This keeps the chicken juicy and also adds flavor to it.

You can eat the vegetables; they taste good, too.

Remove the chicken after the 15 minutes to a plate to cool; or cool in the refrigerator. Cool the broth in the refrigerator overnight for the fat to congeal. The next day the fat will have congealed on top of the broth, so lift it off. You can use the soup broth in many dishes.

When the chicken is cold, you can use immediately in many of our chicken recipes, such as casserole dishes, Shepherd's pies, chicken pies, salad or sandwiches; or see our "Ready Cooked Chicken" recipes.

Tip: It is much better to use a paper towel than cheesecloth, which you have to wash; and besides the paper towel clears the broth beautifully. Throw the paper towel away. No sweat, or tears!

Cook Once For Twice Chicken, Beef And Broth

to make soups, a chicken dish and a meat dish with the "Ready Cooked" chicken and beef

Cut a *3½ pound chicken* into 9 pieces leaving the breast whole.

Cut a *1¾ pound whole piece of chuck* into 3 pieces or use *a piece of whole round steak weighing the same* and cut into its sections. We like the chuck best.

Peel and cut each into 3 pieces, *2 carrots, 2 medium onions, 1 large stalk branch of celery or leaves.*

Put everything into a large pot. Add about *11 cups water.*

Bring to a boil. Add *2 teaspoons salt.*

Turn the heat to low. Cover. Cook until the chicken is done, which usually takes about 45 minutes.

Remove the chicken. Continue to cook the beef until it is done, which takes about 60 minutes longer. Altogether, it cooks 1 hour 45 minutes.

Strain the broth. Let meat and chicken get cold.

You can use the chicken and meat in dishes of your choice right away or put in refrigerator and use them as you wish the next day, or you can freeze. We sometimes make a beef pie or a chicken pie or Shepherd's pies or grind and stuff into a meat or a chicken roll or make turnovers. Turn to the index for "Ready Cooked" beef and "Ready Cooked" chicken for other ideas.

Chicken Stuffing For Crepes And Patty Shells (Pancakes) Stuffed With Chicken

with a delicious sauce and can be made ahead and can be frozen also!

The Chicken Stuffing

Cut *2 cooked chicken breasts* with a scissors into very small cubes or pieces.

Chop fine *1 small onion—about ¼ cup, ½ stalk celery—about ¼ cup.* Put into a skillet with *2 teaspoons oil* and *1 teaspoon margarine.* Cook, stir 2 minutes. Cover. Turn heat to low, simmer about 10 minutes until soft and onions are clear. Drain the fat.

Chop fine or use *1 can chopped (2½ ounces) drained mushrooms.*

Chop fine *2 tablespoons parsley.*

Mix these vegetables with the chicken.

Stir *½ teaspoon curry powder, ½ package instant chicken bouillon powder* into *½ cup Hellmann's Mayonnaise* and *1 tablespoon dry vermouth.* With 2 forks gently mix the chicken mixture in. Add a *good grind of pepper, salt to taste* and *⅛ teaspoon grated nutmeg.*

Spoon into the middle of each pancake.

Roll up.

Arrange in a glass or other pretty baking dish that can be brought to the table.

This can be refrigerated or frozen. When you plan to use these, defrost them.

Heat in 400° oven, covered with foil, about 20 minutes; or put on a low shelf and broil-bake.

When hot, sprinkle grated Parmesan cheese on top and broil. Watch it so it doesn't burn—takes only a few minutes. Serve.

Tip: We wash and chop fine our fresh parsley and freeze in packages of 1 tablespoon each to have ready when we need them. This way they don't get old and have to be thrown away, and when freezing them, the flavor is still there.

Sauce For Crepes Stuffed With Chicken Or Stuffed Patty Shells

you can try both of these sauces . . . they both taste good and then you can decide which will be your favorite

Sauce Number 1:

Sauce to use separately to pour over the stuffed pancakes at the table.

Melt *4 tablespoons margarine*. Take off heat. Stir in *4 tablespoons flour*. Stir in *¼ teaspoon onion powder, ¼ teaspoon dried thyme leaves, ¼ teaspoon curry powder, a pinch of freshly grated nutmeg, 3 chicken bouillon powders, a touch of tabasco, a grind of pepper* (white if you have it) and *2 cups milk*. Cook, stir 10 minutes.

Before using stir in *1 teaspoon margarine or butter.*

Sauce Number 2:

Filling to Stuff Pasta:

Stir *½ cup skim milk into 1 (3 ounce) package cream cheese with chives.*

Stir in a *pinch of dried ginger, ¼ teaspoon thyme, 1 teaspoon chopped fine parsley* and *2 tablespoons Vermouth.* Bring to a simmer. Cook, stir 2 minutes.

Chicken Stuffing For Pancakes And Jumbo Pasta Shells

you need your "Ready Cooked" chicken or you can use "Ready Cooked" beef, veal or pork—or even tuna fish and that's the easiest because you didn't even have to "Ready Cook" it at all!

This is stuffing for 8 jumbo pasta shells for 2.

Chicken Stuffing or the equivalent meat.

Grind or chop very fine *enough "Ready Cooked" chicken or equivalent to make 1 cup.*

Stir in *3 tablespoons Hellmann's mayonnaise, a good grind of pepper, ¼ teaspoon onion powder, ½ teaspoon dried tarragon, a pinch of ground nutmeg,* and *salt to taste.*

Tip: We buy the nutmeg that looks like a hard nut and grate it on our grater. The smell and taste are divine!

Crepes For Stuffed Chicken Or Other Stuffing

since the crepes are so light and delicious they are always a treat . . . besides chicken, you can use tuna fish, canned salmon, ground ham, chopped spinach and grated cheese, etc.

These can be made ahead, stuffed, kept in the refrigerator until needed later in the day or whenever or for a longer time can be frozen. In fact, you can eat some and freeze some.

This makes about 18 thin pancakes or crepes.

You need an 8 inch skillet. The Teflon lined ones that are rounded are nice and if you have a ¼ metal measuring cup, it's a help.

Spread 3 long sheets of wax paper over a clean surface. You will turn out the baked crepes on these.

Into a large bowl, put *1 cup flour.* Add *¼ teaspoon salt* and a *pinch of sugar.*

Add 1 egg at a time, mixing each time well with a wooden spoon so there are no lumps until you have added *4 large eggs.*

Stir in *1 cup cold tap water* and *1 teaspoon oil.* Let stand 15 to 30 minutes, preferably 30 minutes.

To Bake:

On second highest heat, heat an 8 inch skillet until hot. Brush with oil.

Fill a ¼ cup metal measuring cup *one half* full of batter or you need 2 tablespoons batter. Pour or spoon into the hot skillet. Immediately lift off and rotate the skillet on and off the heat so the batter spreads all over so this will make a thin pancake. Cook, just a minute, just until the bottom is a light brown and when you touch the top it is dry. Turn quickly over onto the wax paper. You do not need to brown the other side. Continue until all are done.

Chicken Stuffing Number 1:

Cut with a scissors *2 cooked or enough canned chicken breasts* into very small cubes or pieces or grind it.

Chop fine *1 small onion*—about ¼ cup, *½ stalk celery,* about ¼ cup.

Put into a skillet with *2 teaspoons oil* and *1 teaspoon margarine.* Cook, stir 2 minutes. Cover. Turn heat to low, cook about 10 minutes until soft and the onions are clear. Drain the fat.

Chop fine *1 can (2½ ounces) drained mushrooms* and *2 tablespoons parsley.* Mix with the chicken.

Stir *½ teaspoon curry powder, ½ package instant Chicken Bouillon powder* or cube into *½ cup Hellmann's Mayonnaise.* Stir in *1 tablespoon Dry Vermouth.* With 2 forks, gently mix the chicken mixture in. Add a *good grind of pepper* and *salt to taste* and *⅛ teaspoon ground nutmeg.*

Chicken Stuffing Number 2:

This is the easiest ever stuffing for crepes and it is very good tasting.

Grind or chop very fine enough "Ready Cooked" or canned *chicken* to make *2 cups.*

Stir in *6 tablespoons Hellmann's Mayonnaise, a good grind of pepper, ½ teaspoon onion powder, 1 teaspoon dried tarragon, a pinch of ground nutmeg* and *salt* to taste.

Spoon into the middle of each pancake on the brown side. Roll up.

Arrange in a glass or other pretty baking dish that can be brought to the table. This can be refrigerated covered with foil or frozen. When you plan to use, if frozen, defrost them first.

Heat oven 400°.

Cover the pan with foil. Bake about 20 minutes or put on a low shelf and broil/bake.

When hot, sprinkle grated Parmesan cheese on top and broil. Watch it so it doesn't burn—takes only a few minutes. Serve.

Sauce For Chicken Stuffed Crepes Or Other Stuffings

Sauce Number 1

Sauce to use separately to pour over the stuffed pancakes at the table.

Melt *4 tablespoons margarine*. Take off heat. Stir in *4 tablespoons flour*. Stir in *¼ teaspoon onion powder*, *¼ teaspoon dried thyme leaves*, *¼ teaspoon curry powder*, a *pinch of nutmeg*, *3 chicken Bouillon Powders or cubes*, a *touch of Tabasco*, a *grind of pepper* (white if you have) and *2 cups milk*. Cook, stir 10 minutes.

Before using, stir in *1 teaspoon margarine or butter*.

Sauce Number 2

Stir *½ cup skim milk* into *1 (3 ounce) package of cream cheese with chives*.

Stir in a *pinch of dried ginger*, *¼ teaspoon thyme*, *1 teaspoon chopped fine parsley* and *2 tablespoons Dry Vermouth* and *1 cup canned chicken or Chicken Bouillon broth*.

Cook, stir until it simmers. Cook, stir 2 minutes.

Serve over stuffed chicken crepes.

Brunswick Chicken Stew

with a Pennsylvania Dutch touch

Cut a *3 or 3½ pound chicken* into 10 pieces. (Cut the backbone into 2 pieces.) Remove the fat.

Remove the carrots from 1 package frozen "stew" vegetables. Set aside.

Heat a large skillet on medium high heat with *2 tablespoons oil* and *1 tablespoon soft margarine*.

Without crowding, brown the chicken pieces. Remove to a plate.

Put *4 cups water* into a large pot. Add *3 teaspoons chicken bouillon powder* and *¼ teaspoon salt*. Bring to a boil.

Add the browned chicken pieces, *¼ cup chopped onions, ¼ cup chopped celery*, the *package "stew" vegetables (with the carrots removed)*. Bring to a boil.

Turn heat to low. Put lid on. Simmer 30 minutes.

Add the *frozen carrots* and *1 cup frozen lima beans*. Bring back to a boil. Turn heat to low. Simmer 30 minutes.

Add *1 cup corn, frozen or canned.*

Add *salt*, if necessary, and *pepper* to your taste.

Make some Pennsylvania Dutch "rivels."

Drop *1 egg* into a bowl.

Add *1 cup flour.*

With your fingers blend into tiny balls or flakes.

Let the stew come to a gentle boil.

A little at a time, drop ¼ cup to ½ cup "rivels" into the stew.

Cook 10 to 15 minutes until everything is done.

This is a real "hearty" dish, perfect for a cold winter day.

Don't let this recipe fool you. If may sound hard, but it's very easy.

Top Stove Chicken And Vegetables With Its Own Sauce

a simple dish that is sparked with dumplings and surprised with sausage or meat balls

Peel and cut into halves *2 medium onions, 4 medium potatoes*, cut into quarters, *3 carrots* each cut into 1 inch pieces and *2 stalks celery* cut into 1 inch pieces.

Chop *2 tablespoons fresh parsley* fine. Set aside.

Remove any fat and skin from a *3 or 3½ pound chicken* cut into portion size pieces. Put these and the skin (not the fat) into large saucepan or casserole.

Add *5 cups water, 1¼ teaspoons salt*. Bring to a boil. Add the onions, carrots, celery. Bring to a boil. Turn heat to low. Cook 30 minutes.

Put into a bowl *½ pound ground beef, ½ slice bread* with crust cut off. Add *2 tablespoons nonfat milk*. Crumble together until the milk is absorbed.

Grate *1 small onion* over ground beef. Add *½ teaspoon salt* to taste, *¼ teaspoon pepper, ½ teaspoon dried Italian Herb Seasoning,* or *¼ teaspoon each oregano, basil and thyme.*

Drop the meat balls into the chicken and vegetables. Cook 15 minutes more.

The Dumplings:

Mix *½ cup flour* with *¾ teaspoon baking powder, ¼ teaspoon salt* and *2 tablespoons finely chopped parsley.*

With a pastry blender or 2 knives mix *2 teaspoons margarine* in the flour mixture until it looks somewhat crumbly, takes a minute.

Mix *1 egg* with a fork. Stir in *1 tablespoon nonfat milk.* Pour into the flour mixture. Barely mix.

Dip a tablespoon into the boiling broth; then dip the spoon into the batter. (The batter will not stick to the spoon.)

Drop by spoonfuls into the boiling broth. Continue until all have been dropped in.

Cover immediately. Turn heat to medium low or low; cook 12 minutes without removing cover. This makes about 10 dumplings.

Your dinner is now ready.

Barbecued Chicken With Tiny Meat Balls

a very nice dish

Use either *2 breasts cut in halves and ½ pound ground beef* or *4 thighs and ½ pound ground beef* for four.

You can make your own barbecue sauce as follows; or use your favorite "bought" barbecue sauce. We use Heinz Barbecue Sauce and dilute it with 1 cup water.

You can make this an oven casserole dish or a "skillet" dish. This dish freezes beautifully.

The Barbecue Sauce:

Mix together *1 cup catsup, 1 cup water, ¼ teaspoon onion powder, ¼ teaspoon garlic powder, ⅛ teaspoon celery powder or seeds, 2 tablespoons brown sugar* and *2 teaspoons Worcestershire Sauce.*

Cook and stir 15 minutes.

If baking in the oven, heat oven 375°.

Salt the chicken pieces lightly. Let stand 10 minutes.

Make the tiny meat balls the size of marbles.

Put ½ *slice bread with crusts cut off* into a bowl.

Add ¼ *cup nonfat milk*. Crumble together until all the milk is absorbed.

Grate about *1 tablespoon onion* over this. Add *1 teaspoon dried oregano*, ⅛ *teaspoon garlic powder* and ½ *of an egg*.

Mix everything together adding *salt and pepper to taste*. Shape into meat balls the size of marbles.

Heat a skillet with *2 tablespoons oil* until hot.

Dip the chicken pieces into *flour*. Shake off excess. Brown nicely, meaty side down; then turn and brown the other side. Remove to a baking dish or casserole.

Dip the meat balls in *flour;* shake off excess.

Brown in the *oil*, adding more *oil as needed*. Don't crowd the meatballs, as they will steam instead of brown.

Remove to the casserole; arrange around the chicken pieces.

Bring the barbecue sauce to a boil. Pour over the chicken mixture. Cover with foil.

Bake in 375° oven about 15 minutes. Remove the foil. Bake 15 minutes more. Check if it is done. Serve.

This is nice with boiled new potatoes and a salad.

I sometimes add a can of niblets corn the last 10 minutes of baking—kids like this—"grown-up" kids, too!

Old Fashioned Chicken Shortcake With Cornbread

these are good for a change

Preheat oven 425°.

You need an 8 inch square baking pan.

With a pastry blender mix *1 cup cornmeal* with *1 cup flour, 1 teaspoon salt, 3 teaspoons baking powder, 1 tablespoon sugar* and ⅓ *teaspoon poultry seasoning*.

Mix *2 eggs* with a fork.

Stir in *2 tablespoons oil* and *1 cup milk*.

Stir into the cornmeal mixture.

Pour into a greased baking pan.

Bake in 425° oven about 20 to 25 minutes.

Fry ¼ *cup chopped onion* and ¼ *cup chopped celery* in *2 tablespoons oil* until onions are soft and clear. Strain. Put the vegetables back in the skillet.

Stir in *1 can cream of mushroom soup* mixed with *⅓ cup milk.*

Heat and stir so it doesn't stick.

Add *2 cups canned or cooked chicken diced.*

Add *1 cup drained peas.*

Heat until hot only. Add *salt* and *pepper*, if needed.

When the chicken is bubbly hot, spoon it between and on top of cornbread squares. Eat hot.

Party Chicken Wings

they're delectable!

Cut off wing tips from *chicken wings* and save in the freezer to use when you make chicken broth.

Cut the "wing stick" from the wings, so they can easily be held in your hands to eat.

Make our "Make and Bake":

With a pastry blender mix together *1 cup bread crumbs, ½ cup flour, 1 teaspoon cornstarch, 1¾ teaspoons onion powder, 1¾ teaspoons garlic powder, 1¾ teaspoons poultry seasoning, 1 teaspoon Paprika, 1¼ teaspoons salt* and *1 teaspoon sugar.*

Add *1 tablespoon and 2 teaspoons oil*, and with your fingers mix until well combined. You will feel no oil—just crumbs.

Heat oven 400°.

Dip each piece of chicken first into *melted margarine*, then into the "Make and Bake."

Arrange in a baking dish. Cover with foil.

Bake in 400° oven ½ hour. Remove foil. Bake 15 minutes longer.

Serve hot.

Can be served cold, too, because they are so tasty.

Broiled Cornish Hen

if you like broiled chicken, you'll love these . . . and it's a 30 minute dinner . . . this is for two

Defrost overnight in the refrigerator a *1½ pound Cornish hen.*

Cut hen in half. Clean the insides carefully and remove any fat.

Brush the halves with *1 teaspoon melted margarine* and *½ teaspoon salt*. Let stand 15 minutes.

Preheat the broiler 15 minutes, putting the oven rack on the second shelf from the broiling unit.

Place the halves, breast side up, on a shallow broiling pan. We do not use a rack in the broiling pan. Broil until browned, about 3 to 5 minutes, but don't go away, as it will burn. When browned, put on oven rack second from the bottom and continue to broil 10 minutes.

Turn the halves over and broil 15 minutes.

Sprinkle a little *dried tarragon leaves* over the breast and thighs and broil 1 minute.

Serve with a nice salad, some cranberry sauce, a fresh steamed vegetable such as broccoli, spinach or peas, some boiled parsley potatoes, and some fresh fruit, or a deep dish fruit pie for a special treat and that is a meal!

Chopped Livers

chopped livers make a special hors d'oeuvre . . . delicious without using a lot of fat . . . the new way to chop livers

Hard cook *3 eggs*. Cool and peel.

Slice *4 medium onions*.

Fry in *2 or 3 tablespoons oil* until soft and clear. Remove onions with a slotted spoon out of the oil.

Wipe out pan.

Heat skillet on medium heat.

Add *2 or more beef bouillon powders* with *2 tablespoons or more water*, and bring to a boil.

Add *1 pound chicken or turkey livers*. Cook, stir until no red shows, not dry.

Remove to a plate to cool.

Strain the broth and keep.

Put the liver, onions and eggs through a grinder. Grind only once or twice as you prefer.

Add the broth as needed to have a soft, juicy chopped liver.

Add *salt* to your taste.

This is a nice luncheon dish, too, served on a pretty lettuce leaf with radishes, sliced tomatoes, a dill pickle and some good sliced dark Danish, Russian or pumpernickel bread—take your choice.

Another Chopped Chicken Livers

people who don't like liver, like this liver

Hard boil *2 eggs*. Let get cold.

Slice *2 medium onions* about ¼ inch thick.

Heat a skillet on medium heat with *4 tablespoons oil* and the onions.

Turn the heat to lowest heat. Cover. Simmer 30 minutes until soft. Do not brown or burn. Drain over a bowl and save the oil. Let the onions get cold on a plate.

Put the oil back in the skillet and heat.

Add *½ pound chicken livers*. Cook on medium heat or low, depending on your stove, and turn until cooked but not browned, just until no blood shows. Takes about 5 minutes.

Remove to a plate to get cold. Strain the oil and juice left in the pan in a strainer covered with a paper towel and put over a bowl. This is a good tip when straining to get a clear liquid.

Let the livers get cold.

When all the ingredients are cold, put through a grinder as follows: Put in first some of the hard boiled eggs, then on top, some of the onions, then on top, some of the livers, then grind together.

Continue to do this until all is done.

Add about *½ teaspoon salt* to taste and mix.

Spoon into a bowl and refrigerate.

This makes an easy dinner served with, in season, tomatoes, and a first course of fresh "sweet" corn, also in season.

Check the index for my recipe under H, how to buy and store "sweet" corn for 2 days and many times 3 days.

Fruit "Garnish"

makes a plain meal fancy . . . lovely with chicken or turkey or even a roast.

Cut *1 banana* into 1 inch pieces.

Drain *1 can (1 pound, 13 ounces) Fruits for Salad* (not cocktail).

Put into a skillet.

Grate a *pinch of ginger* over, *¼ teaspoon nutmeg* and *¼ teaspoon cinnamon.*

Add *¼ cup walnuts, ¼ cup raisins* (preferably yellow), *2 tablespoons sherry* (American sherry is fine), and *3 tablespoons margarine.* (You can omit the sherry.)

Cook 15 minutes; check that it doesn't stick or burn.

Put under broiler, baste and brown.

Delicious served with chicken or cornish hens, lamb, or veal or beef roast.

A good sherry that isn't expensive and is a dessert sherry, which means a sweet sherry, if you like a cream sherry, is Emilio Cream Sherry. Emilio Lustaw are the shippers. Zerez and London—I paid only $2.95 in Florida in December, 1976 at a "Publix" supermarket. I just thought you would like to know.

Spiced Crisp Duck

what could be better? . . . as expensive as ducks have become, this can be a once in a while treat . . . you will love the crispy skin

Defrost a *4 to 5 pound frozen duck* in the refrigerator—takes about 2 days.

When defrosted remove any fat you can. Wipe the duck well.

Mix together *1 teaspoon salt, ½ teaspoon onion powder, 1 teaspoon garlic powder, ½ teaspoon ground allspice* and *½ teaspoon ground ginger.*

Cut *3 bay leaves* each into 3 pieces.

Put duck, back up, on a piece of foil large enough so later you can enclose it. Rub the spice mix over the duck lightly, then turn breast up and rub the spice mix over being sure to smear generously on the breast. Enclose in the foil. Put back in refrigerator to season overnight.

To roast—

Heat oven 450°.

Remove the duck from the refrigerator.

With a fork prick the duck all over the skin and fat but not into the meat.

Place a rack with legs in a shallow baking dish 15½" × 10½".

Pour about *4 cups water* into the pan being careful that the water is beneath the rack.

Place the duck breast side up on the racks or rack.

Use a brush to "mop" (not to remove the ground spices) *1 tablespoon melted margarine* over the duck.

Put in 450° oven.

Roast 20 minutes. With a fork punch the skin to release the fat.

Turn the duck over breast side down.

Roast 15 minutes—punch again to release the fat.

Turn the heat to 325°. Turn the duck breast side up.

Roast 1½ hours, punching the skin but not the meat every 15 minutes to get out more fat.

Turn breast down, roast 25 minutes and with the fork prick the skin to get the fat out.

Remove from the oven. Let cool.

The water in bottom of the baking dish has turned to a lovely broth.

When it cools, put in the refrigerator overnight so that the fat will congeal and then be removed easily.

You can make some bean soup out of this or you can cook some beans in it.

When ready to eat the duck—

Heat the broiler. Put the cooked duck on a rack in the shallow pan. Put on the middle rack of the oven. Broil breast side down, use the fork to get as much fat out as you can. Don't let the duck burn—just let the skin get nice and crisp. Broil about 10 minutes. Turn breast side up, broil 10 minutes as you did the back to brown and get more fat out.

Serve at once.

Did you ever taste a more crispy delicious duck?

Black Cherry Sauce For Chickens Or Ducks

delicious with Cornish hens, or ducks and also broiled chicken

Strain *1 cup canned pitted black cherries.*

Stir/cook *1 cup Burgundy wine, ¼ cup sugar* until it boils.

Reduce heat; cook 2 minutes and add 1 cup pitted black cherries.

Off heat, combine *2 teaspoons water* with *2 teaspoons cornstarch* and stir into the wine/cherry mixture. Cook/stir until it clears and thickens. Serve over each portion of chicken or duck.

PAN FRY is to brown on higher heat; turn to low to finish cooking.

GRILL means to broil.

PAN BROIL means to heat a skillet hot, brush with fat and brown each side fast; then turn heat down and cook until it is as you like it, turning the food as necessary. You can pan broil by sprinkling a very little salt on a hot skillet and keep turning. Turn the heat down to finish when it has browned.

What Is Sophie's Special Cut Blade Beef Roast

Sophie's Special Cut Blade Beef Roast is a blade roast that has two tender parts that can be used as steaks and one center part that looks pretty, and you think it is tender, but it is tough.

That tough piece you either braise or pot roast, make a stew out of, or make different kinds of "Swiss steak," or grind to make hamburgers or other ground beef recipes. This piece of beef needs liquid of some kind—broth, tomatoes, water, beer or wine to keep it moist and tender. Also slow, lowest heat helps to tenderize it both on top of the stove or in the oven. The result is a very tasty dish. You also need some kind of herb or spice to season it and some flavoring vegetables, such as onions, celery, carrots, and, of course, a scant amount of salt and some pepper, preferably freshly ground, and a pinch of sugar.

Tip: A smart Penny Pincher buys when on sale as many blade roast or steaks, preferably roasts, as her pocketbook can afford and freezer space can hold. Watch the newspapers for the sales.

Following are some very inexpensive recipes.

Three Ways To Cook The Tender Blade Steaks

from the two tender parts of the blade roast

Strip Steak Stir Fried

Cut the *2 tender parts* into strips about ½ inch thick and 2½ inches long. This is a tip from the Chinese who have to save fuel and is a quick way to get a juicy steak.

Heat a skillet with *1 tablespoon oil* until hot.

Add the beef strips. Cook, stir just long enough to fry it as you like it, medium rare, medium, or well done. Steaks are always juicier when only medium rare or medium.

Remove from skillet immediately to a heated plate and eat.

Sprinkle a little *salt* on if you wish, and a "grind" or "shake" of *pepper*.

This is about the easiest way to "cook" a steak and one of the best ways.

Sliced Pan Broiled Tender Blade Steaks

Slice the *tender steaks* into slices.

Heat a skillet with *1 or more,* if needed, *tablespoons oil or margarine*. Put in the steaks without crowding.

Brown on one side. Turn; brown the other side. Keep turning and browning to get the steaks as you like them, medium rare, medium, or well done. Eat at once.

Broiled Blade Steaks

Cut the *2 tender parts of the blade roast* into as thick as possible 1 inch or 1¼ inch slices.

Heat the broiler hot. Put steaks on a rack in a broiling pan.

Broil 6 minutes on one side, 4 minutes on the other, or more as you like it.

Blade Beef Stew

made from the "tough" part of a blade roast . . . you use the tender parts as steaks . . . the blade roast is the least expensive beef, and you get the most out of it

Remove any fat or gristle from the *center piece of the blade roast.* Cut it into 1 inch pieces. Set aside.

Slice *2 large onions;* cut into 4 pieces a *stalk of celery;* peel and cut into 4 pieces *1 carrot.*

Heat a casserole or saucepan with *2 tablespoons oil* on high heat.

When hot, put in some of the beef pieces without crowding them. (They won't brown if you crowd them.) As the beef pieces brown, remove to a plate and brown the rest.

Put *¼ cup beef broth* from 1 can (12½ ounces) Campbell's Beef Broth into a screw-top jar. Add *¼ cup flour* and shake until combined. Set aside.

Put the *rest of the can of beef broth* into the casserole, and add *1 more can of beef broth.* Bring to a boil.

Shake the flour mixture and stir into the boiling beef broth. Cook, stir a few minutes until it starts to thicken.

Add the vegetables and browned beef pieces. Bring back to a boil. Turn heat to low. Cover; simmer about 2 hours until the beef is tender.

Remove the beef to a plate. Put the rest through a food mill or strainer.

Return the beef to this sauce, and you have your stew.

Add *pepper* to taste.

This stew reheats well and freezes well.

This can be made as written or, after bringing the stew to a boil, put lid on, and put into preheated 325° oven. Bake until the meat is tender, about 1½ hours or more, as needed.

Swiss Steak From Sophie's Special Cut Blade Beef Roast

the large flavorful, less tender piece of beef from Sophie's Special Cut Blade Beef Roast

Rub the less tender *piece of beef* from Sophie's Special Cut Blade Beef Roast with *flour,* but don't salt.

Heat the skillet. Add *1 teaspoon margarine,* and brown the beef nicely.

In a saucepan put *½ can tomato soup* with *½ cup water.* Bring to a boil.

Pour over the beef, and bring back to a boil. Turn heat to low; simmer 1 hour.

This makes quite a bit of sauce. If you would like to use some of this sauce in other dishes, brown some of the hamburger meat from Sophie's Special Cut Blade Beef Roast, add the sauce to it, and pour over some hot biscuits made with "Quickie Mix."

Or you can make a mini-meatloaf from the hamburger meat, and you can have the sauce to go along with your mini-meatloaf.

Swiss Steak With Stewed Tomatoes

This will make enough for 2 portions.

Cut into *four,* the tough *piece of beef* from Sophie's Special Cut Blade Beef Roast, rub *flour* in, and brown in *2 tablespoons margarine* in hot skillet.

Heat *1 can (16 ounces) stewed tomatoes* (use the store brand) until it boils.

Pour the stewed tomatoes over the beef. Bring back to a boil; turn heat to low; simmer 1 hour.

This is very tender, tasty and healthy.

Swiss Steak With A Delicious Oniony Flavor

Cut *1 medium onion* into thin slices. Fry in *2 tablespoons vegetable oil* until soft and yellow. Remove. Strain the onions and put the fat into a skillet.

Rub the flavorful, *less tender cut from Sophie's Special Cut Blade Beef Roast* with *flour* and brown on medium heat in the oil and add *1 teaspoon margarine* if needed.

Bring to a boil *1 beef bouillon cube* in *1 cup water.* Add this to the browned beef.

Add the onions. Bring back to a boil. Put lid on; turn heat to low; simmer 1 hour until tender.

If you prefer, you can use the cup of broth which you

made out of the bones from Sophie's Special Cut Blade Beef Roast.

If you prefer a thicker sauce—and many people do—put *2 tablespoons cold water* in a screw-top jar, add *1 tablespoon flour,* shake, stir into the boiling broth before adding the beef.

To make broth from the bones, put the bones in a small saucepan, add 2 cups water. Season; bring to a boil; turn heat to low; simmer 1 hour. You get approximately 1 cup beef broth. The bones should have a little meat left on them.

Swiss Steak With A Rich Mushroomy Taste

made from the center piece of blade beef roast

Rub *flour* into *1 slice* of flavorful, less tender piece of *beef* from Sophie's Special Cut Blade Beef Roast.

Brown in hot skillet with *1 teaspoon margarine.*

In a small saucepan put *½ can mushroom soup* and *½ cup water.* Bring to boil.

Pour over the beef. Bring back to a boil; turn heat to low; simmer for 1 hour until tender and delicious.

For a change, after bringing back to a boil, put this in the preheated 325° oven and bake about 1½ hours or until tender.

You can use the other half can mushroom soup for another meal.

Dilute with ½ cup water. Brown some hamburger meat from Sophie's Special Cut Blade Beef Roast and some sliced onions until onions are soft and yellow. Pour this over hot biscuits made from "Quickie Mix" for another happy meal.

A Meal In A Dish

Fry *1 medium onion* with *2 tablespoons oil* and *2 sliced carrots* until onions are soft and yellow. Remove.

Rub *flour* on flavorful *less tender cut from Sophie's Special Cut Blade Beef Roast.* Brown in *1 teaspoon margarine.*

Heat 1 cup broth made from *1 beef bouillon cube* and *1 cup water.* Bring to a boil.

Put *2 tablespoons water* in a screw-top jar, add *1 table-*

spoon flour and shake until mixed. Stir into the broth. Cook and stir until it thickens.

Pour into the skillet with the beef, onions and carrots. Bring back to a boil.

Put lid on; turn heat to low; simmer about 1 hour until tender.

You have a meal in a dish, no sweat, no tears—just good eating.

Chicken Steaks in Sauce

"chicken steaks" are tender strips of beef cut from the blade part of chuck

Cut *beef* into strips.

Chop *1 medium onion* and cut *1 small, sweet green pepper* into small strips.

Heat skillet on medium heat until hot. Add *1 tablespoon margarine or oil.*

Put in strips of beef, don't crowd, so the strips will brown quickly. Remove browned strips and continue until all have been browned, adding *fat as needed* a little bit at a time. This helps to brown the meat nicely. Remove to a plate.

Add fat to the skillet if needed. Put in chopped onions and strips of pepper. Cook, stir 5 minutes until onions are soft and clear.

Stir in *1 cup canned beef broth or beef broth made from 1 bouillon powder or cube and 1 cup water.*

In a small bowl mix *2 tablespoons cornstarch* with *¼ cup wine*. Stir into the sauce. Cook, stir until clear and thickened, takes about 1 or 2 minutes.

Add the beef strips; simmer together to blend the taste and heat the beef piping hot, takes about 2 minutes.

Eat while hot.

Talking About Arm Roasts

You get a lot of beef and plenty of taste when you buy an arm roast. It is never as cheap as a "blade roast," but it has the advantage of more meat and most times less fat. No, it does not have those two delicious, tender parts that the blade roast has.

When the arm roast is on sale, it's prudent for you to buy as many as you can afford if you have a freezer. Again, I repeat, a freezer is a money saver and a time saver.

What can you do with an arm roast? You can make a pot roast or many kinds of stews. This is important, you can ask your meat cutter, or do it yourself, to slice the arm roast into ½ inch or ¾ inch or 1 inch slices, depending on what you will want to do with them. We use ours just as we do our round steaks when they are on sale, as they have lots of flavor. See Index under "A" for Arm Roasts or under "R" for Roasts, then look for Arm Roasts.

Like the round steaks, the arm roast cut into slices of the thickness you prefer, taste much richer if baked in the oven. The arm roast using the round steak recipes are, if anything, more juicy and more flavorful since it comes from the chuck.

Watch the newspapers to see when the arm roasts are on sale.

Another tip for "sale bought" arm roasts, ask the meat cutter to grind some of the arm roast into ground beef or hamburger meat. If you want to make a stew of the arm roast, don't ask the meat cutter to cut it into small pieces, especially when the beef is on sale. He might refuse, and it really wouldn't be fair to take him away from his work when you can easily cut them at home.

What we need to remember is that beef marked stew meat, cut up and packaged is usually higher than the same beef you can buy in one piece. They are usually some part of the chuck, such as the blade roast, 7 bone roast, shoulder roast, arm roast or pieces "left over" from other parts that the butcher wants to get rid of. Be smart, do your own cutting. You not only "penny pinch" and "dollar save," but you know what you have.

A Family Favorite Pot Roast

a family favorite . . . no wonder, it's so full of flavor and the gravy is delicious

Heat oven 450°.

Rub *1 teaspoon salt* over a *5 pound arm roast.* Let stand 15 minutes.

Put into a casserole. Sprinkle *3 tablespoons flour* over the beef.

Place in 450° oven. Let get brown, takes about 20 minutes.

Slice *3 large onions*. Peel and cut into quarters *4 carrots* and *4 potatoes.*

Make *6 cups bouillon broth* out of 3 chicken bouillon powders, 3 beef bouillon powders and 6 cups water. Bring to a boil. Remove the beef to a plate.

Make a bed of ½ of the onions. Put the beef, browned side down, on the onions.

Sprinkle *3 tablespoons flour* on top of the beef. Place back in the oven to brown, takes 20 minutes.

Put *1 large bay leaf* cut into 4 pieces and *6 whole allspice* on top of the beef. Put the rest of the onions on top. Pour 4 cups broth around but not on top of the beef.

Arrange the carrots and potatoes around the beef. Bring to a boil on top of the stove.

Place in oven with lid on. Turn heat to 325°. Bake 1½ hours. Turn.

Add the other 2 cups bouillon broth. Put lid on. Bake 1½ hours.

Test whether the beef is done. The beef should be juicy and the gravy flavorful.

Let stand 10 to 12 minutes before slicing. Serve with the gravy.

This reheats beautifully!

Good And Easy Pot Roast

Fry *4 to 6 large onions, sliced,* in *4 tablespoons vegetable oil,* adding more if needed. Onions should be soft and golden in color, not brown. Remove to a plate.

Rub *2 tablespoons flour* into a *3 or 4 pound arm chuck roast or* the *center cut of a blade roast* and brown. Remove.

Make a bed of the onions; put roast on top.

Bring to a boil *½ bottle catsup* mixed with *2 cups water* and *2 beef or chicken bouillon powders*. Cover.

Simmer slowly on lowest heat about 2½ to 3 hours.

The beef will add flavor to the sauce, and the sauce will add flavor to the beef.

You can add vegetables to this for a meal in a dish.

Pot roasts roast beautifully in the oven, but to conserve electricity and "penny pinch," "top stove" is the answer.

New Way Pot Roast

an easy "new way" to make a pot roast for families that have to eat dinner at separate times, like when you have to go to a Parent-Teachers meeting, a Scout meeting, a 4-H Club, or whatever

This serves 4.

You need a *3 or 3½ pound arm roast.*

Peel and cut *4 large onions* into slices.

Heat a casserole on medium high heat until hot.

Add *1 tablespoon oil* and *1 tablespoon margarine.* Add the sliced onions and cook, stir about 2 minutes.

Turn heat to low. Cover. Simmer 10 minutes.

Stir in *3 tablespoons flour.* Take off heat; stir in *3 chicken or beef powders* and *2 cups cold tap water or 1 can beef broth,* and *enough water to make 2 cups.* Add *1 bay leaf* cut into 3 pieces and *4 whole allspice* and *½ cup catsup.*

Add the roast. Cover; place in 325° preheated oven. Bake, basting now and then, about 2½ to 3 hours until the beef is tender. If you prefer, cook on top of the stove on lowest heat. Let simmer until tender.

If the family is eating together, it's ready! If members of the family are eating at different times, the meat is sliced ready for them to remove to a saucepan, heat and eat.

Pot Roast "Flavored" With Beer

you cook it; don't drink it, please

Buy a *3 or 3½ pound pot roast* such as a chuck arm roast, chuck shoulder roast or chuck blade roast.

Wipe the thick piece of pot roast with a dry paper towel.

Peel and slice *4 large onions,* cut *4 carrots* into 4 pieces each, cut *3 stalks celery* into 4 pieces each *or* use some large bunches of *celery leaves.*

Heat a heavy (preferably) casserole that has a lid on high heat with *3 tablespoons oil.*

Add the vegetables. Stir, fry a minute or so until hot. Turn heat to low. Cover; let cook 10 minutes until the onions are soft and clear. With a slotted spoon remove to a plate and leave the fat in.

Add *2 tablespoons oil* to the oil left in the casserole. Turn the heat to medium high, let get hot. Brown the meat nicely on both sides. Remove to a plate.

Mix together *½ teaspoon salt* and *¾ teaspoon Italian herbs* or *¼ teaspoon basil* and *½ teaspoon oregano.* Rub over the browned meat. Set aside.

Stir in *3 beef bouillon powders* into *2 cups water* to make 2 cups cold beef bouillon broth. Put ¼ cup of this broth into a screw-top jar. Add *¼ cup flour* on top. Shake well to combine. Set aside a minute.

Bring to a boil the rest of the bouillon broth and *1 bottle (7 ounces) or 1 cup beer.* Shake the flour mixture well, and stir into the boiling broth. Cook, stir about 1 minute.

Put the browned beef into the casserole. Add the vegetables. Bring to a boil.

Add *1 bay leaf* cut into 4 pieces and *4 whole allspice.*

Put lid on, turn heat to low. Simmer on top of the stove about 2½ hours until beef is tender. Or you can place in heated 325° oven and bake until tender, about 2 to 2½ hours.

Add *salt,* if necessary, and *pepper* to taste.

This pot roast freezes well and reheats well.

We usually serve the carrots with the beef and put the rest of the vegetables with the sauce through a food mill or strainer so that nothing is wasted.

Romantic Table Made Sliced Steak

the Japanese call it Sukiyaki . . . a two-step dinner that takes 15 to 20 minutes to cook . . . the preparation takes a little longer

Cook *1 cup rice* as usual. You can make it early and reheat. We like to cook the rice right before we start preparing the vegetables, etc.

Peel and slice thin *1 large Bermuda onion* or a regular onion.

Wash, slice *½ pound fresh mushrooms.*

Wash carefully *4 cups watercress or fresh spinach,* enough for 4 (you can use frozen spinach but don't defrost).

Drain *1 can (3½ ounces) bamboo shoots.*

Drain and run under cold water *1 can (16 ounces) bean sprouts.*

Cut into 1 inch strips the green part of *scallions, enough to make ½ or ¾ cup,* cut enough *celery stalks* on a slant into 1 inch pieces *for 4.*

You can ask your butcher to cut top round steak into ⅛ inch *thin* slices, enough for 4 people, or use the tender steaks from a Blade Roast and cut into as thin slices as possible (these are delicious, see what I mean if you're in doubt . . . check index under "Blade Roast" for tender steaks or you can use 4 packages frozen beef steaks which are sliced paper thin. Don't buy frozen chopped steaks, and also check that the steaks in the package are really steaks, as one half of them may be some kind of chopped Lord Knows What . . . !).

Before you start cooking, make this sauce:

Mix together *2 cups chicken broth, 1 cup saki or dry sherry wine, 2 tablespoons sugar, 6 tablespoons soya sauce (Kikoman brand).* Set aside.

Prepare this Chicken Broth mixture ahead in a cup with a handle for easy pouring.

On a large platter you can arrange each food separately so they look beautiful like an appetizing picture, the sliced onions, the watercress or spinach, the celery, the bamboo shoots, the sliced mushrooms, the sliced steaks.

Also in a cup, put *½ cup oil* to have handy. You will not use this much oil. Also you will need 2 large spoons, so have them ready.

Have everything ready on the table to cook at the table. Use an electric skillet or your large skillet over a hot plate.

Heat the skillet with 2 or 3 tablespoons oil. When hot, add the onions, cook, stir about 5 minutes, as you want them crisp and not browned.

Add the celery, cook, stir 5 minutes, adding some sauce to cook this, no more oil.

Add the bamboo shoots, the bean sprouts and the sliced fresh mushrooms. Cook, stir about 3 minutes adding sauce as needed.

Add the steaks next. Stir, fry just until no color shows.

At the last add the fresh watercress or fresh spinach. If you are using the frozen chopped spinach—cook it, continually using two forks to scrape off the cooked spinach, so it stays bright green and cooks fast.

Pour the sauce over so everything is hot, hot; but don't keep cooking. Serve at once over the hot rice.

This is a non-fattening dish. It reads like a lot of trouble but honestly it's one of the easiest dishes to make . . . it's fun to cook and most fun to eat.

PS—You can make this dish with sliced chicken breasts or a turkey breast.

Real Juicy Steak

you roast it in the oven like a baked tenderloin

Ask the butcher for a thick *top round roast that weighs 4 or 5 pounds.*

Preheat oven 500° 15 minutes at least.

Rub *soft margarine* and sprinkle *salt* lightly over the top round steak roast.

Put on a rack in a shallow roasting pan. Put enough water to cover bottom of the pan well being careful it does not touch the rack.

Bake 45 minutes for rare, the juice spurts out, it's that juicy; add 5 minutes at a time to get the steak the way you want it.

Cut into thin slices to serve. This is the English way, and you know the English have a "know how" with roasts.

You can do the same with the "eye" of the round.

Tip: If you don't use all the steak, don't worry. You can make delicious stew out of the rest the next day or another day.

T-Bone Steak Pan Broiled

pan broiled and succulent! . . . Penny Pinchers splurge when they get a raise!

You need *T-Bone or Porterhouse Steaks* for four (try to cut down on the portions and buy less)—the Porterhouse steaks have larger tenderloin than the T-Bones. The steaks can be about ½ or ¾ or even 1 inch thick as you like them. Remove any outside fat.

Heat a large skillet, large enough to hold 2 steaks at a time without crowding, on high heat until hot.

Put a drop of water on, and if it sizzles or skitters around, the skillet is hot enough.

Brush a *little oil or margarine* over the skillet. Place the steaks in. Brown lightly, then turn. Brown the other side.

Lower the heat to medium. Turn and brown until you get the steak as you like it. You usually do not have to add any more margarine. For rare, it takes about 5 to 7 minutes only; for medium rare or well done, you cook it longer. The length of time depends on the thickness of the steak as well as how you like it.

Once you do it this way you will know how long to cook it and also what thickness you like best.

Remove to heated plates. Sprinkle a little *salt* on and a grind of *pepper*.

You've got it made!

To use no fat, sprinkle the hot skillet very, very lightly with salt; then follow the rest of the recipe.

Stir Fried Sliced Flank Steak

Slice *flank steak into ½ inch slices* against the grain; then cut each in half.

Mix together *2 tablespoons cornstarch, 2 tablespoons teriyaki or soy sauce, 2 tablespoons sherry, ½ teaspoon sugar, ¼ teaspoon dried ginger* and *⅛ or ¼ teaspoon garlic powder*.

Add to the beef; toss to coat.

Let stand 15 minutes, turning now and then.

Heat skillet with *1½ tablespoons oil*.

Add beef and stir fry until it loses its redness, about 1½ to 2 minutes—never more than 2 minutes.

Add *pepper* to taste.

This is a quick dish, so have plates hot and eat immediately.

Have rice cooked and waiting, because the steaks can't wait.

Barbecued Steakettes

on tasty open faced, toasted rolls

Buy a package of frozen *Steakettes* (10 ounces). Select the least fatty package. These steakettes are thin. Also, buy a package of *hamburger rolls*.

You also need either *Heinz Barbecue Sauce with Mushrooms or Grandma's Molasses Barbecue Sauce*. Both are good.

Heat the broiler.

Take out 8 frozen "Steakettes." (Do not defrost.)

Heat a skillet hot.

Brush with *margarine.*

Put in the Steakettes.

Keep turning with a metal spatula, and cook about 1 minute until no pink shows.

Remove to a cookie sheet.

Brush each Steakette with 1 tablespoon Barbecue Sauce.

Put under the broiler, takes about 4 minutes to cook.

When it is almost ready, open 4 hamburger rolls, spread with margarine and put on the cookie sheet. Watch carefully, do not burn; remove as soon as browned.

Remove the broiled, sauced Steakettes to the open faced rolls. Cut each roll in half. Serve at once.

Everyone likes these easy to make Barbecued Steakettes.

Beef Stroganoff

a party dish made the Penny Pincher way in a casserole

This recipe is for four. Multiply for more.

Buy a whole piece of *round steak* or a piece of sirloin steak on sale and have it cut ¼ inch thick. Usually the whole round is less expensive than buying it in sections.

Cook *1 cup rice* now or do it while the beef is in the oven.

Cut the steak into ½ inch long by ¼ inch wide strips. Heat a skillet hot with *2 tablespoons oil.* Add *1 tablespoon margarine.* Put in without crowding only enough of the strips to brown quickly. Remove to a plate as it browns and brown the rest. Leave the good brownings in the skillet but mop up the fat from the skillet.

Strain *1 can onion soup* and remove fat from *1 cup fresh or canned chicken broth.* Mix *1 cup cold tap water* with *1 Vegetable Bouillon Powder or cube.*

Add *3 tablespoons margarine or butter* to the skillet. Cook, stir on low heat until the fat is melted. Take off heat and stir in *4 tablespoons flour.* Gradually stir in all the broths.

Cook, stir on medium heat until it comes to a boil and gets thick. Stir in *1 tablespoon and 1 teaspoon A-1 sauce* and *1 tablespoon Worcestershire Sauce.* Cook, stir 5 minutes.

Add *1 can (4 ounces) sliced mushrooms* and its juice and the steak strips. Add *salt* and *pepper* to your taste.

Pour into a casserole. You can set aside, put in the refrigerator and bake in oven when ready to use.

Place in a 325° oven. Cover. Cook until meat is fork tender. You can cook as long as an hour. Serve piping hot with the rice.

Right before serving you can do as the Russians do if you wish, slowly stir a little of the sauce into some sour cream until you add enough to make the sauce warm, then stir this back into the sauce and this way it won't curdle. The Beef Stroganoff is good just as is without the sour cream, especially when you make it for a Dinner Party.

Beef Stew

Beef for stew is cut into 1 to 2 inch squares. Use beef from chuck, such as blade 7 bone, shoulder, arm roast, round steak, brisket or short ribs.

How to cook a beef stew: all stews are covered and cooked very slowly in a flavorful liquid with taste-giving vegetables, herbs and spices. Never, never boil the stew. Cook on lowest heat possible.

Here is how to vary the stews:

You can cook the stew on top of the stove or in the oven.

You can marinate the meat, or not.

You can brown the meat, or not.

You should remove the fat on the stew meat.

The liquid can be water, broth, wine, beer, canned or fresh tomatoes, tomato sauce or canned soups.

You can cook the meat in a lot of liquid or a little.

You can thicken the stew, or not.

You can skim, strain and season the sauce partway through the cooking of the stew, or at the end.

You can serve the stew with the vegetables you cooked with the stew, or you can use the vegetables just to flavor the stew and remove them.

What is a stew? A stew is meat that is browned, cooked in a slightly thickened sauce made with a broth or stock preferably, rather than water. Sometimes wine is added. It is cooked with herbs, spices and/or flavoring vegetables. Sometimes the stew is served just with its sauce; other times with the vegetables cooked right along in the stew.

Stew Meat: The most flavorful meats for stews are the less expensive cuts, chuck, round steak.

The meaty chuck, like the arm roasts, 7 bone roasts, are not as dry and apt to become tender more quickly than round steak. Round steak has less fat and is all meat, so it is a good buy for the slow, slow cooking stew, but chuck has more flavor.

Rump is tasty and makes a nice stew, but it is expensive.

Boned shoulder is a meaty, flavorful piece of chuck, more expensive usually than the arm roast but still may be a good buy.

Compare prices of these cuts. Include bones, fat, and the juiciness of the different cuts to help you decide which is best. Remember, chuck is both juicy and flavorful.

Remember, too, you can cut the beef yourself and save money.

Tips on making all kinds of stew:

Cut the meat into bite size pieces, cooks more quickly and is more flavorful.

Simmer, never boil, stews.

Brown the meat before adding any liquid.

To thicken, sprinkle flour on browned pieces of meat; or stir into the fat used to cook the vegetables or meat.

Stew meat browns quickest and easiest on high heat. Be sure to leave plenty of space between the pieces. Add more meat as you remove the browned pieces until all have been browned. This is a quickie method, and the meat browns instead of steaming, as it does when you crowd the meat.

Good Old Fashioned Beef Stew With Vegetables

you need a casserole that fits the meat and vegetables and a large skillet

Cut about *2 pounds chuck* into bite size pieces, about 1½ inches.

Peel and cut *3 large onions* into cubes.

Put *3 tablespoons vegetable oil* into a large skillet. Add the onions. Turn heat to high. When it sizzles, turn heat to simmer, put lid on, cook 10 minutes. Remove to a casserole.

Peel and cut into chunks *4 carrots* and *4 medium potatoes.* Put potatoes into cold water.

Add *2 tablespoons oil* to the skillet, and heat on high heat.

Add pieces of meat, don't crowd. Brown on high heat. Add *oil as needed*. Remove browned pieces to a casserole.

Stir in *4 tablespoons flour*. Cook 3 minutes. Stir in *4 cups beef bouillon broth.*

Add the broth to the beef in the casserole. For more flavor add *¼ to 1 teaspoon dried thyme* and *½ teaspoon parsley, chopped fine.*

Add the carrots and potatoes. Bring to a simmer. Turn heat to lowest heat; simmer 1 hour, or more—until tender.

You've got a meal in a dish.

Tasty Beef Stew

Cut the beef stew meat into 1½ inch cubes.

Heat a skillet hot. Add *2 tablespoons oil.* Without crowding, brown the cubes of beef. (Beef will steam instead of browning if you crowd them.)

As the beef browns, put into a casserole that fits.

When all are in the casserole, sprinkle 1 tablespoon at a time, shaking the casserole each time, adding *3 tablespoons flour* so the beef is covered well.

Pour *1½ cups water, 2 beef bouillon powders* and *1 onion powder* into the skillet. Stir to mix the brownings into the broth. Let come to a boil. Pour over the beef in the casserole.

Tear *1 bay leaf* into 4 pieces and arrange on the meat. Add *4 allspice.*

On medium high heat bring to a simmer. Cover with a piece of wax paper; then put on lid. Simmer about 1 to 1½ hours until the beef is tender.

A green or orange vegetable, some "Rice Potatoes" (see Index for recipe under "R"), and a fresh fruit for dessert, and you've got a good meal. How about your homemade or even "bought" whole wheat bread to mop up the good gravy?

Meat, Potato, Onion Pie

a man's dish . . . and what woman can resist!

You need an 8 inch "deep" pie dish or casserole.

Heat oven 400°.

You need *4 cups bite size "ready cooked" beef, 2 cans Campbell's Beef Broth* and *2 cans chicken broth.*

Chop *3 cups onion* and *½ cup carrots.*

Cook, stir *⅓ cup or 6 tablespoons oil* with the 3 cups onions and ½ cup carrots 3 minutes. Turn heat to simmer. Cover. Cook 10 minutes until onions are soft and clear. Set aside 1 cup of this sauteed onion mixture.

With a spatula stir the "ready cooked" meat into the skillet with the rest of the onions and carrots. Add *salt* and *pepper* to taste.

Slice enough *young potatoes to make 2 cups.*

Cook in water to cover with *½ teaspoon salt*. Let come to a boil; turn heat to low; cook 5 minutes. Drain. Gently mix with the cup of sauteed onion mixture. Stir in *6 tablespoons flour*. Cook, stir 3 minutes.

Stir in *2 cans Campbell's Beef Broth (or 4 cups),* and *2 cans (or 2⅔ cups) chicken broth.* (If you have homemade soups, they are best). Cool.

While it cools, make the bottom and top pie crust from our "Pastry Dough" recipe as follows:

Pastry Dough

Put *1¾ cups flour* into large bowl. With a pastry blender mix in *½ teaspoon salt* and a *pinch of sugar.*

Add *⅔ cup vegetable shortening.* With the pastry blender mix into large crumbs. Push ⅓ aside and mix the rest into fine crumbs.

Put some ice cubes into a bowl of *water.* When ice cold, measure 6 tablespoons into a cup. A little at a time pour the ice water, mixing with a fork or your hands, using as much water as necessary until it forms a soft, but not sticky, ball. Throw this ball from one hand to the other 20 times.

Divide into halves. Roll one piece on a clean floured surface to fit the 8 inch deep pie dish and put in. Roll out the top crust. Let stand to have ready.

Spoon the filling onto the bottom crust. Immediately place the top crust on. With a sharp knife, cut a small hole in the center and 6 slits around it.

Brush the crust with a little *milk.*

Immediately place in the 400° oven. Bake about 1 hour until the crust is a lovely brown. If the pie starts to bubble out, after 20 minutes reduce the heat to 375°.

Serve hot and enjoy.

Tip: To prevent the crust from getting soggy, brush the

bottom crust with butter—not margarine. Put in the refrigerator until it hardens.

"Ready Cooked" Beef Salad For A Hot Day

it's different . . . hardly anything to do

Slice *4 hard cooked eggs.*

Cut cold *"ready cooked" boiled beef* into thin slices. Place on a platter.

Cover with thin, thin *slices of onion.* (The red ones are nice.)

On one side arrange the eggs. On the other side arrange *1 can drained red kidney beans.*

At one end arrange sliced *dill pickles.*

On the other end arrange *sweet pickles* and *olives.*

Pour your favorite *Italian dressing* over the beef and beans. Put a *spoon of mayonnaise* over the eggs.

With some crusty bread and fruit for dessert, what could be better for a hot day?

A Tempting Shepherd's Pie

tastes as good as it looks, make with whipped potatoes

Heat oven 400°.

Grease a 2½ quart casserole.

Wash and peel *5 medium potatoes.* Cook in *water to cover* with *1 teaspoon salt.*

While they are cooking, cut *1 pound "ready cooked" beef* into bite size cubes. Add *3 tablespoons dried onions, 4 cups mixed, frozen vegetables, 1 can Campbell's Chicken Broth* and *1 can and ¼ cup Campbell's Beef Broth.*

Put into a 2½ quart casserole.

Make the whipped potatoes as follows:

Drain the water off the cooked potatoes. Shake over burner a second to dry out.

Put through the "ricer," or mix until there are no lumps.

Add *3 tablespoons margarine* and *½ cup hot milk.*

Add ½ cup of the whipped potatoes to the meat mixture to thicken it.

Spoon the rest of the whipped potatoes on top. Sprinkle a little *paprika* on top.

Place in 400° oven. Bake 45 minutes.

Serve at once.

Homemade Meat Pies

the "store bought" ones never tasted like these

For 4 individual pies you need *2 cups "ready cooked" beef*. The ready cooked beef can be from your boiled beef dinner or from your pot roast, or another roast, or even from your Swiss steak or other steak. It's the second time around and is many times even better than the first time.

Dice *2 medium onions*. In a skillet put *¼ cup oil* and the onions. Cook, stir on medium heat 2 minutes. Turn heat to low. Cover. Cook 10 minutes. Drain in a strainer over a bowl. Remove the onions to a large bowl.

Put the oil back into the skillet. With a scissors cut 2 full cups bite size cubes of your ready cooked beef.

Brown the beef quickly in the leftover oil from the onions. Drain. Add the beef to the onions in the bowl.

Peel and cut into quarters *2 medium potatoes*. Boil in *salted water* to cover about 7 or 8 minutes. Drain. Mix with the meat mixture being careful not to mash them.

Add *salt* and *pepper* to taste. Divide into 4 small foil pie pans 4½ inches round.

Bring *1¼ cups homemade beef broth or Campbell's Beef Broth* to a boil. Put into a screw top jar *½ cup water, 1 beef bouillon powder*. Shake well. Add *2 tablespoons flour*. Shake until the flour is combined. Stir into the boiling broth. Turn heat to low. Cook, stir 5 minutes. Pour over the individual pies. Place in refrigerator to get cold.

Make our Pastry Dough recipe, as follows:

Remove 2 tablespoons flour from 1 cup flour.

With a pastry blender mix in *¼ teaspoon salt* and a *pinch of sugar*.

Add *⅓ cup vegetable shortening*. Mix with the pastry blender into large crumbs. Push ¼ aside. Mix the rest into fine crumbs. Mix together.

Make some *iced water* with ice cubes. Sprinkle as much of *3 tablespoons* of the *iced water* over flour mixture as you need. Mix with a fork or your hands to make into a soft, but not sticky, ball. Throw hard from one hand to the other 20 times and divide into 4 pieces. Roll each piece, one at a time, to fit a pie pan.

Place on top of each pie. With the back prongs of a fork, press down to close the edges. Make small slits in the center of each pie. Put foil around the edges. Brush crust with *milk.* Do this to all.

Bake the pies in preheated 425° oven on a baking sheet until crusts are browned, takes about 45 minutes.

If you plan to freeze these, do not put the milk on the crust. Do this when you are ready to bake them.

FOR BEGINNER PIE CRUST MAKERS—see recipe index "Pie Crusts—Beginners" for page.

What To Do With

the 3 pound ground beef specials the supermarket puts out for families at lower prices . . . but check these prices . . . are they lower than the 1 or 2 pounders? . . . and can you use this quantity? . . . have you a freezer to store them?

If you are a busy person, and who isn't these days, you don't have to cook the ground beef, but you can "prepare" them into meal size portions of your family's favorite dishes and freeze them.

Out of the 3 pound ground beef specials you can choose from our many ground beef recipes. See recipes Index "B" for Beef.

1. Barbecued Meat Balls
2. Meat Loaf
3. American Hamburgers
4. Stretch It Hamburgers
5. Chili Con Carne
6. Spaghetti Sauce
7. Hamburger Scramble

American Hamburgers

these are the kind we do not add fat to when we fry them . . . instead, we try to get the fat out!

Lightly shape *1 pound ground beef* into 4 hamburgers. Wrap in foil with wax paper in between and freeze.

When ready to use, either defrost or cook frozen.

Heat a large skillet hot on high heat.

Sprinkle a *little salt over the skillet, about ¼ teaspoon.*

Put the 4 hamburgers in. Brown on one side quickly. Sprinkle a *little salt* on the skillet as you lift each hamburger to turn it over. No more salt please. Turn the hamburgers over about 4 times.

Turn the heat lower. If you like the hamburgers rare, they will be ready. Keep turning the hamburgers, without pressing them down, until they are as you like them.

Eat while hot, and please don't let them cook dry.

Tip: Don't press the hamburgers down, as the juice should stay in the hamburger.

The "Stretch It" Hamburger

it's magic . . . you get 6 hamburgers instead of 4 out of 1 pound of ground beef and it "puffs" up, too

Cut the brown crust off *2 slices white puffy bread.*

Put into a large bowl. Add *½ cup milk.* Crumble together until the milk is absorbed.

Grate *1 medium onion* over. Add *1 egg, ¾ teaspoon salt* and *1 pound ground beef.*

Mix with your hands, a spoon, 2 forks or a pastry blender.

Divide into 6 portions, and shape each into a hamburger about an inch thick.

Put the hamburgers with wax paper in between (to keep from sticking together) on a piece of foil large enough to make a drug store wrap. Wrap and freeze.

When ready to use, heat a large skillet hot. Add *1 tablespoon oil* and *1 tablespoon margarine.*

Put the hamburgers in without crowding. Brown on one side quickly. Turn, and let start to brown. Immediately put the lid on and turn the heat to low or simmer. Cook 5 minutes.

See how they have "puffed" up? Serve immediately.

Hamburger Scramble

singles, doubles, families, children, all make this over and over again . . . it's a favorite

Boil *1 cup elbow macaroni* according to directions on

package, only boil 9 minutes. Run cold water over the macaroni. Drain.

Make the hamburger scramble:

Chop *1 medium onion,* dice *1 red or green pepper,* cube *½ cup cheddar cheese.*

Drain *1 can (15½ ounces) chick peas.*

Heat a large skillet on medium heat with *2 tablespoons oil.* Add the chopped onion. Cook, stir 2 minutes. Turn heat to low. Cover. Cook 8 minutes until the onions are soft and clear.

Add the chopped pepper. Cook, stir 2 minutes.

Stir in *1 pound ground beef.*

Crumble in *2 chicken bouillon powders or cubes, ¼ teaspoon ground allspice, 1 bay leaf* cut into 4 pieces, *¼ teaspoon garlic powder* and some *pepper.* Cook, stir 5 minutes.

Add the cooked macaroni, the drained chick peas and the ½ cup cubed cheddar cheese.

Taste; add a little *salt,* if necessary.

Serve piping hot.

Homemade "Burger Queens" Or "Big Smackaroo"

whatever that means . . . make your own! . . . why bother to drive . . . save on gas!

Make these toppings. (Put each on a separate plate.)

Chop *onions.*

Chop *tomatoes.*

Chop *romaine or iceberg lettuce.*

Chop *sweet pickles or sweet relish.*

Mix *½ cup salad dressing* with *2 tablespoons catsup* and *lemon juice* to your taste or *½ cup* your favorite *mayonnaise* with *catsup* and *lemon juice* to your taste. Set aside.

You can make your own hamburger patties or "Queens" 8 to *1 pound of ground beef;* or for quarter pounders make 4 patties to 1 pound.

Fry quickly on one side; turn, fry the other side. Put on *4 rolls.*

Put some of the lettuce, tomatoes, sweet pickles or relish and onions on top. Quickly spoon some of the dressing on top. Put the top of the roll on.

Eat and enjoy!

With the money you save, you can make your hamburgers "quarter pounders" easily. You might even have two. How about that?

Stuffed Patties

a glorified hamburger . . . do ahead and have in freezer as a quickie dinner . . . if you double this recipe, you can cook once, then eat one and freeze one

To *1 pound ground beef* add ½ *teaspoon salt,* a good grind of *pepper* and ⅛ *teaspoon garlic powder*. Mix.

Make into 8 thin patties.

Mix together ¼ *cup chopped stuffed green olives* with ¼ *cup grated sharp cheddar cheese.*

Spread *1 tablespoon catsup* on each of the 4 patties. Divide the stuffing into 4 portions, and spread on the catsup patties.

Top each with the unstuffed patties. Pinch the edges together well.

Fry in a hot skillet with *2 tablespoons oil* until nicely browned on both sides.

Hamburger On A Bun

Make this "American Hamburger."

Put ¼ *pound ground beef* on a large plate.

Shape into a patty, but don't handle too much.

Heat a skillet until hot on medium high heat. (To test whether it is hot enough—sprinkle a drop or two of water on the skillet. If the water skitters around and evaporates quickly, the skillet is ready.)

Sprinkle ¼ *teaspoon salt* over the hot skillet.

Place the hamburger in the skillet.

Let brown on the bottom, takes about 1 minute.

Turn and brown the other side, takes about 1 minute.

Turn a few times to cook the hamburgers as you like them; rare, medium or well done.

The hamburgers should not be cooked over 3, 4 or 5 minutes at the most.

Open a bun. Smear a *little margarine* on each.

Put the buns on a shallow baking dish under the broiler.

Watch it so it doesn't burn. Use a hot pad so you won't burn yourself.

Put the hamburger on the bottom of the bun.

Put as much or as little of the following on top of the hamburgers; catsup, mustard, a slice of onion, sweet relish, a slice of tomato, a piece of lettuce.

Close the bun.

Can you open your mouth wide enough? Have fun eating!

Cheeseburger

Cook the *hamburger*. (See Index for "American Hamburgers.")

Open a bun. Lay it flat on a cake pan.

Put the cooked hamburger on the open bun.

Place a *slice of cheese* on top.

Put on the middle rack under the broiler until the cheese melts. Watch it.

Close the bun and eat your cheeseburger.

Put some catsup on, if you like.

Pizzaburger

takes a few minutes and makes a "quick hurry up" meal with fresh fruit for dessert

Put into a bowl *1 pound ground beef*.

Sprinkle over *1 teaspoon salt* and *1 teaspoon onion powder*. Mix. Divide into 4.

You can flatten each between 2 pieces of wax paper until it measures about 7¼ inches across—about the size of a salad plate. (This is because they shrink as they fry.)

Let stand while you make the sauce.

Open *1 can (15½ ounces) Progresso or your favorite Pizza Sauce;* put into a saucepan.

Add *1 teaspoon dried oregano* and *¼ teaspoon garlic powder*.

Bring to a simmer. Cook 5 minutes.

Open *4 buns*. Toast the 4 buns and put on individual plates, opened.

Heat a large skillet. When hot, put in the "burgers." Brown on one side. Turn, brown the other side. Do this again. The whole frying takes about 2 minutes altogether.

Divide *½ to 1 cup shredded mozzarella cheese* on the cooked burgers. Put the lid on. Cook a minute or two until it melts. Remove lid.

Place each one on an open bun.

Spoon some of the sauce on top, being careful not to have it run all over.

Sprinkle *½ cup grated Parmesan cheese* on top.

Close the Pizzaburgers and eat.

Tip: Save any sauce you have left to use another time as this sauce freezes well.

Chili Con Carne

this is a "1 pounder" chili . . . you might want to double it or even more . . . whatever you do with the "3 pound ground beef special" depends on what your family likes . . . you can most certainly make more of what your family likes . . . we make more meat loaves because they're handy since we live in the country and in the summer you know how people drop in just before lunch!

You can prepare chili 2 ways, one is to freeze it in a 1 pound package; and when you plan to use it, defrost it the night before. If you forget to defrost it, don't panic. Put it in the heated skillet and cook, stir until you've got it apart.

The second way is to do a little more work. Chop *1 large onion, 1 green pepper* and mince *2 cloves garlic* and freeze them.

When ready to cook:

Defrost the *ground beef.* If the beef is not defrosted, cook, stir it in a skillet until no red shows.

If you have not frozen the *vegetables,* chop them now.

Either way, heat a large skillet with *3 tablespoons oil* and the vegetables, and cook, stir until they simmer. Put lid on. Turn heat to low. Let simmer 10 minutes.

Take off lid. Stir in the defrosted beef. Cook, stir until no red shows.

Stir in *2 cans (1 pound) tomato sauce, 1 can tomatoes,* cut up, *3 teaspoons chili powder (sweet or hot,* as you like it), *½ teaspoon cumin, 1¼ teaspoons salt* and *1 teaspoon garlic powder.*

Cook, stir 25 minutes.

Add *2 cans (16 ounces) kidney beans* that have been

washed under running water. (We like Progresso.) Cook 5 minutes.

Eat some, freeze some.

Another Chili Con Carne

a Mexican dish that Americans love

Place *1 pound ground beef* on a large plate.

Sprinkle *1 teaspoon salt* on the ground beef and *pepper to taste.*

Grate *1 large onion* over the ground beef.

Let stand 10 minutes to season.

Heat a large skillet until hot.

Add *4 tablespoons oil.*

Add the seasoned ground beef. Cook/stir 5 minutes.

Add *1 can Progresso Pizza Sauce* or other sauce and *½ teaspoon dried oregano, ¼ teaspoon salt, 1 tablespoon sweet (not strong) chili powder* and *1 can (1 pound) drained red kidney beans.* Cook/stir 10 minutes until all the flavors are combined.

Now you have "Chili con Carne."

Tip: You can use "hot chili" powder as you wish.

Barbecued Ground Beef

fine on heated buns

You need *1 pound ground beef,* the least fatty kind.

Grate *1 onion* over the ground beef. Let stand 10 minutes.

Heat a skillet with *1 tablespoon oil* on high heat. (If you have fatty ground beef, you won't need any fat.)

Cook/stir until no red shows.

Drain the fat off. To the beef add *1 can tomato sauce (15½ ounces), 1 can (8 ounces) stewed tomatoes, ½ teaspoon dried mustard, ¼ teaspoon ground ginger, 1 tablespoon brown sugar, 1 teaspoon Worcestershire Sauce* and *2 drops Tabasco.*

Cook and stir until it comes to a boil.

Simmer 15 minutes on low heat. Stir in *1 can (8 ounces) niblet corn* and *1 can (8 ounces) green lima beans.* Heat until hot.

Heat *4 buns.*
Spoon the hot barbecued ground beef on the heated buns.

Ground Beef-Rice Skillet Dinner

tastes as good as it looks

Bring *1½ cups water* with *¾ teaspoon salt* to a boil.
Drop in *¾ cup long grain rice.* Let come back to a boil. Put lid on. Turn heat to low. Cook 25 minutes.
Chop *1 red or green pepper* and *1 large onion.*
Heat a large skillet. Add *2 tablespoons oil* and the chopped pepper and onion. Turn heat to medium. Cook and stir 2 minutes. Put lid on. Turn heat to low. Cook 10 minutes.
Stir in *1 pound ground beef.* Sprinkle *1 beef bouillon powder* over it. Cook, stir 5 minutes.
Add *1 can (10¾ ounces) Tomato Soup, 1 can (12 ounces) Niblets Corn* and the rice. Cook and stir 5 minutes.
Yes, it does taste as good as it looks!

Kidney Beans And Rice Dinner

with ground beef, too, they really "go together," especially in a skillet

The cooking time only takes 25 minutes.
Chop *1 cup green pepper, 1 medium onion* and *1 cup celery.*
Run under cold water *1 can (1 pound) kidney beans* and drain.
Heat a skillet hot. Add *1 pound ground beef.* Cook and stir until no red shows. Remove to a bowl. Sprinkle *salt* to taste. Let stand.
Put into the skillet the onions, green pepper, celery, kidney beans, *1 can (4 ounces) sliced mushrooms and its broth, 1 teaspoon salt,* the cooked ground beef and *2½ cups chicken broth,* fresh, canned, or bouillon broth.
Cook, stir and bring to a boil.
Add *1 cup rice.* Mix well. Do not let the rice stay on top. Cook, stir until it comes back to a boil. Cover; turn heat to low. Simmer about 20 minutes or more, if necessary.
Taste; add *salt and pepper only if necessary.*
Serve hot, hot!
A "quickie meal."

Meat Balls And Potatoes

a man's dish that women like, too

Cut off the crust of *2 slices bread.* Place in a large bowl.
Add *⅓ cup milk.*
Crumble together until all the milk is absorbed.
Put *1 pound ground beef* on top.
Grate *1 medium onion* over the beef.
Beat *1 egg* well with a fork. Add to the beef mixture.
Add *1 teaspoon salt.*
Mix everything together lightly.
Shape into balls the size of golf balls.
Place on 2 large plates.
Open *3 cans of Chicken Broth.* Remove 3 tablespoons to a bowl or cup.
Put the rest of the broth into the casserole and add *1 cup water.*
Place the casserole on the heat. Turn heat to high. Let come to a boil.
One by one, drop the meat balls in until all have been added.
Bring back to a boil.
Put *2 tablespoons flour* into a screw top jar.
Add the 3 tablespoons chicken broth from the bowl.
Close the screw top and shake until no flour shows (no lumps—strain it if there is).
Slowly stir into the meat ball mixture.
Stir/cook 5 minutes; turn the heat down.
Drop in *4 potatoes,* peeled and cut into eighths, *4 carrots,* peeled and cut into 1 inch pieces, *2 stalks celery,* diced, and *6 scallions* with green stalks, cut and diced.
Bring back to a boil; turn heat to low. Cook and stir now and then 45 minutes. Sprinkle *2 tablespoons finely chopped parsley.* Serve piping hot.

Meat Balls In Mushroom Sauce

and vegetables . . . a meal in a dish

Cut off crusts from *2 slices bread.*
Pour over *⅓ cup milk.*
Crumble together until all the milk is absorbed.
Put *1 pound ground beef* on top.

Grate *1 medium onion* over the beef.
Beat *1 egg* with a fork.
Add to the meat mixture.
Sprinkle over *1 teaspoon salt.*
With your hands mix lightly.
Shape into balls the size of a golf ball.
Open *1 can Cream of Mushroom Soup* and *1 can Cream of Celery Soup.*
Put into a casserole.
Cook/stir and add *1 cup milk.* Let come to a boil.
One by one drop in the meat balls.
Bring back to a boil. Add 4 cups of a mixture of *frozen broccoli, carrots* and *cauliflower.*
Bring back to a simmer. Put lid on. Cook 30 minutes.
You have your meat and vegetables all in 1 dish.
Yes, you could have a salad of greens and a fruit dessert, either fresh or canned, or a deep dish pie or some Jell-O.

Porcupine Balls

these will surprise you after they cook

Cut the brown crust off *2 slices bread.*
Put the bread in a large bowl. Add *½ cup milk.*
Crumble the bread and milk together until all the milk is absorbed by the bread.
Lay *1 pound ground beef* on top.
Grate *1 medium onion* over it.
Break *1 egg* in a deep saucer. Mix with a fork. Add to the beef mixture.
Sprinkle *⅓ cup rice* over the mixture. Use your hands to mix lightly. Shape into balls the size of golf balls. Place on a large plate.
Into a large saucepan or casserole put *1 can Campbell's Tomato Soup, ¼ cup catsup, ¼ teaspoon dried basil* and *½ cup water.*
Place on medium heat. Let come to a boil.
Heat a skillet hot on medium heat. Add *1 tablespoon oil* and *1 tablespoon margarine.*
Put as many of the meat balls in without crowding, and brown them quickly. As they brown, drop them with a pair of tongs into the sauce.
When all are browned and in the sauce, let the sauce come

back to a boil. Turn heat to simmer. Put lid on. Simmer 15 minutes.

Surprised? See the rice porcupine quills sticking out of the meat balls?

Tasty Beef Balls

you can double or triple this recipe because they freeze so well . . . nice to have on hand for unexpected company

Cut off the crust from *1½ slices of white pulpy bread,* the kind all supermarkets sell. Put into a large bowl.

Add *½ cup nonfat milk.* With your clean hands crumble together until the milk is absorbed.

Grate *1 medium onion* over this. We freeze some onions whole with their skins for grating, as they grate beautifully frozen and you don't cry either. Try it.

Add *1 egg* and *¾ teaspoon salt.* Mix together well.

Add *1 pound ground beef.* Mix with your clean hands or a spoon and keep it light.

Shape into balls the size you wish from large marbles to walnuts or whatever.

Use as the recipe of your choice tells you.

German Beef Balls

you guessed it . . . it has sauerkraut

Peel and cut into quarters enough *Idaho potatoes for 4.*

Cook until done.

In the meanwhile, make Tasty Meat Balls out of *1 pound ground beef* the size of golf balls. (See Index for recipe under M.) Set aside.

Bring to a boil *1 can (16 ounces) sauerkraut* (drained) with *1 can (16 ounces) stewed tomatoes, 1 teaspoon sugar* to taste, and *2 tablespoons white wine,* if you wish (Johannesberg Reisling).

Brown meat balls. Drop one by one into the sauerkraut mixture. Bring to a simmer. Simmer 30 minutes.

Rice the potatoes or whip the potatoes.

Pour the meat ball/sauerkraut mixture over the potatoes.

This is a "quickie" meal.

Barbecued Meat Balls

these just have to become one of the family's favorites

Cut off the crusts from *1½ slices white soft, pulp bread,* the kind all the supermarkets sell. Put into a bowl. Add *½ cup nonfat milk.* With your hands crumble together until the milk is absorbed.

Grate *1 medium onion* over this.

Add *1 egg* and *¾ teaspoon salt* and mix together well.

Add *1 pound ground beef.* Mix with a fork or your hands, but keep it light.

Shape into balls the size of large marbles.

Put on a plate to use at once; or freeze as follows: Put a piece of wax paper on a cookie sheet. Arrange the balls on top. Freeze. When frozen, store in a plastic bag.

When ready to use:

Chop *1 medium onion* and *1 green pepper.*

Bring to a boil *1 jar Heinz Barbecue Sauce.* Add the onions and green pepper. Bring back to a boil.

Drop in, one at a time, the meat balls. Bring back to a boil.

Turn heat to low. Cover. Simmer 30 minutes.

Serve over or with riced potatoes or cooked rice, groats (kasha), small pasta shells or macaroni. Canned great northern beans, kidney beans, lima beans, black eyed peas or chick peas would go along fine with this. No work either, these are the good foods that come in cans and save us work.

New Orleans Gumbo Casserole With Meat Balls

it's got flavor . . . takes ½ hour to cook and everybody says, "More!"

Cut the crusts off *2 slices bread.* Place the bread in a large bowl.

Add *¼ cup milk.* Crumble together until the milk is absorbed by the bread.

Put *1 pound ground beef* on top.

Grate *1 medium onion* over the beef.

Sprinkle on *1 teaspoon salt.*

Open *1 egg* into a bowl and mix well with a fork. Add to the meat mixture.

Mix together lightly with your hands. Shape into large marble size balls, and put on a large plate.

Open *3 cans Campbell's Chicken Gumbo Soup.* Pour into a casserole or saucepan.

On high heat, cook and stir until it comes to a boil.

One by one, drop the meat balls in. Let come back to a boil.

Turn heat to low. Put lid on. Cook 30 minutes.

Tasty Meat Loaf

always good and as good cold as hot if there's any left!

Cut off the brown crust from *2 slices of "puffy" white bread.* Put into a large bowl. Add *½ cup milk.* Crumble together until milk is absorbed.

Grate *1 medium onion* over. Add *1 egg* and *¾ teaspoon salt.*

Add *1 pound ground beef.* Mix with your hands lightly; or use a spoon or a pastry blender or 2 forks.

Spoon the mixture onto a sheet of foil shaping it into a "loaf" without mashing it down. It will be a "rough" looking loaf, which makes it taste better.

Freeze; then close with the drug store wrap.

When ready to use:

Heat oven 450°.

Grease a 1½ quart casserole.

Remove the foil from the frozen loaf and put in the center of the casserole.

Make the sauce:

Put *½ cup catsup* into a saucepan. Stir in *1 chicken or beef bouillon powder* and *1 cup water.* Bring to a boil.

Pour ¼ cup around the meat loaf.

Place in the 450° oven. Bake about 15 minutes. Turn heat to 325°; bake about 30 minutes. Remove from oven.

In the meantime, bring the sauce to a boil. Turn heat to low. Cook, stir now and then 10 minutes.

When the meat loaf is done, bring the sauce to a boil; serve the sauce with the meat loaf.

Cold Meat Loaf
For The Next Day's Dinner

tastes just as good cold and some people say even better . . . be sure and cut into thin slices, tastes better that way . . . a no-work meal

In the winter serve some hot, homemade split pea soup, if you have some in your freezer; or open a can of split pea soup and mix with ½ to 1 can chicken broth with fat removed. Serve this soup with the meat loaf, as follows:

For each person slice the *"ready cooked" cold meat loaf* into slices and put on a plate in a bed of *shredded lettuce.* Slice some rings of *green pepper or red pepper* on top.

Drain *1 can (1 pound) green beans* and arrange them on top.

Pour your favorite "bought" *salad dressing* on top; *or* just open a jar of *3 Bean Salad.*

See? No cooking!

In the summer a macaroni salad or a bean salad would be nice, too.

For a no-work dessert, what could be better than a crunchy, crisp apple with a piece of cheese as a "go with."

Meat Loaf

for a meat loaf dinner and a second day "no cook" dinner

Grease a 3-quart ovenproof glass casserole.

Preheat oven 450°.

You need *2 pounds ground beef.*

Cut off the crust from *3 slices white bread.*

Crumble together with *1 cup nonfat milk* until the milk is absorbed.

Add *2 eggs, 1½ teaspoons salt* and a *good grind of pepper.*

Grate *2 medium large onions* over above.

Mix everything together well.

Lay the ground beef on top.

Mix together with your clean hands. Taste to see if salt or pepper is needed.

With your hands or a large spoon scoop into the middle of the greased casserole into a free standing "shaped meat loaf." Smooth the top with your hands lightly to make it look pretty. The meat loaf tastes better if you don't handle it too much.

Place in the preheated 450° oven. Bake 15 minutes. Turn the heat to 325°. Pour about ¼ cup sauce over the meat. Bake 45 minutes or until done.

Serve hot the first day with the vegetable that you baked along with it in the oven and serve sliced cold for a second dinner.

Sauce—Put ½ cup catsup into a saucepan. Stir 1 chicken or beef bouillon powder or cube in. Stir in 1 cup water. Cook, stir until it comes to a boil.

If you wish, you can peel and quarter Irish potatoes and put around the meat loaf to bake along with it or cut sweet potatoes in halves and bake along with it.

Italian Meat Loaf

if the Italians don't make this meat loaf, they should . . . at any rate it's an interesting meat loaf with its vegetables and cheese . . . try it, please

Chop *½ cup onions* and *½ cup celery.*

Grate *½ cup Parmesan cheese* and *1 cup mozzarella cheese.*

Drain *1 can (4 ounces) mushrooms.* Save the broth. Cut the mushrooms into pieces.

Slice *1 green pepper* into rings.

Open *1 can (15 ounces) Hunt's Sauce with Bits.*

Saute in *2 tablespoons oil* the ½ cup onions and ½ cup celery until the onions are soft and clear, takes about 10 minutes. Drain.

Put into a large bowl *2 pounds of ground beef,* the sauteed onions and celery, *1 cup seasoned bread crumbs, 1½ teaspoons salt,* a grind of *pepper* and ½ cup grated Parmesan cheese.

Mix *2 eggs* with a fork. Stir in *1 cup milk.* Add to the meat mixture and mix together. Taste. Add *salt* if necessary.

Spoon into a shallow casserole or baking dish. Shape gently into a loaf.

Pour around it the heated mushroom broth. Place in 375° oven. Bake 45 minutes.

Pour 1 can Hunt's Tomato Sauce with Bits around the loaf.

Sprinkle the meat loaf with the grated mozzarella cheese

and the mushrooms, and arrange the green pepper rings on top.

Dot with a very little *butter or margarine*. Bake 15 minutes. This is good both served hot or cold. Served cold, it makes delicious sandwiches if you use very thin bread and smear it with our "Mustard Mayonnaise." See Index for recipe.

Three Layer Meat Loaf

it's different . . . you have your meat and vegetables cooked together saving fuel and time and getting the best bargain, easy cooking and good taste

Heat oven 450°.

Make *1 cup beef bouillon broth of 1 package beef bouillon powder stirred in 1 cup water.*

Defrost *2 cups frozen mixed vegetables* and *1 box (12 ounces) frozen, chopped spinach.*

Hard cook *2 eggs*. Chop fine.

Cut off the crusts from *3 slices bread*. Crumble the bread into *¼ cup nonfat milk*. Let stand until the milk is absorbed.

Stir in *1 egg.*

Grate *1 medium onion* over *1 pound ground beef.*

Sprinkle *1 teaspoon salt* over, a *pinch of nutmeg* and some *pepper* to taste. Add the bread mixture. Mix everything together.

Squeeze the water out of the defrosted spinach. Chop fine.

Mix with the hard cooked, chopped fine eggs. Add *salt* and *pepper* to taste. Mix in *1 tablespoon unsweetened mayonnaise.*

Divide the ground beef mixture into 3 portions.

Spread 1 portion in the shape of a meat loaf in the bottom of a 2 quart casserole.

Spread the defrosted vegetables, mixed with 2 tablespoons mayonnaise, over the loaf but leave 1 inch all around the beef.

Spread the second portion of beef over this.

Repeat with the spinach mixture.

Spread the last ground beef mixture over this.

Pour ½ cup of the beef bouillon broth around the meat loaf.

Mold the sides closed with your hands.

Bake in 450° oven 15 minutes.

Pour as much of the ½ cup beef bouillon broth around the meat loaf as is necessary to keep the loaf moist. It should only come ¼ inch up the sides of the meat loaf.

Turn heat to 350°. Bake 45 minutes to 1 hour until done.

Serve with a sauce made by mixing together *1 cup catsup* with *2 beef bouillon powders* and *2 cups water.* Bring to a boil. Serve boiling hot separately.

Layered Beef With Whipped Potato Topping

a casserole dish baked in the oven

Grease a heatproof 1½ quart glass casserole.

Heat oven 400°.

Peel, cut into quarters and boil until tender *4 large mealy potatoes.* Shake over heat to dry.

Put the potatoes through a ricer; or use your potato masher or electric mixer. (The ricer makes the fluffiest whipped potatoes.) Add *2 tablespoons margarine, 1 beaten egg, ⅓ cup milk, salt and pepper* to taste. Mix well. This is a potato puree.

Make broth out of *1 beef bouillon powder with ½ cup water.* Set aside.

Cook *1 package kale or spinach.* Add *1 tablespoon margarine, salt* and *pepper* to taste. Set aside.

Grate *1 medium onion* over *1 pound ground beef.*

Mince *1 tablespoon parsley.* Soak *2 slices bread* in *¼ cup milk,* and crumble together. Add to the ground beef and mix well.

Melt *2 tablespoons margarine* in a skillet on medium heat. Add the ground beef, cook and stir about 5 minutes. Sprinkle *2 tablespoons flour* over the beef and cook and stir. Add the ½ cup beef bouillon broth and a little pepper to taste. Cook, stir 5 minutes.

Add the parsley to the beef.

Arrange a layer of beef in the casserole, then a layer of potato puree, then a layer of kale or spinach. Repeat, ending with a layer of potato puree.

Bake in 400° preheated oven until potatoes are golden colored, and everything is hot, takes about 20 to 30 minutes.

Sprinkle some grated *Parmesan cheese* on top. Put under broiler to brown lightly. Serve.

"Big Pot" Macaroni And Spaghetti Sauce

who says you always have to cook spaghetti just because you want to use spaghetti sauce

Chop *1 cup onions* and *1 cup green peppers.* Open *1 can (4 ounces) sliced mushrooms.*

In a large pot, cook, stir *1 pound ground beef* until no red shows. Stir in *1 teaspoon salt.*

Add the onions, green pepper and the can of mushrooms.

Open *2 cans (1 pound each) tomatoes.* Cut the tomatoes into pieces. If you can, buy the tomatoes that have a thick sauce instead of the watery tomatoes with juice.

Add to the pot.

Add *1 can (8 ounces) tomato sauce.*

Bring to a boil. Lay a piece of foil on top of the pot to keep the sauce from spattering all over.

When the sauce boils, drop in *2 cups elbow macaroni.* Bring back to a boil.

Turn heat to low. Cook, stir now and then until the macaroni is done, takes about 20 minutes.

Add *salt* and *pepper* to taste.

Eat hot, hot.

Sprinkle some grated cheese on top; it's mighty nice.

This is a quickie dinner when everyone has to go "somewhere," so all eat at different times.

This reheats well, but if it has to be reheated over and over again, double this.

Spaghetti Sauce

made with 1 pound ground beef

Most people freeze more than 1 pound ground beef, because they cook enough for at least 2 meals of spaghetti sauce, so freeze as many 1 pound or 2 pound packages as you want from the "3 pound ground beef special."

This recipe is for a 1 pounder spaghetti sauce. In this case you freeze only 1 pound package of the ground beef.

When ready to use, defrost the night before, so it will be easy to make the sauce.

Heat a skillet until hot. Cook, stir the *1 pound ground beef* until no red shows.

Sprinkle *1 teaspoon salt* over.
Grate *1 medium onion* over the beef.
Add *4 cans (15½ ounces) Progresso Pizza Sauce*, which is excellent ripe tomato sauce with a basil leaf in it; or use your *favorite tomato sauce (15 or 16 ounces each), 1 teaspoon garlic powder, 2 teaspoons dried oregano* and *2 teaspoons basil or 3 teaspoons Italian herbs* to taste, and *1 teaspoon sugar.*
Cook, stir 15 minutes until the seasoning has flavored the sauce.
Add *1 tablespoon oil.* Cook 1 minute.
The spaghetti sauce is ready.

New Quick Lasagna

you won't believe it . . . we don't cook the lasagna noodles . . . saves time, saves energy

You can use the commercial lasagna noodles. It works, but we use the square Pennsylvania Dutch "Bot Bois," because we like them better. These are squares 2½ × 1¾ inches, and they are more like homemade ones.
Grease a 6 × 10 inch glass baking dish.
Heat oven 400°.
You need *5 cups of your favorite spaghetti sauce.* If it is thick, thin it a little, as it will thicken when it bakes.
Make a layer of the spaghetti sauce, then a layer of *lasagna,* then a layer of sauce, then a layer of *cheese.* (We use Danish Havarti Cheese, but you can use mozzarella, too.) Repeat, starting with lasagna and ending with the sauce.
Cover with foil. Place on a cookie sheet covered with foil.
Bake in 400° oven 45 minutes. Remove foil, bake 30 minutes. Sprinkle grated *Parmesan cheese* on top. Bake until browned, takes a few minutes; or put under broiler to brown.
This tastes very good.
Tip: If you use the commercial lasagna noodles, it will take about 45 minutes covered and 45 minutes uncovered.

Old Fashioned Corned Beef

you can save the broth to make our Bean Soup

Buy about a *2¼ pound corned beef.*
Bring the corned beef to a boil with *water to cover* and

add *3 bay leaves, 6 allspice, 4 peppercorns, 1 large garlic or 2 small cloves garlic,* and *2 medium onions.*

Remove any scum. Turn heat to low. Simmer 1½ hours. Taste to see if the water is salty or not. If salt is needed, add to your taste.

Wash and cut a *cabbage* into halves, then quarters. The cabbage will not fall apart when it cooks. Set aside and add to the corned beef 20 to 25 minutes before the corned beef is done. (Some people place the cabbage around the corned beef at this time and bring back to a boil.)

Turn heat to low and cook 1¼ hours more until the corned beef is done. It has a good flavor and is very soft. We usually test by putting a fork in, and if it goes in easily, it is done. If corned beef is cooked too long, it falls apart and can't be cut well.

Cut the corned beef into thickish slices. Serve with the cabbage and boiled potatoes.

These three go well together. Mustard goes nicely, too.

Pumpernickel or rye bread spread with some margarine or butter adds the right touch, or should I say "taste"?

Corned beef is not cheap, but once in a while, it's mighty nice.

The New Englanders add carrots, as well as cabbage. That's not to be sneezed at either!

Corned Beef And Cabbage

it's canned corned beef and it's quite tasty and inexpensive

Peel and cut *enough large potatoes for 4* into quarters. Put into cold water.

Open *1 can (12 ounces) corned beef,* and cube into large cubes.

Cut *½ head of cabbage* into rough pieces.

Put *4 cups water,* the corned beef, cabbage, *2 allspice, 1 bay leaf* into a casserole.

Bring to a boil. Cover. Turn heat to low; simmer 45 minutes.

Add *salt to taste,* about ⅛ teaspoon.

Add the potatoes. Bring back to a boil. Cook until done, takes about 25 minutes.

Cooked Breast of Lamb

since this is the "Cinderella" of lamb, and like Cinderella you change it from something cheap moneywise, to a beautiful dish, let's begin . . . this is the easy part, one day you cook and have dinner and the next day you have another dinner

Buy *2 breasts of lamb.*

Wash, put into a kettle with *6 cups water, 1 large carrot, 1 medium onion, 1 bunch celery leaves or 1 stalk celery,* cut into thirds.

Bring to a boil. Turn heat down; simmer until lamb is done, takes about 1 hour.

Remove lamb to a plate to get cold. Refrigerate.

Strain the broth. Let get cold. Put in refrigerator. The next day remove fat, and there is plenty of fat to remove.

You can use the broth to make:

An Inexpensive But Good Bean Soup

Wash, drain and bring to a boil *1 pound great northern the day before . . . you can also use other broth or onion, chicken or beef bouillon broth . . . this is where you get two good, nutritious meals out of two inexpensive lamb breasts*

Wash, drain and bring to a boil *1 pound great northern beans* in *5 cups water.* Put lid on. Let stand 1 hour.

Peel and cut in half *2 medium potatoes.*

Chop fine *1 large carrot, 3 small onions or 1 medium one,* and *2 stalks celery.* Mince *2 tablespoons parsley,* fresh or frozen. (We always mince some of our fresh parsley when we buy it, freeze it in 1 tablespoon portions and have ready when we need it.)

Remove any fat from the lamb broth or other broth. You should have 5 cups of lamb broth.

Put into a soup kettle with the "soaked" beans and any "soaking" water left. Bring to a boil.

Add the prepared vegetables, *1 bay leaf,* and *4 whole allspice.*

Bring back to a boil. Turn heat to low. Cover. Simmer about 1 hour until the beans are tender.

Add *salt and pepper* to taste, and add the parsley. Cook 5 minutes.

Push 2 cups of the beans and the potatoes through a food mill or a strainer; then stir back into the soup to thicken it.

Bring to a boil when ready to eat. Eat and enjoy.

Barbecued Lamb Breasts

Cut the *lamb breasts* each into 1 rib pieces. You will have about 14 ribs. You will see a thick piece of fat on each one. Cut off the thin piece of meat on top of the fat. Then cut off the thick piece of fat. Do this to all the ribs.

Use your *favorite barbecue sauce,* either homemade or commercial. The commercial one we use is "Heinz Barbecue Sauce" and for a complete change "Grandma's Molasses Barbecue Sauce."

Put the ribs and pieces of thin lamb on a shallow broiling pan or a cookie sheet with sides. Don't use a rack.

In electric oven put oven rack as close to the broiler unit as you can. Preheat broiler. Spoon the barbecue sauce on top of each rib and meat.

Put under broiler, meaty side up, and broil until beautifully browned, takes about 5 minutes.

With tongs turn over and spoon barbecue sauce over this side, and broil until done, takes about 3 minutes.

Remove to a heated platter, spooning any barbecue sauce left in the pan over the ribs.

These are crisp and delicious ribs.

Tip: To strain the broth put a strainer over a large bowl or utensil.

Instead of using cheese cloth, which is messy to clean, put 2 paper towels, one on top of the other, and pour the broth slowly through. The broth will be clear, and you can throw away the paper towels. Easy?

Casserole Breast Of Lamb Flavored With Vegetables

this is one of the bargains in meat . . . this time lamb . . . even the "lamb don't likers" will like this . . . it's different and we promise it will become one of your favorites

Heat oven 400°.

Buy a *whole breast of lamb.* It is inexpensive. Cut off the "no bone" portion. This is the part to use for this recipe. The rib part can be used to make recipe. Put the rib part in the refrigerator or freeze to use another time. Today we will casserole the other part of the breast.

Wipe the "no bone" breast part with a wet towel. Dry.

On medium heat, heat a fireproof casserole with *2 tablespoons oil* until hot. Put the breast of lamb, meaty side down in. Brown nicely on this side only. Remove to a plate. Leave the juice in.

Mix together *2 tablespoons soft, not melted, margarine or butter* with *¼ teaspoon garlic powder* or if you prefer onion powder, a *good grind of pepper* and *¼ teaspoon salt.* Rub the top part with this. Cut a *bay leaf* into 10 small pieces and arrange on top of the breast. Let stand to season.

Cut *1 large onion* into thin slices. Peel and slice ¼ inch thick enough *potatoes for 4.*

Stir *¼ cup chicken broth* into the good brownings.

Make a layer of the potatoes into the bottom of the casserole.

Sprinkle lightly with *salt and pepper.* Layer the onions on top.

Make a layer of *1 can (1 pound) drained Great Northern Beans.*

Cover with the lamb meaty side up.

Pour enough chicken broth to come halfway up the lamb. Do not cover the lamb completely. Bring to a boil. Place in 400° oven. Turn heat to 325°. Cover. Roast 1½ hours.

Mix together *2 cups plain crumbs* with *4 tablespoons melted margarine, some pepper, salt to taste,* and *¼ teaspoon onion powder* and *2 tablespoons chopped parsley.*

Spoon on top of the lamb pushing the crumb mixture on top so it adheres to the lamb.

Roast uncovered about ½ hour until lamb is tender.

Wasn't I right?

Rolled Breast Of Lamb

you use the rib breast of lamb part to bake another dish and you use the meaty part that has no bones to roll and bake this dish

Heat oven 400°.

Cut the meaty part that has no bones in the *breast of lamb* off. The butcher usually hides this under the breast with the ribs when he prepackages the breast.

Wipe the meat with a wet towel, then wipe dry.

Mix together *7 tablespoons soft margarine* with *¼ teaspoon onion powder, ¼ teaspoon garlic powder, ½ teaspoon salt* and *a good grind or shake of pepper*. Smear/rub over the lamb.

Roll up tightly like a jelly roll. Tie with kitchen cord every 3 inches. Cut each one. Place on a rack, cut side up. Broil.

Peel enough new small, red preferably or small white, *potatoes for 4*. Peel and cut *3 carrots*, each into 1 inch slices, and if you are an onion lover—glaze 8 or so of the very small onions in a skillet just until they become coated—and add.

Arrange the vegetables around the rolled lamb. Add *½ cup chicken broth* or enough to come 1 inch from the bottom.

Bring to a boil. Place in the 400° oven. Turn heat to 325°. Cover. Roast ½ hour. Baste. Continue to roast ½ hour. Remove lid. Roast, basting now and then, about ½ hour until the breast is tender. Slice in thin slices and serve with the vegetables.

Of course, you have cut off the strings!

Lamb Breast With Stuffing

this is a double bargain . . . some bean soup and roasted breast with stuffing . . . all from one lamb breast

Since lamb breasts are so fatty, the best way to get rid of the fat is to cook them first.

Bring to a boil the *lamb breast, 1 medium onion, 1 carrot, 1 bunch celery leaves, 6 cups water* and *1 chicken bouillon powder*.

Turn the heat to low. Cover. Cook about 1 hour until most of the fat is in the broth.

Remove the breast and the vegetables to a plate.

Put 2 pieces of paper towels (we use Bounty) in a strainer over a large bowl. Gently pour the broth through the paper covered strainer. Place the broth in the refrigerator overnight for the fat to congeal. The next morning remove the fat and make some quick bean soup.

A Quick Bean and Macaroni Soup

Chop each, about ⅓ *cup, onions, celery, carrots.* Wash under running water ¼ *cup pearl barley* and *2 cups beans.*

Bring the *broth* with *1 cup water* added to a boil.

Add the vegetables, the macaroni and bring back to a simmer. Cover. Cook/stir now and then until beans and barley are tender. Taste, add salt if necessary and some pepper and mash a few of the beans to thicken the soup.

Breast of Lamb and Stuffing

The Stuffing—Put *2 cups Pepperidge Farm Seasoned Bread Stuffing* into a bowl. Chop each *1 medium onion, some celery leaves* or *stalk, a small carrot* and *2 tablespoons parsley.*

Heat a skillet with *2 tablespoons oil, 1 tablespoon margarine* and the vegetables. Cook/stir 2 minutes. Turn the heat to low. Cover. Cook 10 minutes.

Pour over the bread crumbs and mix gently.

Beat *1 egg* with a fork. Stir in *2 tablespoons chicken broth.* Pour over the stuffing and mix lightly.

Grease a shallow baking dish that will fit the cooked breast of lamb.

Make a bed of the stuffing. Remove as much of any visible fat from the lamb breast as possible. Place the breast on top of the stuffing.

Slice enough onion into thin slices, dip each one into a small saucer of oil, then arrange on top of the breast.

Place in 400° oven. Bake about 20 minutes until the onions are cooked. Put under broiler to brown.

Serve at once.

Lamb Riblets

cut a breast of lamb into individual riblets . . . you pay more for them when the butcher slices them and packages them . . . it's very easy for you to cut them and you will be glad to save some money!

Put the *riblets* into a saucepan or casserole with *6 cups of water, 1 large onion, 1 carrot* (peeled and cut into 4 pieces), *1 branch or rib of celery,* and *1 chicken bouillon powder.*

Bring to a boil. Turn heat to low. Cook until the riblets get done—about 1 hour. Strain.

Let the riblets get cold. Put the broth in the refrigerator overnight for the fat to congeal.

Remove the fat. Make some bean, split pea or lentil soup with this broth.

Remove any fat that you can from the ribs.

Heat the broiler.

Dip the ribs into *oil or melted margarine,* then dip into *crumbs.*

Put on a broiling pan. Broil on one side, then the other. Serve at once with a grind or sprinkle of pepper.

These are very tasty.

You can use seasoned bread crumbs if you wish.

Baked Lamb Shoulders Chops

you will like these and you have your meal in a casserole and "the price is right"

Have the butcher cut *6 lamb shoulder chops* thin, about ¼ to ½ inch thick.

Heat oven 325°.

Wipe the lamb chops and rub over with about *¼ teaspoon ground allspice.* Sprinkle lightly with *salt.* Set aside.

Slice *1 medium onion.*

Open *1 can (1 pound) Progresso Chick Peas* and drain. Put the beans in a bowl.

Heat a casserole on medium high heat with *4 tablespoons oil.*

Add the onions. Cook, stir 2 minutes. Cover. Turn heat to low. Cook 10 minutes.

Strain the oil. Put the oil back in the casserole. Set aside.

Add the onions to the beans and add *1 jar (2 ounces) drained, cut pimentos* and *1 cup rice*. Set aside.

Heat the casserole with the oil. Without crowding, put in the chops. Brown on one side; then the other side. Remove to a plate. Sprinkle on some *pepper*.

From the casserole remove any fat, but leave the good brownings in.

Stir *2¼ cup chicken broth* into the brownings in the casserole. Add *1 bay leaf*. Add the beans, rice, onion mixture.

Place the browned lamb chops on top. Bring to a boil. Cover.

Place in 325° preheated oven. Bake 30 minutes until chops are tender.

Mix together *1 cup seasoned bread crumbs* with *2 tablespoons melted margarine*. Spoon over the chops.

Put under broiler and brown. Serve at once.

Oven Barbecued Veal Ribs

no work . . . no sweat . . . no tears

Cut ribs apart. *Salt* lightly. Place in shallow baking dish that fits.

Heat oven 350°.

Pour over *"Grandma's Molasses Barbecue Sauce."*

Close tightly with foil. Place in 350° oven. Bake 45 minutes. Remove foil. Baste now and then and put foil over lightly.

Cook 15 minutes; then continue to baste and cover lightly until tender, takes about 30 minutes more.

Put under broiler to brown. Serve.

Breast Of Veal With Stuffing

this is a very easy, time saving stuffing dish and you have veal that is tasty and moist, unlike most veal which gets dried out

You need a *breast of veal* and have the butcher cut the ribs. Don't let him make a pocket, as you will want to carve them when cooked.

Make the stuffing:

Chop *1 cup onions, 1 cup celery, ¼ cup scallions* and grate *1 carrot*.

Put the vegetables in a skillet with *½ cup oil.*

Cook, stir until it comes to a simmer. Turn heat to low. Cover. Simmer 10 minutes.

Heat the oven 325°.

Put *4 cups seasoned cubed bread stuffing* into a large bowl. Pour the vegetables and the oil over the bread stuffing. Mix gently together. Beat *2 eggs* with a fork. Gently mix with the stuffing. Add *salt and pepper* to taste. Set aside.

Wipe the veal. Heat a heavy casserole that fits the veal with *2 tablespoons oil.* Brown the meaty side of the veal slowly until it is a pretty brown color. Just brown this side. Remove to a plate.

Pour *1 cup chicken broth* into the casserole. Arrange the veal, meaty side up, in the casserole. Rub *¼ teaspoon ground allspice* on top and cut *2 bay leaves* each in 4 pieces and arrange on top of the veal.

Peel *enough potatoes for 4.* Arrange on one side of the veal.

Peel *4 carrots;* arrange on the other side of the veal. Sprinkle *salt and pepper* lightly over the potatoes, veal and carrots.

With your hands arrange the stuffing on the veal. Bring to a simmer. Place in 325° oven. Bake about 2½ to 3 hours. Check now and then to see if the veal is done.

Remove to a platter. Serve the meat, stuffing and vegetables all cooked in one dish.

This makes a beautiful dish.

Veal Ribs In Sauce Southern Style

you'll be surprised what the molasses does to the sauce and it only bakes about 1 hour

Preheat oven 325°.

You need *4 meaty veal ribs*, the kind that isn't expensive, because they're older and more meaty.

Heat a casserole with *1 tablespoon oil* until hot.

Put in 2 meaty veal ribs and brown on both sides. Remove to a plate and brown the other 2 ribs. Remove to the plate.

Put *½ bottle (1 pound, 4 ounces) Grandma's Molasses Barbecue Sauce* into the casserole. Stir in *1 can Campbell's*

Beef Broth. Arrange the veal ribs in one layer. Bring to a boil. Cover with foil. Put lid on; place in 325° oven.

Bake 45 minutes. Take off lid. Turn heat to 300°. Bake 20 more minutes. The veal ribs should be tender and tasty.

Serve over mashed potatoes or rice or kasha (groats). Try one at a time and see which your family likes best.

If you like, you can thicken the sauce with cornstarch.

Smothered Veal With Onions And Green Peppers

barbecued with a bonus of a wonderful sauce and this is an inexpensive meat dish

Have the butcher cut *1 veal breast into ribs or riblets.*

Wash, seed and slice *1 large green pepper* and slice *one large onion.*

When ready to use, wipe the riblets. Cut the loose meaty parts off the bones leaving some veal on the bones.

Salt the veal lightly.

Oil a shallow baking dish.

Pour *1 bottle Heinz Barbecue Sauce (with onion)* into the pan.

One at a time, turn the veal and bones in the sauce to be sure that all sides are covered with sauce.

Arrange the onions on top and cover with the green peppers.

Cover with foil tightly.

Place in 325° oven. Bake until veal is done, takes about 2½ or 3 hours.

Serve with rice on the side, or potatoes, or groats.

Veal Chops

how can a Penny Pincher afford these? . . . by buying shoulder veal chops, cut thin, and on sale

Rub a little oil over the *shoulder veal chops. Salt very lightly* and *pepper;* sprinkle a *little Italian Herbs* over them. Let stand 15 minutes.

Set aside *1 cup chicken or veal broth.*

Heat a skillet with *4 tablespoons oil* until hot.

Dip, one chop at a time, into *crumbs* lightly and put into the skillet. Continue, one by one, until all are crumbed and put into the skillet.

Brown the chops without burning on one side, then the other, until all are browned. Remove each as they brown to a plate.

Strain the fat, but leave the good brownings in. You can save the fat in the refrigerator to use another time.

Put the skillet on medium heat. Immediately stir in ½ cup of the chicken or veal broth, more as needed. Cook and stir, scraping up the good brownings. When all have been scraped up. return the chops to the skillet. Bring to a simmer. Cover.

Turn heat to low. Simmer until chops are tender, which takes from 20 to 30 minutes, adding more of the broth as needed while it cooks.

Where do we get the veal broth? We collect in our freezer the bits and pieces and also the bones we have cut off various pieces of veal. Not being a butcher and not having sharp knives like the butcher has, we have a little meat clinging to the bones. When we have "enough" collected, we make some veal broth or stock, as it is usually called.

The chops served with a side dish of small zucchini, sliced thinly, with their skin on and cooked a few minutes in oil, then cooked with some cut-up bite-sized canned tomatoes (they're canned when vine ripened and have more flavor than out of season tomatoes) which means, of course, in season use your "home grown" tomatoes. Sprinkle very lightly with salt and a good pinch of sugar to taste and stir in a little flour just to barely thicken it.

A Simple "Easy Do" Ham

an honest to goodness easy way to cook and everyone loves it . . . good sliced cold . . . makes a tasty sandwich sliced thin

Heat oven 400°.

Remove the gelatin from a *1 pound can of ham.*

Put the ham in a casserole that fits.

Pour *1 cup sweet pickle juice* over the ham. (We like the juice from Heinz Sweet Pickles or Gherkins; it's so flavorful!)

Rub *¼ teaspoon ground cloves* mixed with *2 tablespoons brown sugar* over the ham. Bring to a boil.

Place in 400° oven. Bake 30 minutes with lid on.

Turn heat to 325°. Turn ham over; bake 30 minutes with lid on.

Remove from oven. Can be eaten hot, or remove ham to a dish to cool.

Keep in refrigerator covered until used. Can last a week in refrigerator, but it won't last that long—it's that good!

You can do a larger canned ham the same way increasing the sweet pickle juice and the cloves and brown sugar.

Ham Loaf

You need a 1½ quart baking dish or 10″ × 6″ × 2″.

Mix together *2 slices bread with crusts cut off* and *½ cup milk* until the milk is absorbed. Stir in *1 egg*.

Grind *1 can (1 pound) Plumrose ham* or your favorite ham. Add to the bread mixture.

Grate *1 large onion* over the ham.

Spoon into the baking dish. With your hands shape into a loaf.

Mix *2 tablespoons marmalade* with *2 teaspoons water*.

Spoon the marmalade mixture over the ham.

Place in 400° oven.

Bake about 30 minutes, basting now and then with the orange marmalade.

Spoon *1 tablespoon melted orange marmalade* mixed with *1 teaspoon water* over the top of the ham loaf.

Put under the broiler to brown nicely, takes about 10 or 15 minutes.

Ham Loaf And Glazed Yams

in a casserole with a touch of orange

Heat oven 350°.

Peel and cut *1 small onion* into 4 pieces.

Remove the gelatin and any fat from a *1 pound canned ham*. (Save the gelatin to cook with some green beans.)

Cut the crusts from *2 slices bread*. Put the bread in a large bowl. Tear the bread into pieces.

Add ¼ *cup milk.* Crumble the bread and milk together until the milk is absorbed.

Cut the ham into pieces to fit into a meat grinder. Grind the ham and the onion together into a bowl or chop fine.

Add the ground ham to the bread mixture.

Beat *1 egg* with a fork. Add to the ham mixture. Mix together with your hands.

Spoon the ham mixture down the middle of a square, 8 inch, glass baking dish. Shape it into a loaf.

Pour ⅓ *cup water* around the ham, not over it.

Place the ham loaf in the 350° oven. Bake 30 minutes.

While this is cooking, open a *can (1½ pounds) yams.* Strain the yams over a bowl. Put the yams and *1 can (6 ounces) concentrated frozen orange juice,* defrosted, into a bowl to marinate.

When the ham has baked 30 minutes, arrange the yams on either side of the ham loaf.

Spoon the orange juice over the yams.

Place in the oven. Bake 10 minutes. Baste with the orange juice.

Put under the broiler. Baste now and then. Broil until the ham loaf and yams are browned lightly, takes about 5 minutes.

Open Faced Ham And Bean Sandwich

Toast *4 slices bread.* Spread with *mustard mayonnaise.*

Put *4 slices ham* on top.

Divide a *can (16 ounces) of your favorite beans* on top.

Place a slice of *cheddar or American cheese* on top of each.

Place under broiler and broil until cheese is melted and beans are hot.

Ham Roll In Pastry

Heat oven 425°.

Remove fat from cooked or canned ham to have ½ *pound ham.*

Grind or chop fine the ham, *1 small onion,* and *5 sweet, small gherkins.*

Stir in *5 tablespoons margarine* and *½ teaspoon Dijon type or Gulden's mustard.*

You need *2 pie crusts* to make 2.

Roll out 1 pie crust at a time into a rectangle about 8″ × 10″. (We used 2 balls of our Pie Mix Pastry and let it come to room temperature in 2 hours. You can use any of our crust recipes. See Index for pie crust recipes.)

Spread the filling over it to within 1 inch of the edges. Roll up.

Place on a cookie sheet. Shape into a half moon. Cut slits at 1 inch intervals. Do not cut through. Spread apart.

Brush with *egg wash.* (See Index for recipe.) Bake in 425° oven about 20 minutes.

With some homemade vegetable, split pea or lentil soup, this makes a nice meal. And dessert? Why, fruit, of course!

This roll freezes beautifully. To reheat, wrap roll in foil. Bake on a rack on a cookie sheet 25 to 30 minutes, if frozen, and 20 to 25 minutes, if defrosted.

Ham Pudding

tasty and never fails, easy to make, almost like a special kind of pudding

Heat oven 400°.

Grease a 1½ quart glass, ovenproof casserole with *margarine.* Sprinkle the casserole with *plain crumbs.* Shake out any excess crumbs.

Grind enough canned or ready cooked *ham to make 1 cup.*

Mix in *½ teaspoon onion powder,* a *good grind of pepper, 2 tablespoons fresh chopped parsley or 1 tablespoon dried.* Set aside.

Separate *3 eggs.* Put the yolks in a small bowl. Put the whites in a large bowl.

In a saucepan melt, don't burn, *3 tablespoons margarine.* Take off heat. Stir in *4 tablespoons flour.* Then stir in *1 cup nonfat milk.*

Place on medium high heat. With a wooden spoon cook, stir, taking off and on heat until it gets thick. Put into a large bowl. Use a rubber scraper (spatula) to get all the "white sauce."

Stir in, 1 yolk at a time, until all 3 yolks have been mixed in.

Mix in the ham mixture. Let stand.

With a rotary beater or electric beaters, beat the whites until frothy. Add a pinch of *salt*. Beat until the whites hold a straight peak in the bowl when the beaters are lifted out.

Add a mixing spoon of whites to the yolk mixture. Mix together to lighten it. "Fold" the rest of the whites in quickly so as not to deflate the whites. Pour into the casserole.

Place in the 400° oven. Immediately turn the heat to 375°. Bake 30 minutes.

Test with a cake tester; and if it comes out clean, which it usually does, remove from the oven.

This can wait 5 minutes without falling, so plan to eat at once.

This reheats beautifully. Place in a 375° preheated oven, takes about 10 minutes to reheat.

It can also be eaten cold.

What's different between this pudding and a souffle? The texture is different.

A Super Surprise Casserole

simple and simply delicious . . . yes, buy a pork shoulder roast and have the butcher cut it into ½ inch shoulder chops

You need *as many pork chops as there are mouths to feed.*

Heat oven 350°.

Grease a 2 quart casserole that is fireproof. A fireproof casserole is one you can put on a burner on top of the stove as well as in the oven.

Peel and slice thin *1 medium onion, 2 carrots* and *2 large potatoes.*

Strain *1 can great northern or other beans, or black eye peas*. Run under cold water.

Wipe enough pork chops for 4.

Heat a skillet with *1 tablespoon oil* and *1 teaspoon margarine.*

Brown the pork chops quickly on both sides; don't burn.

Sprinkle lightly with *salt* and *pepper* and arrange on the bottom of the casserole.

Top with ½ of the onions, then arrange ½ of the potatoes on top, then a layer of all the carrots, a layer of the rest of the potatoes, a layer of the rest of the onions, then spoon the beans on top.

Bring *2 cups chicken broth* to a boil. Pour over the casserole.

Cook the casserole until it bubbles. If you do not have a fireproof casserole, just put it in the oven instead and let it cook until it bubbles.

Cover. Bake in 350° oven about 30 minutes. Remove lid. Taste. Add *salt* and *pepper* as needed.

Sprinkle *½ cup seasoned crumbs* on top. Bake, uncovered, 15 minutes or until the chops are tender. Serve.

If there is some left over, serve it as a soup the next day.

A Whole Meal In Minutes

as pretty as a picture with tasty "healthy" sausages and vegetables . . . a dinner in a dish . . . healthy? . . . these sausages have no "nitrate" in them

You need *1 package Swift's Premium Brown 'N Serve Sausage (The Original)*. These are found in the freezer case of your supermarket.

Put the sausages into a skillet with a *little water* on high heat. Cook until the water evaporates; then cook and turn until browned nicely and the fat has run out.

Remove the sausage to a paper towel. Wipe any fat off. Cool. Without cutting through, cut down the middle lengthwise. Open. Place like spokes into a heatproof, round, large pie plate or other dish large enough and fireproof, as you will broil this dish.

Put *a small can (8 ounces) sauerkraut,* drained, in the center.

Spoon *a can (8 ounces) pork and beans,* drained, down the middle of the open sausages.

Arrange spoonfuls of *1 can (8½ ounces) mixed vegetables* in between the sausage "spokes."

Sprinkle grated *Parmesan cheese* on top of the vegetables.

Put under the broiler close to the heat about 8 to 10 minutes to heat and brown; don't burn.

Summertime Stuffed Peppers

with the kind of filling everyone likes

Grease a heatproof dish that will hold 8 green pepper halves.

Cook *1 cup rice.*

Cut *4 large green peppers* in halves.

Defrost *6 Swift's Frozen Brown 'N Serve Smoked Sausages* and cut each into 6 pieces; then mash them.

Bring *water* to a boil in a saucepan. Drop in the pepper halves. Bring back to a boil. Parboil the peppers 2 minutes. Drain. Run under cold water to cool instantly.

Cook, stir the sausage, getting the fat out. Drain the fat. Remove the sausage to paper towels and wipe off the fat clinging to the sausage. Wipe out the fat in the pan, too.

Drain *1 can (16 ounces) Frijoles Negros (black beans).* Run cold water over the beans.

Put into a large bowl the beans, sausages, 2 cups cooked rice, *1 can (8 ounces) stewed tomatoes* (cut the tomatoes into smaller pieces), *salt* and *pepper* to taste, a *few drops of Tabasco, ¼ teaspoon dried basil* and *⅛ teaspoon garlic powder.* Mix.

Spoon into the 8 halves.

Bring *¼ cup water* and *2 tablespoons oil* to a boil. Pour around, not on top, the filled peppers; or use some chicken bouillon broth instead.

Place in 400° oven. Bake about 20 minutes until done.

Skillet Made Sausage And Potatoes

it's very tasty

Defrost *2 packages (8 ounces each) frozen Swift's Patties or Links,* Premium Brown and Serve Sausages—the Original. (Tip: be sure to get the ones marked "the original," since they have no nitrite or nitrate in them, which some say is not healthy for us.) Cut the sausage into small cubes.

Chop a large *onion to make about 1 cup.*

Peel and cube *4 potatoes to make about 2 cups.* Put into a saucepan with *water to cover* and *½ teaspoon salt.*

Put on high heat. Let come to a boil. Turn heat to medium. Cook 7 minutes. Drain in a strainer over a bowl.

Heat a skillet with *2 tablespoons oil* on medium heat. Add the chopped onions. Cook, stir 2 minutes. Turn heat to low. Put lid on. Cook 8 minutes. Drain in a strainer over a bowl. Put the onions on a plate.

Wipe the skillet with a paper towel.

Put the cubed sausage in. Turn heat to low. Put lid on. Cook 10 minutes. Remove lid. Turn heat to medium and brown the sausages, takes about 5 minutes. Strain over a bowl. You will be surprised how much fat you removed. You don't need the fat.

With a paper towel, mop up any fat left in the skillet.

Add the potatoes, onions, sausages and *1 tablespoon oil.* Turn heat to medium. Cook and stir gently so you won't crush the potatoes until everything is hot, takes about 5 to 8 minutes.

Add *salt and pepper* to taste.

Eat while hot. It's very tasty.

"No Make" Dinner For Singles and Doubles

you bake it . . . it's ready made, and it tastes almost as good as you or I could make from scratch

Heat toaster-oven 400°.

Place on top of a frozen, cooked *macaroni and cheese, 3 Swift's Frozen Sausages, The Original,* for 1 person or 6 for 2 people.

Place in 400° oven.

Bake 15 minutes. Turn the browned sausages over to brown the other side. Bake 15 more minutes. Sausages are done and the macaroni and cheese is bubbling.

Serve with a salad, some steamed spinach, a juicy McIntosh or Golden Delicious apple, and you have a meal!

No bread? You've got that nice macaroni.

Of course, you can double the amount for 4.

No Watch Barbecued Franks

you bake these

Cut *4 frankfurters* into bite size slices.

Put into a heatproof baking dish or skillet *½ cup catsup, 4 teaspoons dried instant minced onion, 1 teaspoon lime or lemon juice or vinegar, ¼ teaspoon dried mustard, ½ teaspoon wet mustard, ⅛ teaspoon dried ginger, 1 teaspoon Worcestershire Sauce, 1 drop Tabasco Sauce, pinch of salt* and *2 teaspoons brown or white sugar.*

Bring to a simmer on medium heat.

Add the bite size "hot dogs." Bring back to a simmer.

Place in 375° oven 15 minutes.

It's ready to eat.

How about a dish of sauerkraut to "go with" it, and some cornbread or biscuits would be nice, too. Of course, if you prefer dill pickles instead of the sauerkraut, by all means, eat it.

10. FISH

POACHING is to cook a food in a liquid just to cover it and cook at a heat that will just make the water move gently or barely move.

Fish And Vegetable Bake

would you like a deep dish pie for dessert? . . . then make one . . . but first make the deep dish pie so the whole meal cooks together . . . saves electric energy and best . . . your energy miles . . . we have recipes in the cookbook using fresh fruit in season or one of the pie fillings

Heat oven 400°.

Lightly *salt and pepper fillet of sole* or other fillet on both sides. Place in the middle of a baking dish.

Mix together *½ teaspoon dried tarragon, 1 tablespoon toasted dried minced onions* and *2 tablespoons melted margarine.*

Spoon over the fish.

Place in refrigerator.

Peel and slice *3 carrots, 4 small potatoes* and *1 small onion.*

Bring to a boil *1 cup water* and *1 chicken bouillon powder.* Add the vegetables.

Cook 10 minutes. Drain, but save the liquid.

Take the fish from the refrigerator.

Arrange the carrots on one side, the potatoes mixed with the onions on the other.

Spoon the broth over all. Cover with foil.

Bake in 400° oven 20 to 25 minutes.

Your meal is ready. How about some whole wheat bread and did you make that Deep Dish Pie treat for dessert? Tip: The deep dish pie put in the preheated oven first, while you make the fish dish, will be baked at the same time as the fish dish and both will come out of the oven the same time, so while they bake, have a relaxing talk with your husband and the children. How about that?

Quick Flavorful Fish Stew

the work is in the chopping and the fun is in the eating and all in all, it's quick!

Cut *enough fish into portions for four.*

Keep in refrigerator until ready to use. If frozen, defrost in the refrigerator overnight.

Bring *6 cups water* to a boil with *4 chicken bouillon powders, 1 onion bouillon powder, ¼ cup brown rice, 1 large bay leaf* and *4 whole allspice.*

Turn heat to low; cook 15 minutes.

While it is cooking, chop fine *½ cup carrots, ½ cup celery, 1 medium onion, 1 medium potato, ½ cup green pepper* and *2 tablespoons parsley.*

Measure *¼ cup tiny pasta,* "roco" or other tiny pasta.

Add everything to the rice broth except the parsley and the green pepper.

Bring to a boil. Cook 10 minutes.

Add the green pepper. Cook 10 minutes.

Add the fish and the chopped parsley, *pepper* and *salt,* if needed.

Cook about 4 to 5 minutes until the fish is done. Don't overcook; they should not fall apart by any means.

This dish takes about ½ hour.

Serve with thick slices of Whole Wheat Bread. (Hopefully, made by you when and if you have the time.) See Index for recipe for Homemade Whole Wheat Bread; also under "Breads."

PS: Don't be surprised if everyone asks for seconds.

Fish Stew

Put into a large saucepan or fireproof casserole *1 can chicken broth, 5 cups chicken bouillon broth, 4 tablespoons chopped onions (or ¼ cup), ¼ cup rice, ¼ cup carrots plus 2 tablespoons,* minced fine, *¼ cup celery,* minced fine and *¼ cup macaroni.* Bring to a boil.

Turn heat to low. Cook 5 minutes.

Add *1 small yellow crook neck squash or zucchini* cut into slices or cubes depending on the size of the squash and *¼ cup cubed green peppers.* Cook 5 minutes.

When the vegetables are cooked, add the fish cut into bite

size pieces. (I use any fish filet with the least bones—flounder, red snapper, cod, halibut, striped bass.)

Add *salt* if necessary, a *good grind of pepper* to taste and a good *pinch of ground allspice* to taste. The ground allspice puts this into the "gourmet" class! Add 2 tablespoons minced parsley.

Cook until done, takes about 5 minutes.

This is very tasty, and even the "I don't eat fish" people will like it. This freezes well.

Tip: We always have minced parsley packaged in 1 tablespoon foil packages which we make when we buy a bunch of fresh parsley and freeze after making and mincing. We do this because it seems no matter how we tried to use up our fresh parsley there was always some that went bad because we couldn't use it all. This is a money saver and a "blessing" when we need parsley for so many of our dishes. It's ready when we're ready!

The Next Day's Fish Salad

from the "cook once for twice" fish stew . . . this fish has more flavor because it was cooked in the seasoned broth of your fish soup

Chop *1 stalk celery, ½ small onion to make 2 tablespoons, 2 tablespoons scallions, 4 tablespoons green pepper.*

Put into a large bowl.

Add the cooked filet of turbot cut into bite-size pieces.

Add *⅓ cup unsweetened mayonnaise.*

Add a *grind of pepper* and *salt* to taste. Add a tiny *sprinkle of cayenne pepper.*

With your clean hands, gently mix together without crushing the fish.

Pan Fried Whole Fish

these are delectable

You can use small Red Snappers in the south or even Pompano if it doesn't cost a million dollars or any other small fish that is not too fatty.

You can choose a small bass, a small blue fish, a Norfolk Spot or whatever small fish you prefer or any filets.

The secret is threefold. Heat the skillet hot. Add 3 or 4 tablespoons oil and 1 tablespoon margarine. Secret #2 is to salt the fish all over lightly and the most important gourmet touch is not to flour the fish until you are "ready to put it in the pan" and be sure to flour the fish "lightly" and shake off any excess.

Also, don't go away, be there to check how the fish is frying.

Let brown into a beautiful golden brown color, turning the heat down a little as necessary. Also, turn the fish over and brown that side. You might have to turn again to get the fish just cooked but not dry. Flake one open just a little to see whether the fish is still opaque or whether it's done.

A grind of pepper, a quarter of lemon (a slice is hard to handle), some homemade lovely whole wheat bread—see our recipe Index under "Whole Wheat Bread"—and that's a gourmet meal. . . . Oh, yes . . . in the summer some slices of home grown tomatoes, a light sprinkle of salt, then thin slices of onion for our onion eaters and that's a meal!

Spanish Style Baked Turbot Fish

the frozen turbot fish is usually cut into fillets, so you have to cut it into portions

Defrost in refrigerator overnight a *package of frozen turbot fish*—enough for four; or use fresh fillet of fish.

Salt lightly with about *½ teaspoon salt*. Let stand 15 minutes in refrigerator.

Melt *2 tablespoons margarine*. Spoon over the fish.

Mix together *1 can (14½ ounces) stewed tomatoes* with *3 tablespoons dry vermouth* and a *pinch of sugar*. We used Noilly Prat French Extra Dry Vermouth.

Put foil tightly on top of the dish.

Bake in 400° oven about 20 to 25 minutes.

Be sure to serve the sauce with the fish—it's light and delicious.

Turbot In Fresh Stewed Tomatoes

in the good old Summer time or early Fall when homegrown tomatoes are plentiful . . . it's then you'll say "never was anything so good"

You can use fresh or frozen *turbot fillets,* or any other fillet is fine.

Make these stewed tomatoes:

Peel and cut enough *tomatoes to make 2 to 2½ cups.*

Wash, remove seeds and cut into pieces a *small green pepper.*

Chop *¼ cup celery, ½ cup onions* or save time and use instead frozen chopped onions.

Put these vegetables into a large skillet with *2 tablespoons oil.* Cook and stir, adding *½ teaspoon dried basil* or *fennel,* a *pinch of garlic, salt* and *pepper* to taste. Cook about 15 minutes.

This makes about *3 cups heavenly stewed fresh tomatoes.*

(Of course, out of season use canned tomatoes.)

When the tomatoes are done, drop in the pieces of fillet of turbot; bring back to a boil. Cook just until done—about 5 minutes.

Serve.

Flavored Italian Fish

for those who don't like fish, they'll love this . . . you will always have juicy fish this way even with dry King Fish

Line a shallow baking dish with foil—no messy washing.

Smear with *butter or margarine.*

Heat oven 400°.

Cut *fish* into portion size. Sprinkle lightly with *salt, pepper* and a *little lemon juice.* Put in refrigerator for 15 minutes.

Smear *mayonnaise* thickly over the fish on both sides.

Spread grated *Parmesan cheese* thickly on the mayonnaise.

Cover with *Italian Seasoned Bread Crumbs* mixed with *chopped parsley.*

Put into the shallow baking dish.

Bake in heated 400° oven about 20 to 25 minutes, depending on the thickness of the fish.

Oven Fried Fish

the easy, tasty way . . . we use frozen turbot because that's one of the best fish frozen

Heat oven 425°.

Defrost overnight in refrigerator *2 pounds fillet of frozen turbot.*

Cut the turbot into 5 pieces or portion size pieces.

Sprinkle *1 teaspoon salt* over lightly on both sides of the fish.

Put in refrigerator for 15 minutes.

Put *¼ cup margarine* into a small saucepan and melt on low heat.

Pour into soup plate.

Put *½ cup corn flake crumbs* in another soup plate.

Dip each piece fish first in the melted margarine, then into the crumbs, and then put into the baking dish.

When all have been done, close the top tightly with foil.

Place in the middle of the 425° oven.

Bake 20 minutes. Remove foil. Bake 5 minutes more.

The fish is ready.

Our Batter Bread goes nicely with this and if you're lucky enough to have made our Whole Wheat Bread by all means serve it.

Broiled Fillet Of Fish With Mustard Mayonnaise

not only is our mustard mayonnaise delicious in a sandwich, try it on broiled fish! . . . it's delectable

Heat the broiler.

Salt and pepper lightly fresh or frozen fillet of sole, flounder, turbot, red snapper, striped bass or other fish. Put into refrigerator.

Make our Mustard Mayonnaise. You can keep in the refrigerator and use as needed: Stir your favorite *mustard* (ours is Dijon type Belgian mustard . . . when we can afford it or a French Dijon mustard, or Gulden's), *¾ teaspoon* to taste into *½ cup of your favorite unsweetened mayonnaise.*

Brush the underside of the fish lightly with the mustard mayonnaise, then a little heavier on the top side.

Place on a shallow broiling pan or a cookie sheet. Place under broiler about 3½ or 4½ inches from the heat.

Broil the fish without turning until cooked, takes about 1 to 4 minutes or more depending on the thickness of the fish, and golden brown on top. Do not turn the fish.

Sprinkle a little finely chopped *fresh parsley* on the fish right before serving or a little bit of *dried tarragon* ½ minute before removing from the broiler.

Also serve with a wedge of lemon and pass some extra mustard mayonnaise for those who like the extra accent of this delicious mayonnaise.

Cucumber Sauce For Fried Fish

or fried crab cakes . . . simple to make

Grate only enough and strain the juice of part of a *cucumber* to make *2 tablespoons of the strained juice.*

We do not use the pulp.

Stir the 2 tablespoons cucumber juice into *½ cup of unsweetened mayonnaise.*

Use as a sauce with fried fish or crab cakes.

This is fresher tasting than the commercial tartar sauce.

Another Sauce For Fish Or Crabs

Soak *1 teaspoon dried tarragon* in hot water to cover 5 minutes, then drain well. Chop fine *1 tablespoon parsley.*

Stir the tarragon and the chopped parsley into *½ cup unsweetened mayonnaise.* Stir in *2 squirts* (about ¼ teaspoon) *lemon juice* into the mayonnaise mixture.

Fillet Of Flounder
Stuffed With Crab Meat

this is not a Penny Pincher dish but just once make it for a special treat

Cut *fillet of flounder* portion size to fit 4 greased-with-butter individual shallow baking dishes. Sprinkle *salt* on lightly and a *grind of pepper* and refrigerate 15 minutes.

Stir *6 tablespoons heavy cream* into *½ cup unsweetened mayonnaise.* Gently mix with *½ can lump crabmeat* (picked over and any shells removed) but try not to crush the crabmeat.

Spoon this over the fillets. Dot with *butter,* sprinkle on *paprika* lightly and add a light grind or shake of *pepper.*

Bake in preheated 375° oven about 15 to 20 minutes until the flounder is cooked but juicy and the top is a golden brown color.

Maryland Crab Cakes

these are the very best crab cakes . . . they are made with "back fin" or otherwise called "lump crab meat" . . . and they are expensive, but once you make these, you will see what a treat they are . . . why "Maryland Crab Cakes?" . . . we believe Eastern Shore, Maryland, has the sweetest crab meat in the USA

You need *1 pound can fresh or pasteurized lump or back fin crab meat.* You can use the much less expensive crab meat, but follow this recipe.

Place the crab meat in a large bowl. Pick over to remove any shells.

Mix together *¼ cup unsweetened Mayonnaise, ¼ teaspoon freshly ground pepper, ½ teaspoon salt* and *1 teaspoon dry mustard.*

With your hands mix very gently the crab meat so as not to break the lumps of crab meat.

Beat *1 large egg* with a fork. Gently add to the crab meat mixture, and gently fold or mix without breaking the lumps of crab meat.

Heat a large skillet until hot.

Put in *enough oil to cover skillet about ¼ inch from the bottom.* Let get hot.

Add *2 tablespoons margarine.* Don't burn. As soon as it sizzles, drop in a large mixing spoon of the crab mixture until the skillet is filled with crab cakes, but be careful not to crowd.

Turn heat to second high heat and brown nicely and quickly. Turn and brown the other side.

Put the cakes on a heated plate with a paper towel on it. Blot any fat quickly with another paper towel.

Remove immediately to a heated plate and serve.
Aren't they delicious?

"Crabmeat Special" Cakes

this crabmeat tastes just as sweet as the expensive Back Fin Crabmeat and is enough for four people

You need a *12 ounce can Pasteurized or Fresh Crabmeat (Special);* this crabmeat is as sweet as sugar!

Heat serving plates in low oven.

Put the crabmeat in a large bowl. Remove any shells.

Mix together *½ cup unsweetened Mayonnaise, ¾ teaspoon dry mustard, and ¼ teaspoon freshly ground pepper.*

Mix with the crabmeat, being careful not to mash.

Beat *1 egg* with a fork and very gently stir into the crabmeat. Don't overmix.

Heat a large skillet on high heat with about *¼ inch oil* until hot.

Drop a full tablespoon of the crabmeat mixture into the hot fat, adding more tablespoons to fill the skillet without crowding.

Brown on both sides quickly. Remove to a plate covered with a paper towel to drain the fat, or put on a rack for a second to drain.

Quickly remove to the heated plates and serve.

Our Potato Salad and our Slaw make this a complete meal with our Open-Faced Cherry pie as dessert.

Fried Soft Shell Crabs

this is not penny pinching but you might want this for a special treat

With a fork beat *2 eggs* and a pinch of *salt.*

Stir in *2 tablespoons milk.*

Place *flour* on a large piece of wax paper.

Heat skillet hot. Add about *½ inch oil.* When hot, add *2 tablespoons margarine.* Test if hot enough by putting edge of crab into hot fat, and if it sizzles, fat is ready.

Dip 2 soft shell crabs, one at a time, into the egg-milk mixture. Then dip in flour.

Place in the skillet without crowding.

Fry on one side about 5 minutes. Turn, brown the other side about 4 or 5 minutes.

Place on heated plates covered with a paper towel to drain any fat off.

Remove to a heated plate and serve at once.

Continue to do the same until all are done.

Tip: For a crisp, delicious taste don't crowd the crabs. Follow our directions.

Imperial Crab

nothing could be better!

Heat oven 375°.

You need *1 can fresh Pasteurized "Special" Crabmeat.*

Mix together *½ cup unsweetened Mayonnaise,* with *1½ teaspoons dry mustard* and *1½ teaspoons wet mustard, 1 teaspoon Worcestershire sauce, 1 teaspoon brandy,* a good grind of *pepper* and *4 drops of Tabasco.*

With your hands mix with the crabmeat so as not to mash.

Spoon into shells or deep saucers. The ceramic kind are nice, too.

Lightly smear the tops with *mayonnaise.*

Bake in preheated oven about 15 to 20 minutes until hot.

Yummy!

We use Dijon type mustard or Gulden's Mustard.

Sliced tomatoes are especially good with these or a tossed salad is nice. We serve a salad of thinly sliced cucumbers and thinly sliced onions mixed with yogurt and salt to taste. We put this in the refrigerator early, ready to eat at dinner time.

A baked potato also goes nicely, and what could be better than 2 medium zucchini or yellow crookneck squash, not too large, sliced ¼ inch thick, dipped in 2 eggs mixed with 2 tablespoons milk and then coated with a mixture of 1 cup crumbs and 1 tablespoon wheat germ.

Fry in ¼ cup oil and 1 tablespoon margarine on high heat, being careful not to burn. When browned on both sides, put on a plate covered with a paper towel, and use another towel to wipe the fat off the top of the zucchini. Remove to a heated plate and serve.

Baked Fresh Bass In A Wine Sauce

you can use a striped bass or a Red Snapper, or Blue Fish, and the French have nothing on us . . . our sauce is good too, even if we don't have rich cream in it!

Heat oven 450°.

Grease a heatproof glass baking dish that will fit the fish.

Slice *1 medium large onion* thin and *1 carrot* (not sweet) into very thin slices.

Sprinkle *salt* over and in the bass lightly, or whatever fish you have.

Sprinkle a *little lemon juice* over the fish.

Put in the refrigerator to marinate. Cover.

Heat a skillet with *4 tablespoons oil* until hot.

Add the onions and carrots. Cook, stir about 2 minutes. Turn heat to low. Cover. Let simmer 10 minutes until soft and clear. Drain over a bowl.

Put the oil back into the skillet.

In a saucepan, add *½ teaspoon tarragon leaves, ½ cup dry white wine* (a Reisling or Johannesburg Reisling or dry Vermouth or a California white wine which you can drink while you're eating the fish—it doesn't have to be expensive), and *1 cup chicken broth*, fresh or canned. Bring to a simmer. Simmer about 10 minutes. Set aside.

Heat the skillet with the flavored oil and add *2 or more tablespoons oil* until hot. Wipe the fish as dry as possible. Brown quickly (but don't cook). Brown on one side—then the other.

Remove to the greased baking dish. Sprinkle a few tarragon leaves on the fish and arrange a few slices of the cooked onions on top.

Bring the rest of the onions and the carrots to a boil in a saucepan. Pour around the fish.

Place in the 450° oven. Cover. Let come to a simmer. Takes about 10 minutes. Turn the heat to 350°. Bake 45 minutes until done.

Poached Whole Bass In The Oven

fantastic to look at and fantastic to eat baked-poached in white wine, sprinkled with herbs and flavored with aromatic vegetables . . . it's a dish to relish

Our bass was a huge bass weighing 4½ pounds. We named the bass "The Loud Mouth Bass!" It was a gift from a dear friend, who had just caught it, cleaned it, and we baked-poached it in the oven as follows. (You can use any good large fish!)

Wash the bass carefully. Put soft *margarine* over and in the bass.

Sprinkle *salt* inside and all over the bass lightly.

Make 3 slanted slashes across the bass.

Let stand in refrigerator while you cook the aromatic vegetables.

Bring to a sizzle, but don't burn, *2 cups sliced onions, 2 cups sliced carrots* (not sweet carrots), and *4 tablespoons oil.* Cover. Turn heat to low. Cover. Cook, steam 30 minutes until carrots are tender. You might have to cook longer.

Add *2 cups dry white wine, 1 large dried bay leaf*, cut into quarters, a sprinkle of *fresh* or *dried dill, 4 cloves garlic,* a tiny piece of *dried red hot pepper* and *2 tablespoons fresh or frozen chopped parsley.* Tip: We freeze our own chopped parsley in 1 tablespoon foil packages. Bring to a boil.

Pour into a baking dish large enough to hold this "King of All Bass." Makes a "bed."

Heat oven 450°. Place in oven. Bake until it bubbles. Arrange the bass on top of the bed of vegetables.

Sprinkle *pepper* and a light sprinkle of *dried tarragon* on the bass. Bake until the sauce bubbles, takes about 10 minutes. Cover tightly with foil.

Bake about 50 minutes, basting once or twice.

Remove foil, brush with *margarine* and another sprinkle of *tarragon.* Bake 10 minutes more. Serve with its vegetables.

As I said before, once in a lifetime you might catch or be given a bass of this size, so if yours is a smaller one, poach it this way, only shorten the time.

Tip: The sauce has a wonderful taste. (Please, never, never use sugar.) We used a dry white wine.

Another tip: When poach-cooking fish in the oven, the aromatic vegetables have to be cooked on top of the stove to release their flavors to the fish. You can poach a whole chicken this same way and achieve a masterpiece of flavored chicken. Be sure to use the tarragon with the chicken, too. Simple, and simply delicious!

Another tip: Don't add water to make the sauce. It dilutes the flavor. We usually are sparing of the wine in our cooking, but this time we discovered it makes all the difference.

A last big tip: If you live in a town where you can't buy fresh fish, try to find a friend, like ours, who loves to fish!

Fresh Caught Bass Or Striped Bass

cooked in white wine it's well—the best! . . . (I must admit it's not such a Penny Pincher dish . . . but if your husband or boy friend caught it . . . isn't it?)

Be sure after you have cleaned the bass that you remove all the scales. Go over it again to be sure!

Sprinkle salt lightly all over the fish including the inside. Place in the refrigerator.

Peel, slice very thin *1 to 3 carrots* (depending on the size of your bass) (the best carrots for this dish are the non-sweet variety), slice *1 or 2 medium onions* very thin, get *2 branches of your frozen celery,* if you have saved it by freezing, *or* cut into 2 inch pieces *1 stalk of celery.*

Heat oven 450°.

Put the vegetables into a saucepan with *1 cup water or water to cover well.* Bring to a boil. Cook about 10 minutes. Strain and save the water.

Arrange the fish in a baking dish that fits.

Mix the water with an equal amount of *dry Vermouth. . . .* We like the French Vermouth "Noilly Prat." Bring to a boil. Pour around the fish. Rub a little *butter or margarine* all over the fish. Arrange some of the sliced carrots and the onions on the fish and also *1 large green dried bay leaf* torn into 4 pieces on it. Add to the broth *2 whole allspice* and *1 dried bay leaf* cut into 4 pieces and the rest of the carrots, celery and onions. Sprinkle a little *pepper* on the fish. Dot with butter or margarine. Cover with foil.

Put into the preheated oven. Let get hot. Turn the heat to 400°.

How long to bake? That depends on the size of the fish.

We have baked a very large one an hour and 15 minutes, but most of the time it takes 30 to 45 minutes until done.

Lift the foil off, stick a fork in to see if the fish isn't raw looking but please don't overcook. The fish should be juicy and delectable.

Serve with the "sauce" (juice) spooned over and around the fish . . . no one ever leaves any of it! Have spoons handy for each one.

Boiled parsley potatoes go nicely with this but please take advantage of the stove and bake the new red or white potatoes, rubbed with butter, right along (the medium size not the large size). We find we don't need to use the higher priced Idaho potatoes. In fact we like the other kind better and we eat every bit of the skin too. I must admit there is thick sour cream on the table; also, some prepared horseradish and some mayonnaise with some lemon juice mixed with it. We use the commercial unsweetened mayonnaise.

Can you bake another fish this way? Of course, striped bass from the fish man or supermarket is also very good . . . but if you can marry a man who just loves to fish that's the best!

How To Steam Shrimp

we have steamed shrimps in beer, in herbs and spices, in a mixture of seasoning vegetables—but this simple way is for me the best

For *1 pound medium shrimps* in their shells bring *3 cups water* and *2 teaspoons salt* to a rolling boil.

Add the shrimps. Bring back to a boil quickly.

Boil 2 minutes until the shrimps turn pink. Taste one; it should be done. If not, cook 1 minute longer.

Pour into a strainer to drain the water off quickly. Some people let the shrimps cool in the water. I prefer not to. Check which way you like them best.

These shrimps, so simply cooked, are a delight with a cocktail sauce made of *Chili Sauce, lemon* and *horseradish* with a drop or two of *Tabasco,* or dipped into a sauce made with *unsweetened mayonnaise, Gulden's mustard* and a *dash of brandy.*

Scampi Shrimp

this started out being Italian but ended up being Alsatian . . . why? . . . because the Alsatian cooks have a delicate touch

For 2 you need *1 pound of very large shrimps* which amounts to about 10 shrimps and costs a fortune. (You can use the regular size shrimp. We do most times.)

Run the shrimps under running water.

Cut each one down the middle of the outside shell, leaving the end shell tip and peeling off the rest of the shell.

Butterfly the shrimps by cutting down the back, but not through it. Remove the dark vein and spread the shrimps. (This is butterflying them.)

Set aside in the refrigerator.

Mince very, very fine *3 cloves garlic, 3 of the white bulbs of the green onions, 2 tablespoons parsley* and *1 teaspoon fresh dill*; or we sometimes use ¼ teaspoon dried green dill. (Don't ever use dried, brownish ones—they're long overdue for the trash can.)

Mix together *½ cup chicken broth* and *3 tablespoons dry Vermouth.*

Preheat broiler until hot, hot. Place broiler rack on second rack from the heat.

Arrange 5 of the butterflied shrimps each in 2 greased with oil, shallow, heatproof baking dishes (individual size that fits the shrimps).

Brush the shrimps with a *little oil.* Sprinkle very lightly with *salt* and lightly with *pepper.*

Leave most of the finely chopped garlic and shallots to use with the broth, but sprinkle a little broth, shallots and garlic over the shrimps. Mix the rest into the broth mixture with the minced parsley and the dill.

Spoon the broth mixture around the shrimps. You will have some left to baste with.

Place the baking dishes on a cookie pan with sides, so you can handle them when broiling.

Put into the hot broiler about halfway in the oven. Broil and baste often with the chicken mixture and brush with *oil.* Don't go away. You have to stand and baste. Broil 5 minutes.

Now move the rack closer to the flame or heat. Brush the shrimps with *oil.*

Broil until shrimps are cooked and start browning, basting once or twice, takes about 2 minutes. Taste one to be sure the shrimps are done, but be careful not to dry the shrimps. They should be deliciously sweet, and be sure to serve a spoon to spoon up the delectable sauce.

The whole broiling time takes about 7 minutes, so it's a "quick cooking" dish. The work is in the mincing and peeling.

A simple green salad goes nicely with this. You might eat the salad as a first course.

A fruit pie or a key lime pie would be nice for dessert.

Salmon Casserole

for 2 and you can multiply for as many as you need . . . it's a dinner in a dish with a salad as a first course, please

Cut off the crusts from *1 slice bread* and tear the bread into pieces (not too small).

Mix *1 egg*. Stir in *4 tablespoons (¼ cup) nonfat milk.* Pour over the bread. Mix without mashing the bread, keep in pieces.

Chop *1 teaspoon parsley*. Add to the bread mixture.

Add *1 can (7¾ ounces) salmon*. Grate *½ small onion* over it.

With 2 forks mix gently without crushing the salmon or the bread.

Spoon into 2 small greased casseroles.

Slice *1 small fresh tomato thin* and arrange on top *(or* use *canned tomatoes, drained)*. Sprinkle lightly with salt.

Sprinkle with *crumbs.* (We use seasoned crumbs.)

Dot with a little *margarine.*

You can bake it now, or refrigerate until you are ready for it.

Heat oven 400°. Bake about 15 to 20 minutes.

Serve piping hot.

If you have the time, make our jelly roll (the easy way) for dessert. See index. It seems to make a hit.

Of course, the easiest dessert which can't be beat is fresh fruit.

Salmon Cakes

Put *1 pound can salmon and its juice and bones* into a bowl.

Grate *1 medium onion* over the salmon.
Mix *2 eggs* with a fork and add.
Tear *2 pieces white bread* into small pieces and add.
Mix together with a fork but don't mash.
Heat a skillet hot.
Add about *6 tablespoons oil.*
Drop by tablespoons into the hot oil.
Brown on one side; turn, brown the other side.
This takes a few minutes only and tastes especially good.

Salmon Stuffed Pastry

with Cream of Mushroom Soup or Cream of Tomato Soup this makes a nice supper . . . a salad and fresh fruit complete the meal

For 2:
Mix together *1 can (3¾ ounces) drained salmon* with *2 tablespoons mustard mayonnaise* made by mixing *½ teaspoon Belgian or French Dijon type mustard, or Gulden's Mustard* into *2 tablespoons Hellmann's Mayonnaise.*
Stir in *1 tablespoon drained capers.*
Roll out *½ of our Never Fail Pie Crust.* (See Index for recipe under P.)
Fill with the salmon mixture. Roll up tightly like a jelly roll.
Place in 400° preheated oven. Bake 20 minutes.
Serve hot with a plate of either Campbell's Cream of Mushroom Soup or Campbell's or Heinz Cream of Tomato Soup mixed with ½ cup nonfat milk and cook, stir until boiling hot.

The Best Ever Tuna Fish Salad

we add a special touch

Drain *1 can (7 ounces) tuna.* (You can use your favorite kind.) Put into a large mixing bowl. With a pastry blender mix until flaky.
Chop *2 tablespoons onions, 2 tablespoons scallions (green tops too), ¼ cup celery, ½ cup nonsweet mayonnaise.*
This is our favorite tuna salad. For a change we sometimes

substitute ½ of the mayonnaise with our "Mustard Mayonnaise."

Some people like chopped green pepper added and others like chopped sweet gherkins added to the tuna salad.

Tip: Don't mash or mush the tuna—just flake with the pastry blender.

Baked Pancakes Supper Dish

it's a perfect dish when you're too tired to either cook or do a lot of preparation

Heat oven 425°.

Put into a 1½ quart glass, deep baking dish *3 tablespoons margarine* and put into the heated oven for 10 minutes.

Drain *1 can tuna fish or salmon.* Break into chunks. Drain *1 jar (2 ounces) pimentos.* Drain *1 can corn.*

Mix *2 eggs* with a fork. Stir in *½ cup nonfat milk.*

Put *½ cup Quickie Mix* into a bowl. Stir in the egg-milk mixture. Add the tuna or salmon, pimentos and corn. The batter will have lumps.

Pour this batter into the melted margarine.

Place in the oven. Bake 15 or 20 minutes. It will be puffy and the texture will not be a pancake or an omelette or a souffle. It's different, but it's good.

Tip: While it is baking, you can heat some of your frozen, homemade soup; or open a can of your favorite soup and eat it.

For dessert, what requires the least amount of work? Yes, fresh fruit, and some of our whole wheat or our own bread which you had in your freezer or the store bought whole wheat bread that tells you all the "goodies" that are in it.

Caponata Tuna Roll

Caponata is an Italian appetizer which we add to our tuna and stuff into our easy to make dough—easy to make—easy to eat

Heat oven 375°.

You need *1 can (4¾ ounces) Progresso Egg Plant Appetizer, called Caponata.*

Mix together the Caponata, *¼ teaspoon dried tarragon, 1*

can tuna fish, drained (7 ounces), *1 jar (2 ounces) filled green olives,* drained, *salt* and *pepper* to taste.

Stir in *2 tablespoons mayonnaise.*

Put into a large bowl *2 cups Quickie Mix* (or a commercial mix). Add *⅓ cup milk.* Stir with a fork until it forms a soft, but not sticky, dough. Place on a floured surface, knead and smooth into a ball.

Roll on a lightly floured surface into a rectangle, 8″ × 10″.

Put the stuffing on the bottom side. Roll up like a jelly roll. Place on a cookie sheet. Curve the roll into a half moon shape. Cut slits at 1 inch intervals from the outside, but don't cut all the way through. Turn the dough up a little so it looks pretty when it bakes.

Brush with an egg glaze made by mixing *1 egg yolk* with *2 teaspoons cold tap water.* This makes a lovely glaze.

Bake in 375° oven for 30 minutes.

A vegetable soup rounds this meal out beautifully. A "home made" soup makes it "gourmet." A good canned soup like Progresso's Minestrone soup with a little chicken broth, fresh, canned, or Bouillon broth added is very acceptable.

Pancakes Stuffed With Fish

what fish? . . . tuna, of course . . . all you have to do is open the can . . . no work . . . and it's always popular too!

Make the pancakes. (See recipe "Pancakes for Stuffing.")

Drain and run cold water over *2 cans (7 ounces) tuna.*

Put into a bowl and mash fine.

Saute *1 finely chopped, small onion* and *½ stalk finely chopped celery* until onion is soft and clear.

Chop fine *2 hard boiled eggs.*

Drain and chop fine *1 can or jar (2½ ounces) pimento.* Put into a bowl. Add *½ cup Mayonnaise.*

Gently mix together.

Put a tablespoon of the filling on the bottom part of each pancake.

Roll up.

Place in a pretty, heatproof, shallow baking dish. Cover with foil.

Heat in a 400° oven; or put on a low oven rack to heat the pancakes so they are hot through, takes about 10 minutes.

If you wish, put under broiler when hot with a sprinkle of *Parmesan cheese.*

Don't let burn; just let brown.

For those who like a sauce:

Stir *½ cup milk* slowly into *1 can Cheddar Cheese Soup.*

Bring the soup to a simmer. Stir in *¼ cup Velveeta cheese,* cut up.

When the pancakes are ready to serve, serve hot, hot with the pancakes.

Or a richer sauce:

Stir *¾ cup milk* into *1 can Cheddar Cheese Soup* and *½ cup grated Swiss cheese.*

Tuna Mushroom, Celery, Vegetable Macaroni Casserole

a meal in a baking dish

Heat oven 400°.

Grease a 6 × 10 inch glass baking dish or use a round casserole.

Mix together *1 can (10¾ ounces) Cream of Mushroom soup* and *1 can Cream of Celery Soup (10¾ ounces), 2 eggs.* Stir in *1 cup nonfat milk.*

Add *2 cups frozen mixed vegetables* and *2 cups elbow macaroni* (uncooked).

Spoon one-half into the baking dish or casserole.

Drain and flake *1 can (6½ ounces) chunk light tuna.*

Spoon over the macaroni mixture and cover with the other half of the macaroni mixture.

Cover with foil.

Place in 400° oven. Cover. Bake 15 minutes. Remove foil.

Spoon melted margarine on top. Bake 15 minutes until macaroni is done.

The Quickest Quick Way Chicken Dinner

this is a Chinese technique with a Southern accent and ends up into a good meal

Cook thin noodles, rice, barley, groats, spaghetti, or even pasta shells to "go with" this dinner.

Cut *enough skinned chicken breasts or dark meat* into bite size pieces *for 1, 2 or 4 portions.*

Chop *1 small onion.* A quick way to chop an onion is to hold the onion in your hand. Cut off the tail of the onion but not the stem, so it doesn't fall apart. Slice down but not to the end; then slice in opposite direction. Put the onion down and slice across. The onion is ready. If you use a large onion, chop it.

Chop *1 stalk celery*—enough for your family.

Heat a skillet with *2 to 4 tablespoons oil*, depending on the amount of onions and celery. Cook, stir them until the onions are soft and clear. Remove to a plate. Strain the oil and save.

Cut enough *Swift's Frozen Italian Style Sausage*, partially defrosted to make it easy for you to slice for your family.

Add a *tablespoon water* in a skillet and cook, stir (called defat) the sausage. You will see the fat coming out. Cook, stir until the water is evaporated and the sausage slices start to brown, but don't burn. Remove the sausages. Wipe out the fat. Put the oil from the onions back in, add the chicken and cook, stir a minute or two.

Add the sausages and the onions. Cook, stir until all are hot, takes a minute or so.

Grind a *little pepper* on.

Serve over the *rice or noodles*, whichever you have chosen to "go with."

Tip: If you are making this dinner for a whole family, you can omit the sausage and use more chicken. You can use a large skillet and at the same time, first remove the chicken, onions and celery after it has almost cooked and add to the skillet a fresh vegetable of your choice that you have par-boiled, or better still, steamed, just until it is a quarter done. Then add a little oil to the skillet and stir, fry a minute; then put a lid on to cook until done, takes a few minutes so don't overcook.

You can then return the chicken to one side of the skillet and the vegetables to the other side. Heat and serve immediately—on heated plates, please.

Where to heat the plates? In your oven on lowest heat for about 3 to 5 minutes. A heated plate makes a world of difference in the taste of any hot food, especially when cooking "Chinese style."

Casseroled Chicken With Batter Bread

a real treat when you eat with Batter Bread

Heat oven 425°.

Grease a 2½ quart glass or metal casserole with soft *margarine.*

Grease a 9-inch glass deep pie dish with *margarine.*

Mix together in a large bowl *2 cans (10¾ ounces) Cream of Chicken Soup* with *2 cups milk.*

Add *¼ teaspoon salt, 1 teaspoon dried parsley, 1 package (10 ounces) frozen, defrosted peas and carrots, ¼ cup minced onions, ¼ cup minced celery* and *2 cups "Ready Cooked" chicken,* diced.

Pour into the casserole. Cover top tightly with foil.

Place in 425° oven. Bake 15 minutes. Let it continue to bake while you make the Batter Bread.

Batter Bread

Put *1 cup Quickie Mix* into a bowl.

Separate *2 eggs.*

Stir the egg yolks with a fork; then stir in *½ cup cold water.*

Stir into the mix.

With a rotary beater, beat the 2 egg whites until stiff.

Fold the egg whites into the batter.

Pour the batter into the greased deep pie dish.

Bake about 15 minutes until the Batter Bread is golden brown and done.

Remove both the Chicken Casserole and the Batter Bread from the oven.

Now you can start to eat.

Chicken, Carrots And Tomatoes

for two we used 1½ chicken breasts cut into halves lengthwise with the bone and skin left on

Slice *1 small onion*, and slice very thin *1 small carrot.*

Heat a large plate until warm in the oven.

Salt and pepper chicken breasts lightly.

Wipe the chicken breasts dry.

Heat a skillet that will hold the breasts without crowding. Add *2 tablespoons oil.*

Coat the chicken breasts with *flour*. Shake off any excess.

Heat the skillet until hot.

Place the chicken in the skillet, meaty side down. Brown until golden brown. Turn and brown the other side.

Place on the heated plate. Sprinkle *salt and pepper* over.

Stir into the skillet on high heat *⅓ cup dry white wine or chicken broth.* Cook, stir the good brownings into the wine or chicken broth. Turn the heat to medium. Add the sliced onion. Cook, stir 5 minutes. Add the browned chicken, the carrots, a *clove of garlic,* and *1 can (8 ounces) stewed tomatoes.* Cook 25 minutes until the breasts are done.

Put the breasts on heated plates. If the sauce is thin, cook, stir on high heat until it thickens. Pour the sauce over the chicken.

Tip: For 4 people, double this recipe; and since it's so easy to make with the "dinner in a dish," by all means make it for your family or guests!

"Quick Chick" Bake

which adds up to chicken with cornbread topping . . . it's easy out of a can and out of a box . . . you do this when you're just too tired to start from scratch and yet want a nutritious meal

Heat oven 425°.

Put into a saucepan *1 can Campbell's Alphabet Vegetarian Vegetable Soup, 1 can Campbell's Chicken Vegetable Soup, 1 can Great Northern Beans,* or *Red Kidney Beans, 1 can Veg-all (15 ounces).*

Add any of these you have in the refrigerator or freezer: *tops of celery,* cut roughly, a little *frozen or fresh chopped onions,* some *chopped green or red peppers* from your freezer or refrigerator, or whatever else you have "ready cooked." (Called "leftovers" by some people.)

Bring to a rolling boil.

Add *2 cans (5 ounces) chunk white chicken* cut into big pieces.

Immediately pour into a heatproof glass or metal baking dish. Put into 425° oven.

Make the topping as follows:

Put into a bowl *1 box Jiffy Corn Muffin Mix.* Mix *1 egg* with a fork.

Stir in *⅓ cup milk.* Batter should be lumpy.

Drop by spoonfuls on top of the bubbly broth.

Place in the 425° oven. Bake 15 minutes until the tops of the muffins are a golden brown color.

Serve at once.

There's no law against serving this with a spoon to make eating a pleasure.

The oven should be preheated, and the "stew" bubbling before you drop on the topping.

Chicken, Carrot, Potato Casserole

simple to make and simply delicious to eat . . . all this and easy, too

Heat oven 450°.

You need a 9″ × 13″ heatproof, glass baking dish to bake and serve in. Grease with *margarine.*

Cut a *3 pound chicken* into portion size pieces.

Shred *2 carrots* with a vegetable peeler or grater.

Slice thin *enough potatoes to make 2 cups,* and put into water.

Slice very thin *enough onions to make about ½ cup or a little more.*

Brush the chicken pieces with *1 tablespoon melted margarine.* Brown, meaty sides up, in broiler quickly. Don't burn and don't brown the other sides. Remove to a plate.

In the casserole make a layer of the carrots, top with potatoes, then the onions.

Sprinkle *salt and pepper* on each layer.

Melt 2 *tablespoons margarine,* and sprinkle over the layers.

Pour 2 *cups chicken broth,* fresh, canned or bouillon broth, over the vegetables. The broth should cover the vegetables but not the chicken.

Arrange the browned chicken pieces, meaty side up, on top of the vegetables. Sprinkle *salt and pepper* on, and brush with *1 or 2 tablespoons margarine.*

Cover the dish tightly with foil. Place in heated 450° oven. Bake 15 minutes.

Turn heat to 400°. Bake 15 minutes. Remove the foil.

Sprinkle some *dried tarragon* over the chicken. Bake 15 minutes.

Test to see if chicken is done. If not, bake 5 or so minutes longer.

Enjoy your dinner in a dish.

We sometimes substitute ½ cup white wine for ½ cup of chicken broth.

You might want to thicken the chicken broth with cornstarch or flour, but we like ours "runny" and full of that fine chicken taste.

Chicken With Delectable Macaroni And Stewed Tomatoes

just the kind of dish you like!

Heat oven 350°.

Remove any fat and skin from *2½ or 3 pound fryer chicken cut into 8 pieces.*

Sprinkle *1 teaspoon salt* over the chicken pieces. Let stand 15 minutes.

Put *3 cups water* and *1 teaspoon salt* into a saucepan. Bring to a boil.

Add *1 cup macaroni* slowly. Bring back to a boil. Boil 7 minutes. Drain in a strainer.

Dice *1 small red or green pepper.*

Put *1 can (14½ ounces) stewed tomatoes* into a bowl. Cut the large pieces tomatoes into smaller pieces.

Add *1 tablespoon minced instant onions,* the cooked macaroni, the diced red or green pepper, *1 box (10 ounces) or 2 cups frozen peas* and *1 cup chicken bouillon broth* made from 1 chicken bouillon powder or cube mixed with 1 cup water.

Place *¼ cup flour* on a plate.

Coat the chicken pieces with flour. Remove any excess flour by patting it off.

Heat a large skillet on high heat until hot. Add *3 tablespoons oil* and *1 tablespoon soft margarine.*

With a pair of tongs put the chicken pieces, meaty side down, into the skillet. Brown, turning the heat to medium high. Turn over, brown the other side. Do not cook, just brown quickly.

As the chicken pieces brown, remove them to the baking dish.

When all have been added, pour the stewed tomato mixture into the baking dish. Cover tightly with foil.

Place in 350° oven. Bake 1 hour.

This dish is now ready to eat.

Tip: If you make this dish early or freeze it and want to reheat it, change the recipe to 1 can (14½ ounces) stewed tomatoes and add 1 can (8 ounces) stewed tomatoes and make 1½ cups chicken bouillon broth. The rest of the recipe is the same. Now you will have juice to reheat this dish.

Chicken, Peas, Rice Dish

here's a meal in a baking dish, and it's not a gooey mixture either . . . the chicken looks so pretty on top of this dish

Heat oven 375°.

Clean, cut up one *3 or 3½ pound chicken* into 8 pieces.

Salt lightly. Let stand 10 minutes.

Get out a rectangular baking dish about 9 × 13½ inches.

If you have made our *"Toasted Dried Onion Mix," use 3 tablespoons* of it; otherwise make it as follows:

Put 3 tablespoons minced dried onions into a small skillet on medium high heat. Cook and stir the onions, taking the skillet off and on the heat so the onions don't burn but turn a golden brown color. This takes about 3 minutes. This "toasting" adds a subtle flavor to the onions.

Cool immediately by spreading out on a piece of wax paper or on a large plate.

Now make our "Homemade Dried Onion Mix":

Put into a large bowl *2 Herb-Ox Instant Onion Broth powders, 2 Herb-Ox Instant Beef Broth powders, ¼ teaspoon sugar, ¼ teaspoon celery salt, ½ teaspoon oil* and the 3 tablespoons Toasted Dried Onion Mix. Mix together with your hands or a large spoon.

Remove 2 tablespoons and set aside to use later.

To the remainder add *1 cup uncooked rice* and *1 box (10 ounces) frozen peas*, broken apart. Mix all together.

Make a layer of this mixture in the baking dish.

Bring to a boil *4 cups water* mixed with *2 chicken bouillon powders.*

Pour over the rice layer.

Arrange the chicken pieces on top.

Grind a *little pepper* on, and sprinkle the 2 tablespoons Dried Onion Soup Mix over the chicken pieces (flavors and browns them).

The chicken broth should not cover the tops of the chicken.

Cover the baking dish tightly with foil.

Place in 375° oven; bake 30 minutes. Remove foil. Baste chicken. Bake uncovered 30 minutes.

The rice, chicken and peas are ready.

For a change you can substitute frozen mixed vegetables for the peas.

This is a casserole dish you will make over and over again.

Chicken Vegetable Casserole

has all the "goodies" in one baking dish . . . and the "goodies" taste as good as the chicken

You need an 8¾ × 13½ inch baking dish.

Cut a *3 or 3½ pound chicken* into 8 pieces. Remove the backs; cut off the wing tips. Remove the skin and any fat.

Salt lightly with *¾ teaspoon salt.* Let stand 15 minutes.

Chop *½ cup celery, ½ cup onion* and *½ cup green peppers.*

Heat a skillet on medium high heat. Add *2 tablespoons oil.* Stir in the chopped onion, celery and green pepper.

Cook and stir 2 minutes. Put lid on. Turn heat to low. Cook 5 minutes. Drain over a bowl. Save the oil.

Pour *1 can (10¾ ounces) Chicken Noodle Soup* and *1*

can (12¾ ounces) Cream of Chicken Soup into a large saucepan.

Add *1¼ cups milk* and the onion mixture. Cook and stir 5 minutes. Remove from heat.

Put *1 box (10 ounces) frozen mixed vegetables* into a bowl. Stir in *½ teaspoon salt* and *⅛ teaspoon pepper*. Add to the soup mixture. Let stand.

Dip the chicken pieces into *¼ cup flour*. Shake off excess.

Put the oil from the bowl and *3 more tablespoons oil* into the skillet. Heat until hot.

Place, without crowding, chicken pieces, meaty side down, into the skillet. Brown quickly and nicely. Remove to a plate and brown the rest of the chicken pieces. Brown on meaty side only. As the chicken browns, remove with a pair of tongs to a plate. When all are browned, place down the middle of the baking dish.

Bring the soup mixture in the saucepan to a boil. Pour over the chicken pieces. Cover tightly with foil. Bake in 350° oven 1 hour and 15 minutes.

Chicken Shortcake

Bake *Baking Powder Biscuits,* split and spread with *margarine.*

Fry *¼ cup chopped onion, ¼ cup chopped celery* until onions are soft and clear in 2 tablespoons oil.

Stir in *1 can Cream of Mushroom Soup* mixed with *⅓ cup milk.*

Heat and stir so it doesn't stick.

Add *2 cups canned or cooked chicken* diced.

Add *1 cup drained peas.*

Heat until hot only.

Add *salt* and *pepper,* if needed.

When the chicken is bubbly hot, spoon it between and on top of the biscuits.

Old Fashioned Skillet Dinner

with "everything" in it

Chop *1 cup onions, 1 cup celery* and mince *1 cup carrots.*

Heat a large skillet hot. Cook, stir *1 pound ground beef*

until no red shows. Remove to a plate. Sprinkle *1 teaspoon salt* over and mix.

Wash and wipe the skillet.

Put *1 cup whole groats* into the skillet.

On high heat, cook, stir the groats, taking off and on the heat. Cook, stir about 5 minutes. Don't burn. Take off heat. Stir in *2 tablespoons margarine.*

In a saucepan bring *2½ cups chicken broth*, the chopped onions, celery, carrots and *1 can sliced mushrooms* (4 ounces) and the ground beef and its juice to a rolling boil. Pour the boiling mixture over the groats in the skillet. Bring back to a boil. Cover. Turn heat to low. Simmer about 15 to 20 minutes.

Add *salt* and a good grind or shake of *pepper* if needed.

Serve hot, hot!

This is a quickie dinner.

Beef Chow Mein Skillet Dinner

"Sophie style" . . . everything into the skillet

Chop *½ cup onions, ½ cup scallions* and *1 cup celery* cut on the slant.

Drain *1 jar (4 ounces) pimento* and cut into small pieces.

Open *1 can (16 ounces) bean sprouts.* Run under cold water and drain.

Open *1 can (8 ounces) water chestnuts*, cut into quarters or slices, *1 can (4 ounces) sliced mushrooms* and *1 can bamboo shoots*, drained. If you wish, add *½ to 1 box (12 ounces) frozen snow peas.*

Heat a large skillet hot. Add *1 pound ground beef.* Cook, stir until no red shows. Sprinkle *½ teaspoon salt* over and mix.

Add the vegetables and *2½ cups chicken broth.* Bring to a boil.

Add *1 cup rice.* Stir well, so the rice doesn't stay on top but is mixed through. Mix in *1 teaspoon salt.*

Bring back to a boil. Cover; turn heat to low. Simmer about 25 minutes until rice is done.

Serve hot, and pass some soy sauce if you like.

Sprinkle on top some chow mein canned noodles; or see our recipe under "H" for Homemade Chow Mein Noodles, and make them ahead of time.

Beef And Vegetable Skillet Dinner

yes, the whole dinner is cooked and served right in the skillet and it looks and tastes tempting! . . . a true Penny Pincher . . . it's made on one burner

Buy a whole piece of *Round Steak* cut ½ inch thick—about 1¼ pounds.

Peel and cut *3 large carrots* into 2 inch pieces, *3 large red or white new potatoes* each into quarters (we leave the skins on especially the red ones) and *3 large onions* cutting so they won't fall apart each into quarters. Tip: The root, not the tail, part will hold it together if you cut the hairy part off but leave the white part underneath to hold the onions. Chop *2 tablespoons parsley fine.*

Cut the round steak into 2 inch wide and about 3 inch long pieces.

Heat a large skillet with *2 tablespoons oil* until hot on second high heat. When hot put in some of the pieces of steak without crowding and brown. Continue until all are browned and place on a large plate. Sprinkle *salt and pepper* on.

Put into the skillet *1 can (10½ ounces) Beef Broth, 1 Beef Bouillon Powder, 2 cups water* and any juice that runs onto the plate where the beef is.

In a screw top jar put *6 tablespoons water* and *5½ tablespoons flour*. Shake well so there are no lumps.

Bring the beef broth mixture to a boil. With a wooden spoon keep stirring as you pour the thickening in. Cook, stir until the sauce thickens. Add *1 large bay leaf* cut into 4 pieces.

Arrange the potatoes, carrots, onions and the beef pieces so they look nice. Sprinkle a little *salt* and *pepper* on the potatoes, carrots and onions.

Bring to a boil. Turn heat to low. Cover with a piece of wax paper or preferably foil, then put a lid on top.

Simmer 1 hour. The steak will be done and so will the vegetables. Taste to see if it needs salt or pepper but don't oversalt.

Serve the skillet dinner in the skillet. Doesn't it look pretty?

Ring Around The Skillet

what is? . . . why, beef and cabbage and red, red tomatoes and plump potatoes with a sauce to accent everything . . . and it's your dinner in a skillet . . . takes only an hour to cook

Buy a ½ inch whole *Round steak*—about 1¼ pounds. Cut into 2 × 3 inch pieces. Set aside.

Set the following vegetables aside each one separately: Shred *1 head green small cabbage* after washing. Peel and cut into thin slices *2 large new red or white potatoes.* Slice thin *1 large onion.* Drain *2 cans (2 pounds) whole tomatoes* in a strainer over a bowl. Without mashing the tomatoes squeeze out the seeds over the strainer.

Heat a large skillet with *2 tablespoons oil.* When hot, brown the steak slices without crowding and without burning the skillet. Remove the steaks to a large plate but leave the good brownings in the skillet. Sprinkle *salt* and *pepper* lightly over the beef, also over the vegetables. Don't use a heavy hand.

Melt *3 tablespoons margarine or butter* in the skillet. Take off heat. Stir in *6 tablespoons flour.* Stir in *2 cups broth* and *1 tablespoon Worcestershire Sauce.* Strain if you feel any little pieces in the skillet. Cook, stir until the sauce comes to a boil and thickens. Remove ½ of the sauce.

Arrange as follows in circles. Make a circle of the shredded cabbage around the outside rim of the skillet. Next arrange the beef around the skillet, next the potatoes in the center and the onions on top.

Sprinkle salt and pepper lightly over each food. Pour the rest of the sauce over the beef.

Arrange the tomatoes on top of the cabbage cutting the tomatoes in halves to add a pretty accent to the dish.

Melt *¼ cup margarine or butter.* Pour over the onions and potatoes.

This makes a pretty picture. Bring to a boil on high heat. Turn heat to low. Cover with a piece of foil, then a lid. Let simmer gently 1 hour. It is ready to serve. Sprinkle *2 tablespoons chopped parsley* over the onions and potatoes. Serve.

Skillet Made
"Beef And Stuffing" Dinner

and the vegetables too, a true Penny Pincher, since it's made on one burner

You need *1 package frozen (18 ounces) Far Eastern Vegetable Mixture* or other fresh or frozen vegetable mixture.

You need *1¼ pound piece of Whole Round Steak* cut ½ inch thick. Cut this into 2 × 3 inch strips. Set aside.

Heat a large skillet hot with *2 tablespoons oil.* Without crowding, brown the pieces of steak until all have been browned. Put onto a bowl. Salt lightly and mix with your hands. Set aside.

Peel and slice thin *2 medium potatoes.* Set aside in water.

Make the Bread Stuffing: You need *½ package (16 ounces) Cube Stuffing* (Herb Seasoned). Put into a large bowl. Chop fine *1 cup onions, ½ cup celery,* peel and grate *1 small carrot.* Heat a skillet with the onions, celery and *½ cup margarine or butter.* Cook and stir 2 minutes. Turn heat to low. Cover. Cook until onions are soft and clear—about 10 to 15 minutes. Add to the bread stuffing and also the grated carrots. Mix gently. Beat *1 large egg* with a fork. Mix with the bread stuffing. Set aside.

Put about *1⅔ cups chicken broth* into the skillet, scraping up the good brownings, with *1 chicken bouillon broth* and *1 cup water.* Bring to a boil. Into a screw top jar put *5 tablespoons water* and *3 tablespoons flour.* Shake well so there are no lumps.

Turn the heat under the broth so it boils gently. Stir in the thickening and cook, stir quickly so no lumps form and it thickens. If there are any lumps, don't panic, just strain and put back in the skillet.

Add *salt lightly* to the package of frozen Far Eastern Vegetables or other vegetables and mix gently into the sauce.

Arrange the meat strips on top. Cover well with the potato slices overlapping them. *Salt lightly* with salt shaker and *pepper.*

Spoon the stuffing on top. Melt *2 tablespoons butter or margarine* and sprinkle over the stuffing.

Turn the heat to high. Let come to a boil. Turn heat to low. Lay a sheet of foil on top. Cover with lid.

Simmer 1 hour until done.

If you like a soft stuffing, eat as is. For a crisp topping, put on the middle shelf of your heated broiler and broil. Watch until the stuffing is crispy on top. Takes about 10 to 15 minutes.

Be careful to use a hot pad on the handle as it is hot and heavy.

Beef, Peas With Mushroom Sauce Skillet Dinner

yes, all cooked in 1 hour on top of the stove and no watching it either . . . it cooks by itself . . . why not read the paper and rest a bit?

You need *1¼ pound Whole Round Steak* and this Pasta is called *"Twisted Spaghetti."* Why? I wouldn't know because it doesn't resemble spaghetti at all. It's little 2 inch twisted pasta that looks like twisted rope and in Italian it's called Cut Fusilli. Anyhow it's good. You need 2 cups.

Cut the round steak into strips 2 × 3 inches long.

Heat a skillet with *2 tablespoons oil.* Brown, without crowding, the steak strips and put into a bowl. Mix with *1 beef bouillon powder.*

Into the skillet stir in *1 can (10¾ ounces) Cream of Mushroom soup* and *½ cup nonfat milk,* scraping up the good brownings. Stir in *1 cup water* and *1 chicken bouillon powder* and the juice that has collected from the browned strips of beef. Bring to a simmer.

Add *1 box (12 ounces) frozen green peas,* the beef strips and the pasta. Bring to a simmer.

Lay a piece of foil over. Put lid on. Turn heat to low. Simmer 1 hour when all will be done.

Your skillet dinner can be eaten at once or it can wait or it can be frozen as it reheats well.

Round Steak On Sale

Round steak is all beef and at a "penny pincher" price is one of the best buys. Watch the newspapers. You'll save money and have luscious meals. Buy as many as you can afford, and make each one into a different dish.

We have recipes that you will make over and over again.

A whole piece of round steak consists of the eye of the round, the top round and the bottom round.

Oven Baked Round Steak With Mushroom Sauce

the mushroom sauce is smooth and full of flavor

Heat oven 325°.

Cut a *1½ or 1¾ pound whole round steak,* which consists of the eye, top and bottom, into its natural sections cutting the large piece in half.

Heat a skillet with *2 tablespoons oil* until hot.

Wipe the pieces of steak.

Put *1 cup flour* into a soup plate.

One at a time, flour the round steaks and put immediately into the hot skillet without crowding. Brown quickly on one side, then quickly on the other side, adding *1 tablespoon oil* at a time *as needed.* If necessary, not to crowd the steaks, fry twice. Don't cook; just brown them.

Put the browned steaks into a heatproof, fireproof, heavy casserole. In a saucepan bring to a boil *1 can cream of mushroom soup, 1 can (4 ounces) sliced mushrooms* and *½ cup chicken broth.* Pour over the beef. Bring to a boil. Cover.

Place in 325° oven. Bake about 2 hours.

Tip: You will notice we made extra sauce here because everyone loves the sauce over whipped potatoes.

Round Steak Stuffed With Vegetables

once you've made it and it's in the oven, you can go about your business, and everyone will say, "what smells so good" ... when you eat it, it will taste just as good!

Heat oven 325°.

Chop *1 cup celery, 1 cup onions* and *3 tablespoons parsley.* Grate *¼ cup carrots*; cube into small cubes *1 cup potatoes.*

Wipe *1 whole piece round steak* cut about ½ inch thick. This is a very good buy on sale. Cut any excess fat off on the outside. Cut the round steak in half lengthwise following its natural separation. One piece will be used for the bottom, and the other half will top the stuffing.

Sprinkle both pieces lightly with *salt* on both sides.

Heat a skillet with *3 tablespoons oil* and *1 tablespoon margarine.* Add the 1 cup chopped onions. Cook, stir until soft and clear, takes about five minutes.

Put into a large bowl the onions, carrots, celery, potatoes and parsley. Add *¼ teaspoon salt* and a good grind of *pepper.* Mix together lightly.

Heat the skillet hot with *3 tablespoons oil.*

Flour both sides of the steaks. Shake off excess flour. Brown the beef on one side quickly; then the other side.

Lay 1 piece into a heavy casserole.

Cut 2 pieces foil as long as the meat is and about 3½ inches wide. Put 1 inch of this foil under the meat on each side and let the rest of the foil stand up to enclose the filling. Spoon the filling in. The foil will keep the filling from falling out.

Put the other browned slice of steak on top. You do not cover the top piece of steak with foil, as we want it to bake and not steam.

Bring to a boil *½ cup canned beef bouillon broth* with *1 cup canned chicken broth.*

In a screw-top jar put *3 tablespoons water, 2 tablespoons and 1½ teaspoons flour.* Shake until dissolved. Stir this thickening into the boiling broth. Cook, stir 2 minutes.

Spoon the sauce around the meat but not on it. Bring to a boil. Cover.

Place in 325° oven. Bake about 1 hour and 45 minutes until the beef is tender.

Serve hot with the hot sauce.

For a change, instead of the gravy, use 1 can (1 pound) stewed tomatoes.

Oven Baked Round Steak With Stewed Tomatoes

and a touch of onions and green peppers

When round steak is on sale, you can stock up on as many steaks as you can afford and either freeze them or make one into this recipe and the rest into recipes that follow. This means you'll have "good eating with no work" as all of these Round Steak recipes are delicious reheated.

Our "bargain" steaks weigh about 1¾ pounds and are a little over ½ inch thick. We have ample portions for 4. The steaks are the whole piece of round, the top and bottom round, and eye of the round.

Cut the *round steak* into its natural pieces, cutting the large piece in half. You will have 5, 6 or 7 pieces.

Wipe the beef dry.

Heat a large skillet with *2 tablespoons oil.* Tip: Put some oil in a cup; it's easier to measure and spoon out of the cup than the bottle.

When the skillet is hot, *flour* each piece, one at a time, and put it into the hot skillet. Brown on one side, then the other. If you need more *oil,* add 1 spoonful at a time as needed. As the beef is browned, arrange in a heavy, fireproof, heatproof casserole. Do this until all are browned.

Make the sauce:

Mix together in a saucepan *2 cans (8 ounces) stewed tomatoes, ¼ cup chopped onions, ¼ cup chopped green pepper* and *1 can (6 ounces) V8 Juice.* Bring to a boil.

In a screw-top jar put *¼ cup cold tap water* and *2 tablespoons flour*. Shake until all the flour is combined.

Stir into the boiling vegetables. Cook, stir until it thickens, takes a few minutes.

Pour over the beef.

Heat oven 325°.

Place the casserole with cover on the middle rack of the oven.

Bake about 1 hour 45 minutes to 2 hours.

Tip: Depending on your stove, after cooking at 325° for 1 hour, you may have to reduce temperature to 300°.

Oven Baked Beans And Rice With Round Steak

the rice gets a little "gooey" but all in all it's very tasty

Heat oven 325°.

Cut a *1½ or 1¾ pound whole round steak,* which consists of the eye and the top and bottom round steak, into its sections, cutting the large piece in half.

Heat a skillet with *2 tablespoons oil* until hot.

Wipe the pieces of steak.

Put *1 cup flour* into a soup plate. One at a time, flour the round steaks and put into the hot skillet and brown quickly on one side, then the other, adding *oil* as needed. Remove to a preferably heavy casserole, putting the steaks on one side.

In a bowl mix together *1 cup brown rice* with *1 can (15 ounces) kidney beans,* washed under running water.

Arrange on the other side of the casserole.

Pour *2¼ cups and 2 tablespoons chicken broth* over the rice-bean mixture.

Bring to a boil. Cover.

Place in 325° oven. Bake about 1 hour and 45 minutes.

Oven Baked
Round Steak With Sauce

this is very rich tasting

Heat oven 325°.

Cut a *1½ or 1¾ pound whole round steak,* which consists of top, bottom and eye, into its natural sections, cutting the largest part in half.

Heat a skillet with *2 tablespoons oil* until hot.

Wipe the pieces of steak dry.

Put about *1 cup flour* into a soup plate.

One at a time flour the round steaks and put in the skillet until all have been browned, but don't crowd. Do this twice, if necessary. Brown on both sides, adding more *oil* as needed, a tablespoon at a time. Tip: Put the oil in a cup for easier measuring.

As the steaks brown, remove to a heatproof, fireproof casserole.

Put into a saucepan *1 can beef broth, ½ can chicken broth* and *¼ cup red wine*. Bring to a boil.

Put into a screw-top jar *¼ cup chicken broth* and *2 tablespoons flour*. Shake well until the flour is absorbed.

Stir into the boiling broth. Cook, stir about 2 minutes.

Pour over the meat in the casserole.

Put on top *4 whole allspice, 2 large dry bay leaves,* each cut into halves, and *¼ teaspoon onion powder*.

Bring to a boil on top of the stove.

Cover. Put in the 325° oven. Bake about 2 hours.

You might want to turn the heat to 300° if the steak is cooking too fast.

Top Stuffed Steaks

one of the easiest ways to have a delicious stuffing without too much work . . . just pop it in the oven and it bakes to luscious goodness—oh, yes, and it makes a nice sauce, too!

Heat oven 325°.

Cut a *whole piece of round steak, about 1¾ pounds,* into its natural sections, cutting the largest piece in half. (A whole piece of round steak, when on sale, is a great bargain.) *Salt* steak lightly on both sides.

Heat a skillet with *3 tablespoons oil* until hot.

Flour the steak pieces; shake off excess.

Brown quickly on one side; turn and brown the other side.

Arrange in one layer in a heavy casserole or Dutch oven.

Make the stuffing:

Into a large bowl put *4 cups Pepperidge Farm cubed seasoned stuffing.*

Chop *enough onions to make 2 cups,* grate *enough carrots to make ½ cup,* chop *enough celery to make 1 cup.* (We use the stalks of celery with leaves, which we always have handy in our freezer.)

Saute the onions in a skillet with *¼ cup oil* and *2 tablespoons margarine* until soft and clear; don't brown.

With 2 large spoons mix the carrots and the celery with the bread cubes. Add the sauteed onions and mix gently together. Mix in *¾ teaspoon salt* and a good grind of *pepper* and *3 tablespoons chopped parsley.*

Mix *1 large egg* with a fork. Gently mix with bread cubes mixture.

Shape gently into large balls, don't flatten, and arrange on top of the browned beef.

Make the sauce:

Bring to a boil *1 cup canned beef bouillon broth and ½ cup canned chicken broth.*

In a screw-top jar put *3 tablespoons cold tap water,* add *1 tablespoon and 1½ teaspoons flour* on top. Shake to combine. There should be no lumps. If there are, strain it.

Stir into the boiling broth. Cook, stir one minute.

Carefully, so as not to use too much and not to pour over

the filling, pour just enough sauce to come just below the beef, not on top. Save the rest of the sauce to use later.

Bring the casserole with the meat and stuffing to a boil.

Put into 325° oven. Bake 1 hour. Check whether there is still sauce in the casserole. Bring the sauce to a boil and add as you did before. If necessary, turn the heat to 300° if it is bubbling too much. Continue to bake until meat is tender, takes about 1 hour and 45 to 50 minutes.

Meat Loaf

for a meat loaf dinner and a second day "no cook dinner"

Grease a 3 quart oven-proof glass casserole.

Preheat oven 450°.

You need *2 pounds ground beef.*

Cut off the *crusts from 3 slices white bread.* Crumble together with *1 cup nonfat milk* until the milk is absorbed.

Add *2 eggs, 1½ teaspoons salt* and a good *grind of pepper.*

Grate *2 medium large onions* over.

Mix everything together well.

Lay the ground beef on top. Mix together with your clean hands.

Taste to see if salt or pepper is needed.

With your hands or a large spoon, scoop into the middle of the greased casserole into a free standing shaped meat loaf. Smooth the top with your hands lightly to make it look pretty. The meat loaf tastes better if you don't handle it too much.

Place in the preheated 450° oven. Bake 15 minutes. Pour about ¼ cup sauce over the meat. Turn the heat to 325°. Bake 45 minutes or until done.

Serve hot the first day with the vegetables that you baked along with it in the oven. Serve sliced cold for a second dinner.

Tip: The best way to grate onions without crying is to freeze them and they will grate beautifully. We use a flat grater. It fits nicely over a bowl.

Vegetables For Meat Loaf Dinner

you bake these in the oven along with the meat loaf

Mix *1 chicken bouillon cube* with *1 cup water.*

Bring to a boil.

Peel and cut *4 good tasting carrots,* medium size, into slices and *4 medium potatoes* into quarters. Put into a heatproof casserole that fits and will fit in your oven.

Pour the boiling broth over the potatoes and carrots. Place in the 325° oven and bake along with the meat loaf until the meat loaf is cooked, which is about 45 minutes. Taste to be sure they are cooked; if not, cook until they are.

You have your meat loaf and two good vegetables ready for your dinner.

Sauce For Meat Loaf Dinner

Mix together *½ cup catsup* with *1 teaspoon onion, chicken or beef bouillon powder.*

Stir in *1 cup water.*

Cook/stir until hot.

You can serve this sauce with the hot meat loaf and also pour a little on the meat loaf and around the meat loaf after it has been browned and the heat is turned to 325°.

Custard For Dessert For The Meat Loaf Dinner

with custard for dessert cooked at one time in the oven to save energy—yours and the electricity

Heat oven 325°.

Mix *2 eggs* with an egg beater or fork.

Stir in *⅓ cup sugar* and *⅛ teaspoon salt.*

Stir in *2 cups milk* and *1 teaspoon vanilla.*

Spoon into 6 custard cups.

Place in a shallow pan of hot water.

Sprinkle a little *nutmeg* on top of each.

Place in 325° oven.

Bake 25 to 30 minutes.

A 20-Minute Fish Dinner

that means 20 minutes only to bake the fish . . . the "get ready" needs some chopping

You need enough *"fillet" of fish for four:* turbot, sole, striped bass, red snapper, whiting. Keep in refrigerator until you are ready to cook it.

You need a shallow baking dish. Grease with *oil or margarine.*

Preheat the oven 400°.

Chop *2 tablespoons dill* or *parsley* fine.

Grate *2 carrots* very fine.

Chop very fine a *medium onion* and *1 stalk celery.*

Make *¼ cup soft bread crumbs.*

Sprinkle a little *salt* and *pepper* over the fillets.

Make a bed of the onions, carrots, celery. Give it a grind of pepper.

Arrange the fish on this bed.

Make the sauce as follows: Melt *1½ tablespoons margarine.* Take off heat. Stir in *1½ tablespoons flour.* Stir in *2 cups chicken broth* and *½ cup nonfat dry milk.*

Cook/stir, bring to a boil. Turn heat to medium high. Cook/stir 2 minutes. Add 2 tablespoons chopped dill.

Pour over the fish, and the rest of vegetable mixture.

Place in 400° oven. Bake until fish is done. Test by sticking a fork in and if the fish is no longer translucent, the fish is done. How long does it take to cook? That depends on the thickness and size of the fillets. It can be 20 minutes.

Tip: If you have a shallow baking pan that can cook on direct heat (as on top of the stove) and also is heat proof in the oven, this makes for shorter cooking time in the oven, as you bring the fish (or other food) to a simmer on top of the stove and then put in the oven to bake. It takes a dish much longer to come to a simmer in the oven than on direct heat on top of a burner.

Why all this? Because, if you need to buy a shallow baking dish, it pays in the long run to buy one that does both these jobs. What would I suggest? The best is an iron one with heavy porcelain covering it all over inside and out. Can serve on the table; or aluminum ones with Teflon (easier to wash) are O.K. So is a Corning one (watch that it doesn't stick) . . . can use on the table as well and washes easy after soaking.

Fish Chowder

a meal in a soup plate . . . this isn't French or Italian . . . this is plain American . . . for those of us who can get fresh fish and for those of us who have to "do with" frozen fish

You need *enough fish fillets for 4*. Keep in refrigerator until ready to cook.

In a deep, large, fireproof casserole put in *2 cans (13¾ ounces) chicken broth* (makes almost 4 cups) and *2 chicken bouillon powders* with *4 cups water* to make 8 cups broth.

Add *½ cup green pepper, cubed, ½ cup chopped onions, ½ cup chopped celery, ¼ cup chopped scallions* and *½ cup minced carrots.*

Add *1 cup potatoes, ¼ cup rice, ¼ cup Orzo pasta, 2 bay leaves* and *2 whole allspice.*

Cook 20 minutes. Remove bay leaf. Cook 10 minutes. You can let this stand until you are ready to eat. Steam or cook *½ of a fresh cauliflower* cut into tiny little flowerets, takes about 3 minutes to steam. Set aside.

Right before eating, add the fish in large bite size pieces and *1 can (1 pound) stewed tomatoes*. Cook about 5 minutes.

Add steamed cauliflower. Cook 2 minutes.

Add *salt and pepper* to taste and a *dash of Tabasco.*

Serve piping hot.

Fish Soup Or Chowder

almost like a stew and your whole meal—vegetables and protein—all deliciously merged into your soup plate . . . you cook once for twice—a real bonus!

You need *2 fresh or frozen fish.* We use Turbot fish fillets. One you keep whole; the other you cut into bite-size pieces.

Cut roughly into pieces *½ cup each onion, celery, green pepper, scallions, carrots.*

Cut into large cubes *1 cup potatoes*. Put into *cold water.*

Measure *¼ cup rice* and *¼ cup Orzo* (a pasta that looks just like rice); or use elbow macaroni.

Open *1 can (1 pound) tomatoes,* strained so that there are no seeds in the juice.

In a large saucepan or kettle put in *2 cans (13¾ ounces) chicken broth or 4 cups chicken broth and 4 cups water* and

2 chicken bouillon powders or cubes. (This makes 8 cups broth altogether.)

Add all the vegetables including the potatoes.

Bring to a boil.

Add ¼ cup rice, ¼ cup Orzo (or elbow macaroni), *2 bay leaves* and *2 whole allspice.*

Bring back to a boil. Turn heat to medium. Cook 20 minutes.

Remove the bay leaves.

Put in the whole fish fillet. (This is for the next day's fish salad dinner. Remember? You're cooking "once for twice.")

Let cook 10 minutes. With a slotted spoon remove the whole fish fillet to a plate. Put in refrigerator, covered.

When ready to eat, bring the vegetable mixture to a boil.

Drop in the bite size pieces of fish.

Cook about 5 minutes until the fish is done. Taste it to see. Don't overcook.

Add the tomatoes and tomato broth. Cook 2 minutes.

Add *salt and pepper* to taste and *a little shake of cayenne pepper* to taste.

We always have on hand when we make this fish dish either steamed cauliflower flowerets or tiny broccoli flowerets. This we add at the last minute with the fish as an added vegetable to make this a "Dinner in a Dish."

Nutritious as well a delicious!

Tip: To "strain" the tomatoes, after you have opened 1 can (1 pound) tomatoes, put a strainer over a bowl.

Pour the tomatoes into the strainer.

Open a tomato (one at a time) *over the strainer.* With your fingers remove the seeds letting them fall into the strainer. Cut the piece of hard stem off the pulp. Place the pulp tomatoes onto a plate. In this way you get the pulp without the seeds. Set aside. Strain the seeds out, so there are no seeds in the juice in the bowl. Set aside.

Cheese, Salmon Or Tuna, Mixed Vegetable Omelette

a meal in an omelette

Heat broiler.

Drain a *can (7¾ ounces) salmon or tuna.* With a fork cut into chunks. Cube *½ cup Velveeta Cheese.*

With a fork beat *enough eggs for four.* Add *salt* and *pepper* to taste.

Heat a large skillet with a fireproof handle or cover the handle completely with foil.

Add *3 tablespoons oil* and *⅓ cup water.* Add *1 box (10 ounces) mixed vegetables.* Bring to a boil; turn heat to medium. Cover. Cook until done. If there is any water left in the skillet, remove it.

Add the salmon or tuna and the cheese. Let cheese start to melt.

Pour the eggs over. Lift the edges as they cook, so the raw eggs run under and cook. When the bottom of the eggs are browned, place under broiler, takes a few minutes only for the top to brown and cook.

Hold the handle with a hot pad, not to burn yourself, and serve.

We usually heat some canned stewed tomatoes and serve it in deep saucers to go with this omelette.

For a change you could sprinkle grated Parmesan cheese on top of the omelette, instead of the cubed cheese.

This is certainly a "quickie" dish and enjoyable, too.

Baked Casserole Of Veal Chops, Potatoes And Beans

with potatoes to flavor the veal . . . the veal flavors the potatoes . . . and the onions take care of both

Heat oven 325°.

You need *shoulder veal chops* cut thin, about ¼ inch thick.

Heat a fireproof, heatproof casserole with *2 tablespoons oil.* When hot, brown the veal on one side, then the other. Remove to a plate.

Rub *salt, pepper* and *1 teaspoon Italian Herbs* over the veal.

Peel and slice *enough potatoes* about ⅛ inch thick and *1 large onion for four.*

Make a bed of ½ of the potatoes; then put ½ the onions on top. Sprinkle a little *salt* and *pepper* on. Make a second layer. Arrange the veal chops on top.

Add a *cup of beef broth or chicken broth.*

Cover with foil; then put a lid on. Bring to a simmer.

Put in 325° oven. Bake until tender, takes about 30 to 45 minutes. Remove the lid. Sprinkle *seasoned bread crumbs* on top. Spoon melted *margarine or butter* on top.

Bake until crumbs brown; or we prefer to put under broiler to golden brown the crumbs.

Broiled Mixed Grill

a quickie for Working Mothers or Fathers, too

Drain *1 can (1 pound) whole small potatoes.* Dip into *4 tablespoons oil or melted margarine.* Place on a shallow broiling pan.

Slice into thick slices enough *tomatoes* for the family. Set aside.

Put *1 package Swift's Frozen Sausages* on the broiling pan.

Broil the sausages and potatoes about 5 minutes. Turn over.

Put the thick, sliced tomatoes on the broiling pan. Sprinkle some *Parmesan cheese* on top.

Arrange in a heap *1 can pork and beans, removing the pork,* which is only a hunk of fat and nothing else, and sprinkle a little *brown sugar* and some *melted margarine* on top.

Drain *1 can zucchini squash.* Put on the broiling pan. Sprinkle on some *melted margarine* and some grated *Parmesan cheese.*

Broil about 5 minutes.

For a change, substitute canned hominy topped with margarine instead of the potatoes, and add it when you add the tomatoes.

A Broiled Ham
Sweet Potato Dinner

and "done" in minutes

Slice and remove fat from *4 (½ inch thick) slices of canned ham.* If some of your "eaters" want a slice more, add it.

Place at one end on a cookie sheet lined with foil (for easier washing). Brush with *soft margarine.* Put a *slice of pineapple* over each slice of ham.

Drain *1 can thick, sweet yams or sweet potatoes.* Arrange next to the ham. Don't crowd. Spoon a *little of the juice* over the potatoes.

At the other end put *thick slices of tomatoes.* Brush with *softened margarine.* Sprinkle a little *salt* on.

Heat broiler.

When ready to eat, put cookie sheet on the middle rack of your broiler-oven. Broil 5 minutes.

Brush the tomatoes with some *margarine.*

Sprinkle some *grated cheese*, Parmesan or Romano or other hard cheese, over the tomatoes.

Broil 5 minutes more.

Everything should be ready to eat.

Another Broiled Ham Dinner

you've got it made right in your broiler . . . and so tasty and good . . . and quick

Cut a *1 pound canned ham* into 4 slices and place on a shallow broiling pan (no rack).

Mix together *¼ teaspoon ground cloves* with *¼ cup brown sugar.* Rub over the tops of the ham slices.

Put 2 foil pans on the broiling pan.

Put *1 can (1 pound) sauerkraut* into one.

Put *1 can (1 pound) cut green beans,* with some of the canned ham broth (gelatin) over it into the other foil pan. Dot with *margarine.*

Put under broiler. Broil about 10 minutes.

You can broil some peach halves along with this, sprinkling a little brown sugar on.

Broiler Franks And Beans

Make slits about 1 inch apart in *enough frankfurters for the family* (or even for 1 or 2 persons), but don't cut all the way through. Put on a piece of foil on a cookie sheet.

Into 1 or 2 foil pans or fireproof dishes, put *1 or 2 cans vegetarian beans or pork and beans* (remove the piece of fat). Stir in *1 or 2 tablespoons catsup.*

Into another foil pan or fireproof dish, put *1 can (1 pound) sauerkraut, or 2 cans* depending on the family's appetite. Put on a cookie sheet.

Turn broiler on.

Place the cookie sheet on second rack from the bottom of the oven. Broil until everything is piping hot, takes about 10 to 15 minutes.

Serve at once.

Broiled Hamburger Dinner

you broil everything at once and it's all ready to eat

Mix together lightly *2 tablespoons catsup* with *1 pound ground beef* and add *½ teaspoon salt.*

Make into 4 patties and put on a shallow broiling pan.

Drain *1 can sliced potatoes.* Melt *4 tablespoons margarine.* Dip each slice of potato into the margarine and arrange on the broiling pan.

Drain *1 can green beans.* Mix with *1 tablespoon melted margarine.* Put onto foil, shaping up the ends to make a large cup to hold the beans. Sprinkle grated *Parmesan cheese* on top.

Broil until the hamburgers are cooked as you like them, turning once to brown the other side.

Pork, Sauerkraut And Potatoes

Preheat oven 450°.

Grease a heatproof casserole.

Slice *enough potatoes for 4.* Put into cold water.

Slice *1 large onion* very thin.

You need *1½ pounds pork chops*—enough for 4.

Heat a skillet hot with *3 tablespoons oil* and *1 tablespoon margarine.* One at a time, *flour* the pork chops and put in the skillet and brown. Remove to a plate. Sprinkle *salt* and *pepper* over the chops.

Leave the good brownings in the skillet, but remove any oil.

Add in the skillet *1 can (1 pound) sauerkraut* and *1 can (1 pound) stewed tomatoes* and a good *pinch of sugar.* Cook, stir until it comes to a boil.

Pour this into the casserole.

Arrange the pork chops on top. Make a layer of the onions on top. Then top with the potatoes. *Salt* them lightly and sprinkle some *pepper* on. Dot with *margarine or butter*. Shake some *Paprika* on top.

Cover. Place in 450° oven. Let come to a simmer. Turn heat to 350°. Bake 1 hour.

Sausage, Macaroni, Vegetable Melange

an inexpensive protein dinner that tastes good, and it's "easy cooking"; you cook "once for twice"

Cook *4 ounces macaroni* according to directions on package. Drain.

Wash *1 cup lentils* under running water. Cover with *1 cup cold tap water*. Let stand 1 hour.

Defrost *1 package Swift's Frozen Sausage,* preferably Italian Style or Smoked, or The Original. (None of these have nitrate in them. Many people like Jones' Frozen Sausage which also has no nitrate in them.)

Cut the sausage into ¼ inch slices. No matter which sausage you use, get the fat out as follows: heat the sausages with 2 tablespoons water until the water is evaporated, gently punching with a fork to help get the fat out.

Turn the heat down. Cook, stir until the fat comes out of the sausages and the sausages brown lightly, takes about 5 minutes. Remove the sausages, not the fat, to a plate covered with a paper towel. Mop the fat up with another towel.

Wash enough *zucchini squash* being careful to rub off or wipe off any "prickles" on the skin of the zucchini. Don't remove the skin, though. You can also use yellow squash *to make 3 cups* sliced ¼ inch thick.

Put *3 cans (15 ounces) Hunt's Tomato Sauce, Special,* or other tomato sauce that has onion, celery and green pepper in it (read the labels) into a large fireproof casserole or "kettle." Bring to a boil. Add the lentils, the sliced zucchini and *¼ teaspoon basil.*

Cook, stir; bring back to a boil.

Turn the heat to medium low, cook, stir now and then for 15 minutes.

Add the sausages, the macaroni, *2 tablespoons burgundy wine*. Cook, stir until hot adding *salt and pepper* to taste, takes a few minutes only.

You can eat one for dinner and freeze the rest. Easy cooking? Yes.

"Gallo" Burgundy of California wine is fine and inexpensive; and for those who drink wine with their meals, this is nice to drink, too.

Zucchini Squash Skillet Dinner

a delicious meal in minutes . . . yes, you can use yellow crook neck squash or cubes of peeled hubbard squash

Steam *4 cups cubed squash*, takes about 8 minutes, or cook in small amount of boiling water and drain well.

Put in a large skillet *1 can (12 ounces) niblet corn, 1 can (1 pound) green lima beans* strained, *1 can (14½ ounces) stewed tomatoes, 2 tablespoons flaked dried onions*, the *4 cups steamed squash, 1 teaspoon dried basil leaves, 2 tablespoons dried parsley* and *¼ teaspoon salt.*

Bring to a simmer.

Add *8 ounces Velveeta cheese,* cubed.

Cook, stir until melted, takes about 3 minutes.

Your dinner is ready.

A Dinner In An Egg

with a salad, some whole wheat bread or "Quickie Mix Biscuits" and a dessert . . . this is a quick satisfying meal

Preheat broiler.

Put 4 heatproof shallow baking dishes on a cookie sheet.

Mix together in a saucepan *1 (1 pound) can tomato sauce, 1 can (1 pound) stewed tomatoes, 1 can (4 ounces) chopped mushrooms* (optional). You can add a *few drops of tabasco* if you wish. Bring to a boil.

Pour into the four baking dishes.

Drop *2 eggs* in each dish without breaking the yolks and sprinkle a little *salt* and *pepper* on.

Put the cookie sheet with the baking dishes on the second shelf under the broiler heat.

Broil (cook) just until the whites congeal and you can see it; takes about 10 minutes.

If you wish you can sprinkle a little Parmesan cheese on top of each and let quickly brown (we usually don't).

Serve hot, hot. The yolks are runny and make a sort of a sauce, too. This mixture tastes good.

A salad made with our "House Dressing" goes lovely with this. Watercress on sale for Penny Pinchers makes a wonderful, fresh salad.

Split Pea Vegetable Protein Stew Or Vegetable Stew

a meal in a soup plate with no meat but you still have good protein, vegetables and good taste . . . how about adding an accent of Whole Wheat Muffins on the side, takes minutes to make and a pleasure to eat

Tip: While you cook this for one meal, double this so you can save electricity or gas and also save your energy by "Cooking Once for Twice," or as we also say "Eat one, freeze one."

Wash under running water *2 (12 ounces) packages yellow* or *green split peas.* Put into a large pot with *8 cups water.*

Peel, chop *1 large onion, ½ cup celery* and cube *3 large potatoes.*

Bring the water, split peas, onions, celery, potatoes to a boil.

Add *1 package (16 ounces) frozen mixed vegetables, 1 teaspoon Italian Herbs, 1 cup macaroni* and *¼ teaspoon garlic powder.* Bring back to a boil. Turn to simmer. Simmer 30 minutes. Taste. Add *salt to* taste. Simmer 30 more minutes.

Cheese, Zucchini, Cut Ziti Skillet Dinner

no meat today but it has protein and Good Taste!

You need about *1 pound zucchini, 1 pound yellow crook neck squash,* either *hard cheese or Velveeta cheese, 1 large green pepper* and either *cans of pureed tomatoes* (read the label to be sure it's tomatoes, not tomato paste) or *tomato sauce*—about *37½ ounces,* and *2 cups "cut Ziti"* which is a Pasta and comes in a box or package.

Measure the 2 cups Ziti. Set aside.

Wash, cut into ½ inch slices (don't peel) and put on 2 separate plates the zucchini and the yellow squash. *Salt* lightly. Let stand 15 minutes.

Wash, remove seeds, cut the green pepper into thin slices.

Bring some water in a saucepan to a boil. Drop in the sliced peppers. Boil 5 minutes. Strain. Remove to a plate. Let stand.

Wipe the squash.

Heat a large skillet with *2 tablespoons oil* until hot, adding more as needed. Without crowding, brown lightly all of the sliced zucchini on both sides. Put on a large plate covered with a towel to drain the fat, adding another towel on top if necessary. Set aside.

Do the same with the yellow squash. Set aside.

Put the tomato puree or sauce into a large deep saucepan.

Add *2½ cups water, 2½ teaspoons sugar, 1¼ teaspoons salt* or to taste, *1¼ teaspoons basil, 1 teaspoon oregano,* and *¾ teaspoon garlic powder.*

Bring to a simmer. Turn heat to low or simmer. Simmer 5 minutes. Stir in *1 tablespoon oil.* Remove from heat.

Wipe the skillet.

Pour in 1 cup of the sauce to cover the bottom of the skillet.

Arrange the Ziti in it in one layer. Cover with some of the sauce.

Slice the cheese very thin and make a layer on top. *A hard cheese* is best in this recipe. If you use a soft cheese like *Velveeta* cut into small chunks to make *1 cup.* Use ½ cup on this layer.

Arrange the green pepper on top.

Cover with the squash in a circle.

Cover with slices of cheese or ½ cup Velveeta. Spoon the sauce over.

Bring to a boil on top of the stove. Turn the heat to low or simmer. Lay a piece of foil on top. Cover with a lid. Simmer 30 minutes.

You can finish this at once or you can refrigerate and use later or you can freeze this dish. It does all three well.

When ready to use, preheat the broiler 15 minutes.

Sprinkle *1 cup grated Parmesan cheese* on top.

Put on the second shelf from the top burner and let brown lightly, takes about 10 minutes.

This is a lovely change from meat and you don't have to mortgage your home either.

12. VEGETABLES

BLANCHING is to boil water and put a raw food in; then boil for a short time, a few minutes only, then quickly cool the food by running under cold water. You prepare the food this way and finish cooking them by a different method. This saves "cooking time" and also "sets" the colors of vegetables.

SAUTE is to cook foods in a skillet in a small amount of fat. The recipe tells you how long.

The best way to GRATE ONIONS is to freeze them; then grate. They never make you cry, and they are much easier to grate.

Whipped Potatoes

Wash *4 mealy potatoes*. Potatoes that are not too large and are the same size cook quicker and better.

Place in a large saucepan with *water to cover*. Bring to a boil on high heat. Put lid on. Turn heat to medium high.

Cook until potatoes are soft. It takes about 30 minutes. Test by putting a fork into a potato, and if it goes into the potato easily, it is done.

Careful, not to splash, drain the potatoes in a colander.

Peel the potatoes as soon as you can handle them. Shake over heat to dry.

Cut the potatoes into quarters.

Push the potatoes through a ricer into a large bowl. They will look like rice.

Add *¼ cup soft margarine* and mix in.

Heat *½ cup and 2 tablespoons milk* until hot. Pour a little of the hot milk at a time into the potatoes, beating as you add the milk.

You may not need as much milk as we said, or you may need more milk. It depends on how many and how large the potatoes are.

Add *salt* to your taste, a little at a time until you get it to your taste. Remember, you cannot remove the salt if you add too much.

Beat the potatoes so they will be fluffy.

Our way is a "no lumps" way.

Tip: A ricer makes fluffier whipped potatoes than an electric mixer.

Hashed Brown Potatoes

Use *2 cups of your "ready cooked" potatoes, or* peel and cube *enough potatoes to make 4 cups.*

To cook, bring to a boil with *water to cover*, and *½ teaspoon salt*. Turn heat to low. Cook until done.

Drain. Shake over heat to dry. Don't burn. Let get cold.

Chop *enough onions to make about ½ cup.*

Heat a skillet hot. Add *2 tablespoons oil.*

Add the onions. Cook, stir until soft, about 5 minutes.

Add the potatoes and mix together and mash some and break up some of the potatoes.

Let cook on medium high heat 5 minutes.

Turn the heat to low.

Let brown on the bottom, takes about 30 minutes.

Use a metal spatula to see whether the bottom has browned.

Put under the preheated broiler to brown the top, takes about 10 minutes.

If you have a skillet that has a plastic handle that will burn in the oven or broiler cover it with foil, and it won't burn This is also a good tip when you want to use a skillet to bake in the oven.

Potato Pancakes

from the Sacher Hotel in Vienna, Austria to the good old USA . . . everyone loves these potato pancakes

Peel and grate *4 mealy type potatoes.*

Pour out most of liquid formed.

Stir in *1 egg* mixed with a fork, *2 tablespoons flour* and *salt to taste.*

Heat a large skillet hot with *⅓ cup oil.*

When hot, not before, spoon the potato mixture into thin cakes into the skillet and brown quickly on one side, then the other. They should be "crispy."

Remove to a plate or cookie sheet covered with paper towels.

Place in lowest heat in oven to keep hot while you fry the rest.

If you wish, you can make these early as above, but do not place in oven or overlap the fried potato cakes. Place the fried potato cakes on a foil-lined cookie sheet to reheat. Place in preheated 425° oven for 10 minutes. These are crispy thin potato cakes.

Riced Potatoes

the best ever!

These potatoes are feather light, need no fat or seasoning, even an invalid wouldn't refuse these. Be prepared, they'll beg for more! The secrets are:

Cook them right before you sit down to dinner.

You need a ricer which is not expensive, and you can also make the very best light whipped potatoes with it.

Have the rest of the dinner ready on heated plates, so you can "rice" the potatoes on each plate, or use a heated bowl.

Here is the recipe:

Peel, cut into quarters *enough potatoes for 4* (or the size of the family). Put into a saucepan with *cold water to cover.*

Add *salt* to taste.

Add *1 small peeled onion*, if you wish, just for flavor.

Bring the potatoes to a boil. Cover. Cook about 20 minutes until done.

Pour off any water left and remove the onion. Shake the pan over high heat, off and on the heat until there is no water left and the potatoes are absolutely dry. Don't burn. Shake over the heat to dry.

To serve hot, put the potatoes in the ricer and quickly push down holding over the plates or bowl, so the potato rice is not pushed down but comes out light as a feather. Be careful not to press down on the riced potatoes or plate as they will get mashed. If you wish, you can add a small lump of butter or margarine on top.

For a change: Peel and cut some carrots into slices and cook them along with the potatoes. Rice them right along with the potatoes. You will like how they look and how they taste.

Ready Cooked Riced Potato Cakes

the second time around better than the first, if that's possible

When you cook your potatoes to make "Riced Potatoes,"

see Index for recipe under Potatoes. Double the amount, so you will have enough to make another meal of them.

Add *¼ teaspoon onion powder* to the *2 cups "ready cooked" riced potatoes.* Stir in *2 tablespoons melted margarine, 1 egg* beaten with a fork, *salt* and *pepper* to taste.

Shape into cakes. Roll the cakes in *flour.*

Heat a skillet with *4 tablespoons oil* until hot. Add *1 tablespoon margarine*, then add the potatoes without crowding and brown on both sides.

Place on a heated plate with a paper towel on it. Drain the potato cakes on this.

Serve the potatoes hot.

Potato Bake With "Ready Cooked Potatoes"

good with chicken, pork chops or veal chops

Scoop *2 cups "ready cooked" potatoes* out of their skins without breaking the skins. Set the skins aside. Mash the potatoes with a potato masher or fork (not fine though).

Smear a 9-inch pie dish with *margarine* very well.

Heat oven 400°.

Mix together the potatoes, *1 tablespoon minced, dried onions, salt and pepper to taste, 1 tablespoon minced parsley, ½ cup plus 2 tablespoons boiling chicken or beef bouillon broth.*

Bring back to a boil.

Pour into baking dish. Dot with a *little margarine or butter.*

Bake in 400° oven 20 minutes.

Put under broiler to brown.

This is one of the dishes we make when we boil enough new potatoes for two meals and "cook once for twice." What do we do with the shells? We use the "ready cooked" baked potato skins, and brush the skins with *margarine* and bake the skins in the oven. Everyone loves the skins baked this way. It's a treat.

We also sometimes sprinkle *cheese* on the inside of the skins and put under the broiler to brown when we want to stretch the protein in our dinner—and we get good taste at the same time.

Fried Potatoes

a two-step method, saves time and saves fat

Peel and slice thin enough *potatoes*—about *1 pound*—to make *2¾ cups.*

Bring to a boil in water to cover with *1¾ teaspoons salt.*

Turn heat to low. Put lid on. Cook 4 minutes.

Drain in a strainer. Put on a plate.

The potatoes can be put in the refrigerator and browned when ready to eat.

Mop with a paper towel to dry.

Heat a skillet on high heat with *2 tablespoons oil* until hot. Test with a small *piece of bread.* If it starts to sizzle immediately, the skillet is ready.

Add the sliced potatoes.

Cook about 1 minute. Turn the heat to medium high. Cook and brown.

Add *oil, 1 tablespoon* at a time as needed—about *2 tablespoons* more oil—*4 tablespoons altogether.*

The potatoes take about 15 minutes to brown.

If you want fried potatoes with onions, see our recipe for Fried Onions and add the browned onions to the potatoes and heat.

Yams, Gingered, Oranged And Nutmegged

or use sweet potatoes

Peel and slice 2 *yams or sweet potatoes.*

Mix together *½ cup water, 3 tablespoons orange marmalade, a good grind of ginger and nutmeg* and *a good pinch of salt, 2 tablespoons margarine* and *a little lemon or lime juice, about 1 teaspoon.* (If you have a choice, the lime is better.)

Cook, stir until melted.

Pour over the yams or sweet potatoes.

Bring to a simmer. Place in 400° oven. Bake ¾ hour.

Baste now and then. Delicious!—the lime juice does something special to this, and there's nothing like fresh yams or sweet potatoes. Yes, you can use canned sweet potatoes with this sauce; keep basting, and, of course, don't cook so long.

Tip: The reason we suggest yams is because it usually is a deeper orange color and so has more Vitamin A. There are some sweet potatoes that are a deep orange, so be a selective shopper.

Fresh Stewed Tomatoes

in the good old Summertime when fresh tomatoes are plentiful . . . you can never get the wonderful taste from canned tomatoes that you get from fresh, farm picked tomatoes, so make this

Peel and cut *enough tomatoes to make 2 to 2½ cups.*

Wash, remove seeds, and cut into pieces a *small green pepper.*

Chop *¼ cup celery* and *½ cup onions.*

Put these vegetables into a large skillet with *2 tablespoons oil.*

Cook and stir, adding *½ teaspoon sweet smelling dried basil* or *fennel, a pinch of garlic powder, salt and pepper to taste.* Cook about 15 minutes.

This makes about 3 cups heavenly stewed tomatoes.

Of course, out of season use canned tomatoes. Good brands are Progresso, Contadina, and one of the best—F & P. Some of the store brands are good, but these you will have to test yourself.

Baby Zucchini And Tomatoes Cooked Together

it's a perfect marriage . . . and you can use baby crook neck squash and it's just as good

Wash, slice *enough baby zucchini or yellow crook neck squash to make about 2 cups* or 1 pound thin slices.

Drain *1 can (1 pound) stewed tomatoes.* We use F & P brand. Strain the tomatoes. Add *enough water* to the juice *to make 1 cup.*

Put the squash, the tomatoes and the juice in a saucepan.

Sprinkle over *1 tablespoon flour.* Mix gently to combine.

On high heat bring to a simmer. Stir in *½ teaspoon sugar,* a pinch of *salt* and *1 teaspoon sweet butter or margarine.*

Bring back to a simmer. Cover. Turn heat to low. Simmer 20 to 30 minutes until the squash is cooked. Don't let squash get too soft. It tastes better if it has a little bite.

Tip: Fresh, frozen or canned corn may be added to this.

Mediterranean Zucchini, Tomato, Onion Specialty

this is not a highly seasoned dish . . . it has all the goodies of fresh, country cooking . . . and for once this is a dish that does not feature garlic

Slice thin *1 medium zucchini* to fit a shallow baking dish. (Pyrex or other glass baking dishes are nice to bake in and serve in—a 9 inch glass baking pan is fine or a 10″ × 6½″ baking dish.)

Smear the dish well with *margarine, butter or oil.*

Arrange thin slices of the zucchini in a single layer. Brush with *melted margarine or oil.*

Sprinkle lightly with *salt* and a light grind of *pepper.*

Arrange a layer of very thin sliced *onions* on top. Brush with *oil.*

Top with very thin sliced *tomatoes* placed so that part of the zucchini is exposed. Brush with *oil.* Sprinkle lightly with *salt* and *pepper* and a sprinkle of *dried basil.*

You can cover with foil and place in refrigerator until ready to bake.

Preheat oven 400°. Bake 10 minutes covered. Remove foil; bake 10 minutes.

Sprinkle *Parmesan cheese* on top lightly.

Put under broiler to brown.

This is a "fresh tasting" and delicious dish.

Ratatouille

a "melange" of vegetables that tastes good and freezes fine, so eat one, freeze one

Wash *1 eggplant* that weighs about 1 pound and *1 pound small zucchini.* Be careful to run your hand over the zucchini to rub off any grit.

Cut the eggplant into ½ inch slices. *Salt* lightly. Place in a strainer over a bowl. Put a plate on with a heavy weight to get the bitter juice out. Let stand 1 hour.

Cut the zucchini into ½ inch slices, then into large cubes. *Salt* lightly.

Peel and cut into large dice *1 large onion.*

Strain *1 can (1 pound) tomatoes.* Save the juice to make Tomato Soup.

Remove the seeds as best you can from the tomatoes. Cut the hard ends off. Cut the pulp into large pieces.

Wash *1 red or green pepper.* Remove the seeds and cut into large cubes.

Heat a skillet with *4 to 6 tablespoons oil* and the diced onions. Cook, stir about 2 minutes. Put lid on; turn heat to low. Cook about 10 minutes until onions are soft and clear.

Wipe the eggplant slices. Cut into large cubes. Add to the skillet with *4 garlic cloves* and cook 15 minutes with lid on.

Stir in the zucchini, red or green pepper and *½ cup celery diced large.* Cook 10 minutes.

Add the tomatoes.

Add *1 teaspoon dried basil, 1 teaspoon dried oregano, salt* and *pepper* to taste. Cook 10 minutes. Stir now and then with 2 rubber spatulas. Do not crush the vegetables.

This makes two casseroles, so eat one, freeze one. It reheats beautifully. Also, if you add cheese, either Parmesan, Muenster or mozzarella, you can have your protein, so you have a meal in a dish.

Eat some whole wheat bread for a nourishing meal.

Summertime Stuffed Tomatoes

when tomatoes are in season, that's the time to make these . . . it's easy to make and easy to eat and it can be made ahead . . . of course, you can make these in winter, too!

Heat oven 400°.

Wash and cut the tops off *4 medium large tomatoes.* With a spoon scoop out the insides leaving thick shells.

Sprinkle *salt* lightly over the inside of the shells and a little *pepper.*

Arrange in a heatproof glass pie plate or in individual heatproof shallow baking saucers like Pyrex 6-inch glass saucers. You can serve in these as well as bake in them, and they look pretty, too.

Make the stuffing.

Put into a large bowl *1 can (7¾ ounces) salmon, 3 tablespoons Progresso Italian Flavored Bread Crumbs*, a good grind of *pepper, ½ teaspoon lemon juice, 1 tablespoon chopped fine parsley, salt* to taste and *1 egg*. Mix with a fork gently.

Spoon into the 4 tomatoes. Don't mash down.

Mix together *2 tablespoons Progresso Italian Seasoned Crumbs* and *2 tablespoons grated Parmesan cheese.*

Spoon over the stuffing.

Melt about *2 tablespoons butter or margarine*. Pour over the crumb mixture.

You can put in refrigerator until ready to use.

When ready to bake, heat oven 400°.

Pour about *2 tablespoons V8 Juice* around the tomatoes in each individual baking dish, or more if using the pie plate.

Bake in 400° oven about 30 minutes.

Don't bake the tomatoes until soft and squashy—they should be firm, though baked.

This is a nice dish served with baked potatoes and a green salad.

What's for dessert? Fresh fruit, of course.

Cooked Frozen Spinach

watch and cook method . . . takes up to 5 minutes

Bring *2 tablespoons water* to a boil.

Put in a *10 ounce package of frozen, chopped spinach* into a saucepan that fits.

Put on medium heat.

With 2 forks keep scraping and turning the cooking spinach until all the spinach is defrosted, and it will be cooked. You cannot leave the spinach or it will burn. Turn the heat down as necessary.

By this method you don't waste the Vitamin A in water which you usually throw down the drain. The Vitamin A remains in the spinach you eat.

The spinach retains its beautiful green color, is not overcooked, and—best of all—you have all the good vitamins to eat (not to nourish the sink drain).

Penny Pincher Creamed Spinach

cream? . . . nonsense, we do tricks with our dry milk

Steam *1 package (10 ounces) frozen spinach* or cook in a saucepan, breaking and tearing the spinach apart with 2 forks as it cooks until it is defrosted. When defrosted, it is hot and cooked. Take off heat. Drain.

Chop the spinach as fine as you like it.

Stir in *¼ cup instant nonfat dry milk* until absorbed. Add *¼ cup skim milk* and *1½ teaspoons margarine*. Cook, stir until hot. Serve. Can be made ahead and reheated.

Spinach that is cooked fast never gets that awful taste that makes people say "I say it's spinach and to Hell with it"; instead they say "more please!"

Spinach Timbales

for those small bits of "leftovers"—a wonderful way to use them up and you can cook them in heatproof baking cups on top of the stove! . . . what could be easier! . . . you can also bake these in the oven or use a skillet to put the timbales in and cook on top of the stove

Grease 4 (6 ounce) glass baking cups with margarine.

Sprinkle with seasoned bread crumbs. Shake out excess.

Cook, tearing apart, *1 package (10 ounces) frozen spinach* over high heat, using 2 forks. Don't go away. This is a quick way to "cook" the spinach. When the spinach is defrosted—it is cooked. Put in a strainer and push with two paper towels and squeeze out as much of the liquid as you can.

Chop the spinach fine.

Put in a saucepan *1 tablespoon oil*. Stir in *1 tablespoon flour* and *1 chicken Bouillon Powder*. Then stir in *1¼ cups nonfat milk*. Cook, stir until it comes to a boil. Cook, stir 2 minutes. Add *¼ cup grated cheese*, if you like.

Mix *3 eggs*. Stir into the sauce. Add a *few grains of cayenne pepper* and *salt to taste*. Spoon into the baking cups.

Put water in the skillet to be high as the filling in the cups and let come to a simmer. Put the cups in. Cover with a piece of foil, put a lid on. Let simmer until done. Test by putting a knife in and if it comes out clean, it is ready.

Tip: Check now and then to be sure the water is simmering (not boiling, please!).

Tip: Whatever you have—"Ready Cooked" (leftovers) such as chicken, meat, beans or vegetables such as squash, broccoli and even cauliflower—you extend your small portion of Ready Cooked by chopping them and you can combine small portions of "Ready Cooked" foods. Check your refrigerator before your "Ready Cooked" become "Leftovers" or "Throw Aways." These can be made into a different dish, Timbales, or a large Timbale. Also, the Timbales don't collapse like a Souffle does and it can be reheated and it tastes good cold too.

Fresh Corn On The Cob

the very best of the summer crop!

How to buy sweet tender corn on the cob.

Supermarket corn is not sweet corn, sometimes it may be tender but I've never tasted a sweet corn in a supermarket that was sweet.

You either buy it fresh picked on a farm or the farmer brings it to town or there are farmers' markets that bring in the corn, young, tender and sweet.

But, you be the tester taster. Buy one corn (the seller will look at you as if you have lost your mind). Ask the price of the ear of corn and pay for it. (It's well spent money.) Husk part of the ear of corn enough to take a bite of it. Is the corn *sweet* and tender?, then buy your required amount. If it is not, then you've saved yourself money and the family a disappointment.

Take the "sweet" corn home immediately. Immediately remove the husks and the hair and put 6 or 8 into a plastic bag and close with a tie. Put immediately into the refrigerator. Then continue to do as you did until all are "husked," bagged and put in the refrigerator. You have now done your good deed for the day.

When you are ready to eat, bring to a boil a large pot filled with water leaving room to add up to a dozen ears of corn. When the water comes to a rolling boil, drop in, one by one, up to 12 ears of corn. Bring back to a boil. Cover. Boil 5 minutes.

Remove the corn with a pair of tongs to a heated platter.

Some will brush the corn with melted butter or soft margarine, salt lightly, while others will eat corn as is because the corn will be juicy and sweet as sugar. We do not like melted butter or margarine as well as "soft" spreadable butter or margarine.

Of course if you are like my family, you will probably want about 4 or 5 ears of the corn for each person.

We never eat corn except when it is in season.

Now here's a real good tip:

You can buy this luscious corn not for just one day's eating but for two days' and many times three days' eating because if you do as we directed you to do, the corn will remain sweet and tender in the refrigerator up to three days. But the corn must be sweet and tender when you buy it! I asked a scientist from the U.S.D.A. why this was so and he said taking off the husks and refrigerating kept the corn from maturing—so it remains sweet, instead of turning into starch.

Steamed Butternuts

a quickie vegetable, and everyone will love it if you call it "Butternuts" instead of squash

Slice and peel *enough butternuts* ¾ inch thick, and cut into large bite size cubes *to make 3 cups.*

Put into a steamer. Sprinkle *a little salt* in.

Steam 5 minutes.

Mix gently with *1 tablespoon margarine.*

Serve.

Pattypan Fritters

fine with chicken or meat

Wash *young, small pattypan squash.* Remove stem. Cut pattypan in half through the center lengthwise, so you can remove the seeds. Scoop out the seeds with a small spoon.

Grate over a bowl enough pattypan to make *1 cup grated pattypan.* We use the juice, too. (We use the flat grater.)

Stir in *5 tablespoons flour, 1 teaspoon baking powder, 1 tablespoon oil, 1 tablespoon wheat germ* and *1 egg* beaten with a fork.

Heat a skillet on second high heat until hot.

Pour *a little oil* in so the fritters won't stick, but not a lot of oil. Brush over the skillet.

Drop the batter by spoonfuls. Brown one side, then the other. Serve hot.

These are very tasty and can be used as a fine tasting vegetable—even the "meat and potato man" will like them.

Tip: Don't crowd the pancakes. As in all frying, when you crowd them, they steam instead of frying and won't brown.

Candied Butternuts

Slice, peel *1 small butternut squash* into 1 inch thick slices. Remove any seeds.

Melt in a saucepan that fits *¼ cup margarine, ¼ cup dark brown sugar, ¼ teaspoon dried ginger* and *a pinch of salt.*

Remove about ¼ cup to pour over the top.

Arrange the sliced butternuts in the syrup mixture.

Pour the ¼ cup left over the top.

Add *2 teaspoons water*. Bring to a boil. Cover.

Turn heat to low. Let simmer 15 minutes. Baste.

Turn heat to medium low. Cook 15 minutes, covered.

Remove cover and cook uncovered. Watch it. Cook 10 minutes.

Remove any fat in the pan.

Your butternuts are ready.

Top Stove Butternut, Gingered And Oranged

delicious enough so you don't need a dessert . . . it's a dessert in itself . . . it goes perfect with chicken, pork and veal . . . and—whoever refuses to eat this with meat? . . . no one!

Slice, peel and cut into 1 inch thick slices *1 small butternut squash* and scoop out the seeds with a teaspoon.

Mix together *¼ cup margarine or butter, ½ cup orange marmalade and 2 tablespoons grated orange rind, a pinch of salt* and *¼ teaspoon dried, ground ginger.*

Divide in half.

Put ½ into a saucepan that fits the sliced squash.

Melt.

Spoon the other ½ margarine mixture over and into the butternut slices.

Arrange on top of the melted margarine mixture.

Add *2 tablespoons orange juice.*

Bring to a simmer. Put lid on. Simmer 15 minutes.

Turn to low. Baste. Cook 15 minutes with lid on.

Baste again. Remove lid. Cook on high heat without lid 10 minutes until done.

Tip: We freeze grated orange rind, 1 tablespoon each, in wax paper and freeze in a plastic bag to have on hand when needed, or just use foil cut into small pieces to close well the 1 tablespoon each of grated orange rind.

Corn And Butternuts

what are butternuts? . . . a lovely vegetable

Slice, peel and cube *enough yellow gold butternut squash to make 2 cups.*

Steam 4 or 5 minutes.

Put into a saucepan.

Add *1 can (7 ounces) whole corn, or use fresh corn.*

Melt *2 tablespoons margarine.* Add to the butternut, corn mixture.

Add a *sprinkle of pepper* and *salt to taste.*

Lightly mix.

Heat and eat.

Whipped Butternuts

tastes as good as whipped sweet potatoes

Wash, slice, peel, remove seeds and cube *enough butternut squash to make 4 cups.*

Steam or cook 4 minutes until soft.

Mash.

Mix together *½ cup peanut butter, 2 tablespoons margarine, ¼ teaspoon salt, ½ teaspoon dried ginger* and *¼ cup milk.*

Stir into the butternuts.

Bake in 400° oven about 5 minutes until top is lightly browned and the dish is hot.

Squash Chips

we like them just as well as potato chips

Slice enough of a *large green zucchini squash* into very thin slices, about 1/16 of an inch, for 2 people, about 50 slices. They're so delicious, you have to have enough.

Heat a large skillet with about *5 tablespoons oil* on high heat.

Put into a soup plate *1 egg* mixed with *2 tablespoons milk.*

Put about *1 cup flour* mixed with *¼ teaspoon salt* into another soup plate.

When the oil is hot, put the sliced zucchini first into the egg, then into the flour, then into the hot skillet. Continue until you add enough slices to fill the skillet, but don't crowd them.

Turn heat to medium; and with a pair of tongs, turn the slices over as they brown. When browned, not burned, put on a cookie sheet covered with 2 pieces paper towels.

Continue until you fry 2 panfuls. You may have to add a little more oil for the second panful.

After frying the second panful, you will have to let the skillet cool and then wipe it out and replace with *fresh oil* and fry 2 more panfuls.

You can eat at once; or you can make early and reheat. You can also freeze these and reheat. To reheat, place in a preheated 400° oven on a rack or a cookie sheet and bake until hot and crisp.

There's only one trouble with these Squash chips—everyone can eat and eat them, and if you are the "fryer," you'll need a helping hand.

Squash Quiche

Heat oven 400°.

Make the "Never Fail Pie Crust"—see recipe index under Pie Crust.

Bake pie crust in 400° oven 8 or 9 minutes, no more, as it will bake later.

Remove from oven and cool.

Turn heat to 375°.

Make the filling:

Peel and cut into cubes *2 cups Zucchini squash.*

Place in a skillet and cook and stir to evaporate the liquid. Don't burn.

Add *3 tablespoons oil, ¼ cup dried onion flakes, ¼ teaspoon dried basil, ¼ teaspoon dried parsley, ½ teaspoon salt* and *pepper* to taste.

Bring to a simmer. Cover. Cook 5 minutes.

Uncover, turn heat to medium. Cook 5 minutes to evaporate the juice.

Cool slightly.

Mix *3 large eggs* with a fork.

Stir in *1½ cups milk.*

Fold in the cooked squash.

Spoon or pour into the partly cooked shell.

Sprinkle *¼ cup Bacon Bits* over the top.

Bake in preheated 375° oven about 30 minutes until sharp knife comes out clean at the edge and a little particle of the custard can stick to the knife when tested in the middle.

Remove from oven. Cool.

Rice-A-Lentil

Wash *1 cup lentils* under running water.

Soak the lentils in *2 cups cold water* mixed with *2 onion bouillon powders* for 1 hour.

Cook *1 cup rice* in *2 cups water* mixed with *2 chicken bouillon powders* and *1 tablespoon oil or margarine*. Bring to a boil. Put lid on; turn heat to low. Simmer 25 minutes. Run a fork through to fluff.

Bring the lentils and the water left to a boil. Turn heat low. Cover. Cook 15 to 20 minutes until lentils are tender but not mushy. Drain any broth left.

Lightly mix the lentils with the rice, and you have a new vegetable, "Rice-A-Lentil."

It's good with meat, chicken or fish.

Cauliflower With Cheese Sauce

Wash *1 whole cauliflower*. Cut off the stem. Steam or cook.

Make the sauce:

Heat *1 can Campbell's Cheese Soup* with *¼ package Velveeta Cheese or other cheese.*

Pour over the cauliflower.
Sprinkle *Parmesan cheese* on top.
Place under broiler until Parmesan is lightly browned.
Serve at once.

"Easy Cook" Delicious Vegetables

well flavored . . . goes wonderful with chicken or fish or any meat now that I think about it

Chop *1 small onion.*

Peel, slice and cube *1 large carrot or 2 smaller ones, 1 large mealy potato.*

Wash and cube without peeling *1 medium or 2 small zucchini* and *2 baby yellow crookneck squash.*

In a skillet bring the carrots, potatoes and onions in *1 cup water and 1 chicken bouillon powder* to a boil, or use 1 cup canned, fat removed, chicken broth. Turn heat to medium. Cook 10 minutes.

Add the zucchini and the yellow squash. Cook until done, about 5 to 8 minutes. Do not overcook. This tastes super if served as soon as done. We hope this will become one of your favorite vegetable melanges.

Tip: Don't buy "limp" zucchini or yellow crookneck squash. Be sure they are crisp and have a fresh look. Also smaller zucchini and yellow squash have fewer seeds and are not apt to be "puffy."

Summertime Vegetable Melange

whatever you have in the way of fresh vegetables

Chop roughly *1 cup onions, 1 cup sweet green pepper (Cuban), or Bell Pepper, 4 cups green cabbage.* Peel *2 large cloves garlic.*

Cube *4 cups potatoes* and put into cold water.

Wash and cut the leaves in half removing the stems of *fresh spinach.*

Wash and cut into large cubes *3 ripe tomatoes or use whole cherry tomatoes.*

Parboil the potatoes, but don't let get soft. Drain.

Put in a casserole the chopped onions and *3 or 4 tablespoons oil.*

Cook, stir until it comes to a simmer.

Add the drained potatoes. Bring back to a simmer. Cover. Turn heat to low. Simmer 15 or more minutes until potatoes are almost tender.

Add all the vegetables to this except the spinach.

Add to taste some dried *Italian herbs* and *salt* and *pepper.*

Cook, stir on high heat until it simmers. Cover. Cook until cabbage is cooked but still crisp, about 5 minutes.

Add the spinach. Cook, stir gently until the spinach is cooked but still a beautiful green, takes about 3 to 5 minutes.

A Vegetable Melange

good served hot or cold

Chop *1 small onion.* Mince *2 tablespoons parsley.*

Wash and cube *3 small zucchini,* about 2 cups.

Cube *enough tomatoes to make 2 cups.*

Add *2 cups fresh, frozen, or canned corn.*

Wash, dry and cut *enough bell green peppers or Cuban sweet peppers to make 1 cup.*

Heat a large skillet with *4 tablespoons oil* and *1 tablespoon margarine.*

Add all the vegetables except the tomatoes.

Bring to a simmer. Turn heat to low. Put lid on. Cook 10 minutes, adding salt and pepper to taste.

Add the tomatoes plus *¼ teaspoon dried basil.*

Cook about 3 or 5 minutes.

German Style Sweet And Sour Red Cabbage

certainly puts "pizzazz" into the cabbage

Remove the outer leaves (wilted ones) of a *red cabbage* and wash under running water.

Quarter, core, and shred the cabbage to make 2 cups.

Don't peel, dice *3 red apples.*

Heat a large pot with *2 tablespoons margarine* and the shredded cabbage and cook, stir 3 minutes.

Add *4 tablespoons vinegar,* the apples, *2 cups water, ¾*

teaspoon salt, 2 tablespoons brown sugar, 1 bay leaf torn into 4 pieces, *4 whole allspice.* Mix together with 2 spoons.

Bring to a boil. Turn heat to simmer. Simmer until cabbage is tender, takes about 1 hour. Serve hot.

This dish reheats well so you can make it early and reheat for dinner.

Buckwheat Groats

when cooked this is called "Kasha"

We like the whole buckwheat groats.

We cook it this way: Put *½ cup whole buckwheat groats* into a skillet.

Cook, stir, don't burn, on high heat, takes about 5 minutes. This is called "toasting."

Add *1 tablespoon margarine.*

Bring to a boil either *1¼ cups water or 1¼ cups Chicken Bouillon Broth.* This must be boiling, or the buckwheat will turn into a mush.

Add. Cover. Bring back to a boil.

Turn heat to low. Cook about 20 to 30 minutes as you prefer the groats.

You can saute onions and/or mushrooms to add to the groats for a change, or combine with cooked noodles or macaroni or smallest pasta shells.

Groats are very tasty with fish, veal, chicken, and other meat, including lamb.

If you are using your oven, you can bake it in the oven, too.

"Kasha" or Groats is old fashioned, and nutritious goodness. Try it, you'll like it!

How To Cook Fresh Pumpkin

it's especially nice for Thanksgiving, and it's equally as good any time of the year because you can find the pumpkin ready and waiting in your supermarket in a can

To cook fresh pumpkin for your pie or pudding is a tedious job. You have to cut the pumpkin in halves or quarters, remove the seeds, then bake in a 325° oven. It takes a long time. It took us 1 hour and 45 minutes. Then we had to peel it and strain it. This is not a money saver, as you have to use your oven too.

We found this a better method: Cut the pumpkin into thin slices; then cut the meat off the skin like you do a cantaloupe when you want to cut a cantaloupe up. We cut the pumpkin meat into smaller pieces and steamed them. Yes, you can use a pressure cooker, too.

We used our food mill instead of a strainer, and that was the easy part. Our pumpkin was not watery because we steamed it.

The easiest way and a time saver is to use a can of pumpkin, and no one has refused our pumpkin pie!

Tip: I must admit the pie made with the steamed fresh pumpkin had an extra fresh, special good taste and every fall we celebrate!

How To Make "Toasted Instant Minced Onions"

makes an ordinary taste into a "something special" taste

Put your *jar or can of instant minced dried onion* in a large skillet.

With a wooden spoon, cook, stir, first on high heat, then turn to next heat, medium high, taking the skillet off the heat now and then so the onions do not burn or brown. Take off and on heat about 5 minutes until the onions turn to a golden color. Beautiful! And the flavor is enhanced!

Be careful; don't burn. Keep taking the skillet off and on the heat. Also, when golden, turn immediately into a large plate to cool.

When cold, put back in container it came in. Check, we did and bought the largest size we could find because we saved money and this is a good, flavorsome product, which we use often. And to you fresh onion lovers, we use fresh onions most of the time, of course, but sometimes these toasted dried onions "hit the spot" for taste, too!

Tip: We use no fat to "toast" the onions. Also we cook, stir and lift the skillet never leaving the stove.

Marinated Mushrooms

inexpensive, tasty and costs less than the "bought" kind

Drain *1 jar or can (4½ ounces) small button mushrooms* and save the broth.

Mix together in a bowl *2 tablespoons oil, 3 tablespoons wine vinegar, 1 teaspoon dried tarragon* and *6 tablespoons mushroom broth* from the can of mushrooms.

Add the mushrooms.

Put in the refrigerator to marinate overnight.

This is very tasty as an hors d'oeuvre or served with cold chicken or meat.

Cooked Onions

or steamed onions in water to cover

In a saucepan cover the sliced onions with water. Remove onions with a slotted spoon.

Bring *water* to a boil. Add *onions*. Bring back to a boil. Turn heat to low. Cover; cook 5 minutes. Strain the onions.

The onions are ready to use with any dishes that need steamed or cooked onions, as in some fish and casserole dishes.

Penny Pincher's Lima Bean Barley Soup

this is as pretty to look at as it is good to eat . . . we always have some of this soup for company that just drops in

Wash *1 pound dry baby lima beans* under running water.

Wash *¼ cup pearl barley* under running water.

Wash, peel *3 carrots,* cut into quarters; peel *1 large onion,* wash *1 large branch of celery leaves.*

Put into a large pot *11 cups water,* the lima beans, the pearl barley, the carrots, celery, onions and *2¼ teaspoons salt.* Bring to a boil. Cover. Simmer 2½ hours.

Put through a food mill or a strainer 1 cup of the cooked limas, the onion and celery. Cut the carrots into small pieces. Put all this back into the rest of the soup.

Bring to a boil. Serve hot.

The soup definitely doesn't need anything else added. It's just good as is!

Tasty Old Fashioned Bean Soup

about as good as the famous "Senate Bean Soup"

Wash under running water *1 pound great northern dried beans.*

Bring to a boil with *10 cups water.* Boil 2 minutes. Remove from heat. Cover. Let stand 1 hour, or you can soak the beans overnight.

Peel and chop *1 large onion,* about 1½ cups, *1 branch celery or stalk* to make about 1 cup, and *2 carrots,* about 1½ cups.

Chop fine *2 tablespoons parsley.*

Put the chopped onions, carrots and celery into a large soup kettle.

Add *4 tablespoons oil.* Bring to a simmer. On medium heat cook, stir 2 minutes. Don't burn or brown. Turn heat to low. Cover; simmer 15 minutes.

Stir in *1 tablespoon flour.* Cook, stir 1 minute. Take off heat.

Add the soaked beans and the water. Bring to a boil. Turn heat to low. Cover; simmer 30 minutes.

Add *1 teaspoon salt.* Cover; simmer 30 minutes until beans are done.

Remove 1 cup beans and push through a food mill or strainer. Stir back into the soup.

Add *½ teaspoon salt* and *pepper to taste.*

Add *½ cup Bacon Bits* and the 2 tablespoons chopped parsley.

Taste. Bring to a boil. Cook 5 minutes.

Another Penny Pincher Bean Soup

tastes good, too

Mix together *6 cups water, 3 packages Onion Bouillon Broth* and *3 packages Beef Bouillon Broth.*

Bring to a boil.

Add *1 can (15 or 16 ounces) lima beans, ½ cup elbow macaroni, 1 bay leaf, 2 allspice, 1 tablespoon minced dried onions, 1 carrot minced,* and *½ stalk celery minced.*

Bring to a boil.

Turn heat to low. Simmer 20 minutes.

Taste, add *salt and pepper to taste.*

Serve hot.

An Inexpensive But Good Bean Soup

made from the broth of two lamb breasts you cooked the day before . . . (you can also use other broth or onion, chicken or beef bouillon broth) . . . this is where you get two good, nutritious meals out of two inexpensive lamb breasts

Wash, drain and bring to a boil *1 pound Great Northern Dried Beans* in *5 cups water.* Put lid on. Let stand 1 hour.

Peel, and cut in half, *2 medium potatoes.*

Chop fine *1 large carrot,* chop *3 small onions or 1 medium one,* and *2 stalks celery.* Mince *2 tablespoons parsley,* fresh or frozen. (We always mince some of our fresh parsley when we buy it, freeze it in 1 tablespoon portions and have ready when we need it.)

Remove any fat from the lamb broth or other broth. You should have 5 cups of lamb broth.

Put into a soup kettle with the "soaked" beans and any "soaking" water left. Bring to a boil.

Add the prepared vegetables, *1 bay leaf* and *4 whole allspice.* Bring back to a boil. Turn heat to low. Cover. Simmer about 1 hour until the beans are tender.

Add *salt* and *pepper to taste,* and add the parsley. Cook 5 minutes.

Push 2 cups of the beans and the potatoes through a food mill or a strainer; then stir back into the soup to thicken it.

Bring to a boil when ready to eat.

Bean Tomato Soup

we started out making bean soup and kept adding and adding until—here, this is it

Wash under running water *1 pound great northern dried beans.*

Bring *12 cups water* and the beans to a boil. Boil 2 minutes.

Remove from heat. Cover. Let stand 1 hour.

Peel and cut in half *1 large onion.*

Peel and cut into 8 pieces *1 large carrot.*

Wash *1 large branch celery or 1 rib celery* cut into thirds.

Bring to a boil the soaked beans and the water they were soaked in, the vegetables, *½ bay leaf* and *3 whole allspice.*

Turn heat to low. Cover; simmer 30 minutes.

Add *1 teaspoon salt.* Cover; simmer 1 hour until beans are soft and the carrots cooked.

Push through a food mill or strainer.

Add *salt to taste.*

Add *2 cans (10¾ ounces) tomato soup,* a *pound can of tomatoes,* cut up, *1 teaspoon A-1 Sauce, 3 tablespoons dry sherry* and a good *grind of pepper.* Bring to a boil before serving.

This will make a lot of soup, so be prepared to call the neighbors in, or freeze some.

Split Pea Soup

our protein soup

In a large kettle bring to a boil *6 cups broth* (homemade, canned chicken or canned beef broth), and *5 cups cold water, 2 cups split peas,* either green or yellow, washed under running water, and *1 celery stalk, 1 large onion, 1 large carrot* . . . all cut into quarters.

Add *1 teaspoon salt* to taste.

Turn heat to low. Put lid on. Stir now and then as it simmers. Simmer about 1 hour until peas and other vegetables are soft.

Push all through a food mill. Put back in kettle. Bring to a simmer. Simmer 5 minutes.

Correct seasoning if necessary.

Eat some; freeze the rest.

No Meat Split Pea Soup

you'd say for sure this soup had meat in it, it's that good and rich

You need *1 package (1 pound) green or yellow split peas, 1 can (6 ounces) V8 Juice, McCormicks Bacon Bits*—not Bacos. (We use Bacos in other recipes but not this one.)

Chop *2 cups onions, 2 cups celery, leaves and stems,* and slice *4 carrots.*

Put the onions into a large pot with *¼ cup margarine or butter.* Place on high heat. Don't go away, or it will burn. Cook, stir until it comes to a simmer. Turn heat to low and cover. Cook 10 minutes.

Add *12 cups water,* the celery and the carrots. Bring to a boil.

Wash the split peas in a strainer under running water. Add to the soup. Bring back to a boil.

Add *1 tablespoon plus ¾ teaspoon salt, 1 can (6 ounces) V8 Juice* and *4 tablespoons or ¼ cup McCormicks Bacon Bits.* (You can omit this if you wish; it tastes very good without the "bits," too.)

Bring to a boil. Cover. Turn heat to low. Simmer 1 hour, stirring now and then.

Your soup looks appetizing and tastes rich.

For variety you can put through a food mill or strainer.

A Melody Of Split Pea Soup

why a melody? . . . because everything is in harmony

Peel and chop *1 large onion, 1 large or 2 small carrots, 1 branch celery leaves or 1 stalk celery*. Set aside.

Wash under running water *1 pound split peas.*

Bring *10 cups water, 1 teaspoon salt* and the split peas to a boil. Turn heat to low. Put lid on. Cook, stir now and then ½ hour until soft.

Push through a food mill or strainer.

Put back into the soup kettle; add *1 teaspoon salt* and bring to a boil.

Add the onions, carrots, celery, *1 bay leaf* cut into half, *4 whole allspice* and *¼ cup brown rice.*

Bring to a boil. Turn heat to low. Simmer 15 minutes.

Add *1 tablespoon chopped fine parsley* and *1 tablespoon tops of shallots or scallions* chopped fine, and *½ cup elbow macaroni.*

Simmer 15 minutes more with lid on until done.

Tip: If you like a thicker soup, cook without a lid on high heat, being careful to stir now and then so it doesn't burn.

Lentil Soup

Esau sold his birthright for this soup . . . it was that good, and it still is

You need *1 package (16 ounces) dried lentils.*

Peel and cut into halves *2 Idaho potatoes.*

Cut *3 large onions* into quarters leaving the "mustache" on, so the onions don't fall apart.

Cut *4 carrots* each into 3 pieces.

Cut *4 celery stems and leaves* from 1 large celery stalk. This is the part that has so much flavor and is usually thrown away. We freeze ours and have it handy for cooking.

Put *¼ cup and 1 tablespoon margarine or butter* and the onions into a large pot. Turn heat to high. Cook, stir until it simmers. Turn heat to low. Cover; cook 10 minutes.

Add *14 cups cold tap water,* the potatoes, celery and the carrots. Bring to a boil.

Wash the lentils in a strainer under running water. Add to

the soup. Bring back to a boil. Cover. Turn heat to low; simmer 2 hours, stirring now and then.

Taste the soup. Add *salt* to your taste.

Put ¾ of the soup and the potatoes, carrots, celery and onions through a strainer or a food mill. Bring back to a boil.

This is a protein rich soup. With slices of homemade whole wheat bread, it's a perfectly delicious meal.

How about some fruit and a little cheese for dessert?

Italian Lentil Soup

the only way to describe this is—it's delicious!

Bring to a boil *10 cups water, 1 ham bone or a ½ pound piece of chuck, 2 smallish or 1 large carrot, 1 large onion, 1 clove of garlic* and *1 branch of celery or large stalk.*

Add *1 teaspoon salt.*

Cover. Turn heat to low. Simmer 1 hour.

Strain *1 cup lentils* under running water and add.

Add *½ teaspoon salt.* Cook about 30 minutes.

Peel, seed and cut into small pieces *2 fresh tomatoes in season or use 1 pound can of tomatoes and its juice.* Remove seeds and cut tomatoes in very small pieces and add *1 can (6 ounces) V8 juice.*

Add *½ cup pasta.* Bring to a boil. Cook 12 minutes.

Quick Lentil Soup

it takes time to soak, but a short time to cook

Wash *1 cup lentils* in a strainer under cold tap water.

Put the lentils in a bowl with *2 cups cold water.* Let stand 1 hour.

Peel and shred *1 carrot.* Chop *enough onions to make 4 tablespoons.* Chop *enough celery to make ¼ cup.* Chop *1 medium potato.*

Bring the soaked lentils and any water it was soaked in, *4 cups chicken broth, 1 bay leaf* cut into quarters, *4 whole allspice* and the vegetables to a boil. Turn heat to low. Cook 20 to 25 minutes until the lentils are cooked.

Push this mixture through a food mill or strainer.

A Bargain Soup

has protein in it, the inexpensive kind, and tastes very good, too . . . you also save on fuel . . . how? . . . make it, and you will see

Soak *1 cup lentils* in *1 cup cold tap water* 1 hour.

Put into a large saucepan.

Add *1 can tomato sauce (15 ounces) with tomato bits.* (Hunt's have the only ones at this time. Others should follow.)

Add *3 cups water, 1 chicken bouillon powder, 1 can vegetable beef alphabet soup, 1 can Campbell's Tomato Soup, 1 teaspoon sugar* and *pepper* to taste.

Cook, stir and bring to a boil. Turn heat to low. Cook 20 minutes.

The soup is ready. With a slice or two of whole wheat bread, this makes a quick meal.

The protein is hidden in the good taste of the lentils.

Vegetable Soup

one of the best of the best . . . and lots of it

Chop *2 cups celery, 2 green peppers, 1 large onion, 1 cup scallions* and shred *1 small green cabbage.*

Skin, seed over a bowl in a strainer, using your fingers to remove the seeds from the pulp, *4 or 5 fresh tomatoes* in season only; *or use canned tomatoes.* Save the tomato juice and put the pulp on a large plate.

Into a large soup pot, put *2 cans Progresso Minestrone Soup, 1 can Campbell's Vegetarian Vegetable Soup, 1 can Progresso Chick Peas* and its broth, *2 cans Progresso Macaroni and Bean Soup, 4 cans College Inn or R & R or Campbell's Chicken Broth* with the fat removed, and *4 cups of your Homemade Chicken Broth,* the chopped vegetables, the shredded cabbage, the tomatoes and tomato juice, *2 boxes (10 ounces) frozen mixed vegetables or 1 bag (24 ounces),* if it is cheaper.

Bring to a boil. Add *½ teaspoon dried thyme leaves* and *½ teaspoon garlic powder.*

Turn heat to medium high. Cook 10 minutes or until the frozen limas are done. Remove from heat when done.

This soup can be made ahead, freezes beautifully, reheats beautifully, and is a meal in itself.

Of course, you can divide this recipe in half; but if you have a freezer, this is a wonderful soup to have on hand.

You can make a crab soup by dropping in the crab meat at the last minute. Heat and eat.

If you drop in a small amount of chicken or meat to enough of this vegetable soup and thicken it with cornstarch, you can have a chicken stew one day, a meat stew another day.

If you pour this soup over rice, you have a chow mein, but don't forget the canned cooked noodles, or make our Chinese noodles.

If you add shrimp, you have a shrimp chow mein.

Serve with whipped potatoes and you have a vegetable shepherd's pie.

This soup never goes to waste!

Iranian Vegetable Soup

who, what, where is Iran? . . . in the past it was the far away romantic Persia . . . what makes this soup different? . . . it's made from lamb, but don't get scared . . . the way we make it, you'll love it . . . and it's truly still one of the biggest bargains, because we use breast of lamb, which at this time costs about $1.59 for the whole breast and you get 2 meals out of it—one the vegetable soup, and the other—small boned, breaded lamb riblets that are crunchy and delicious!

What do you do about the fat? We show you how to get rid of it!

Put *8 cups water* over the breast of lamb. Add *2 cans Campbell's Chicken Broth or 2 chicken bouillon powders or cubes* (we like HerbOx), *1 large carrot, 1 large onion, 1 branch of celery leaves or a stalk of celery, 1 bay leaf* and *3 whole allspice*. Bring to a boil. Turn heat to low. Cover. Cook until lamb is tender, takes about 1 hour or more.

Remove the lamb. Let get cold and refrigerate.

Put 2 paper towels in a strainer over a bowl.

Strain the broth through this. Put the broth into the refrigerator.

The next day, lift off any fat or remove any fat.

Peel and chop *2 carrots, 1 medium onion, 1 branch or*

stalk of celery, 2 medium large potatoes and wash in a strainer under running water *¼ cup barley.*

Bring the broth to a boil. Add the vegetables, the barley and *1 can (1 pound) stewed tomatoes.*

Bring to a boil. Turn heat to low. Cover. Cook about 1 hour until barley and vegetables are soft. Add *salt* and *pepper* to taste.

Open a *can of Great Northern Beans.* Put in a strainer and run cold water over them. Add to the vegetable soup. Bring to a boil. Turn heat to low. Simmer 5 minutes.

Fill everybody's plate full and pass your hearty Whole Wheat Nut and Raisin Muffins. See Index for recipe. Or slice some of our Whole Wheat Mini Loaves, and you've got one heck of a meal!

The lamb? That can make another meal.

Cut the cooked breast into *riblets.* Remove any visible fat, being careful to cut so they don't fall apart.

When ready to eat, have the rest of the meal ready, such as vegetables, including potatoes, because you will broil these.

Turn the broiler on to get hot in the meantime.

Make our *"Make and Bake," or* use *Progresso or other seasoned crumbs.* We have used both ways.

Put some *melted margarine* in one soup plate and seasoned crumbs in another soup plate. Dip the riblets first in the melted margarine, then in the crumbs.

Broil in a shallow broiling pan (no rack please) a few minutes only. Serve piping hot.

Crunchy? Good? And truly a "penny pincher" if ever there was one.

Magic Vegetable Soup

what's so magic about this soup? . . . it doesn't taste like lamb at all . . . it is a beautiful basic soup that can be made into a vegetable soup, a bean and barley soup or a split pea or lentil soup . . . you make the choice

Preheat oven 450°.

Wash, peel and cut into 4 pieces each *2 carrots, 1 large onion or 2 medium ones.* Wash *2 stalks celery* and cut each into 3 pieces.

Wash under running water *1 whole lamb breast.* Put into a

large pot. Add *8 cups cold tap water,* the vegetables, *1 beef bouillon powder or cube* and *2 vegetable bouillon powders or cubes.*

Bring to a simmer. Cover. Simmer 1 hour to 1 hour and 10 minutes until the breast is tender.

Remove the breast and vegetables from the broth.

Put 2 paper towels (we use Bounty) into a medium or large strainer over a bowl. Using a cup, pour the broth into the paper covered strainer to strain the broth.

We usually put the broth into the refrigerator overnight for the fat to come to the top. If you wish to use right away, remove the fat first with a spoon, then use pieces of paper towels.

Chop the vegetables you removed from the broth into small cubes or pieces. Put back in the soup.

Heat and eat.

Homemade Vegetable Soup

that's what makes a house a home

Soak overnight *1 cup Great Northern Dried Beans or Kidney Beans* in *2½ cups water* to soften; or bring beans and water to a boil. Boil 2 minutes, take off heat. Soak 1 hour in same water with lid on.

Add beans and water to *12 cups broth (chicken or beef).* Bring to a boil.

Add *½ cup each chopped celery* (not too fine), *onions, 1 pack (24 ounces) frozen assorted vegetables, 1 can (1 pound) stewed tomatoes, 1 teaspoon salt* and a *pinch of sugar.*

Or you can substitute 1 cup each fresh or frozen vegetables—carrots, peas, green beans, corn and green lima beans—and bring to a simmer. With lid on simmer about 1½ hours.

Add *1 small green cabbage,* shredded. Cook 1 hour longer to get a delicious taste. Add some *pepper* and a *little salt* if needed.

Let cool. Keep in refrigerator to season overnight. Then eat some, freeze the rest. Makes about 13½ cups, or 8 pints soup.

You work only once, but you will enjoy this delicious soup many times.

French Strained Vegetable Soup

Wash *2 cups Great Northern Beans.*

Bring *5 cups water* and 2 cups beans to a boil. Boil 2 minutes. Take off heat. Soak 1 hour in same water with lid on.

Add beans and water to *12 cups broth (chicken and beef).* Bring to a boil.

Add *1 cup chopped celery* (not too fine) and *1 cup chopped onions, 2 packs (24 ounces each) frozen assorted vegetables, 1 can (1 pound) stewed tomatoes, 1 teaspoon salt* and a *pinch of sugar.*

Bring to a simmer. Simmer with lid on 1½ hours.

Add *1 small green cabbage, shredded.*

Cook 1 hour longer.

Add some *pepper* and a *little salt,* if needed.

Push through the food mill.

Eat some; freeze the rest.

Chicken, Beef "Large Pot Soup"

this makes ready cooked chicken . . . ready cooked beef . . . and ready cooked broth to make many dishes from 1 cooking . . . this is a "go about your business" dish to make into a very large pot or kettle of soup

Put into large pot or kettle *one 3½ pound chicken* cut into 10 pieces, a *1¾ pound piece of chuck.* You can use the center part of a blade roast, or you can use the more expensive arm roast, which is also chuck, or you can use a whole piece of round steak, or the less expensive bottom round steak.

Wash, peel and cut into 3 pieces *2 carrots, 1 nice bunch of the celery branches, 2 medium onions.* Add to the soup.

Pour *enough cold tap water to come well over the meat and vegetables,* about 11 cups.

Bring to a boil. Spoon the scum off. Add *1 teaspoon salt.* Bring back to a boil.

Turn heat to low. Cover. Simmer about 45 minutes until the chicken is cooked but not overcooked. Remove the chicken to a plate. Continue to cook the soup until the beef is tender, takes about 1 hour 15 minutes. Altogether the soup has cooked 2 hours.

This makes 9 cups of broth after the fat is removed. You

make 3 soups using 2¾ cups of this broth for a split pea soup, 2¾ cups for lima bean soup and 3½ cups for lentils.

While the beef and soup are simmering, remove the skin and bones from the chicken. Place the skin and bones in a saucepan. Cover with cold tap water. Bring to a boil. Turn heat to low. Cover. Simmer until the broth tastes like chicken broth, takes about 2 hours. Strain. Let get cold. You can use this broth to make some of our soups, too.

Out of the chicken, skin and bones broth you use 2¾ cups to make a green split pea soup, and you add to the 2¼ cups left ½ cup of canned chicken soup to make another lima bean soup.

For these recipes, see the next pages.

Green Or Yellow Split Pea Soup From The Chicken, Beef "Large Pot Soup"

good any time

Wash *1 cup dry yellow or green split peas* under running water.

Put into a pot the *2¾ cups broth* and *2¾ cups cold tap water, ½ stalk celery, 1 carrot* cut into quarters, *1 medium onion* and *½ teaspoon salt* and the 1 cup split peas.

Bring to a boil.

Turn heat to low. Cover. Simmer. Stir now and then as it simmers. Simmer about 1 hour until the peas and the other vegetables are soft.

Push through a food mill.

Put back into the pot and bring to a simmer. Simmer 5 minutes. Add *pepper* to taste.

You eat whenever you are ready, as this reheats well and also freezes well.

This makes about 4½ cups soup.

Lima Bean Soup From The Chicken, Beef "Large Pot Soup"

a protein soup that tastes like more

Wash *1 cup dried lima beans,* either baby or large, under running water.

Wash under running water *2 tablespoons large, whole barley* called "Pearl Barley."

Cut into small pieces *2 tablespoons dried mushrooms,* and soak in a *small bowl of cold water* 15 minutes.

Put into a pot *2¾ cups of broth, 2¾ cups cold tap water,* 1 cup lima beans, 2 tablespoons "pearl" barley, the mushrooms and the liquid they soaked in, *½ stalk celery, 1 medium onion, 1 small carrot* and *½ teaspoon salt.*

Bring to a boil. Cover. Let simmer. Stir now and then. Simmer about 1½ hours until the barley and beans are soft.

Push ¼ cup of the limas and the rest of the vegetables through a food mill.

Put back into the rest of the soup. Bring to a simmer. Simmer 5 minutes. Taste. Add *salt and pepper* to taste.

This makes about 4½ cups.

This soup freezes well.

Lentil Soup From The Chicken, Beef "Large Pot Soup"

a protein soup that you will make over and over

Wash under running water *1 cup dried lentils.*

Put into a pot *3½ cups broth, 3½ cups water, 1 small mealy potato* cut into halves, *½ stalk celery, 1 large onion, 1 carrot,* all cut into quarters, *½ teaspoon salt, ½ bay leaf* and *1 whole allspice.*

Bring to a boil. Cover. Let simmer, stirring now and then. Simmer about 1 hour and 15 minutes until soft.

Push ¼ cup of the lentils and the rest of the vegetables through a food mill; or you can push all the lentils through the food mill.

Bring to a simmer. Add *salt* and *pepper* if you wish.

This makes 6 cups of soup.

Like the other "protein" soups, this freezes well.

A Very Quick Easy Onion Soup

made from our "Homemade Dried Onion Soup Mix"

How to make Toasted Dried Minced Onions:

Put *3 tablespoons dried onions* into a small skillet. Don't go away. Cook, stir over medium heat about 3 minutes, taking the skillet off and on the heat so it doesn't burn, takes about 3 minutes until golden brown and toasted.

Spread on a large plate to cool at once.

This is our "Toasted Dried Minced Onions."

Homemade Dried Onion Soup Mix (no artificial flavors):

Mix together *3 Herbox or other Instant Dried Onion Bouillon Broth* and *2 Herbox Instant Dried Beef Bouillon Broth* with *¼ teaspoon sugar, ¼ teaspoon celery salt, ½ teaspoon oil* and the 3 tablespoons "Toasted Dried Minced Onions."

Stir in *4 cups water*. Bring to a boil. Turn heat to low.

Simmer 5 minutes.

Serve hot with Cheese Toasted Topping Bread if you wish.

Cheese Toasted Topping Bread:

Diagonally slice *French bread or Italian bread* into thickish slices and toast until well toasted on both sides.

Sprinkle grated *cheddar cheese or Gruyère* and top with grated *Parmesan cheese*. Toast top side only until melted and browned. Don't burn.

Float on top of soup. Eat at once.

Our supermarket pulpy bread is not good for this, because it gets soggy.

Tomato Soup

a good way to use up "leftover" (ready to use) tomato juice

Put *2 cups tomato juice, ½ cup water, 2 tablespoons rice, 1 tablespoon chopped onions, ¼ cup shredded carrots*, a *pinch of salt* and *¼ teaspoon sugar* into a saucepan.

Bring to a boil. Turn heat to low. Stir now and then. Cook 10 minutes.

This is a very refreshing soup.

Reheats well.

For a meal in a soup plate, drain 1 can (wet pack) small shrimp (4½ ounces). Run cold water over the shrimp. Drain. Add to the soup. Bring to a boil. Serve.

Turkey Soup

from a roasted turkey which you have "ready cooked" . . . some people call them "leftovers"

Into a large kettle put all the *bones, skin, giblets and tiny odds and ends of the roasted turkey.*

Add *12 cups water, 1 large carrot, 1 large onion, 2 stalks celery, ½ piece bay leaf* and a *parsnip* if you have one.

Bring to a boil. Add *1 teaspoon salt.*

Turn heat to low. Simmer 3 hours. Add *salt* to taste. Strain. Put in refrigerator overnight for the fat to come to the top.

Remove all the turkey pieces from the bones. Cover; refrigerate.

In the morning remove the fat. Place the broth in a kettle.

Chop fine *2 carrots, 1 stalk celery* and *1 small onion.* Add to the soup with *½ cup rice, 1 can (8 ounces) stewed tomatoes, 1 large potato* chopped into small pieces and the pieces of turkey.

Bring to a boil. Turn heat to medium low. Cook until rice is tender, about 20 minutes.

Add *salt and pepper* to taste.

Manhattan Clam Chowder

Cut out the hard stems from *2 cans stewed tomatoes (8 ounces),* and cut the tomatoes into bite size pieces.

Put into a saucepan. Add *2 cans V8 Juice (6 ounces), or a larger can, 2 cans minced clams (8 ounces), 2 whole dried bay leaves, ¼ to ½ teaspoon dried thyme leaves,* according to your taste, a good *grind of pepper* and *salt* to taste. Bring to a boil.

A little extra *chopped onion, celery* and *green pepper,* added to the chowder, enhances the chowder.

Cook 10 minutes.

You can add *1 tablespoon oil, butter or margarine.* Cook, stir 1 minute. Serve piping hot.

Tip: Do not buy canned chopped clams, as they are tough; buy the *minced* clams.

Chicken Salad

a very quick dish for singles, meaning for one person . . . you can multiply for as many as you wish

Open *1 can chicken (5 ounces).* This makes ¼ pound chicken.

Chop *2 tablespoons celery, 2 tablespoons onions,* and *1 tablespoon scallions.*

Mix together with *3 tablespoons mayonnaise, 2 tablespoons sweet pickles,* a *good grind of pepper* and *salt to taste.*

Gently mix into the chicken.

For two hearty eaters, double everything.

Summertime Chicken Salad

everything is in it including, of course, your Ready Cooked Chicken and all the vegetables . . . it's a meal in a salad

Cut enough *Ready Cooked Chicken, about 2 cups,* into the size cubes so you know it's chicken.

Chop *¼ cup celery* and add.

Stir *2 tablespoons water* into *½ cup mayonnaise.* Mix gently with the chicken. Refrigerate.

Boil *enough potatoes to make 2 cups,* cubed.

Drain these: *1 can (8 ounces) cubed carrots, 1 can (8½ ounces) peas* and *1 can (8½ ounces) cut green beans.* (Using canned green beans in a salad is about the best way to use canned green beans.)

Chop *½ cup celery* and *¼ cup scallions.* Chop fine *2 tablespoons onions.*

Put all these vegetables into a bowl. Then mix together *¼ cup oil, 3 tablespoons vinegar, 1 teaspoon sugar, salt* and *pepper* to taste.

Pour over the vegetables and let marinate in the refrigerator ½ hour.

Add *½ cup fresh mayonnaise.* Toss gently with 2 spoons. (Tip: read the label on the jar of mayonnaise to be sure it is fresh. Does it have a date? If not, taste it at home before using. Why? I once had to throw out my salad because the mayonnaise was not fresh. Yes, it broke my heart!)

Put the cubed chicken into a bowl. Add *2 tablespoons parsley,* finely chopped, *¼ cup plus 1 tablespoon mayonnaise, salt* to taste and a good grind or shake of *pepper.*

Arrange on crisp lettuce leaves. Surround with the mixed vegetable salad.

I once had a salad like this in Zurich, which was served on individual plates with the chicken salad (made as a regular chicken salad) in the center and each vegetable, marinated in vinegar and oil dressing (no mayonnaise, the chicken had mayonnaise), and each arranged in a small bunch, separately, around the chicken. This was very nice, as the chicken with its light mayonnaise and the well seasoned oil and vinegar dressing for the vegetables made a nice contrast. Try it.

Hawaiian Style Chicken Salad

it's plain . . . but it tastes fancy

With a scissors cut into large cubes *2 cups "ready cooked" chicken,* chop *½ cup celery, ½ cup onions,* and cut with the scissors *¼ cup scallions with the green tops,* too.

Drain *1 cup cubes of canned pineapple.*

In a large bowl put the chicken, onions, celery, scallions, pineapple and *½ cup unsweetened mayonnaise.*

Mix gently together. Add *salt to taste,* about ¼ teaspoon, and a little *pepper.*

Mix gently.

Chicken And Ham Salad

we use "ready cooked" chicken . . . and when, as our Pennsylvania Dutch say, "We're fresh out," we use boned canned white meat chicken . . . they don't seem to be as oversoft as the canned whole chicken

Combine *2 cups ready cooked or canned chicken* and *2 cups ready cooked or canned ham* cut into cubes with *½ cup each chopped onions, celery, ¼ cup scallions* and *4 tablespoons sweet pickles.*

Stir *1 teaspoon wet mustard (Gulden's)* into *½ cup unsweetened mayonnaise, salt,* and *pepper* to taste.

Gently mix with the chicken, ham and the other vegetables.

Place on bed of shredded lettuce or young green cabbage. Garnish with slices of small, red, crisp radishes and thin, thin slices of cucumber.

Pour a *"Vinaigrette Sauce"* over the lettuce or cabbage, radishes and cucumbers. (See Index for "Vinaigrette Sauce" under dressings.)

"Ready Cooked" Beef Salad For A Hot Day

it's different . . . hardly anything to do

Slice *4 hard cooked eggs.*

Cut the *cold "ready cooked" boiled beef* into thin slices. Place on a platter.

Cover with thin, thin slices of *onion.* (The red ones are nice.)

On one side arrange the eggs.

On the other side arrange *one can drained red kidney beans.*

At one end arrange sliced *dill pickles.*

On the other end arrange *sweet pickles* and *olives.*

Pour your favorite *Italian Dressing* over the beef, eggs and beans.

With some crusty bread and fruit for dessert, what could be better for a hot day.

Instead of the dressing, one of my friends sprinkles a little wine vinegar over the beef. It tastes very good, too. For the eggs you could use unsweetened mayonnaise and the Italian Dressing on the kidney beans.

A Special Crabmeat Salad

this has to be special at the price you have to pay for crabmeat these days

You need *1 pound of fresh or pasteurized "special" or lump crabmeat.*

Remove any shells in the crabmeat.

Hard cook *2 eggs.* Run under cold water. Cool, shell, cube.

Chop *2 tablespoons fresh parsley.* Mince fine *2 tablespoons onion* and *2 tablespoons scallions.* Slice *1 stalk celery* into small, thin, slanted pieces.

Wash and cut into small flowerets *1 head cauliflower.* Steam just until tender, but crisp, takes about 3 to 5 minutes.

Put everything into a large bowl.

Add a *good grind of pepper* and *½ teaspoon salt.*

Mix together *1 cup unsweetened mayonnaise, 1 tablespoon mustard,* preferably Belgian or French Dijon type, and *½ teaspoon dry mustard.*

Stir in *2 tablespoons dry vermouth.* Gently mix together.

Garnish with little *red cherry tomatoes.*

Serve with a side dish of noodles accented with currants and chopped walnuts.

Cook enough medium size noodles for four in slightly salted, boiling water until the noodles are cooked but not squashy soft and have a little bite. Drain.

Add 2 tablespoons soft margarine, salt and pepper to taste, ¼ cup currants and ¼ cup chopped walnuts.

Serve hot.

Very Special Fish Salad

this fish salad tastes better than the usual because we cooked the fish the day before in our Fish Soup, and it absorbed all the good flavors of the vegetables in the soup . . . we cooked "once for twice"

Put *2 cups cooked fillet of fish* cut with a scissors, so it doesn't mash the fish, into a large bowl.

Chop *¼ cup each, celery, green pepper, scallions;* then cut or mince fine *½ of a small onion* (even less than ¼ cup).

Add *¼ teaspoon salt,* a *good grind of pepper, 6 tablespoons mayonnaise* and a *light shake of cayenne pepper.*

Gently mix together; don't crush. Taste.

Serve immediately; or put into refrigerator.

A So Good Mixed Vegetable Salad

you use a ready cooked vegetable with a canned vegetable which also makes it an easy salad to make

We use *1 cup ready cooked flowerets of cauliflower* and about *2 cups cubed, ready cooked potatoes* with *1 can (8 ounces) drained whole green beans,* which we cut in halves.

Chop a *branch of green scallions* and *2 tablespoons onions.* Add *4 tablespoons oil* and *2 tablespoons wine vinegar, salt* and *pepper* to taste, and then gently mix with a little *unsweetened or our Homemade Mayonnaise.*

That's all there is to it. We eat ours as a first course and need no vegetables with our "protein" course. Sometimes I omit the potatoes, but mostly my husband insists on them. He says it does the "right thing" to the salad.

A Two-Way Easy Vegetable Salad Or Hot Vegetable Dish

serve it cold for a hot summer day or heat for a cold winter day and it becomes a hot vegetable dish

For a hot summer day:

Run under cold water *1 can (15 ounces) great northern beans.* Set aside in a large bowl.

Drain *1 can (1 pound, 1 ounce) niblets corn.* Add to the beans.

Chop *1 small onion, 1 branch scallions* and *1 small green or red pepper.* Add to the beans.

Mix together *2 tablespoons lemon juice, 1 tablespoon wine vinegar* with *3 or 4 tablespoons oil* and *1 teaspoon Italian herbs.*

Mix with the vegetables.

For a cold winter day:

Put the above vegetables and sauce into a saucepan and bring to a boil.

Turn heat to simmer. Simmer until the onions are soft and clear, takes about 10 minutes.

Green Bean Salad

Cut *2 cups Ready Cooked green beans* or 1 pound canned, drained green beans into 1 inch pieces. Put into a large bowl.

Chop *¼ cup green pepper, ¼ cup celery, ¼ cup scallions, ¼ cup onions,* and *¼ cup pecan nuts.*

Add to the beans.

Stir into *⅓ cup unsweetened mayonnaise, 2 tablespoons distilled vinegar, ¼ teaspoon sugar, pinch salt,* and *pepper* to taste.

Add to the bean mixture. Stir gently.

A Summer Salad And A Winter Vegetable

summer you eat cold . . . winter you eat hot

Summer Day Salad

Run under cold water and drain *1 can (15 ounces) kidney beans.* Put into a large bowl.

Wash and cut into tiny flowerets *1 small head cauliflower.* Save the stems to steam and use another time as a snack or vegetable.

Chop *1 small or medium green pepper* and *2 tablespoons parsley* fine. Add the rest of these vegetables to the beans.

Make this curry dressing:

In a bowl put *½ cup unsweetened mayonnaise.*

Stir in *½ teaspoon curry* and a *good grind of pepper.*

Stir in *2 tablespoons dry vermouth.*

Stir gently into the vegetables.

Add *salt* and *pepper* to taste.

Winter Day Vegetable

Prepare the vegetables as above.

Steam the cauliflower until done but still a little crisp.

Add the green pepper.

Stir, cook about 5 minutes until cooked but still crisp.

Add the rest of the vegetables to the skillet. Heat.

Stir *½ teaspoon dried curry powder* into *½ cup unsweetened mayonnaise.*

Stir in *2 tablespoons nonfat milk.*

Heat on low heat just until hot, so it won't curdle.

Pour over the heated vegetables and serve.

Bean Salad

Hard cook *3 eggs;* chop.

Strain *2 (16 ounce) cans Great Northern beans.*

Mix the beans and eggs with *½ cup minced fine onions, ¼ cup celery, 8 sweet gherkins or other sweet pickles,* quartered and sliced, *½ cup unsweetened mayonnaise* diluted with *2 tablespoons milk, salt* and *pepper* to taste.

Add ½ minced green pepper for a change.

Tip: With slices of canned meat or corned beef or shredded and fried dried beef, you have a good quickie meal; and don't forget to open a can of peaches, which is usually a good buy.

For a good hot toasted bread, cut an Italian bread down the middle lengthwise, spread with margarine, then put it back together and heat in the oven; or leave it open and put it under the broiler.

Kidney Bean Salad

To take the canned taste from beans, run them under cold water a second; save the bean broth.

Mix *1 can (16 ounces) firm kidney beans* with *2 hard cooked eggs,* diced, *¼ cup each minced celery, onion* and *green pepper, ¼ cup or more to taste unsweetened mayonnaise, ¼ teaspoon salt, ⅛ teaspoon pepper* or to taste and *2 tablespoons milk or bean broth.* Mix gently so as not to crush the beans.

Let season in the refrigerator.

If your family is like ours, double this recipe.

No Work Bean Salad

all you have to do is mix them

Drain *1 can (1 pound) green beans* and *1 can red kidney beans.*

Chop *2 tablespoons scallions* and *2 tablespoons onions* and *½ cup walnuts or pecans.*

Add to the beans with *½ cup Italian Salad Dressing* and a dash of *pepper.*

Place in refrigerator to marinate overnight or at least a few hours.

We serve this in deep saucers.

For a change:

Instead of the Italian Dressing, add ½ cup of our French dressing made by mixing together *½ cup oil* and *4 tablespoons tarragon vinegar,* or *4 tablespoons wine vinegar* and *½ teaspoon dried tarragon.*

Macaroni Salad

Cook *1 (8 ounce) box macaroni* according to directions on box. Don't overcook, drain, cool.

Hard cook *4 eggs.*

Separate, mince the whites and add to the macaroni.

Push the yolks through a strainer; use your clean hands.

Stir the yolks into *¼ cup distilled white vinegar.* Mix with *2 tablespoons prepared mustard* and *2 tablespoons sugar;* then add to macaroni.

Mince *½ green pepper, ¼ cup celery* and *¼ cup onion.* Add with *1 teaspoon salt* to taste, *¼ teaspoon pepper, 1 teaspoon celery seed* and *½ cup unsweetened mayonnaise* to the macaroni gently so as not to mash.

Taste, correct seasoning.

Cucumber Salad

for people who like cucumbers

Cut a *cucumber* into very thin slices to make about *1½ cups.*

Slice *1 small onion* very thin.

Add to the cucumber with *¼ teaspoon dried dill or ½ teaspoon chopped fresh dill.*

Mix together *¼ teaspoon salt, ½ cup yogurt* and *1 tablespoon milk.*

Stir into the cucumber-onion mixture.

Put in refrigerator to marinate until ready to eat.

Potato Salad

the potatoes come from a can and, believe it or not, it tastes quite good when you're in a hurry and everyone wants to eat

Drain *1 can (1 pound) potatoes.* Run cold water over and drain again. (Del Monte Whole New Potatoes is a fine brand, or you can use your favorite.) Cut into cubes.

Hard boil *1 egg.*

Chop *2 tablespoons each, onion, scallions, ¼ cup celery* and *1 tablespoon parsley,* and add.

Chop the hard boiled egg and add.

Add *¼ cup plus 2 tablespoons non-sweet mayonnaise.*

Lightly mix, adding *salt and pepper to taste.*

Homemade Potato Salad

winter or summer it's always welcome

Cook enough medium or small size "not" mealy *potatoes to make* about *2 cups.* Don't use large potatoes as the outside of the potatoes will overcook and become mealy until the center will be done; and, if you cook until the outside is cooked only, the insides will be raw. So cook medium or small potatoes and the inside and outside of the potatoes both will be done at the same time.

Let the potatoes get cold before peeling them.

This is better than to try to peel them when they are hot as they crumble if you cut while they are hot. The flavor you add is supposed to penetrate better if you cut when hot but we prefer not to do this as we don't like mushy potatoes and we let our potatoes "set" long enough before eating for the flavor to flavor the potatoes.

When potatoes are cold, cut into cubes. Tip: Slice with a knife, then cut with a scissors into cubes.

Chop *2 tablespoons onions, 2 tablespoons scallions,* and *¼ cup celery*. Chop fine *1 tablespoon parsley*. Add to the potatoes.

Put *¼ cup unsweetened mayonnaise* into a bowl. Stir in *1 tablespoon white vinegar* to taste. Mix lightly into the potato salad. Add *salt and pepper* to taste.

Sometimes we add *1 hard cooked chopped egg* to our potato salad.

Sometimes we stir the hard cooked egg yolk into the mayonnaise for a pretty color and chop the whites and add to the potato salad. This potato salad looks prettier, too.

Our House Salad

we make this salad often during a week at my house, changing the kinds of lettuce only, or we substitute other "in season" vegetables . . . the rest stays the same . . . for two; double for four

As you follow the directions, put each vegetable into a medium bowl to put in the refrigerator.

Wash, dry and cut into large cubes *1 small tomato*. Put into the medium bowl.

Wash, dry and chop *1 stalk, including the bulb, scallion* and *½ of 1 very small onion.*

Peel and slice very thin *¼ cucumber.*

Wash, dry and slice very thin *4 small red radishes.*

Chop fine *1 tablespoon parsley.*

Wash, dry, tear into bite size pieces the *lettuce of your choice,* Romaine, Boston, Bibb or Iceberg. Gently place on top; don't push down on the cut vegetables. Cover with Saran Wrap. Place in the refrigerator until ready to use.

When ready to use, remove the Saran Wrap. Gently put the lettuce on the Saran Wrap.

Mix *3 tablespoons oil, 1 tablespoon wine vinegar*. We like Japanese Rice Wine Vinegar, and *¼ teaspoon salt.*

Mix with the vegetables but not the lettuce. Taste. Add *salt* and *pepper* to taste. Let stand 15 minutes. (You can be finishing the dinner.)

Gently mix the lettuce with the rest. Taste. Add *salt,* if necessary. Eat at once.

We like this salad because we get fresh vegetables and don't have to cook them and get "all" their vitamins.

Rice Salad

so simple, so good . . . this will also become one of your favorites

Cook 1 cup rice and let get cold; or use your ready cooked rice. To freshen 3 cups ready cooked rice, put into a saucepan with 4 tablespoons water. Cook, shake over high heat 1 minute. Turn heat to low. Cover. Cook and shake about 5 minutes until the rice is fluffy as it was, but also tender. Keeping rice in the refrigerator, even though covered, changes the texture of the rice although it is still grain-by-grain separate.

Put the *"freshened" rice* into a large bowl.

Sprinkle *3 tablespoons oil* over the rice and *2 tablespoons white vinegar*. We use a Japanese Rice Vinegar. With 2 spoons mix together lightly. Let stand.

Chop *¼ cup scallions, ¼ cup onions, ½ cup celery* and *½ cup green pepper.*

Add to the rice.

Drain *1 jar (2 ounces) pimentos* and add.

Add *¼ cup Wishbone Italian Dressing* and a *good grind of pepper.*

Fluff with two spoons.

Lynda's Salad

with Lynda's tart lemony dressing

This is one of our favorites!

Arrange *slices of a sweet cantaloupe,* cut into half moon slices, on one side of each individual salad plate.

Put *slices of tomatoes* on the other side. This is a nice contrast in texture and taste.

Make the dressing:

Put into a bowl *1 8 ounce jar Kraft's Miracle Whip Dressing.*

Stir in *½ clove garlic, crushed, 6 tablespoons strained lemon juice, 1 tablespoon wine vinegar* and *¼ teaspoon paprika* until smooth.

Serve over the tomatoes.

Marie's Slaw

Chop *enough cabbage to make 2 cups* (not too fine).

Add *2 tablespoons chopped green pepper* and *¼ teaspoon celery seed.*

Put *¼ cup mayonnaise* into a bowl.

Stir in *1¾ teaspoons sugar* and *⅛ teaspoon salt.*

Fold, don't stir hard, *2½ teaspoons cider vinegar,* or a little more to taste, into the mayonnaise mixture.

Add to the cabbage mixture and combine.

Place in refrigerator to season.

Spiced Beets

tastes better than any of the "store bought" ones

Mix together *3 tablespoons white vinegar, 3 teaspoons sugar,* a *pinch of salt, 3 allspice* and *1 bay leaf* cut into 3 pieces.

Put *1 can (8 ounces) of small whole beets* into a bowl. (These usually taste better.) Slice the beets.

Stir in the vinegar-spice mixture.

Put in refrigerator to marinate, preferably overnight.

Serve in deep saucers with the tasty juice.

Larry's Cucumber Pepper Relish

the best I've ever tasted . . . an old fashioned recipe handed down from mother to daughter . . . and now we hand it down also from son to son!

Make this in season:

To make it easy, so you don't have to finish this at midnight, start to cut up the vegetables at 10 o'clock in the morning; or figure the time out so that it is convenient for you.

You need a clean cloth bag, preferably made of 2 layers of cheese cloth that you can close tightly. We sometimes make a "make do" one of 2 layers of the cheese cloth, closing it with a strong piece of cord.

We start at 10 o'clock in the morning and wash, then chop into ¼ inch cubes, *8 cups unpeeled cucumbers.* Set aside.

Wash, drain, remove seeds and cube into ¼ inch pieces *2 cups sweet red peppers* and *2 cups sweet green peppers.*

Peel and cube into ¼ inch pieces *1 cup onions.*

Put all of these vegetables into a large container, preferably a ceramic bowl or a large soup kettle lined with Teflon or even an aluminum one.

Sprinkle with *1 tablespoon turmeric.*

Dissolve *½ cup salt* in *8 cups cool tap water.* Pour over the vegetables and mix. Let stand 4 hours.

Drain in a large strainer over a colander in your sink.

Put back in your container. *Cover with cool tap water.* Let stand 1 hour. Drain as before.

Put into a cheese cloth bag (or your homemade one) *1 tablespoon dried mustard seed, 2 sticks cinnamon, 2 teaspoons while dried cloves* and *2 teaspoons whole allspice.* Tie the bag closed tightly, so these spices will not fall out.

Into a large pot put the bag with the spices and *4 cups white distilled vinegar.* (We use Heinz.) Add *1½ cups dark brown sugar*. Bring to a boil.

Pour over the vegetables. Let get cold. Cover with a clean dish towel. Let stand 18 hours in the kitchen.

After the 18 hours, bring a pot full of water to a boil. With this boiling water scald your clean jars, and put your lids into boiling water to have ready as soon as you are ready to fill the jars with the hot relish.

Remove the bag of spices from the relish.

On high heat bring the relish to a simmer. Don't boil! But let get "hot through" by simmering.

Pack hot into the clean, scalded hot jars. Seal at once with the scalded lids.

Let get cold. Store in a cool place.

We also freeze this relish.

This takes time—but it's worth it.

My Husband's Favorite Salad

Put the following into a large bowl:

Chop or cut into small cubes *1 medium good-tasting tomato*. Slice thin *10 small ruby red, crisp radishes*. Cut thin *1 small thin cucumber*, peeled. Chop fine *¼ small onion*. Chop fine or cut with a scissors *enough scallions—the green part too—to make 2 tablespoons*. Chop fine *2 tablespoons parsley*.

These go into the bottom of the bowl. You can do this ahead, if you wish.

Cover with cut up or broken *salad greens*. We use Romaine quite often.

If making ahead, cover with Saran Wrap and refrigerate. If you use at once, stir the salad dressing into the mixed vegetables. Taste. Add *salt and pepper* to your taste. Cover with the greens.

Just before eating, mix everything together.

Serve.

Salad Dressing

Put into a bowl *5 tablespoons oil, 1 tablespoon wine vinegar, salt to taste, a pinch of sugar*.

Mix with a rotary beater until creamy, takes about a minute. Stir in *1 tablespoon rich cream*. Pour over the salad. Mix gently. Spoon into plates.

Vinaigrette Sauce

Mix together *¼ cup Japanese rice vinegar*, or an American wine vinegar that isn't too strong or a French red wine vinegar with *½ teaspoon salt* until dissolved.

Then stir in *1 teaspoon wet mustard* (Dijon type mustard, or Gulden's), *pepper to taste* (ground fresh with a pepper grinder—makes pepper taste and smell wonderful), and a *pinch of sugar*—about ⅛ teaspoon.

Mix this well.

Add slowly, mixing as you add, *¾ cup soybean, safflower, corn oil or cotton seed oil* or use half of any of these oils and ½ olive oil. (Make sure these oils are fresh.) We like a light olive oil. Some people like a heavy one. Test to see which you like best.

For a change you can add a clove of garlic, or crush it into the bowl, or use garlic powder to taste.

You can use part lemon juice instead of vinegar, or all lemon juice.

More changes if you wish—add minced shallots, or 1 or 2 teaspoons minced scallions or ½ teaspoon curry powder, or my husband likes Roquefort cheese, a blue cheese, crumbled into the Vinaigrette Sauce. Some people like red wine instead of wine vinegar; others add some red wine and the wine vinegar (that's me).

Also, here are more choices—hard boiled egg yolks or whites or both; tarragon or other herbs added, such as faithful chopped parsley or chives or chervil.

A tip: My French Alsatian friend always added, when I wasn't looking, a tablespoon or two of real honest-to-goodness heavy cream. How do I know? I peeped!

You can make a delicious salad of watercress and use Vinaigrette Sauce and chopped hard cooked egg yolks. We usually push the yolks through a sieve—looks pretty, too.

Wine Vinegar Salad Dressing

for four salads on four plates

Put *½ cup unsweetened mayonnaise* into a bowl.

Stir in *4 tablespoons French Wine Vinegar.*

Mix together well or

Put ½ cup unsweetened mayonnaise into a bowl.

Stir in *4 tablespoons Spice Island Tarragon Red Wine Vinegar* or your favorite wine vinegar. Mix together well.

We use this dressing over our "Layered Vegetable Salad."

Chop enough *Romaine, Bibb, Boston or Iceberg lettuce to* make 4 nice beds on 4 salad plates.

Drain *1 can whole asparagus.* Arrange on the bed of lettuce.

Pour ¼ of the Salad Dressing over the 4 salads.

Peel, cut and slice thin enough *cucumbers* to make a layer on top of the asparagus. Sprinkle a little *dill* on top—fresh or dried.

Make another layer of thin *sliced green peppers.*

Last make a layer of thin *sliced tomatoes* especially if they are in season and top with very thin *sliced onions* if you like onions.

Pour the rest of the sauce over each salad.

When you serve this, don't bother to cook a vegetable—you've got it all in the salad plate.

A baked or boiled new potato would go nice with the fish, chicken or beef course.

Russian Salad Dressing

it's the lemon juice that gives it "zing"

Mix *½ cup unsweetened mayonnaise* with *¼ cup catsup* and *4 teaspoons lemon juice.*

Three Creamy Dressings

good in potato salad, green bean salad and, when thinned, over salad greens

Blue Cheese Dressing

Mix together *½ cup unsweetened mayonnaise, ¼ teaspoon garlic powder, ¼ teaspoon onion powder* and *¼ cup milk.*

Cut or crumble *2 tablespoons blue cheese* into the dressing. We use Cold Pack Blue Cheese (Treasure Cove).

Thinned Creamy Dressing

fine for salad greens

Mix together *½ cup unsweetened mayonnaise, ¼ teaspoon garlic powder, ¼ teaspoon onion powder* and *¼ cup milk.*

Thick Creamy Dressing

Mix together *½ cup unsweetened mayonnaise, ¼ teaspoon garlic powder* and *¼ teaspoon onion powder.*

This is the one we use to make "Green Bean Salad" or other vegetable salads.

Mayonnaise Sauces

used as a dressing for salads

What mayonnaise? Use your favorite . . . we do and we also make our own when we have the time.

Anchovy Mayonnaise

Stir into *½ cup mayonnaise ½ or 1 mashed anchovy fillet.*

Curry Mayonnaise

Stir into *1 cup mayonnaise ½ teaspoon curry powder, ½ teaspoon dry mustard* and *4 tablespoons dry vermouth.*

Egg Mayonnaise

Stir into *½ cup mayonnaise 2 hard cooked, mashed egg yolks, ½ tablespoon Dijon type wet mustard* and *½ tablespoon* (or 1 tablespoon to your taste) *wine vinegar*. (We use Japanese white rice wine vinegar when we can get it.)

Garlic Mayonnaise

Stir into *½ cup mayonnaise ½ teaspoon mashed anchovy, 1 teaspoon finely chopped parsley* and *½ teaspoon dried garlic powder.*

Herb Mayonnaise

Stir into *½ cup mayonnaise ½ teaspoon finely chopped parsley, chives, chervil* and *tarragon*. If using dried, add ⅛ to ¼ teaspoon each; then add more as you like. Remember, you can always add, but you can't take away. Of course, you can use Italian herbs or French herbs instead of the different herbs. Both the Italian herbs and the French are quite good. Start with ½ teaspoon and add to your taste.

Mustard Mayonnaise

Mix together *½ cup mayonnaise* and *1½ teaspoons Dijon type mustard.* You can also substitute Gulden's as it is quite good. This is wonderful in sandwiches. It makes chicken sandwiches on very thin bread something special.

Tarragon Mayonnaise

Stir into *½ cup mayonnaise ¼ teaspoon* (or ½ teaspoon to your taste) *dried tarragon.*

Tomato Mayonnaise

Stir in *½ cup mayonnaise, 1 tablespoon tomato sauce or puree, 1 tablespoon chopped pimentos* and *⅛ to ¼ teaspoon basil.*

Mustard Mayonnaise

for ham, cold cuts, beef (slices or sandwiches), hard boiled eggs and baloney and that's no baloney!

Mix together *½ cup unsweetened mayonnaise* with *2 teaspoons Gulden's Mustard* and a *tiny, tiny pinch of sugar.*

Dijon Mustard Sauce

delicious in an egg sandwich, as a "pepper upper" with fish and sparks sliced cold beef right into the "gourmet" class . . . and chicken? of course

Mix together *1 cup unsweetened mayonnaise* and *1½ teaspoons Belgian "Dijon Type Mustard."* You can also substitute the French Dijon Mustard, and Gulden's is quite good, too.

Yogurt, Mayonnaise Dressing

Mix together *½ cup unsweetened mayonnaise, ¼ cup*

Dannon Yogurt, 1 teaspoon lemon juice, 1 tablespoon wine vinegar, ¼ teaspoon garlic powder, ¼ teaspoon onion powder, pinch of sugar and 1 tablespoon fresh chopped parsley.

Sour Cream Horseradish Sauce

served with boiled beef . . . it's a divine dish . . . so simple . . . so good

Mix together *½ cup sour cream* and *4 teaspoons prepared horseradish.*

On low heat cook and stir slowly until it gets heated, but do not boil—just heat.

Serve with boiled beef or roast beef.

We many times serve this cold and don't cook it at all.

Our French Dressing

we use this dressing very often . . . this is for 2 people . . . multiply for 4

Put into a bowl *6 tablespoons oil.* (We use safflower or sometimes 3 tablespoons olive oil and 3 tablespoons safflower oil.) Add *2 tablespoons wine vinegar.* (We use Japanese Rice Vinegar, French Wine Vinegar, Spice Islands Tarragon Vinegar, Progresso Wine Vinegar or other red wine vinegar. Of course, you can use your favorite one.)

Add *¼ teaspoon salt* and a *pinch of sugar.* Mix well. We use a rotary beater or sometimes a fork, whichever is handy. We sometimes add 1 tablespoon water if the vinegar is strong!

We pour our dressing over the greens right before serving.

If we make "My Husband's Favorite Salad," we pour this over the vegetables and let marinate while we cook the dinner, if it's a quick meal, say about a 30-minute meal; then we mix this together with the greens right before serving. My husband loves to use this dressing from his salad when I serve steak. Then I increase the dressing and use 9 tablespoons oil, 3 tablespoons wine vinegar, ⅓ teaspoon salt and a pinch of sugar.

Never Fail
Homemade Mayonnaise

it's not only an excellent mayonnaise, but you can make it to your "taste" . . . it takes longer to write this than for you to make it

We find that we must get the "feel" of the mayonnaise as we make it, so we suggest using electric hand beaters (not the stationary kind), a rotary beater or a wooden spoon.

You need a small, deep, narrow bowl (the size of the small bowl of an electric mixer is OK).

Measure *1 cup oil.* Set aside and set aside *¼ teaspoon wine vinegar* plus *¼ teaspoon lemon juice.*

Put *2 egg yolks* into a small deep bowl. (You can freeze the whites to use as an "egg wash" for rolls or breads, or you can make our Silver Cup Cakes or our Chocolate Mousse, or just add them to scrambled eggs.)

Add about *⅛ teaspoon salt, ⅛ teaspoon wet mustard* of your choice, *⅛ teaspoon sugar.* Mix well on lowest speed.

Continue to mix on lowest speed (or slowly by hand). Gradually add ¼ teaspoon oil and combine before gradually adding another ¼ teaspoon oil. Do not add the oil until the one you have added has been absorbed and is thickened. Continue to add ¼ teaspoons oil at a time and let thicken before adding more until you have added about 1 or 2 tablespoons. Then start adding about ½ teaspoon at a time, waiting until each is absorbed before adding more. Gradually you can pour in all the oil by spoonfuls, remembering to let the oil be absorbed before adding more. If it gets thick, and it will, you can add the vinegar and lemon juice. When all the oil has been added, the mayonnaise will be too thick. *Stir in 1 tablespoon cold tap water and then stir in 1 more tablespoon cold tap water.* This lightens the mayonnaise.

Taste the mayonnaise and add a little more *salt* if it needs it and a little more *wine vinegar or lemon juice,* but go very lightly. Mayonnaise can be used in many dishes, and so you want it sort of neutral so you can flavor it when you use it.

A Delicious Cooked Curry Sauce

you won't believe it is so easy to make . . . wonderful with stuffed pancakes, stuffed Pasta Shells, and just as good when you want a curry sauce for chicken

Soften *1 package Cream Cheese with Chives* (3 ounces) by letting soften at room temperature.

Gradually stir in *½ cup milk* until soft. (We use skim milk.)

Stir in *¼ teaspoon garlic powder, a good pinch grated dried ginger, ½ teaspoon curry powder* and *salt to taste.*

Stir in *1 cup chicken broth,* fresh, canned or bouillon broth.

Cook, stir 2 minutes.

This can be heated and served hot; or it can be poured over stuffed chicken pancakes or stuffed pasta shells and baked in the oven.

Curry Sauce

with a touch of celery

Mix together *1 can Campbell's Cream of Celery Soup, 1 teaspoon curry powder, ¼ teaspoon onion powder, ¼ teaspoon garlic powder* and *¾ cup milk.*

Cook, stir until it comes to a boil.

Serve hot.

Can also be used as a sauce to bake with chicken in a casserole.

Curry Dressing

this is delicious

Mix *½ teaspoon dry mustard* and *½ teaspoon curry* into *1 cup unsweetened mayonnaise.*

Gradually stir in *¼ cup or 4 tablespoons dry vermouth.*

Cheese Sauce

when you need a cheese sauce for fish or chicken stuffed pancakes or pasta shells, or whatever!

Stir into *1 can Campbell's Cheddar Cheese Soup* slowly, not to lump, *¾ cup milk.*

Stir in *½ cup grated Swiss cheese or cheddar.*

Cook, stir until hot.

Stir in *1 tablespoon kirsch.* (This isn't a Penny Pincher idea! The one below is!)

Another Cheese Sauce

Stir into *1 can Campbell's Cheddar Cheese Soup ½ cup milk.*

Cook, stir, until hot.

Stir in *¼ cup Velveeta cheese.* Cook, stir until melted and hot.

Tomato, Cheese Sauce

nice to bake with fish, chicken and macaroni

Into *1 can Campbell's Condensed Tomato Soup* add *½ (8 ounce) package Velveeta cheese* shredded.

On "simmer heat," cook and stir about 10 minutes until the cheese is melted.

Take off heat. Gradually, a little at a time, stir in *1 cup milk.*

This is a tasty, smooth sauce.

Homemade Tomato Sauce

it's easy to make because your sauce is "ready cooked" in a can

To *1 can (15½ ounces) Progresso Pizza Sauce* add *¼ teaspoon garlic powder, ¼ teaspoon dried basil, ¼ teaspoon dried oregano,* a *pinch of salt* and *1 tablespoon oil.*

Bring to a simmer. Simmer 8 minutes.

Add *½ teaspoon grated Parmesan cheese.*

Cook 2 minutes.

We like Progresso Pizza Sauce fine because it is red ripe

tomatoes pureed with a basil leaf added, which you can't even taste. You add your own herbs to get a homemade taste.

Sour Cream Horseradish Sauce

delicious with boiled brisket

Mix together *1 cup sour cream* and *1 teaspoon,* or more to taste, of *prepared horseradish,* drained.

For a change use the red horseradish.

Hot Horseradish Sauce

Mix together *1 cup sour cream* and *horseradish,* drained, to taste.

Do not boil but heat on low heat until hot.

If you boil, the sour cream can curdle.

Horseradish Sauce

made with yogurt it almost even fools the sour cream lovers

Mix together *½ cup yogurt* with *2 tablespoons bottled horseradish* to taste.

That's all there is to it and it's good.

Two Sour Cream Dressings

For Beets

these are delicious over canned as well as cooked fresh beets . . . this recipe is for two, so you multiply for four

Tip: Whole, small beets taste better than the sliced beets, so buy the whole ones and slice them yourself.

Mix together *4 tablespoons white distilled vinegar, 1 tablespoon and 1 teaspoon sugar, 4 whole allspice or ¼ teaspoon ground allspice* and *2 large bay leaves* each cut into 4 pieces.

Drain *1 can (8½ ounces) whole beets.* Set the beets into a bowl. Slice them.

Stir the beet juice into the vinegar mixture. Pour over the sliced beets. Let marinate a day.

When ready to use, stir in slowly *¼ cup sour cream.*
Serve in deep saucers.

Another Sour Cream Dressing for Beets:
Drain *1 can (8½ ounces) whole, small beets* and slice. Marinate the beets in *¼ cup Italian dressing* and the juice from the beets.
When ready to eat, stir slowly in *¼ cup sour cream.*
You can substitute yogurt for the sour cream.

Foolproof Way
To Make White Sauce

whether you want a thin or a thick sauce, you will never have lumps with our method

The Foolproof Method for a Thin, Medium or Thick Sauce:
In a saucepan, melt the right amount of fat (further down we tell you how much to make a thin, medium or thick white sauce). Take off heat. Stir in the correct amount of flour. Then stir in 1 cup skim or regular milk.
On medium low or low heat, with a wooden spoon, cook and stir, cook and stir, being careful it doesn't burn. This takes about 10 or 15 minutes to come to a boil and become a thin, medium or thick sauce.
If you wish to do as I do, you turn the heat to high and cook and stir, cook and stir, taking off and on the heat and continue to do this, being careful not to burn, until it comes to a boil and thickens, takes about 3 minutes. Turn heat to low. Cook, stir 2 minutes.
Use as needed. If the sauce has to wait, put a piece of Saran Wrap right on top of the sauce. This will keep a skin from forming.
Here is how much of each ingredient you will need to make a thin, medium, or thick sauce:

Kind	*Fat*	*Flour*	*Liquid*
Thin	1 tablespoon	1 tablespoon	1 cup milk, skim or regular
Medium	1½ tablespoons	1½ tablespoons	1 cup milk, skim or regular
Thick	2 tablespoons	2 tablespoons	1 cup milk, skim or regular
Very Thick	3 tablespoons	3 tablespoons	1 cup milk, skim or regular

Penny Pincher White Sauce

you use dry milk and water

The Method

Put into a saucepan the right amount of fat—margarine, butter or oil—to make a thin, medium or thick sauce. We tell you how much in the table below. Melt on low heat, so it doesn't burn. Take off heat.

Stir in the right amount of flour; then stir in ¼ cup plus 1 teaspoon nonfat dry milk. Gradually stir in 1 cup water.

Put on low heat, cook and stir until it comes to a boil—takes about 10 to 15 minutes. Don't burn. A quicker way is to put on high heat and cook and stir, cook and stir, taking off and on heat, until it comes to a boil. You will have to be extra careful it doesn't burn or lump. It is important to not only stir all the time, but to take off the heat, too (so it doesn't get too hot) as you cook. This takes 3 minutes.

When it starts to boil, turn heat to low. Cook and stir 2 minutes.

HERE IS THE TABLE

Kind	*Fat*	*Flour*	*Instant Dry Milk*	*Water*
Thin	1 tablespoon	1 tablespoon	¼ cup + 1 teaspoon	1 cup
Medium	1½ tablespoons	1½ tablespoons	¼ cup + 1 teaspoon	1 cup
Thick	2 tablespoons	2 tablespoons	¼ cup + 1 teaspoon	1 cup
Very Thick	3 tablespoons	3 tablespoons	¼ cup + 1 teaspoon	1 cup

Tip: If you want to make a sauce instead of a white sauce, use the above; only substitute a broth for the water.

Italian Dressing

this will keep a week . . . so it saves time and money

Put into a bowl *½ cup oil, 2 tablespoons wine vinegar* (rice wine vinegar; Spice Island; French wine vinegar; Progresso wine vinegar; or your favorite supermarket might have a good brand under its own name), *¼ teaspoon garlic powder, ¼ teaspoon Italian herbs, 3 tablespoons water, ½ teaspoon salt, 1 teaspoon sugar, 1 teaspoon lemon juice.*

Mix together with a rotary beater.
Pour into a bottle. Shake well before using.
We save our vinegar bottle to use for our "homemade" dressing.

French Dressing

Put into a bowl *½ cup oil, 2 tablespoons wine vinegar, 1 teaspoon sugar, ½ teaspoon salt, 1 teaspoon wet mustard* (Dijon type is nice or Gulden's), *or ½ teaspoon dry mustard* and *2 tablespoons cold tap water.*
Mix together well. Store in a bottle.
Tip: We do not add any pepper to any of our homemade dressings because pepper tastes best ground fresh over the salad itself.
We vary this by adding one of these herbs: thyme, basil, tarragon or a pinch of paprika.

Easy Sauces For Fish Or Meat

you won't believe how easy it is to make . . . these sauces are "dual" sauces . . . they are good with fish and meat . . . good hot or cold . . . that's doubly good!

Into *½ cup unsweetened mayonnaise* gradually stir in *2½ tablespoons cold tap water.*
You can use this as a cold sauce with cooked cold fish or meat.
For a hot sauce, turn heat to low, be sure it's low heat, so the sauce doesn't curdle. Slowly cook, stir until hot. Spoon over your "American Style Steamed" fish. Your husband will tell you how delicious the sauce is, and he'll think you spent hours making it. Just smile sweetly.

Cold Caper Sauce

delicious with fish

Gradually stir into *½ cup unsweetened mayonnaise 2 tablespoons cold tap water.*
Stir in *2 teaspoons drained capers.*

Serve cold over cold cooked fish or just try it over canned salmon, it's super. How about using with sliced cold veal or chicken? Yummy!

Hot Caper Fish Sauce

Into ½ *cup unsweetened mayonnaise* gradually stir *2½ tablespoons cold tap water* until smooth.

Stir in *2 teaspoons drained capers.*

On low heat, cook, stir slowly until heated hot.

This never curdles on low heat—so don't use higher heat—takes only a few minutes.

Hot Horseradish Sauce

Gradually stir in *2½ tablespoons tap water* into *½ cup unsweetened mayonnaise* until smooth.

Stir in *3 teaspoons white or red horseradish* and a *good pinch of sugar.*

On low heat, slowly cook, stir until hot.

The low heat keeps it from curdling. This is a good sauce with hot boiled beef and also with oven steamed fish.

Cold Horseradish Sauce

good with fish or meat

Gradually stir into *½ cup unsweetened mayonnaise 2 tablespoons tap water* until smooth.

Slowly, stir in *3 teaspoons white or red bottled horseradish* with *a good pinch of sugar.*

Cucumber Sauce For Fried Fish

or fried crab cakes, simple to make

Grate only enough and strain the juice of part of a *cucumber to make 2 tablespoons of the strained juice.* We do not use the pulp.

Stir the 2 tablespoons cucumber juice into *½ cup of unsweetened mayonnaise.*

Use as a sauce with fried fish or crab cakes. This is fresher tasting than the commercial tartar sauce.

Another Sauce For Fish Or Crabs

Soak *1 teaspoon dried tarragon* in hot water to cover for 5 minutes, then drain well. Chop fine *1 tablespoon parsley.*

Stir the tarragon and the chopped parsley into *½ cup unsweetened mayonnaise.* Stir in *2 squirts (about ¼ teaspoon) lemon juice* into the mayonnaise mixture.

Thickenings

Flour

1 tablespoon flour	to 1 cup liquid	= thin sauce or gravy
1½ tablespoons flour	to 1 cup liquid	= medium sauce or gravy
2 tablespoons flour	to 1 cup liquid	= thick sauce or gravy
2½ tablespoons flour	to 1 cup liquid	= thicker sauce
3 tablespoons flour	to 1 cup liquid	= very thick sauce

Procedure for a Thin Gravy or Sauce

Measure 1 cup cold liquid (should be a broth).

Put 1 or 1½ tablespoons flour into a screw-top jar.

Take out ¼ cup or 4 tablespoons of the cold liquid and add to the flour.

Shake the flour and liquid in the screw-top jar until combined. No flour should show, and there should be no lumps. Let stand.

Heat the rest of the liquid in the saucepan on medium heat until it comes to a boil.

Shake the flour mixture again. Gently stir the flour mixture in. Bring back to a boil. Turn heat to low. Cook and stir slowly about 5 minutes.

Cornstarch, Arrowroot or Potato Starch

1½ teaspoons cornstarch, arrowroot or potato starch	to 1 cup liquid =	a thin gravy
2 teaspoons cornstarch, arrowroot or potato starch	to 1 cup liquid =	a thicker but still thin enough to be a good gravy
1 tablespoon cornstarch, arrowroot or potato starch	to 1 cup liquid =	a sauce too thick for a gravy

Procedure to Thicken with Cornstarch, Arrowroot or Potato Starch

Put the amount of cornstarch, arrowroot or potato starch recommended for the thickening you want, either 1½ or 2 teaspoons, into a bowl.

Stir in 2 tablespoons of the cold liquid until combined. Let stand.

Bring the rest of the liquid on medium heat to a simmer.

Mix the cornstarch, arrowroot or potato starch mixture, and slowly stir into the simmering liquid. It will clear in about a minute.

Cook and stir slowly about 2 minutes.

Top Stove Flavorful Rice

this makes any chicken or fish dish "gourmet" even if it is both easy and inexpensive to make

Chop *½ cup onions* and *2 tablespoons parsley.*

Bring to a simmer *2 tablespoons oil* and the chopped onions. Cook, stir 2 minutes. Put lid on. Cook 8 minutes until the onions are soft and clear.

Stir in *1 cup rice.* Cook, stir about 2 minutes.

Bring *2 cups chicken broth* to a boil.

Add the rice, onions and the oil they cooked in.

Bring to a simmer. Put lid on. Turn heat to low. Let simmer 25 minutes.

Remove from heat. Let stand without removing lid 15 or 20 minutes.

Fluff the rice with a fork.

Good, isn't it?

Confetti Rice

this is a "fun" dish to make . . . if there are any children around teach them to make this . . . they'll love it, but be careful with the cutting

Cook *1 cup rice* as usual. Set aside.

Chop *1 large onion, 1 stalk celery with the leaves,* dice *1 medium red or green pepper, chop 4 small carrots,* chop *1 tablespoon parsley,* cube *½ pound Velveeta cheese,* open *1 can (15 ounces) kidney beans* and drain.

Heat a large skillet on medium high heat with *4 tablespoons oil.*

Add the onions, carrots, celery and parsley. Cook/stir 1 minute. Turn the heat to low. Cook/stir 5 minutes until the onions are soft and clear—not brown. Add *¾ teaspoon salt* and *pepper* to taste.

Continue to cook and stir gently as you add the rice, the kidney beans, then the cubed cheese. Cover. Cook on low heat about 5 minutes.

Your "Confetti Rice" will be ready to eat. Pretty too.

Seasoned White Rice

with a chickeny taste and an accent of onion, this is always welcome . . . fine with broiled or roasted chicken

Cook in *2 tablespoons oil, ½ cup onions* about 2 minutes. Put lid on. Turn heat to low. Cook 10 minutes.

Stir in *1 cup white rice.* Cook/stir 2 minutes.

Bring *2 cups chicken broth* and *¼ teaspoon salt* to a boil.

Add the rice. Turn the heat to low. Cover. Simmer 25 minutes. Do not remove cover. Take off heat. Let stand 20 minutes. Fluff the rice by criss-crossing with a fork.

For a change you can sauté with the onions, ¼ cup chopped celery, ¼ cup green pepper.

For another change we sometimes add with the sauteed onions, ¼ cup pine nuts.

You can add the nuts without the onions too.

Enriched Rice

In a saucepan bring *2 cups water, 1 tablespoon oil* and *1 teaspoon salt* to a boil on medium high heat.

Add *1 cup Carolina Enriched Rice or Uncle Ben's Converted Rice.*

Bring back to a boil. Turn heat to simmer. Put lid on.

Cook 25 minutes. Remove from heat. Let stand 20 minutes covered.

Remove lid. Fluff with a fork.

How To Cook Brown Rice

takes longer to cook than the white rice but is more nutritious and the taste is good

Bring *2¼ cups and 2 tablespoons water* and *½ teaspoon salt* to a boil. Add *1 cup brown rice.* Bring back to a boil. Cover. Turn the heat to low. Simmer 45 minutes. Remove from heat. Let stand 20 minutes. Fluff with a fork.

For variety you can add sauteed chopped onions, celery and green pepper, or nuts or raisins, depending on the dish you wish to use with the rice. Add any of these after the rice is cooked or you can add the chopped fresh or sauteed onions, celery and green pepper to the raw rice and cook as usual.

You can also put in ½ to 1 teaspoon curry powder, sauteeing it with chopped onions for a curry rice.

You can substitute chicken broth or beef broth instead of water to cook the rice for a more flavorful rice.

Tip: We found the rice was fluffier if we did not add any oil to the water when cooking the rice.

Easy Pilaf

this more or less Turkish style rice is a fine rice dish . . . it's one of the easy-make dishes

Bring to a boil *1 cup Campbell's Beef Broth, 1 can (16 ounces) stewed tomatoes,* and *1 tablespoon oil, butter or margarine.*

Add *1 cup rice.*

Bring back to a boil.

Turn heat to low. Cover. Simmer 25 minutes.

Let stand covered 15 minutes.

Fluff. Serve or set aside and reheat when ready to use.

Macaroni And Cheese Top Stove

this can be made in a jiffy

Grate *1 cup Cheddar cheese.*

Bring *16 cups water* and *2 teaspoons iodized salt* to a boil. Slowly, not to stop the boiling, gradually add *2 cups macaroni.* Boil 9 or 10 minutes. Drain in a colander. Run cold water over. Drain again. This makes 4 cups cooked macaroni.

Put the macaroni into a saucepan. Place on low heat. Stir in *1 cup nonfat milk.* Cook and stir one minute. A little at a time, add *1 cup Parmesan or other cheese that melts or Velveeta.*

Cook and stir as you add. When all have been added, cook, stir 1 minute.

Add *1 tablespoon margarine* and stir gently. Cover.

Cook 5 minutes. The macaroni and cheese will be ready to eat.

Buttered Noodles

Cook *4 ounces wide noodles* according to directions on package, about 7 to 9 minutes.

Drain. Put the noodles back in the pot. Add *1 tablespoon margarine or oil* and *¼ teaspoon caraway seeds.*

Mix together gently.

These are very good as a side dish.

If you don't have any caraway seeds, the noodles, just with a little margarine or oil, are quite good, too.

French Fried Noodles

wonderful with Chicken Chow Mein . . . and very, very nice as a snack and perfect with drinks

Put a rack on a cookie sheet covered with foil. This is to have ready to quickly drop on the deep fat-fried noodles.

It's nice to have a deep fryer with a basket.

You need as much of a bag of *Medium noodles* (we use Pennsylvania Dutch Egg Noodles) as you wish.

Heat about *2 inches of oil* until hot, test by dropping in a noodle and it should immediately rise to the top and start browning.

To cook the noodles:

Drop the dry noodles into the basket and lower immediately into the hot oil.

Keep a second only, it will start to get golden brown.

Remove immediately and "dump" at once into the rack on the cookie sheet. Salt lightly.

Continue to do this until all have been deep fried.

These noodles are always fresh when used with your Chow Mein . . . unlike the commercial canned ones.

Deep Fried Noodles

the Chinese invented these and if you're using the ones that come in cans, you'll realize how wonderful the ones you make are . . . there's no comparison and . . . these make snacks that go perfect with a glass of wine or a stronger drink and also for a gathering of friends and good conversation

Put wax paper on a clean surface to put the cooked pancakes on.

Measure *1 cup flour,* remove 2 tablespoons and add *1 teaspoon wheat germ, ½ teaspoon salt.* Mix with a pastry blender.

Mix *2 eggs* with a fork well. Stir in *1 cup water* to make a thin batter. Stir into the flour mixture.

Heat a 4 or 5-inch skillet hot on medium heat.

Brush with *oil.* Pour in 2 tablespoons batter and tilt the skillet off and on heat so the batter covers the bottom of the skillet and bake until the bottom side is cooked and when you touch the top side it is not sticky. You only brown very lightly the one side. Remove to the wax paper.

Continue until all are cooked and are cold.

Cut the pancakes into ¼ inch strips.

You can store these with wax paper in between in the refrigerator until you are ready to use them or you can deep fry them as soon as they are cold as they keep well for a few days.

Heat about 4 inches of oil in a deep fry pan or whatever you use to deep fry. It makes it easier if you have a deep fry basket too.

When the oil is hot, test with a small piece of bread and if it rises to the top at once and starts to brown, it is ready. Drop in a small handful of the cut noodles into the basket and fry just until golden . . . takes a few seconds only.

Remove to a rack to cool. Continue until all are done. If you cook these too long they come out hard instead of crisp.

These are very "munchable!"

Noodle Dumplings Or Bott Boi

a Pennsylvania Dutch dish and "good is" this kind of "noodle" . . . sometimes called a dumpling and sometimes "slippery noodle" and commercially it may be called "Bott Boi"

Mix with a fork *1 egg, ¼ teaspoon salt* in a medium size bowl about 1½ quart or so size.

Measure *1 cup flour.*

Gradually add flour, about ½ cup, enough to make a dough that is sticky but you can handle.

Sprinkle some of the flour over the dough as you work it in your hands. Continue to add a little flour at a time working the dough to smooth it until it is hardly sticky.

Cut the dough in half.

Sprinkle some flour over a surface and also over the piece of dough. Start rolling and roll adding flour to the board as you roll so the dough doesn't stick. Roll as thin as possible.

Cut into 1 inch squares.

Roll out and cut the other half dough the same way.

You can use these when making our Pennsylvania Dutch Chicken Noodle Soup. If you make them larger you can use them in your Lasagna.

Our Favorite Spaghetti Sauce

and yours too . . . this is a meat sauce so robust and perfect made with ground beef that it becomes a meal in a dish . . . you only cook it an hour as the canner does the hard work for us

Tip: Cook the sauce without a cover.

Pour *2 cans (2 pounds, 3 ounces) Progresso Italian tomatoes* into a large strainer over a large bowl. With a spoon don't mash—but lift and move the tomatoes so the juice runs out. Get as much juice out as possible without mashing. This is the secret to get a thick sauce. Save the juice though.

Put the pulp through a food mill or push through a strainer placed over a large bowl.

Pour into a large kettle with *5 cans (8 ounces) tomato sauce (either Progresso or Contadina), 1 large stalk celery* cut into 3 pieces, *3 large cloves garlic, 3 teaspoons dry basil,*

1 large or 2 small bay leaves, 2 whole allspice or 1/8 teaspoon ground, 1 teaspoon dried leaf oregano. Let come to a simmer.

Grate *1 large onion* over *2 pounds ground beef.* Let stand 5 minutes.

Heat a large skillet with *4 tablespoons oil* on high heat. Add the onion flavored ground beef. Cook, stir, takes about 3 to 5 minutes only to get the red out.

Take off heat. Stir *1 teaspoon salt,* or more to taste. With a rubber spatula push into the sauce. Bring back to a simmer. Simmer ½ hour, stirring now and then. If the sauce looks too thick, add ½ cup of the tomato juice you set aside.

Cook; stir now and then 30 more minutes.

Add *1 teaspoon sugar* and *1 tablespoon oil (plus 2 tablespoons dry sherry* if you wish).

Cook, stir 3 minutes.

This lovely fresh tasting meat sauce is ready to eat! This freezes beautifully and is also excellent for Lasagna, too.

How To Serve Your Spaghetti Hot

who wants to eat cold spaghetti?

While the spaghetti is cooking, turn oven to its lowest heat.

Put in the plates you will serve the spaghetti on and a large bowl with *1 tablespoon oil* in it. (This will keep your spaghetti hot when you serve it.)

Put a colander in the sink.

When the spaghetti is cooked as you like it, immediately—carefully, not to scald yourself—pour it into the colander to drain the boiling water off.

As soon as the spaghetti is drained, immediately put it into the heated bowl. Toss the spaghetti in the oil.

Serve at once, or put a portion into each hot plate, and spoon some sauce over it immediately.

Tip: Don't cook spaghetti mushy. Cook it a little firm as the Italians call it—"al dente."

Baked Spaghetti

baking the spaghetti makes it an easier meal than rushing around when you make "spaghetti" the usual way . . . this is a fine dish for a "Buffet Dinner"

Break *8 ounces or ½ pound Vermicelli spaghetti* into halves. Cook in *12 cups boiling water* with *1 teaspoon salt* until it comes back to a boil, then boil 7 minutes. Drain. Cool under running water. Drain again.

Divide *1½ pounds ground beef* in half. Spread each on a large plate. Sprinkle *½ teaspoon salt* over each one and grate a *small onion* over each. Let stand 5 minutes.

Heat a large skillet with *2 tablespoons oil.*

Add the beef. Cook/stir until the red is out of the beef, which takes about 5 minutes.

Take off heat. Remove to a bowl.

Make the sauce: In a large saucepan, open *2 cans (15½ ounces) Progresso Pizza Sauce* or your favorite "tomato" sauce, *1 teaspoon garlic powder, 1 teaspoon dried leaf oregano, ½ teaspoon dried leaf basil, 1 teaspoon sugar, ½ to ¾ teaspoon salt* (not too much, so taste).

Bring to a simmer. Simmer and stir about 5 minutes.

Add *pepper* to taste and *1 tablespoon oil.*

Cook and stir 1 minute.

Stir in the cooked ground beef, *½ teaspoon sugar, ½ teaspoon salt, ¼ teaspoon leaf oregano.* Cook, stir 2 minutes.

Pour into a heat-proof greased glass baking dish. Bake in 400° oven about 20 minutes.

Sprinkle *1 cup Parmesan cheese* on top. Put under broiler and brown, takes a few minutes only.

Good Spaghetti Casserole

the spaghetti baked in its own sauce

Heat oven 350°.

Break *4 ounces uncooked (#8) spaghetti* into 1 inch pieces. Set aside in a large bowl.

Cook/stir on high heat *1 pound ground beef* until no red shows. Take off heat. Stir in *¾ teaspoon salt.*

Mix with the broken spaghetti.

Mix *1 jar (16 ounces) spaghetti sauce* with *1 cup water.*

Stir into the spaghetti/meat mixture being careful to mix the meat so that it separates the spaghetti.

Place in 350° oven. Bake 60 minutes.

This is very good spooned and served.

Sauce For Lasagna

Many times when we are in a hurry (and when aren't we?), we start our sauce with any of these sauces: Ragu Meatless Marinara Sauce, Chef Boyar-dee Spaghetti Sauce with Mushrooms, Progresso Tomato Sauce, Hunt's Sauce with Tomato Bits and Buitoni Tomato Sauce. We use others too, but read the labels as to what's in it!

Put *1 jar your favorite spaghetti sauce* in a saucepan. (We used a 15 ounce jar Buitoni this time.)

Stir in *½ teaspoon basil, 2 whole allspice, 1 bay leaf.*

Cook, stir, bring to a simmer. Cook 10 minutes.

Add *1 tablespoon dry Vermouth or a Johannesburg Reisling wine* from California.

Cook, stir 5 minutes.

Use with the Lasagna.

If making the Lasagna with ground beef. stir, fry just until the red is out. Add to the sauce and cook as above.

If using sausage, stir, fry until the fat is out. If in cases, take the sausage out of the cases first to fry. After fat is cooked out, add the sausage to the sauce.

A quick sauce with good flavor can be made from 1 can (1 pound) Hunt's Tomato Sauce with Tomato Bits and 1 teaspoon "Dried Italian Herbs." This saves buying a lot of herbs if you don't use many herbs.

New Quick! Lasagna

you won't believe it, we don't cook the lasagna noodles before we bake it . . . this saves time and energy

Many times we prefer not to use the commercial lasagna noodles because they are so thick and tough. We use the Pennsylvania Dutch Brand "Bott Boi" as it's thinner, more tender. These are squares 2½" × 1¾" or we make our own noodle squares (see recipe index under "N") instead and make them larger.

Grease a 6″ × 10″ glass baking dish.

Heat oven 400°.

You need *5 cups of your favorite spaghetti sauce* (see our recipe under "S" in index).

Make a layer of the spaghetti sauce, then a layer of raw—not cooked—*lasagna or the Pennsylvania Dutch Bott Boi* arranged to cover the sauce, then a layer of sauce, then a layer of *cheese* (Havarti cheese or mozzarella or muenster), then a layer of sauce. Repeat starting with the lasagna (Bott Boi) and ending with the sauce.

Cover with foil.

Place on a cookie pan covered with foil (in case it runs over).

Bake in 400° oven. Cover. Bake 45 minutes.

Remove the foil, bake 30 minutes.

If using lasagna noodles it would take 45 minutes covered and about 45 minutes uncovered or more.

If you wish you can sprinkle *½ cup to 1 cup grated Parmesan* cheese on top after the lasagna is baked and put it under the broiler to brown.

We usually omit it as we feel we have enough cheese in our lasagna.

By the way, this is not an Italian, Italian Lasagna, it's a "Sophie" Lasagna—but friends and enemies both love it!

The Five Cheese Lasagna

an exciting lasagna because the different cheeses came together to make a beautiful taste in your mouth

We used Ronzoni Lasagna (curly edge) and found they were not as thick as some of the others, which to me always makes for a better lasagna. Also, we noticed that no artificial color was used. Good for you and us, Mr. Ronzoni, whoever you are! We also use Pennsylvania Dutch brand "Bott Boi" which are large squares and the dough is like "homemade."

We used a baking dish 8 × 8 inches.

Follow directions on box to cook the *lasagna.*

Drain. Run cold water over. Put into a bowl with cold water, so they will not stick while you make the sauce and get the cheese ready.

The Cheese:

A *4 ounce package of Treasure Cove Blue Cold Pack Cheese.* (Be sure and remove the wax around it and soften the cheese at room temperature.)

A *3 ounce package of cream cheese with chives.* Mix with a spoon to soften.

Enough slices of *Swiss cheese to make 1 layer.*

Enough slices *Velveeta cheese to make 1 layer.*

Grated *Parmesan cheese to cover the dish.*

The Sauce:

Put into a saucepan *1 can Hunt's Tomato Sauce with Tomato Bits (15 ounces), Hunt's Tomato Sauce Special* (has celery, green pepper, onions, and tomato bits in it), *¼ teaspoon Italian herbs* and a *tiny pinch of sugar.*

Bring to a boil. Add *½ teaspoon Italian herbs.*

Cook, stir 10 minutes. Stir in *1 tablespoon dry vermouth.* Take off heat.

Put a layer of this sauce in the bottom of the baking pan, then a layer of lasagna, a layer of cream cheese, a layer of Swiss cheese and some sauce on top, then a layer of lasagna and a layer of Blue Cheese, a layer of Velveeta, a layer of lasagna and the rest of the tomato sauce. Sprinkle the grated Parmesan cheese on top.

Put in 400° oven.

Bake about 20 minutes.

How To Cook Pasta Shells For Stuffing

Cook as follows *as many Jumbo Pasta Shells as you need.* We usually use 4 per person.

Bring *5 quarts water* and *2 teaspoons salt* to a boil. Add the shells.

Cook 45 minutes. Drain. Run cold water over. Drain again.

Stuffed Italian Shells
In Tomato Meat Sauce

these taste as good as they look

The Stuffing:

With a metal spoon mix *2 packages (3 ounces each) Philadelphia Cream Cheese* with *2 teaspoons milk.*

Stir in *1 teaspoon garlic powder, ⅛ scant teaspoon salt.*

With your fingers push *enough dried parsley through a fine strainer to make ¼ teaspoon.* (It's easy!)

Stir this into the cheese mixture. Set aside.

Steam or cook *1 package (10 ounces) frozen chopped spinach,* takes about 5 minutes.

Cool a little.

Put into a double piece of cheese cloth making it into a sort of bag. Squeeze all the water out.

Chop the spinach fine, and put into a bowl.

Melt *2 tablespoons margarine* and stir into the spinach.

Stir in *½ teaspoon nutmeg* and *a little pepper.*

Add to the cream cheese mixture. Stir to combine the two. Set aside.

The Shells:

In a large pot bring to a fast boil *4 quarts water* and *1½ tablespoons salt* and *1 tablespoon oil.*

Drop in *18 Jumbo Pasta Shells* (Ronzoni, San Giorgio or other jumbo shells).

Bring back to a boil. Stir now and then so the shells don't stick, especially to the bottom.

Boil about 15 minutes; drain in a colander. Run cold water over. Drain well.

Put on a large plate to cool.

The Sauce:

Heat a skillet with *1 tablespoon oil.*

Stir in *½ pound ground beef,* fresh or frozen. If frozen,

cook and scrape the beef until all is defrosted. Either way, just cook, stir only until no red shows. (Don't try to brown, as this only dries and toughens the meat.)

Stir in *1 pound jar Spaghetti Sauce*. We use Progresso Spaghetti Sauce with Mushrooms, Ragu, Franco-American, or use your favorite Spaghetti Sauce.

Spoon about ⅓ of this sauce in an 8-inch glass baking dish.

Stuff the cheese/spinach stuffing into the cooked shells with a dull knife.

Place the stuffed shells on the sauce open side up, 6 shells in each row, making 3 rows.

Spoon the rest of the sauce on top.

You can bake at once, or cover with foil and refrigerate or freeze.

When ready to use leave foil on.

Place in a preheated 400° oven. Bake 30 minutes.

Sprinkle about ½ *cup grated Parmesan cheese* on top.

Place under broiler and brown lightly.

Serve hot.

Frozen Baked Stuffed Pasta Shells With Sauce

these are frozen and are a "cooked once for twice" recipe, which means I made one for dinner, and at the same time I made another and froze it . . . saves fuel, time and money!

Put the frozen baking dish of Baked Stuffed Pasta Shells in a 400° oven.

Cover with foil. Bake 1 hour. Remove foil.

Sprinkle grated *Parmesan cheese* on top. Put under broiler to brown.

Eat and enjoy.

Chicken Stuffing For Jumbo Pasta Shells

you need your "Ready Cooked" chicken or you can use "Ready Cooked" beef, veal or pork—or even tuna fish and that's the easiest because you didn't even have to "Ready Cook" it at all!

This is stuffing for 8 jumbo pasta shells for 2 with Chicken Stuffing or the equivalent meat.

Grind or chop very fine *enough "Ready Cooked" chicken or equivalent to make 1 cup.*

Stir in *3 tablespoons Hellmann's mayonnaise, a good grind of pepper, ¼ teaspoon onion powder, ½ teaspoon dried tarragon, a pinch of ground nutmeg,* and *salt to taste.*

Tip: We buy the nutmeg that looks like a hard nut and grate it on our grater. The smell and taste are divine!

Stuffed Pasta Shells
In Curry Sauce

with ready cooked chicken in a delicious curry sauce, you've got a dish!

Cook *as many Jumbo Pasta Shells as you need counting 4 for each person.*

Bring *5 quarts water* and *2 teaspoons salt* to a boil. Drop in the shells. Be careful not to let the shells stick. Boil 45 minutes. Drain. Let get cold. You might want to follow the directions on the package.

Make the Chicken Stuffing:

Grind or chop very fine *enough "ready cooked" chicken or canned chicken to make 1 cup.*

Stir in *3 tablespoons unsweetened mayonnaise, a good grind of pepper, ¼ teaspoon onion powder, ½ teaspoon dried tarragon,* a *pinch of ground nutmeg,* and *salt to taste.*

Fill the 16 shells.

You can arrange 4 in 4 individual baking dishes, greased with margarine; or you can use one large shallow baking dish.

Make the Sauce:

Soften *1 package Cream Cheese with Chives* (3 ounces).

Gradually stir in *½ cup milk.* (We use skim milk.)

Stir in *¼ teaspoon garlic powder, a good pinch grated dried ginger, ½ teaspoon curry powder* and *salt to taste.*

Stir in *1 cup chicken broth, fresh, canned or bouillon broth.*

Cook, stir 2 minutes.

When ready to eat: pour over the stuffed shells. Cover with foil.

Place in 400° preheated oven. Bake about 20 minutes. Serve.

You can sprinkle a little grated Parmesan cheese onto the shells if you wish, and put under the broiler for a minute or so to brown. Serve at once.

Stuffing For Manicotti Or Pasta Jumbo Shells

Put *½ package,* which is 2 ounces, *Blue Cold Pack Cheese* (Treasure Cove) into a bowl. Let get soft at room temperature.

Stir in *1 package (8 ounces) cream cheese* softened to room temperature, *2 tablespoons chopped fine parsley* and *1 egg yolk.*

Stuff into whatever Pasta or Pancakes you prefer.

A Different Stuffed Manicotti

what's different? . . . you bake it without a sauce . . . but just in case you like yours with a sauce . . . we give you that, too

Cook *manicotti* tubes according to directions on package, about 6 minutes.

Thaw *1 package (10 ounces) frozen chopped spinach.*

Cook, stir until the liquid is out; then squeeze out any liquid left in. Chop fine.

Saute in *1 tablespoon oil 1 chopped small onion* until soft and clear.

Mix together the spinach, *1 (8 ounces) carton of cottage cheese,* drained well, *¼ cup grated Parmesan cheese, 2 tablespoons Seasoned Bread Crumbs, 1 egg* mixed with fork and *salt and pepper* to taste.

Add *1 (2½ ounce) drained jar or can stems and pieces of mushrooms* and the spinach mixed with *¼ teaspoon nutmeg.* Mix together. Taste.

Add *salt and pepper to taste.*
Stuff into the cooked manicotti.
Place in a greased with oil, shallow, baking pan.
Brush the manicotti with *oil.*
Heat *¼ to ½ cup Chicken Bouillon Broth.* Spoon around the stuffed manicotti.
Bake in 400° oven 15 to 20 minutes.
Sprinkle *¼ cup Parmesan cheese* on top of the manicotti.
Put under the broiler to brown.
Serve.
If you like a tomato sauce, which many people do, instead of the chicken broth, mix together your favorite canned or jar of spaghetti sauce with 1 tablespoon grated Parmesan cheese and bring to a boil.
Pour around the stuffed manicotti.
Bake in oven 20 minutes until sauce is bubbling hot and the manicotti is hot, too. Serve.

Clam Sauce And Stuffing For Pasta Or Rotille

Remove the fat with pieces of paper towels from *1 can (10½ ounces) Progresso White Clam Sauce.*
Make a white sauce as follows:
Melt *2 tablespoons margarine or butter.* Take off heat.
Stir in *3 tablespoons flour.*
Stir in *1 cup milk.*
Place back on heat. Cook, stir until it comes to a simmer. Simmer 5 minutes.
Gradually stir in the Clam sauce.
Add *1 can (8 ounces) Doxsee's Minced Clams* (not chopped, they're tough), *½ teaspoon dried oregano leaves* and a *good grind of pepper.* Bring to a boil.
Serve over the hot "Rotille" or serve with the stuffed Manicotti or Stuffed Pancakes, or the Stuffed Jumbo Pasta Shells.

The Stuffing:

Let *½ of a 4 ounce package of Blue Cold Pack Cheese* (Treasure Cove brand) get soft at room temperature.
Stir in *1 package (8 ounces) cream cheese* softened at room temperature, *2 tablespoons chopped fine parsley* and *1 egg yolk.*

Stuff into whatever pasta or pancakes you prefer.

Grease a baking dish that fits the stuffed pasta. Spoon a little sauce into the baking dish about ½ inch or use chicken broth, fresh, canned or Bouillon Broth.

Arrange the stuffed pasta in rows or rings or whichever way is best.

Place in 375° oven. Bake 20 minutes until hot.

Sprinkle a little *Parmesan cheese* on top. Brown under broiler.

In the meantime, heat the rest of the sauce. Each person can pour the sauce over their pasta.

This is truly a fine dish—pasta lovers will make this over and over again.

Stuffed Jumbo Pasta Shells With Red Clam Sauce

you can make them early and bake them later . . . they're a real treat

Mix together *½ package, which is 2 ounces, Blue Cheese, Cold Pack Cheese* (Treasure Cove, aged over 100 days) with *1 package (8 ounces) cream cheese.*

Stir in *2 tablespoons chopped fine parsley* and *1 egg yolk.*

Cook, following directions on package, *19 or 20 Jumbo Pasta Shells* for "little" eaters and double this for hearty eaters. Drain.

We use 8½ or 9 inch round foil pans to bake these in, as these are easy to freeze in, too.

Spoon *½ cup chicken broth,* fresh, canned or bouillon broth, into each pan.

Stuff the pasta shells and arrange them in the pans. The chicken broth should not cover the shells.

With pieces of paper towels mop up any fat from *1 can (10½ ounces) Progresso Red Clam Sauce.*

Stir *1 can Doxsee Minced Clams (8 ounces)* into the Red Clam Sauce.

Spoon some of the clams into the shells. Spoon the rest of the clams and the sauce around the shells.

When ready to bake, place in preheated 375° oven. Bake 20 minutes.

Sprinkle a little *Parmesan cheese* on top. Broil until lightly browned, takes about 3 to 5 minutes.

"Never Fail" Single Crust Or Pastry For Beginners

made with vegetable shortening . . . it's the easiest of all the crusts to make, and it always comes out right

Put into a bowl *some ice cubes and water* to get icy cold.

Put into a large bowl *1 cup flour*. Remove 3 tablespoons flour; replace with *1 tablespoon wheat germ, ¼ teaspoon salt* and a *tiny pinch of sugar*. Mix with a pastry blender.

Measure *⅓ cup vegetable shortening*. Put one-half into the flour mixture. Mix with the pastry blender until the flour looks like fine crumbs.

Add the rest of the vegetable shortening. Mix with the pastry blender until it looks like large crumbs.

Divide the flour mixture into 3 piles. Sprinkle 1 tablespoon of the icy cold water over one pile. Mix with a fork or your fingers together. Do the same with the second pile. Mix the two together. Combine this with as much of the third pile as will make a soft, but not sticky, ball. To any left of the dry mixture add as much of 1 tablespoon water as is needed to make a soft ball. Combine all three into one large ball.

Over a clean surface throw the ball from one hand to the other 20 times. This makes the dough a wonderful texture and smooth.

The dough is now ready to be rolled out and used in the recipe of your choice.

Roll the dough out to fit the pie plate. Roll onto the rolling pin. Unroll over the pie plate or onto the pie filling, depending on the kind of pie you are making. Gently fit the crust in, but don't stretch the crust.

To bake the crust, prick it all over with a fork to keep it from ballooning up.

Cut off any excess dough around the edges. With the back prongs of the fork, press the edges down to make a design and to keep the dough from slipping. If you wish, you can use your fingers to make a fancy design.

Cover the edges of the pie with 1 inch foil to keep from over-browning when baking.

Preheat oven 450° 15 minutes before baking the crust. Bake about 10 to 12 minutes.

We usually preheat the oven before we bake the crust.

"Never Fail" Single Crust Or Pastry For Experienced Pie Makers

made with vegetable shortening

Put into a bowl some *ice cubes and water* to get icy cold.

Put into a bowl *1 cup flour*, remove 3 tablespoons and replace with *1 tablespoon wheat germ, ¼ teaspoon salt* and a *tiny pinch of sugar.*

Mix with a pastry blender.

Divide *⅓ cup vegetable shortening* into half. Add half of the shortening and mix with the pastry blender into fine crumbs. Add the rest of the shortening and mix into large crumbs. Mix the two together.

Put 3 tablespoons of the icy water into a cup. Gradually stir as much of the water as is needed into the flour mixture to make a soft, but not sticky, ball that cleans the bowl.

Over a clean surface throw the ball from one hand to the other 20 times. This makes the dough a wonderful texture and smooth.

Make the crust for the recipe of your choice.

To make a bottom crust roll out to fit the pie plate. Unroll into the pie plate without stretching. Prick with a fork all over so the crust won't balloon up when baking.

Put a 1 inch piece of foil around the edges to keep from burning.

Bake in preheated 450° oven about 10 to 12 minutes.

Use as needed, see recipe index for pie of your choice.

"Flaky, Tender" Single Pie Crust Or Pastry

made with oil, it's probably the healthiest of all the crusts . . . it's a bit touchy but rich-tasting . . . you solve the problem by rolling out between two sheets of wax paper—so there's really no problem after all . . . this is Marie's favorite . . . who is Marie? . . . my good right arm who tests with me and gives me courage to "go on"

Into a large bowl put *1 cup flour*. Remove 3 tablespoons.

Add *1 tablespoon wheat germ, ¼ teaspoon salt* and a *pinch of sugar.*

Into a cup pour *¼ cup oil* and *3 tablespoons nonfat milk.* Mix with a fork until creamy, takes a half minute.

Pour into the flour mixture. Mix with a fork or your hands into a ball. Flatten.

Cut two pieces of wax paper about 12 inches square.

Roll the dough between these two pieces of wax paper into a circle that fits a 9 inch pie plate.

Remove the top piece of wax paper. Invert the crust over the pie plate. Gently peel off the wax paper.

Fit the crust, don't stretch, into or onto the pie filling or pie plate, depending on what kind of pie you are making.

For a bottom crust like in a lemon pie, prick the crust in the pie plate with a fork all over, as this keeps it from ballooning when baking.

Also, put one inch wide strips of foil to cover the edges to keep from over-browning.

Bake in 450° oven about 10 to 12 minutes.

Cool; use as needed.

Tip: We usually preheat the oven before we make the pie or the crust.

"Tender And Foolproof" Single Crust Or Pastry For Beginners

made with margarine or butter, it has a rich taste

Into a bowl put some *ice cubes and water* to get icy cold.

In the meantime put *1 cup flour* into a bowl. Remove 3 tablespoons flour. Replace with *1 tablespoon wheat germ* and add a *tiny pinch of sugar.* Mix with a pastry blender.

Measure *⅓ cup soft margarine or soft, room temperature butter.* Put one-half into the flour mixture. Mix with the pastry blender until it looks like fine crumbs. Add the rest and mix until some of it looks like large crumbs.

Divide the dough into three piles.

Sprinkle 1 tablespoon of the icy water over one pile. Mix with a fork or your fingers just to hold together.

Repeat this with the second pile. Don't overmix, but make these two into one ball. They may be moist enough so you can mix with some or all of the last pile without adding any water. Add as much or as little of 1 tablespoon of the icy water as you need to make a ball. Then with your hands shape into one large ball that is not sticky, but is soft and cleans the bowl.

Over a clean surface throw the ball from one hand to the other 20 times. It does something "good" to the texture and smooths the dough. (This is a French trick given me by my friend, Yolande, who says, "Every French woman knows that!")

The dough is now ready to be used in the recipe of your choice.

Roll the dough out to fit the pie plate. Roll onto the rolling pin, unroll over the pie plate or over the pie filling, depending on the kind of pie you are making.

Gently "fit" the crust into the pie plate. Don't stretch the crust as it will shrink when baking.

To bake the crust, prick it all over with a fork to keep it from ballooning up. Cut off any excess dough around the edges.

With the back prongs of the fork, press the edges down to make a design.

Cover the edges of the pie with 1 inch foil to keep from over-browning when baking.

Preheat the oven 450° 15 minutes before baking the crust. Bake about 10 to 12 minutes.

We usually preheat the oven before we make the pie.

Tip: We usually make our filling first to have ready before we make our crust or crusts.

This is a fine crust for deep dish pies, both fresh and canned, or canned pie fillings, especially if you want a rich crust or pastry.

"Tender And Foolproof" Single Crust Or Pastry For Experienced Pie Makers

made with margarine or butter, it has a rich taste

Into a bowl put some *ice cubes and water* to get icy cold.

Put into a bowl *1 cup flour,* remove 3 tablespoons flour

and replace with *1 tablespoon wheat germ, ¼ teaspoon salt* and a tiny *pinch of sugar.* Mix with a pastry blender.

Divide *⅓ cup soft margarine or soft, room temperature butter* into half. Add half of the margarine or butter and mix with the pastry blender into fine crumbs. Add the rest of the margarine or butter and mix into large crumbs. Mix the two together.

Put *3 tablespoons of the icy water* into a cup. Gradually stir as much of the water as is needed into the flour mixture to make a soft, but not sticky, ball that cleans the bowl.

Over a clean surface, throw the ball from one hand to the other 20 times. This makes the dough a wonderful texture and smooth.

Make the crust for the recipe of your choice.

To make a bottom crust, roll out to fit the pie plate. Unroll into the pie plate without stretching. Prick with a fork all over so the crust won't balloon up when baking.

Put a 1 inch piece of foil around the edges to keep from burning.

Bake in preheated 450° oven about 10 to 12 minutes.

Use as needed; see recipe index for pie of your choice.

"Never Fail" Double Crust Or Pastry Dough For Beginners

made with vegetable shortening . . . for pie crusts or for any fruit dumplings, fruit rolls, meat rolls, turnovers, or any recipe you need a rich "easy to make" pastry dough

Put some ice cubes into a bowl of water to get icy cold. You will use from *6 to 6¾ tablespoons.*

Put into a large bowl *1¾ cups flour.* Remove 1 tablespoon and 2 teaspoons flour; replace with *1 tablespoon and 2 teaspoons wheat germ,* and add *½ teaspoon salt* and a *pinch of sugar.*

Measure *⅔ cup vegetable shortening.* With a pastry blender, mix one-half of this shortening into the flour until it looks like cornmeal. Add the other half and mix into large crumbs.

Divide the flour mixture into 3 piles in the bowl.

Sprinkle 2 tablespoons of the icy water over one pile and

mix into a rough ball. Don't handle too much. Do the same with another pile. Combine the two balls; then combine with as much of the last pile of dry flour mixture as will make a soft, but not sticky, ball. There is usually dry flour mixture left to do this.

Add only as much water (usually about 2 tablespoons up to 2¾ tablespoons, sometimes more) as you need to make that into a soft, but not sticky, ball. Combine with the other ball into 1 large ball that cleans the bowl and is soft, but not sticky.

Over a clean surface throw the ball from one hand to the other 20 times. You will be amazed at the soft, smooth texture it gets. (This is a tip I got from my French friend, Yolande, who says, "Every French woman knows that.")

The dough can be divided in half, one a little larger than the other, using the larger one to roll out for the bottom crust.

See Index for recipes for individual pies.

"Never Fail" Double Crust Or Pastry Dough For Experienced Pie Bakers

made with vegetable shortening . . . for pie crusts or for any fruit dumplings, a fruit roll, meat rolls, turnovers, or any recipe you need a rich "easy to make" pastry dough

Put some ice cubes into a bowl of water to get icy cold. You will use from *6 to 6¾ tablespoons.*

Put into a bowl *1¾ cups flour,* remove 1 tablespoon and 2 teaspoons flour and replace with *1 tablespoon and 2 teaspoons wheat germ,* add *½ teaspoon salt* and *a pinch of sugar.* Mix with a pastry blender.

Divide *⅔ cup vegetable shortening* into half. Add half of the shortening and mix with the pastry blender into fine crumbs. Add the rest of the shortening and mix into large crumbs. Mix the two together.

Put 6 tablespoons of the icy water into a cup. Gradually stir as much of the water as is needed into the flour mixture to make a soft, but not sticky, ball that cleans the bowl.

Over a clean surface throw the ball from one hand to the

other 20 times. This makes the dough a wonderful texture and smooth.

Divide the dough into half, one a little larger than the other, using the larger one to roll out for the bottom crust.

Use as needed. See Index for recipes for individual pies.

"Tender And Foolproof" Double Crusts For Beginners

made with soft margarine or butter

Put some ice cubes into a bowl of water to get icy cold. Altogether you will use about *5½ to 5¾ tablespoons of water.*

Put into a large bowl *1¾ cups flour.* Remove 1 tablespoon and 2 teaspoons flour, replace with *1 tablespoon and 2 teaspoons wheat germ* and add a *pinch of sugar.*

Measure *⅔ cup soft margarine or softened room temperature butter.*

With a pastry blender mix ½ of this fat into the flour mixture until it looks like fine cornmeal. Add the rest of the fat and mix until it looks like large crumbs.

Divide the flour mixture in the bowl into 3 piles.

Sprinkle 2 tablespoons of the icy water over one pile and mix together.

Do the same with 2 tablespoons water over another pile. Combine these two into a ball. Mix with as much of the last pile of flour mixture as will make a soft, but not sticky, ball. There is usually some dry flour mixture left. Add only as much water as you need to make that into a soft, but not sticky, ball, sometimes 1½ or 1¾ tablespoons.

Combine with the other ball into 1 large ball that cleans the bowl.

Over a clean surface throw the ball from one hand to the other 20 times. You will be amazed at the soft, smooth texture it gets. This is a tip I got from my French friend, Yolande.

The dough can be divided, one a little larger than the other, using the larger one to roll out for the bottom crust.

Use both crusts as needed in your selected recipe. See Index for recipes for individual pies.

"Tender And Foolproof" Double Crusts For Experienced Pie Bakers

made with soft margarine or butter

Put some ice cubes into a bowl of water to get icy cold. Altogether you will use about *5½ to 5¾ tablespoons of water.*

Put into a bowl *1¾ cups flour,* remove 1 tablespoon and 2 teaspoons flour and replace with *1 tablespoon and 2 teaspoons wheat germ,* and add a pinch of sugar. Mix with a pastry blender.

Divide *⅔ cup soft margarine or softened room temperature butter* into half. Add half of the shortening and mix with the pastry blender into fine crumbs. Add the rest of the shortening and mix into large crumbs. Mix the two together.

Put 5½ to 5¾ tablespoons of the icy water into a cup. Gradually stir as much of the water as is needed into the flour mixture to make a soft, but not sticky, ball that cleans the bowl. Over a clean surface throw the ball from one hand to the other 20 times. This makes the dough a wonderful texture and smooth.

Divide the dough into half, one a little larger than the other, using the larger one to roll out for the bottom crust.

Use both crusts as needed in your selected recipe. See Index for recipes for individual pies.

A Double Flaky And Tender Pie Crust

it's nutritious too

Put into a large bowl *2 cups flour.* Remove 2 tablespoons flour. Add *2 tablespoons wheat germ* and *½ teaspoon salt.*

Add *½ cup oil* and *6 tablespoons nonfat milk.*

Mix with a fork until creamy, takes a minute.

All at once pour into the flour mixture.

Mix with a fork into a ball. Throw from one hand to the other 20 times.

Divide in half.

Roll one at a time between 2 pieces of wax paper each into a circle to fit a 9 inch pie plate.

For the bottom crust, remove the top piece of wax paper and invert the crust over the pie plate. Gently peel off the wax paper, fit the crust into the pie plate.

Put the filling of your choice in. Cover with the top crust. Make a small hole in the center and 6 slits around it. Crimp the edges closed with a fork. Brush with milk. Put a 1 inch foil around the edges to keep from over-browning.

Place in oven. Follow the recipe of your choice.

Graham Cracker Crust

when you want a different crust

Heat oven 375°.

We make our graham cracker crumbs from 1 package of a 3 package box of graham crackers. It's easy; we put the crackers in a plastic bag and roll with a rolling pin until fine—no sweat, no tears! This makes about *⅔ cup crumbs.*

Put the crumbs into a bowl.

Add *¼ cup sugar*. Then stir in *¼ cup softened margarine or butter.*

Mix well with your fingers preferably, or a fork.

Pour into a 9 inch pie plate. Try to press evenly over the bottom and sides of the plate.

Tip: If you have an 8 inch pie plate, press it firmly over the crust to make the crust an even layer.

Place in the preheated 375° oven. Bake 8 minutes to make a crisp crust.

A Press And Push Pie Crust

which means just what it says . . . with no messy clean up afterwards, you make it right in its pan

Preheat oven 425°.

Into an 8 inch pie plate put *¼ cup oil, 3 tablespoons non-fat milk*. Mix with a fork until creamy.

Add *¼ teaspoon salt* and a *pinch of sugar, ¾ cup and 1 tablespoon flour* and *1 tablespoon wheat germ.*

Mix with a fork into a ball.

With your hands, push and press to cover the bottom and sides of the pie pan. Try to get it evenly distributed.

Prick the crust all over with a fork to keep from ballooning up when you bake it.

Put 1 inch foil around the edges of the crust.

Place in 425° oven.

Bake 8 minutes. Remove foil; bake 4 or 5 minutes more until lightly browned.

Cool on a rack.

Fill with your favorite filling.

A "No Clean Up After" Pie Crust

no mess, no bother . . . it's a good pie crust, too, so there's no excuse when someone says, "How about a pie?"

Heat oven 425°.

Put into a bowl *1 cup flour, ¼ cup vegetable shortening, ¼ teaspoon salt* and a *pinch of sugar*. Mix with a pastry blender or a fork.

Add *3 tablespoons cold water*. Mix with a fork until it forms a ball.

Place between 2 pieces of wax paper that fit an 8 inch or 9 inch pie plate.

Roll out to fit the pie plate.

Lift off the top sheet of wax paper.

With your two hands lift up the wax paper with the crust holding them together at the top and place, crust side down, on the pie plate.

Lift off the wax paper.

Arrange the crust in without stretching.

With a fork prick holes all over the crust.

With the back of the fork prongs, press the edges down. This makes a design and holds the edges up. Cover the edges with 1 inch foil.

Place in 425° preheated oven. Bake 7 minutes. Remove foil; bake 5 or 6 minutes more, as needed, being careful not to burn. Altogether bake the crust about 12 to 14 minutes.

Deep Dish Canned Cherry Pie

when there's snow on the ground, canned cherry pie will bring summer into the house

Make your pie *crust as* usual. (See index for recipe.)

Roll it out to fit the "inside" of your pie dish, no edges, just a round disk.

With a fork, punch holes all over, so it won't balloon up.

Bake on a cookie sheet at 450° until done, about 14–15 minutes. Let get cold.

Make the filling:

Drain *1 can (16 ounces) seeded dark sweet cherries.*

Put the juice into a measuring cup and the drained cherries into the deep pie dish.

Add *3 tablespoons lemon juice* to the cherry juice and *enough water to make 1 cup.*

Put into a saucepan. Stir in *4 tablespoons sugar* to taste. Bring to a boil.

Mix together *2 tablespoons cornstarch* and *2 tablespoons water.*

Stir into the boiling juice. Cook, stir, lifting off and on the heat until it clears, takes about 1 minute.

Pour over the cherries. Let cool.

Put the cold pie crust on top.

Your deep dish pie is ready.

Deep Dish Fresh Cherry Pie

this is delicious fresh and in the winter you can use the frozen cherries you froze in the summer

Heat oven 450°.

Bring *4 cups seeded fresh sour cherries* (Montmorency) with *2 tablespoons water, 2 tablespoons lemon juice* and *½ cup sugar* to a boil.

Stir *3 tablespoons water* into *3 tablespoons cornstarch.*

Stir into the boiling cherries. This clears instantly and thickens.

Pour into an 8¼ inch deep dish pie plate.

Let get cold.

Make *pastry crust.* See Index under "P"—Pie Crusts.

Place crust over the pie dish. Close the edges with the back prongs of a fork.

Crimp 1 inch foil around the edge to keep from burning.
With a sharp knife, make a small hole in the middle.
Around it cut 6 small slits for the steam to escape.
Brush the crust with *milk or half and half.* This helps to brown the crust, especially the "half and half."
Bake in 450° oven for 30 minutes until the crust is browned.

Deep Dish Frozen Cherry Pie

if you're lucky enough to have frozen some cherries in the summer, you can make this pie in the winter

Heat oven 450°.
Put *4 cups frozen sour cherries* (Montmorency) into a saucepan with *½ cup and 3 tablespoons sugar, 2 tablespoons water* and *2 tablespoons lemon juice.* You should have about 2½ cups cherry juice. Bring to a boil.
Mix together *3½ tablespoons cornstarch* and *3½ tablespoons cold water.*
Stir into the boiling cherries. This clears instantly and thickens.
Cook, stir, take off and on heat about 1 minute.
Pour into an 8¼ inch deep pie baking dish.
Make your favorite *crust.* See Index for recipe.
Make a small hole in the center and small slits around it. Close the edges of the crust with the back prongs of a fork. Crimp 1 inch foil around the edges to keep from over-browning. Brush the crust with *milk.* Put on a cookie sheet.
Bake in preheated 450° oven 15 minutes. Remove foil. Bake 10 minutes until the crust is browned.
Tip: The frozen cherries, when cooked, have about 2½ cups liquid.

Deep Dish Fresh Peach Pie

one of the greatest pleasures of summer . . . in the winter, if you have some frozen, everyone will be delighted!

Heat oven 450°.
If the peaches can be peeled easily, do so; otherwise drop *as many whole peaches as you think will make 4 cups sliced*

into a pot of boiling water. (We use 4 very large or 6 medium.)

Let cook about 1 minute only. Remove the peaches to a large bowl of cold water. Take out immediately. Take the skin off the peaches.

Cut into halves, then quarters, then eighths. Put into a large saucepan. Add *¼ cup cold water, ⅓ to ½ cup sugar* and *3 tablespoons lemon juice*. Bring to a boil.

Mix together *3 tablespoons water* with *3 tablespoons cornstarch.*

Slowly stir into the peach mixture. It clears almost instantly. Remove from the heat.

Pour into an 8¼" deep dish pie plate.

Make your favorite crust. See Index for recipe.

Place crust over the pie dish.

Make a small hole in the center and small slits around it. Close the edges of the crust with the back prongs of a fork. Crimp 1 inch foil around the edges to keep from burning. Brush the crust with *milk*. Put on a cookie sheet.

Bake in preheated 450° oven about 15 minutes. Remove foil. Bake 10 minutes until the crust is browned.

Fresh Raspberry Deep Dish Pie

in summer nothing tastes better

Heat oven 450°.

Wash and drain enough *raspberries to make 4 cups.* Put in saucepan with *3 tablespoons lemon juice* and *¾ cup sugar.*

Bring to a boil. Mix together *2 tablespoons cornstarch* and *2 tablespoons cold water.* Stir into the boiling raspberries. This clears instantly and thickens.

Pour into a 9 inch deep pie dish.

Make your favorite crust. See Index for recipe.

Place crust over pie dish.

Make a small hole in the center and small slits around it. Close the edges of the crust with the back prongs of a fork. Crimp 1 inch foil around the edges to keep from over-browning. Brush the crust with milk. Put on a cookie sheet.

Bake in preheated 450° oven 15 minutes. Remove foil. Bake 10 minutes until the crust is browned.

Deep Dish Black Raspberry Pie

makes a summer day seem blessed . . . in winter with snow on the ground, get out those berries you froze and taste again summer's harvest

Defrost overnight *1 package or 4 cups frozen black raspberries.*

Heat oven 450°.

In a saucepan bring to a boil the defrosted raspberries with *3 tablespoons lemon juice* and *¾ cup sugar,* takes about 10 minutes.

Mix together *2 tablespoons cornstarch* and *2 tablespoons cold water.* Stir into the boiling raspberries. This clears instantly and thickens. Cook, stir, take off and on heat about 1 minute.

Pour into 9 inch deep pie dish.

Make your favorite *crust.* See Index for recipe.

Place crust over the pie dish.

Make a small hole in the center and small slits around it. Close the edges of the crust with the back prongs of a fork. Crimp 1 inch foil around the edges to keep from over-browning. Brush the crust with *milk.* Put on a cookie sheet.

Bake in preheated 450° oven 15 minutes. Remove foil. Bake 10 minutes until the crust is browned.

Deep Dish Fresh Apple Pie

always welcome especially if you're watching your calories

Heat oven 450°.

Make a crust of your choice, see recipe index under P—Pie Crusts.

Peel, core, cut into slices enough *apples* to make *5 cups.* Sprinkle with *2 tablespoons lemon juice* and *1 tablespoon melted margarine.* Mix together *1 tablespoon flour* with *¼ cup and 2 tablespoons sugar* and *1 teaspoon cinnamon.* Mix gently into the apples. Spoon into the pie plate.

Roll out the pie crust. Unroll onto the pie plate. Cut off excess crust. Crimp the edges with the prongs of a fork. Make a small hole in the center, then cut 6 small slits around it. Put foil around the edges of the crust to keep it from over-browning. Brush the crust with milk.

Place in 450° oven. Bake 20 minutes. Remove foil. Bake 10 minutes until done. Remove to a rack to cool. Serve warm or cold. Either way it's good—some may like a thin slice of cheese with this.

A Double Crust Apple Pie

This is made the same way, only make a double crust. See recipe index under P—Pie crusts (double crusts).

Deep Dish Frozen Apple Pie

if you grow apples it's nice to slice and freeze in individual packages for individual pies so that you can have apple pies whenever you want them

Heat oven 450°.

Put into a saucepan *5 cups frozen apple slices.*

Add *2 tablespoons lemon juice* and *1 tablespoon melted margarine, ¼ cup and 2 tablespoons sugar, 1 teaspoon cinnamon*, and *2 tablespoons flour.*

Cook and stir until the apples defrost and come to a boil. Pour into the deep dish pie plate.

Make a crust of your choice. See recipe under P—Pie Crusts.

Roll out the pie crust. Crimp the edges with the prongs of a fork. Make a small hole in the center, then cut 6 small slits around it. Put foil around the edges of the crust to keep from over-browning. Brush with milk.

Place in 450° oven. Bake 15 minutes.

Remove foil. Bake 10 minutes until done. Remove to a rack to cool.

A Double Crust Apple Pie

This is made the same way, only make a double crust. See recipe index under Pie—Pie Crusts, double crusts.

Fresh Apple Pie

when you've waited and waited until apples are in season and you make your first pie with Summer Rambo apples, who cares if you eat as many slices as you get ready for the pie?

Preheat oven 450°.

You need a 9 inch pie plate.

Mix gently into *5 cups of peeled, sliced apples 2 tablespoons lemon juice.*

Mix together *½ cup white sugar* with *2 tablespoons flour, ¼ teaspoon salt* and *1 teaspoon cinnamon.* Set aside.

Make *2 crusts* either from scratch; or use 2 balls of pie dough from "Sophie's Mix." (See Index for recipe.)

Roll between 2 sheets of wax paper; or sprinkle a little flour over a clean surface and roll out to fit the pie plate.

Lightly roll it on the rolling pin. Unroll on top of the pie plate. Fit into the pie plate without stretching it.

Roll out the top crust and let stand.

Put apple mixture into pie crust.

Dot *2 tablespoons margarine* over the apples.

Place pie crust on top. With the prongs of a fork press down on the edges, but don't tear. This makes a design.

Put 1 inch wide piece of foil around the edges of the crust to keep the edges from burning. Cut a small hole in the middle of the crust and 6 slits around it to let the steam escape.

Place in preheated 450° oven. Bake about 15 minutes and remove foil. Bake about 10 minutes longer.

Nothing tastes better than a warm pie crust.

Have handy some cheddar or American cheese for those who like cheese with their pie.

Apple Pie

a double crust apple pie spiced with cinnamon and lemon

Heat oven 450°.

Make your favorite double crust, see recipe index.

Peel and slice *4 cups apples,* or if you wish use 4 cups frozen, peeled and sliced apples. Put into a large bowl. Mix lightly with *2 tablespoons lemon juice.* Mix together *¼ cup and 2 tablespoons sugar, 2 tablespoons flour* and *1 teaspoon cinnamon.*

Mix with the apples. If using fresh apples, spoon into the bottom crust. Dot with about *1 tablespoon butter or margarine.* If using the frozen sliced apples, put on the stove, cook, stir now and then until defrosted, then mix in the flour mixture and bring to a boil. Spoon into the bottom pie shell. Dot with 1 tablespoon butter or margarine.

Either way, place top crust on. Close the edge of the 2 crusts together. Cut off excess. Make small hole in the center. Cut 6 small slits around it. Brush crust with milk. Crimp 1 inch foil around the edges to keep from burning while baking.

Place in preheated 450° oven. Bake 15 minutes.

Remove the foil. Bake until done, takes about 10 minutes.

Nectarine And Blue Plum Deep Dish Pie

a wonderful combination . . . you can substitute peaches or apricots for the nectarines . . . also, off season you can use these fruits which you froze to make these pies

Heat oven 450°.

Put into a saucepan *2 cups fresh or frozen sliced nectarines* or peeled peaches or apricots and *2 cups fresh or frozen blue plums.*

Add *1 tablespoon lemon juice, ¼ cup plus 2 tablespoons sugar* and *2 tablespoons flour.*

Cook, stir on medium heat until it comes to a boil and thickens.

Pour into a deep dish baking pie dish.

Make the crust. See recipe index under P—Pie Crusts for your favorite crust.

Roll the crust out to fit the top of the baking pan. Press the edges with a fork to close well. Cut off any excess dough. Make a small hole in the center of the crust. Cut 6 small slits around it. Put 1 inch foil around the edges of the crust to keep it from burning. Brush the crust with some milk.

Place in the preheated 450° oven. Bake 15 minutes. Remove the foil. Bake 10 or more minutes until done.

Double Crust Pie

You follow the deep dish pie recipe but you make 2 crusts instead of one—a bottom crust and a top crust. The rest of the recipe is the same.

Fresh Peach Pie

what could be better?

Heat oven 450°.

Make pastry for a *2 crust pie*. See Index for recipe. Put one crust into an 8 or 9 inch pie plate. Roll out the other. Set aside.

Peel, slice *5 cups peaches* and put into a large bowl.

Combine *½ cup sugar* with *4 tablespoons flour.*

Measure *1 tablespoon lemon juice*. Let stand.

Melt *2 tablespoons margarine.*

Mix together quickly the sugar, flour mixture, the tablespoon lemon juice and the melted margarine, stir into the 5 cups sliced peaches.

Pour or spoon quickly into the bottom pie crust. Put the other crust on top.

With the prongs of a fork press down on the edges, but don't tear. This makes a design. Put 1 inch wide piece of foil around the edges of the crust to keep from burning.

Cut a hole in the middle of the crust and slits around it to let the steam escape as it bakes.

Place in preheated 450° oven. Bake 15 minutes.

Remove foil. Bake 10 minutes until browned nicely.

Glazed Strawberry Pie

it's easy to make and delicious to eat . . . it's an open faced tart

Bake one of our *9 inch pie crust* recipes. (See Index for recipe.) Let get cold. For a Graham Cracker Crust, see Index under "C."

Wash *2 pint boxes* of fresh strawberries in 4 changes of water to remove any sand. Let dry. Remove the stems.

Separate the large pretty berries from the smaller ones.

Crush enough of the smaller berries with a potato masher to make 1½ cups.

Stir *1 tablespoon milk* into a *3 ounce package of cream cheese;* then stir in *2 tablespoons 10X Confectioner's Sugar.* Spread on the cooled, baked crust.

Arrange the large strawberries on the cream cheese mixture.

Bring to a boil the 1½ cups crushed strawberries.

Boil and stir 1 minute.

Mix together *1 cup sugar* and *3 tablespoons cornstarch.*

Stir into the crushed strawberries. Let come back to a rolling boil. Cook, stir 1 minute. Take off heat. Cool.

Spoon over the large strawberries to glaze them; then spoon the rest of the cooked strawberries into the pie, being careful to let the pretty large berries which you glazed show.

Place in the refrigerator until you are ready to serve. Standing in the refrigerator makes it easier to cut.

A Winter Time Cherry Open Faced Pie Or Tart

you use your frozen cherries and you'll agree nothing tastes better in the winter than a fresh baked cherry tart

Make and bake an *8 inch crust.* Set aside to cool while you make the filling.

Put *2 cups frozen cherries* into a large saucepan.

Add *1 tablespoon water, 1 tablespoon lemon juice, ¼ cup plus 1½ tablespoons sugar.* Bring to a boil.

Mix together *2 tablespoons cornstarch* and *1 tablespoon water.*

Stir into the boiling cherries. Take off and on heat until it clears and thickens, takes about 1 minute. Cool.

Pour into the shell.

It looks pretty enough to eat!

Canned Cherry Tart

when fresh cherries aren't in season, you can still make a good tart with canned cherries

Make *pie crust* as usual; see Index for recipe. With a fork prick holes all over. Bake; let get cold.

Make the filling:

Drain *1 can (16 ounces) seeded dark sweet cherries.* Put the juice into a measuring cup and the cherries into a bowl.

Add *3 tablespoons lemon juice* to the cherry juice and enough *water to make 1 cup.* Put into a saucepan. Add *4 tablespoons sugar* to taste. Bring to a boil.

Mix together *2½ tablespoons cornstarch* and *2½ tablespoons water.*

Stir into the boiling juice. Cook, stir, lifting off and on the heat until it clears, takes about 1 minute.

Pour over the cherries. Cool a few minutes. Spoon into the baked, cooled crust.

Using canned cherries rather than the canned prepared pie filling mix costs less, and you get a better tart.

Tip: When you buy the canned cherries, be sure to buy the *pitted* cherries.

Open Faced
Apricot Pie Or Tart

with fresh apricots, nothing but nothing tastes as good

Let *2 packages (3 ounces each) Philadelphia Cream Cheese* get to room temperature.

Make a *crust* as usual; only roll it out thickish to fit a 9 inch pie pan.

When you fit it in your pie pan, only come half way up the sides, so it will be a tart instead of a regular pie.

Prick all over carefully, so it will not balloon up.

Bake in preheated 450° oven about 13 or 14 minutes.

Remove from oven and cool.

Make the filling:

You will need only about *11 or 12 fresh apricots.*

Bring water in a saucepan to a boil. When the water boils, drop in, one by one, the apricots. Cook just long enough to be able to slip off the skins, takes about 1 minute.

Have a large bowl of iced cold water standing close by. With a slotted spoon remove the apricots and drop into the cold water. Slip off the skins. Cut or break in halves. Place on a large plate, domed side up.

Put into a saucer about *4 tablespoons commercial apricot preserves.* (We make our own; see Index for recipe.) Mix with a spoon. With your fingers, gently, one by one, glaze each half apricot and put on a large plate domed side up.

With an electric mixer, or with a spoon, stir 4 tablespoons of the preserves into the 2 packages softened Philadelphia Cream Cheese until smooth.

Spoon over the cold crust to make a bed for the glazed apricots.

Arrange the apricots, domed side up, in a circle starting at the outer edge. Make a second row and put an apricot or two in the center.

The glaze makes the apricots a beautiful shiny color—almost too pretty to eat!

Wild Blueberry Tart

it tastes as good as it looks

If you have some of our "Sophie's 6 Pack Freezer Dough," defrost one and use; or make our "Never Fail Pie Crust." See Index for recipe.

Heat oven 450°.

Roll out *dough* to fit an 8″ or 9″ pie dish.

Don't cover the pie dish rim, just the sides, as this is a tart.

Prick all over with a fork.

Bake in preheated 450° oven 12 to 14 minutes.

Cool.

Make the filling:

Drain *1 can Wild Blueberries*. Put the blueberries into a bowl.

To the blueberry juice add about *2 tablespoons lemon juice,* which makes 1 cup juice altogether.

Put into a saucepan. Stir in *3 tablespoons sugar*. Bring to a boil.

Mix together *2½ tablespoons cornstarch* with *2½ tablespoons cold tap water*. Stir into the boiling juice.

Take off heat. Stir slowly. It will clear at once and thicken.

Put back on heat. Cook, stir slowly 1 minute.

Pour over the blueberries and mix slowly. Let stand until it cools, about 20 to 25 minutes. Pour into the crust.

It's as pretty as a picture.

Keep in refrigerator until ready to eat.

Open Faced Fresh Plum Pie Or Tart

a five minute plum filling and pie . . . the filling tastes fresh because it's hardly cooked . . . and the crust takes only 12 minutes to bake . . . easy? . . . yes

Chop into small chunks *enough washed, seeded prune plums to make 2 cups.*

Mix together *½ cup sugar* with *1 tablespoon flour.* Mix with the prune plums.

Stir in *1 tablespoon lemon juice.*

Cook, stir on high heat until it boils. Cook, stir 5 minutes until thickened.

Spoon onto a large plate to cool.

Make one of our *8 inch pie crust* recipes and bake. Let cool.

Spoon the cold prunes on top.

This could be called an Open Faced Pie or Tart. Either way it tastes mighty good.

Lemon Meringue Pie

one of our favorites

Make and bake your favorite *crust.* Let get cold.

Make the Lemon Filling:

Grate *1 tablespoon lemon rind* and strain *enough lemon juice to make ¼ cup juice.*

Boil enough water to make *1½ cups boiling water.*

Separate *4 eggs,* whites in a large bowl, yolks in a deep saucer.

In a large saucepan mix *1⅓ cups sugar* with *4 tablespoons cornstarch.*

Gradually stir in the egg yolks into the cornstarch-sugar mixture. Then stir in the grated lemon rind and the lemon juice.

Gradually stir in 1½ cups boiling water.

Cook, stir and bring to a boil on high heat.

Turn heat to low; cook, stir 4 minutes. Take off heat. Let cool. When mixture cools, it thickens.

Spoon into cold pie crust.

Preheat oven 350°.

Beat the 4 egg whites until stiff. Add *3 tablespoons sugar* and beat until you feel no grains of sugar when you taste.

Spoon, don't smooth, onto the crust making sure the whites touch the crust all around. Don't leave any space anywhere between whites and crust. Don't smooth the meringue; it looks prettier without smoothing.

Bake in 350° oven about 15 minutes.

Remove and cool.

Squash Pumpkin Pie

it looks like a squash, white with green stripes, and a crook neck, but it's a light orange color when you peel it . . . when you make it into a pie, it tastes exactly like pumpkin

Make a *pie crust*. See Index for recipe under "C"—Crusts.

Wash, peel, and remove the seeds from the squash. Cut into cubes. Steam until tender.

Push through a food mill. Put into a strainer over a bowl and let drain, about ½ hour.

Put into a bowl *6 tablespoons sugar, ½ teaspoon ginger, 1 teaspoon cinnamon, ½ teaspoon nutmeg* and *¼ teaspoon salt*. Mix together.

Stir in slowly *1 cup of the squash* and *1 teaspoon vanilla.*

Stir in *3 eggs.*

Stir in *1 can (13 ounces) evaporated milk.*

Pour into the unbaked pie crust.

Sprinkle a *little cinnamon* over the top.

Place in 425° oven. Bake 20 minutes.

Turn heat to 350°. Bake 20 minutes.

Tip: The little cinnamon on top of the pie does something special to the pie. Also, you can use 1 or 2 tablespoons light rum or brandy for a special occasion.

Pumpkin Pudding Pie

"pumpkin eaters" will certainly like this

Make and bake a *9 inch pie crust*. Let get cold.

Mix together *1 package Vanilla Pudding and Pie Filling* (3 ounces), *¼ teaspoon salt, ½ cup sugar less 2 tablespoons, ½ teaspoon ground ginger, 1 teaspoon cinnamon, ½ teaspoon nutmeg, 1 can evaporated milk, 1 cup canned pumpkin* and *1 teaspoon vanilla.*

Bring to a boil on high heat stirring slowly all the time.

Cook and stir about 3 minutes until thick.

Take off heat. Cool.

Spoon into the cold crust.

Here's your pie!

Easy Pumpkin Pie

always in season because Libby's in a can is always ready and waiting . . . but if you use fresh pumpkin, we found the best way—the least watery way—was to wash the pumpkin, cut it into thin slices, then peel the slices and steam the pieces in a steamer until soft . . . then we put it through a food mill, or you could use a strainer . . . the best pumpkins, with deep orange color and less seeds, are the "Crook Neck" pumpkins . . . once in your life, please use a fresh pumpkin!

Make a *pie crust* (see Index for recipe), and place in a 9 inch pie pan.

Heat oven 425°.

Measure *½ cup sugar and remove 2 tablespoons.*

Add *½ teaspoon ginger, 1 teaspoon cinnamon, ½ teaspoon nutmeg, ¼ teaspoon salt.* Mix together.

Stir in slowly *1 cup pumpkin* and *1 teaspoon vanilla.*

Mix *3 eggs* with a fork and stir in.

Stir in *1 can (13 ounces) evaporated milk.*

Pour into the unbaked pie crust.

Sprinkle a *little cinnamon* over the top.

Place in 425° oven. Bake 20 minutes.

Turn heat to 350°; bake 20 minutes.

Tip: The little bit of cinnamon on top of the pie does something special when baked.

Pumpkin Pie With Meringue

like the Lemon Meringue Pie you bake the crust by itself, so there is never any soggy crust

Bake a *crust* and let get cold. (See Index for Pie Crust Recipe.)

Make the filling:

Separate *3 eggs,* yolks from whites.

Put into a saucepan *½ cup sugar.* Remove 2 tablespoons.

Add *½ teaspoon ground ginger, 1 teaspoon cinnamon, ½ teaspoon nutmeg, ¼ teaspoon cloves, ¼ teaspoon salt* and *3 tablespoons cornstarch.*

Mix with a wooden spoon.

Stir in gradually *1 cup canned pumpkin* and *1 can (13 ounces) evaporated milk.*

Cook and stir the pumpkin mixture on medium heat until it comes to a boil.

Turn heat to low; cook 2 minutes.

Remove from heat.

Mix the egg yolks with a fork. Stir, a little at a time, into the pumpkin mixture until all has been added.

Place on low heat and cook, stir 2 minutes.

Cool. Pour into the baked pie shell.

Make the meringue:

Beat the 3 egg whites in a large mixing bowl (1½ quart size) with a rotary beater until soft peaks form.

Gradually add *3 tablespoons sugar* while you continue beating until the whites are stiff and shiny.

Spoon the whites onto the filling, being careful not to leave any space between the whites and crust.

Do not smooth the meringue; let stay in peaks.

Bake in 350° oven 15 minutes until meringue is golden brown.

Coconut Meringue Cream Pie

one of my favorite pies

See Index under "C" for crust and choose your favorite one.

Make and bake the *9 inch crust.* Set aside to get cold.

Make the filling:

Mix together *6 tablespoons sugar, 6 tablespoons cornstarch* and *¼ teaspoon salt.*

Stir in *2½ cups milk.* Cook and stir on medium heat until it comes to a boil and gets thick.

Cook 1 minute longer. Take off heat. Gently stir in *2 tablespoons soft (tub) margarine, 1 teaspoon vanilla* and *½ cup shredded coconut.*

Put a piece of Saran Wrap right on top of the filling to keep a skin from forming. Let get cold.

Spoon into the pie crust and make the meringue.

The Meringue

Put *4 egg whites* into a bowl. (We always have some frozen in our freezer and then defrost the whites to make the meringue.) Or you can separate 4 eggs, use the whites and later make custards or a cake or whatever with the yolks.

Beat the whites with a rotary beater or an electric beater until foamy. Add *¼ teaspoon cream of tartar* and a *pinch of salt.*

Beat until stiff and test by lifting the beaters out quickly. The peak formed should be straight, not droopy.

Beating all the time, slowly add a tablespoon at a time, *6 tablespoons sugar.* Beat until when you taste the meringue, you will feel no grains of sugar. It should be smooth; also, when you lift the beaters out, the peak is straight.

Tip: The meringue isn't ready until you have beaten enough so you do not feel any grains of sugar—but don't overbeat.

Gently fold in *2 tablespoons grated lemon rind.*

Spoon the meringue onto the filling being careful to leave *no* space between the meringue and the crust. This keeps the meringue from weeping.

Sprinkle about *¼ cup of the shredded coconut* on top of the meringue.

Place on a cookie sheet in 400° oven.

Bake about 10 minutes until the coconut is beautifully browned.

Remove from oven. Cool.

Keep in the refrigerator.

This is best eaten the day it is baked.

Chocolate Cream Pie

you can have it plain or fancy . . . plain? . . . just a chocolate taste . . . fancy? . . . with a whisp of brandy . . . should I say, "Chocolate is nice, but brandy is dandy!"

Make and bake your favorite *9 inch pie crust.* Let get cold.

Push *1/3 cup cocoa* through a strainer into a bowl, so there are no lumps.

Add *3 tablespoons cornstarch plus 2 teaspoons, 1/4 teaspoon salt, 1/2 cup sugar* and mix together.

Slowly stir in *2 1/2 cups milk* and *1/4 cup brandy* (optional).

Pour into a saucepan. On high heat cook, stir until it starts to boil and gets thick.

Turn heat to low. Cook and stir slowly 3 minutes.

Take off heat. Stir in *1 teaspoon vanilla* and *2 tablespoons soft "tub" margarine.*

Put a piece of Saran Wrap right on top of the pudding.

Let get cold.

Spoon into the baked cold crust.

Your Chocolate Cream Pie is ready.

Vanilla Cream Pie

it's a "Penny Pincher" cream pie that tastes much more expensive than it costs

See Index for recipe under "C" for Crust and choose your favorite one.

Make and bake a *9 inch pie crust.* Set aside to get cold.

Make the filling:

Mix together *6 tablespoons sugar, 6 tablespoons cornstarch* and *1/4 teaspoon salt.*

Stir in *2 1/2 cups milk.*

Cook and stir on medium heat until it comes to a boil and gets thick.

Cook 1 minute longer. Take off heat.

Stir in *2 tablespoons soft (tub) margarine* and *2 teaspoons vanilla.*

Put a piece of Saran Wrap right on top of the filling to keep a skin from forming. Place in refrigerator to get cold.

Spoon into the pie crust and make the meringue.

The Meringue

Put *3 egg whites* into a bowl.

Beat with a rotary beater or electric beaters until foamy. Add *1/4 teaspoon cream of tartar* and a *pinch of salt.* Beat on highest speed until when you lift the beaters out, it forms a "droopy" peak.

Gradually as you beat, add a little at a time, *6 tablespoons sugar* until all have been added.

Continue to beat until you taste it and feel no grains of sugar. It will be smooth and glossy.

Pile on top of the filling being sure to see that the meringue touches the rim of the crust with no space in between. (This is to ensure that the meringue won't "weep.")

Place in 400° oven. Bake about 10 minutes.

Remove from oven. Cool.

If you wish, you can grate 2 tablespoons lemon or orange rind and fold gently into the meringue before baking it.

You can use our "Homemade Whipped Cream" (milk) instead of the meringue. See Index for recipe. Or you can whip some honest to goodness whipping cream if you wish.

You can arrange some fresh fruit, such as bananas, sliced and dipped in lemon juice and drained, then arranged on top of the filling or you can arrange the slices on top of the crust and put the filling on top of the fruit. Other fruits you can use are peaches or slightly sweetened berries, such as blueberries, raspberries and strawberries.

You can also use well drained canned fruits.

Tip: For a change in the filling use 2¼ cups milk and ¼ cup Sherry Wine. That's a switch! Worthwhile, too!

Key Lime Pie

the limes give this pie a taste you'll long remember

Bake one of our *pie crusts; or* make the *graham cracker crust,* as follows:

Heat oven 350°.

In a large bowl mix together *1¼ cups graham cracker crumbs* and *¼ cup superfine sugar.*

Stir in *¼ cup room temperature butter or margarine* until well blended with a wooden spoon or your hands.

Press the mixture evenly in a 9 inch pie plate with your fingers. You can shape this by pressing it down with an 8 inch pie plate. Remove the pie plate.

Bake the crust 10 minutes in the preheated 350° oven. Cool.

Separate *4 eggs;* put yolks in the top of a double boiler or a saucepan that will fit over another saucepan. Put the whites into the large bowl of an electric mixer or other large bowl.

Grate as fine as possible *enough lime rind to make 1 teaspoonful.*

Squeeze and strain *key lime juice to make ½ cup.*

Mix the 4 egg yolks just to combine. Gradually stir in *¼ cup sugar,* ½ cup lime juice and the grated rind.

Put the usual amount of water into the bottom pan of the double boiler, and heat until it simmers but does not boil.

Place the egg yolk mixture over the "simmering" water.

Cook, stir with a wooden spoon 10 minutes until the mixture coats the back of a metal spoon. Do not boil; simmer.

Put into a large bowl to cool to room temperature.

When this yolk mixture is room temperature, beat the egg whites with a *pinch of salt* until foamy.

Add *¼ teaspoon cream of tartar.* Beat until soft peaks form.

Gradually beat in *¼ cup sugar.* Beat until the mixture (meringue) is stiff—holds a straight peak when you lift the beaters out.

Stir ⅓ of this meringue into the egg yolk mixture to lighten it.

"Fold" the rest of the meringue into the yolk mixture.

Spoon into the cooled, baked pie crust or the cooled graham cracker crust.

Tip: Some people whip some cream to top this pie.

Lemon-No-Bake-Pie

Make and bake a *graham cracker crust* to fit a 7 or 8 inch pie plate.

Gradually stir into *1 can (15 ounces) sweetened, condensed milk, ½ cup lemon juice.*

Pour into the graham cracker crust.

Put in the refrigerator to congeal.

You can serve as is; or right before serving, slice *bananas* over the pie and serve immediately.

If you are fortunate to grow *red raspberries,* please try some of these on top of this pie as a special treat. Or, of course, for a special occasion you could buy a small box of red raspberries. Don't buy the black raspberries, they must be the red ones.

Fresh *blueberries* are very, very nice, too. Don't get carried away and put a lot on; just put 1 layer on.

To Make Canned Blueberry Pie Filling "Homemade"

Stir *1 can (1 pound, 5 ounces) Wild Blueberry Pie Filling* with *2 tablespoons lemon juice* and *1 tablespoon sugar.*

Make pie as usual; or make a deep dish pie.

You bake a 2 crust pie in 425° oven 25 minutes; then remove the foil from the crust edges and bake 10 minutes more.

See Index for recipe for deep dish pie.

To Make "Prepared Pie Fillings" For Pies

taste more homemade

Put *1 jar or can "Prepared Pie Filling" fruit*—peaches, apricots, plums, cherries, apples, blueberries—into a saucepan or bowl.

Stir in *2 or 3 tablespoons lemon juice* and *3 or 4 tablespoons sugar* to taste.

Follow our directions for "Deep Dish Pie" or "Two Crust Pies."

Tips On Thickening Different Kinds Of Pies

To 1 cup fruit juice:

For a thick filling you can cut, use 2½ tablespoons cornstarch mixed with 2½ tablespoons water.

For a thin, thickish filling use 1½ tablespoons cornstarch mixed with 1½ tablespoons water.

For a more runny filling use 1¼ tablespoons cornstarch mixed with 1¼ tablespoons water.

For a runny filling use 1 tablespoon cornstarch mixed with 1 tablespoon water.

To 2½ cups juice:

For a thickish filling you can cut, use 3½ tablespoons cornstarch mixed with 3½ tablespoons water.

For a tart use 4 tablespoons cornstarch mixed with 4 tablespoons water.

Tips On Frozen Pies

For a better taste, bake the pies you will freeze. They taste better than when frozen raw and then baked.

Tips On What To Do With Little Pieces Of Leftover Pie Dough

When you make a pie and you have little pieces of pie dough left over, don't throw them away. Roll it out into a square if you can; otherwise let it be round and cut it into 4 pieces.

Fill each one with thick *orange marmalade* and *golden or dark raisins* on the bottom of each piece, and fold over the top dough.

With a fork press the edges closed. It makes a pretty design.

Brush with *egg wash* made by stirring 2 teaspoons cold water into 1 egg yolk, *or* brush with *milk.*

Place in preheated 450° oven about 15 to 17 minutes.

You can use any thick preserve and add raisins or nuts or dates.

We are partial to apricot preserves.

How To Make Prepared Fruit Filling Pies

using jars or cans of prepared fillings, peaches, apricots, plums, cherries, apples, blueberries or other fruits

Put the *jar or can of Prepared Fruit Filling* into a saucepan. Stir in *2 or 3 tablespoons lemon juice* and *3 or 4 tablespoons sugar* to your taste.

Put into a heatproof glass (8 inch) deep pie dish.

Make a crust of your choice. Arrange on top of the filling. With the prongs of a fork crimp the edges to the dish.

Make a small hole with a sharp knife in the middle of the crust to let the steam escape when baking. Also, make about 6 little slits around it.

Cover the edges with 1 inch foil to keep from over-browning.

Bake in 425° oven about 30 to 40 minutes.

For a two crust pie:

Select the filling of your choice and make it homemade as above, but make 2 crusts, one for the bottom and one for the top. Bake as you usually do for a 2 crust pie.

How To Freeze Your Fruit Pies

Wash, peel, cut as necessary, the fruit you plan to freeze.

Measure 4 cups of the fruit and put in plastic bag. (For apples measure 5 or 6 cups sliced apples.)

We have a deep, narrow pan that just fits our 2 gallon plastic bags. We put the plastic bag into the pan and fold the top over the rim so the bag is held safely. We then pour the proper amount of fruit to make 1 pie in each bag and freeze immediately. No dilly dallying! We label the bags.

These are the fruits we freeze: black raspberries, cherries, sliced peaches, cut prune plums, 2 cups apricots and 2 cups prune plums (my husband's favorite combination) and peeled and sliced apples.

As I said before, the harvest of the summertime makes delicious eating in the winter and spring.

How To Make Pie
From Frozen Fruit

in the summer when home grown fruit is so plentiful, freeze the fruit in "portion sizes" in plastic bags enough for a pie . . . when winter comes, you'll enjoy the pleasures of the "Fruits" of the summer and fall—raspberries, cherries, apricots, plums, peaches and apples—there's nothing better!

Deep Dish Pies with Frozen Fruit Fillings

Make the Filling:

Defrost the *frozen fruit of your choice* either in the refrigerator overnight or before you make your pie you can put the frozen fruit into a saucepan with *3 tablespoons lemon juice* and *½ to ¾ cup sugar,* depending on the fruit.

Cook, stir until the fruit is defrosted. Bring to a simmer.

Put *2 tablespoons cold tap water* into a bowl.

Stir in *2 tablespoons cornstarch,* depending on your fruit. Stir into the simmering fruit. Cook, stir until it clears and thickens.

Pour into the 8 or 9 inch pie dish. Let stand while you make the crust.

Make the *crust of your choice.* Place on top of the pie plate. Cut off any excess dough. With the prongs of a fork close the edges of the crust. Make a small hole in the middle and 6 slits around it.

Crimp 1 inch foil over the edges of the crust to keep from over-browning. Brush crust with *milk* so crust will brown nicely.

Place in preheated 425° oven. Bake about 15 to 20 minutes or until you see the fruit bubbling. Turn heat to 325°.

Bake until done, about 20 to 25 minutes.

For a 2 Crust Pie:

Defrost the frozen fruit of your choice. Do as above, only make 2 crusts. Put one crust into the pie plate, then make the top crust to have ready. Then make the filling. In this way your bottom crust will not get soggy.

Brush the top crust with milk or margarine, and put foil on the edges.

Make a hole in the top crust and 6 slits around it for the steam to escape.

Put in 425° oven. Bake 15 to 20 minutes.

Reduce heat to 375.° Bake until done, about 20 to 25 minutes.

Tips On Turnovers

to use up any pieces of pastry left when you make your crust or crusts . . . "good to the last piece," as they say . . . here are some tips

There are usually small pieces of pastry dough left when you make a pie crust that you don't know what to do with. Throw it away? No! You will be surprised how little dough you will need to make small turnovers. Roll the dough as near to a square as you can. Cut into 4 equal pieces or squares.

We find that a jelly stuffing is the best stuffing, but no matter how thick it is, it runs out while it is baking. To solve this problem we melt the jelly, and while boiling stir in cornstarch to these proportions: Bring ¼ cup jelly to a boil. Stir in 1 tablespoon cornstarch mixed with 2 tablespoons water. Stir, taking off and on heat, until it thickens, takes about 3 to 5 minutes, but be careful not to burn.

We use orange marmalade, apricot preserves, plum preserves or peach preserves. After we smear the jelly on, we sometimes dot the preserves with golden raisins.

Place the squares on an ungreased cookie sheet. Spoon some of the jelly on each. Fold the dough over to make triangles. With your fingers press the edges together; then use the prongs of a fork to seal the edges. With a fork prick the turnover top all over to let steam out; or put a slit in the center of each turnover.

For a pretty turnover brush with egg wash by stirring 2 teaspoons cold water into 1 egg yolk and brush this on top of the turnovers.

Bake in 450° oven about 14 minutes.

Fruit Turnovers

these only take 15 to 20 minutes to bake and are about as good as pie

Heat oven 425°.

Turnover Filling:

For our turnovers you can use any of these canned fruits,

homemade or commercial: apricots, peaches, apples, plums, pears, or blueberries, canned with sugar (not the water packed kind).

Whatever canned *fruit* you choose, drain well, then cut with a scissors into ½ inch pieces (except the blueberries) to make 2 cups. Add *sugar to taste* but don't overdo. The fruit should be good and sweet, because in baking with the crust that is not sweet, the fruit needs to be sweet by contrast.

The Turnover Pastry:

Remove 6 tablespoons flour from 2 cups flour in a large bowl. Add *2 tablespoons wheat germ, ½ teaspoon salt* and *¼ teaspoon sugar.*

Mix with a pastry blender.

Add *⅔ cup vegetable shortening.* With the pastry blender, mix into large crumbs. Push ¼ of these crumbs to one side. Mix the rest into fine crumbs. Now combine the two. (This helps to make a flaky crust.)

Put *ice cubes* and *water* into a small bowl to let get icy cold. When cold put 1 tablespoon water over a small portion of the crumbs and mix together to make a soft dough. Add another tablespoon to another portion and mix that portion. Do the same with a third tablespoon of water. Combine the 3 doughs and mix with as much of the dry dough as you need to make a soft, but not sticky, dough.

Sprinkle as much of the fourth tablespoon water over the rest of the crumbs as you need and mix. Combine with the rest of the dough into one large soft ball cleaning the bowl.

Sprinkle a little flour on a surface. Put the dough on it and cut into halves.

Roll one-half of the dough into 9″ × 10″. With a sharp knife cut off any dough to straighten it. (Save the dough.) Measure with your eyes and cut into 4 pieces.

Take one piece of dough at a time, turn diamond shape toward you and spoon about 3 tablespoons fruit a little below the center. Without stretching, cover with the top piece of dough thus making the turnover diamond shaped. Put on a cookie sheet or 2 sheets, using a spatula, and press with the back prongs of a fork to close. Prick the top all over with a fork. Brush with *milk or* an *"egg wash."* See Index for recipe.

Place in 425° oven. Bake 15 to 20 minutes.

Cool on rack.

If the fruit needs thickening, the proportion is ½ cup juice to 2 tablespoons cornstarch. Stir 2 tablespoons juice or water (preferably juice) into 2 tablespoons cornstarch. Bring ½ cup juice to a boil. Stir in the cornstarch mixture. Take off heat. Stir. It should clear at once.

If the juice is a light syrup, add sugar before heating for a better taste.

Fresh Apples Baked In A Dough

something different and good

Heat oven 400°.

Make the filling first:

Wash, peel, core, slice, then cube *enough apples to make 3 cups.*

Mix *½ cup sugar* with *1 tablespoon cinnamon* and *2 teaspoons flour*. Mix into the apples.

Add *1 or 2 tablespoons lemon juice* according to the taste of the apples. Mix.

Make our *"Rich Baking Powder Dough."* See Index for recipe under "D."

Cut the dough into half; then each into half to make 4 pieces.

Roll out the dough, one at a time, into 11 × 4½ inch pieces. Smear a *little margarine* down the center of the dough, but not the edges.

Arrange the apples lengthwise down the middle. Dot with a *little margarine.* If you like, sprinkle a little cinnamon over.

Fold the dough, one side lengthwise, over the fruit to enclose it. Pinch the ends together. Brush the top with *soft margarine,* and sprinkle a *little sugar,* mixed with *cinnamon,* on top.

Cut into 5 pieces. Arrange in the baking dish or on a cookie sheet.

Do the same to the rest of the dough.

Place on the second shelf from the heat in the oven.

Bake about 20 to 25 minutes.

You can serve this hot. They also freeze well, reheat well, too. To reheat, put in foil, close, place on a rack or a cookie sheet and bake about 10 to 15 minutes in a 400° oven.

Peaches are delightful made this way; so are prune plums and apricots.

Fresh Apples In A Dough With A Sauce

it's like dumplings and yet it's different, but good! . . . do the same with peaches . . . you'll be glad!

These freeze so well that we bake in 2 foil square pans 8″ × 8″ × 1¾″ and eat one and freeze one. Of course, you can use a large pan that fits depending on the size of your family.

The sauce:

Put *3 cans (6 ounces) of apple or apricot juice,* which makes 2 cups, into a saucepan.

Stir in *1 tablespoon strained lemon juice* and *4 tablespoons sugar.* Put ¼ cup of this juice into a screw-top jar. Add *1 teaspoon flour.* Shake well to combine. Stir into the rest of the juice; set aside.

Make the filling:

Wash, peel, core, slice, then cube *enough apples or peaches to make 3 cups.* Mix *½ cup sugar, 1 tablespoon cinnamon* with *2 teaspoons flour.* Mix into the apples or peaches. Add *2 tablespoons lemon juice,* according to your taste, and mix.

Make our *"Rich Baking Powder Dough"* recipe. See Index for recipe under "D."

Cut the dough into half; then each into halves to make 4 pieces.

Roll out the dough, one at a time, into 11″ × 4½″. Smear a *little margarine* down the center of the dough, but not the edges.

Arrange the fruit lengthwise down the middle. Dot with a *little margarine.* If you like, add a little more cinnamon.

Fold the dough, one side at a time, lengthwise over the fruit to enclose it. Pinch the ends together. Brush the top with *soft margarine* and sprinkle on a *little sugar* mixed with *cinnamon.*

Cut into 5 pieces. Arrange in the baking dishes.

Bring the sauce to a boil. Spoon it quickly around the fruit rolls.

Place on the second shelf from the heat in the oven. Bake about 20 to 25 minutes.

This is mighty good served hot.

They also freeze well. They reheat well covered with foil on a rack or a cookie sheet and baked about 10 to 15 minutes in a 400° oven.

18. PUDDINGS, SWEET SOUFFLÉS AND CREPES

Vanilla Pudding

In a saucepan mix together *¼ cup sugar, 3 tablespoons cornstarch* and *¼ teaspoon salt.*

Stir in *1¼ cups milk.*

Cook and stir on medium heat until it comes to a boil and gets thick.

Cook 1 minute longer. Take off heat.

Stir in *1 tablespoon soft margarine.*

Then stir in *1½ teaspoons vanilla.*

Pour into 4 or 5 cups.

Put Saran Wrap on each custard (not the cup) to keep a skin from forming.

Place in refrigerator.

This is a nice dessert because it not only tastes good, but doesn't use eggs which gives you a chance to eat an egg at another meal.

Chocolate Pudding

you mix and make it yourself . . . how's that? . . . and so easy!

Push *⅓ cup cocoa* through a strainer so there are no lumps.

Stir in *½ cup sugar, 3 tablespoons cornstarch* and *¼ teaspoon salt.*

Slowly stir in *2½ cups milk.*

Pour into a saucepan. Put on medium heat.

Cook and stir slowly with a wooden spoon until it starts to boil and gets thick. Turn the heat to low.

Cook and stir slowly 3 minutes.

Take it off the heat. Stir in *1 teaspoon vanilla* and *1 tablespoon margarine.*

Spoon or pour into 5 glass cups or deep saucers.

Put a piece of Saran Wrap right on top of each of the puddings. This keeps a skin from forming. Refrigerate.

Doesn't this taste good?

Peanut Butter Pudding

a smooth peanutty taste

Put into a bowl *3 tablespoons cornstarch, ¼ cup sugar* and *¼ teaspoon salt.* Mix together well.

Stir *¼ cup peanut butter* until soft in another bowl.

Gradually stir in, a little at a time, *2¼ cups milk.*

Strain in a strainer over a bowl, so there are no pieces of peanut butter.

Slowly stir this milk-peanut butter mixture into the cornstarch mixture.

Place on medium heat. Cook and stir all the time slowly with a wooden spoon until it starts to boil and gets thick.

Cook 1 minute on low heat. Take off heat.

Stir in *1 tablespoon soft margarine or butter.*

Stir in *1 teaspoon vanilla.*

Pour into 4 glass baking cups or deep saucers.

Put a small piece of Saran Wrap right on top of each pudding. This keeps a skin from forming.

Place in refrigerator until you are ready to eat.

Pumpkin Pudding

this is especially nice and you don't have to use any eggs either

Put into a saucepan *½ cup sugar and remove 2 tablespoons.*

Add *3 tablespoons cornstarch, ½ teaspoon ground ginger, 1 teaspoon cinnamon, ½ teaspoon nutmeg, ¼ teaspoon ground cloves* and *½ teaspoon salt.*

Mix together.

Gradually stir in *1 cup canned pumpkin* and *1 can (13 ounces) evaporated milk.*

Bring to a boil. Turn heat to low.

Cook and stir 2 minutes.

Pour into 5 custard cups.

Place a piece of Saran Wrap right on top of each pudding to keep a skin from forming.

Refrigerate.

Butterscotch Pudding

In a saucepan mix together *3 tablespoons cornstarch, ¼ cup brown sugar* and *¼ teaspoon salt.*

Stir in *2¼ cups milk*. Strain.

On medium heat cook and stir until it comes to a boil and gets thick.

Cook 1 minute longer.

Take off heat. Stir in *1 tablespoon soft margarine.*

Stir in *½ teaspoon "Imitation Maple Flavoring."*

Pour into 4 or 5 baking dishes.

Put a small piece of Saran Wrap right on top of each pudding. This keeps a skin from forming.

Place in the refrigerator until you are ready to eat.

Noodle Pudding

if your dinner is short on protein, this makes a nice addition as a dessert

Heat oven 350°.

Steam *1 cup raisins* about 3 minutes. Dry. Set aside.

Grease a 2 quart glass, heatproof casserole.

Melt *¼ cup margarine*. Set aside.

Cook *8 ounces of large noodles* in *12 cups boiling water* with *4 teaspoons salt* for 5 minutes. Put under running water. Drain. Put into a large bowl and stir in the melted margarine.

Drain a *16 ounce carton of skim or whole milk cottage cheese.*

Melt *2 to 4 tablespoons* (depending on your choice of cheese) *margarine* and add to the cheese. Add *¼ cup sugar* and a *pinch of salt,* if needed. Mix together.

Separate *4 eggs*. Put yolks in a saucer and the whites into a large bowl.

Mix the yolks with a fork. Stir into the noodles. Stir the cheese through the noodles. Then stir in the raisins.

Beat the whites until stiff. It will hold a straight peak when you lift the beaters out.

Fold the whites into the noodle mixture. Brush 1 tablespoon melted margarine over the top noodles to keep from drying.

Spoon into the casserole. Bake in 350° oven about 45 minutes.

Serve hot.

Raisin Rice Pudding

this makes its own sauce and is the easiest rice pudding to make that we have ever made—and we have made plenty!

Bring *2 cups water, ½ teaspoon salt* and *1 tablespoon oil or butter* to a boil.

Stir in *½ cup rice* and *½ cup raisins.* Bring back to a boil. Turn heat to low. Cover. Cook 30 minutes.

Mix *2 tablespoons sugar* and *1 teaspoon cornstarch* with *1¼ cups milk* until the sugar is dissolved.

Stir into the rice mixture.

Cook, stir until the rice is slightly thickened, takes a few minutes.

Stir in *1 teaspoon vanilla.*

You can let get cold in the refrigerator or some people like this served warm.

We sometimes strain the rice mixture from the sauce. When serving, put the rice in a mound in each dish and spoon the sauce around the pudding.

Either way, it's good.

A New Different And Delicious Rice Pudding

it's easy, too!

You need *1½ cups cooked rice.*

Steam *¾ cup golden raisins.* Drain. Dry.

Mix together with the cooled rice.

Make this lemon sauce:

Mix together in a saucepan *½ cup sugar* and *1 tablespoon cornstarch.*

Stir in *½ cup water* and *¼ cup strained lemon juice.*

Cook and stir gently on medium high heat until it thickens slightly and becomes clear, takes about 10 minutes.

Remove from heat.

Put the rice in 4 deep saucers or glass bowls into a mound shape.

Pour the lemon sauce over and around the rice mounds.

Very tasty, isn't it?

Rice Pudding With Raisins, Sauce And Sherry

you'll like it! . . . the Sherry does something for the sauce

Rice for the Pudding:

Bring *2 cups water, 1 teaspoon salt* and *1 tablespoon oil* to a boil.

Add *1 cup rice.* Bring back to a boil.

Turn heat to low. Cover with lid.

Simmer 20 minutes. If you like a softer rice, steam instead 25 minutes.

Let stand 15 minutes.

Remove lid. Fluff with a fork. Let cool.

Tip: If you use rice you have cooked the day or so before, put 2 tablespoons water for each cup of rice, and place on high heat fluffing with 2 forks a minute or so. Be careful not to burn. You use ¼ cup water to reheat 2 cups cooked rice.

Make the sauce for 2 cups cooked rice:

In a saucepan, mix together *¼ cup sugar, 3 tablespoons cornstarch* and *¼ teaspoon salt.*

Stir in *2 cups plus 1 tablespoon milk.*

Cook and stir slowly on medium high heat until it comes almost to a boil, takes about 5 minutes and starts to thicken.

Take off heat.

Stir in slowly *2 tablespoons soft margarine,* then *1½ teaspoons vanilla.*

Stir in *3 tablespoons or ¼ cup dry sherry.* This is the sauce.

The raisins:

For 2 cups cooked rice you will need *½ cup raisins.*

Steam to soften, or soften in boiling water.

Drain well; dry.

Mix lightly with the 2 cups cooked rice.

Add ¼ cup sauce and mix lightly together.

Spoon into 6 small glass bowls or deep saucers.

Shape into a mound leaving room around it for the sauce.

Spoon some of the sauce around the rice pudding until all has been used.

You have the rice pudding and sauce in the same dish.

Easy Top Stove Rice Pudding

a perfect time to make rice pudding is when we have some ready cooked rice . . . if not . . . it's easy to cook, so don't wait

We use brown rice because it is more nutritious, but you can substitute the white rice.

Brown rice: Bring *1¾ cups water* and *¼ teaspoon salt* to a boil. Add *½ cup brown rice*. Bring back to a boil. Cover; turn heat to low. Simmer 1 hour to get soft. This is longer than you usually cook this rice. Take the rice off heat.

Put ¾ cup of the cooked rice into a bowl. Add *½ cup raisins* and mix together. Divide this between 5 custard cups.

Make the custard: Beat *2 eggs* with a rotary beater. Stir in *1½ cups nonfat milk* and *¼ cup sugar, a pinch of salt* and *½ teaspoon vanilla*. Pour this custard over the 5 cups with the rice/raisin mixture, coming about ½ inch below the tops of the cups.

Put the cups carefully into a large skillet. Pour hot water from the hydrant into the skillet being careful not to pour any into the pudding, to come up to the top of the custards (½ inch below the custard cups).

Turn the heat to high and bring to the boiling point. Don't boil.

Turn the heat off immediately. Cover the skillet with a lid. Let stand on the stove 30 minutes without moving it; don't remove the lid until the 30 minutes are up. Tip: we put a piece of foil on top of the skillet before putting the lid on, so no water from the steam drips into the custard.

At 30 minutes, test with the sharp point of a knife. The knife should come out clean. If it should happen that a little custard clings to the knife, you can eat as is or cover again and let stand longer. Once you have made this, you will see how easy it is. This is for electric stoves.

Our Favorite Rice Pudding With Raisins Made On Top Stove

Cook *1 cup rice* as usual.

Soften *½ cup raisins* in *boiling water* 2 minutes. Drain and dry.

Into a large saucepan stir *3 cups milk* into *1 box vanilla pudding mix.*

Add *1 teaspoon vanilla* and 2 cups cooked rice. Save the rest to use another time. Cook and stir about five minutes or a little more until thick and creamy.

Add *1 tablespoon margarine.*

Mix *2 eggs.* Take pudding off heat. Slowly stir the eggs into the pudding. Put back on medium heat and cook, stir for a minute or so, but do not boil. The eggs give it a richer taste.

Remove from heat; stir in the raisins.

Cool, push a piece of Saran Wrap or wax paper right on the pudding (not over the pudding) to keep a skin from forming. When cool, put in refrigerator.

Wait till you eat this pudding, you will love it!

For a change you can serve sliced fresh or canned fruit on top, strawberries, peaches, bananas, raspberries or other fruit. You can also, if you wish, stir 2 tablespoons sherry or brandy and remove that amount from the milk before stirring it into the vanilla pudding mix. Can you remove ¼ cup milk and replace with ¼ cup sherry or a liqueur like Grand Marnier, or Raspberry or Strawberry Liqueur? Why not, if you can afford it.

Top Stove Cup Custards

tender and perfect cup custards, easy to make and you bake them on top of the stove, a true Penny Pincher

Beat *4 eggs* with a rotary beater.

Stir in *3 cups milk,* then stir in ½ *cup sugar, a pinch of salt* and *1 teaspoon vanilla.*

Put 6 custard cups into a large skillet or use 2 smaller skillets.

Pour enough hot water into the skillet to come about ½ inch below the tops of the cups.

Pour the custards into the cups to come ½ inch from the top of the cups. Sprinkle a little nutmeg over the custards.

Turn the heat of electric stove to high and bring to boiling point but *do not* boil. Turn off heat.

Cover with a piece of foil and a lid on top. Let stand where it is until cooked, takes 30 to 35 minutes.

These are tender custards and so easy to make.

Top Stove Peanut Butter Cup Custards

something different, something good

You need a large skillet with a lid.
Makes 4 cup custards.
Put *1/4 cup peanut butter* into a bowl.
Mix *2 eggs* with a fork. Gradually stir in *1½ cups nonfat milk.* Stir in *⅓ cup sugar, a pinch of salt* and *1 teaspoon vanilla.*
Gradually slowly stir this egg, milk mixture into the peanut butter until it is combined.
Divide into 4 or 5 custard cups to come ½ inch from the top of the custard cups.
Put the custard cups into a skillet that fits.
Pour enough hot tap water into the skillet around the custard cups (but not on the custard!) to come ½ inch from the top of the cups.
Turn the heat on electric stove to high and *bring* to a boiling point but *do not* boil. Turn the heat off. Cover immediately.
Let stand 30 to 35 minutes until done.
These are tender, tasty custards.

Chocolate Mousse

smooth as silk, tastes rich as cream . . . it's a real surprise and it's more Penny Pincher than our other "Mousse"

Have a bowl ready to put the mousse in after you have made it.
You need an electric mixer, electric hand mixer, or you can use a rotary beater. Whichever you use, once you start, use the highest speed the whole time.
Measure all the ingredients to have ready.
Put *4 egg whites* into the large bowl of electric mixer (or an equivalent bowl).
Measure *1 cup clear Karo Corn Syrup* into a measuring cup.
Measure *4 tablespoons dry, unsweetened cocoa* onto a plate or wax paper.
Beat the 4 egg whites at the highest speed until stiff. You

can tell this by lifting the beaters up quickly, and the egg whites should hold a straight peak, usually takes about 3 minutes.

Pour about ⅓ of the cup of syrup at a time into the beaten egg whites continuing to use the highest speed and a rubber spatula to get the syrup into the egg whites.

Continue until you have gradually beaten in the whole cup of syrup. This makes a "meringue." Stir in the *1 teaspoon vanilla.*

Now, continuing to use the highest speed, stir in 1 tablespoon at a time, the 4 tablespoons cocoa using the spatula to help mix.

Use the rubber spatula to put the mousse into a large bowl, don't crush. Looks pretty, doesn't it?

Place in the freezer. Let get cold before serving. Remove from freezer 10 minutes before serving.

Will keep in the freezer up to 2 days; up to 5 days it then turns magically like an ice cream and yet not an ice cream. Everyone likes it, too.

Tip: The mousse, when made, must be put in the freezer, not the refrigerator, and must be kept in the freezer.

If you wish to make "Creme de Cacao Mousse," after you have stirred in the cocoa with the beaters, beat in 1 tablespoon at a time the 3 tablespoons "Creme de Cacao" liqueur. Then continue to follow the rest of the recipe. Creme de Cacao puts this into the "Gourmet" class.

Fresh Peach Compote

when peaches hang ripe on the trees and you have a special guest for dinner . . . this is not a Penny Pincher recipe, but I just couldn't help giving it to you!

Peel, seed, and cut into halves *enough peaches for 4,* about 6 medium peaches; or you can use only 4 very large peaches.

Bring to a boil *3 cans (5½ ounces) apricot nectar, ¼ cup sugar, 2 tablespoons lemon juice* and *1 tablespoon sweet brandy.* We use Masson's DeLuxe Brandy, which is a sweet brandy. You can substitute an unsweetened brandy and add a little sugar to sweeten it.

Add the halves of peaches. Bring back to a boil. Cook 5 minutes. Remove to a bowl to cool. Refrigerate until ready to serve. Leave it to marinate in the refrigerator overnight. This adds to the taste.

Why did we use apricot nectar? Because we couldn't get peach juice at the supermarket. Anyhow, the touch of apricot adds to the flavor.

Homemade Apple Sauce

tastes twice as good as the "bought ones!"

Wash carefully the apples. You can use the early apples, "Summer Rambo," or the later apples such as "Winesap," or "McIntosh" or any apple that is not mealy but has a sweet and sour taste.

Don't peel or core the apples. Remove the stems.

This is a timesaver tip. Cut the apples into quarters.

Put into a large kettle or saucepan. Add enough water to cover the bottom of the kettle, about 1 inch.

Bring to a boil. Cook, stir now and then.

Cover. Turn the heat to second high heat.

Cook, stir now and then until the apples are soft, takes about one half hour.

Put into a strainer. Don't press, just let the apple juice run through. Set the juice aside.

Put the cooked apples through a food mill or a strainer. The seeds and core will remain in the food mill and the rest will be apple sauce.

Add sugar to taste, adding some of the apple juice if the apple sauce is too thick.

You can freeze the apple juice, then add sugar when ready to use. We use ours to make the sauce for our Fresh Apple Rolls.

This apple sauce is delicious served with potato pancakes that go with an Arm pot roast or boiled Brisket of Beef and is super with duck.

German Pancakes With Glazed Apples

the glazed apples with the touch of lemon and cinnamon make this a dessert to remember

We use a 4½ inch measured on the bottom skillet to cook the pancakes. You can use a larger one if you wish.

The pancakes can be made ahead and so can the apples.

In fact, you can make a batch of the pancakes, leave enough for dessert and freeze the rest. The apples should be made fresh for the best taste.

Cover a clean surface with large pieces of wax paper to put the cooked pancakes on when fried.

The pancakes—With a pastry blender mix together in a bowl *1 cup flour, 2 teaspoons sugar, ½ teaspoon salt*. Make a well in the center. Drop in *4 large eggs*. Mix with a wooden spoon until there are no lumps and the batter is smooth. Gradually stir in *1 cup cold tap water*. Let stand ½ hour.

When ready to fry we put on a large plate a small cup with a little oil, a natural bristle brush, and a ¼ metal measuring cup and a smallish bowl with the batter near the stove to have ready to fry the pancakes. We fill the metal cup a little more than ¾ full to have ready. We heat the skillet hot on second high heat and brush the skillet lightly with oil. Pour in the batter and quickly tilt and swirl the batter to cover the bottom of the skillet and also come up and cover about ½ of the sides. This takes longer to tell than to do. Once or twice as you do this, it will become very easy to do. When the bottom has browned but not burned and as you touch the top of the pancake and it is dry, turn over onto the wax paper. Continue with the rest.

You can make these ahead and use when ready for the dessert or continue and make the dessert.

Mix together *¼ cup sugar* with *1 teaspoon cinnamon*. Set aside.

Peel, core, cut into quarters, then into slices about ⅛ inch thick enough *apples* to cover the pancakes you will need for dessert. We serve one pancake a person. Put immediately in some lemon juice as you slice and then remove to a plate. This keeps the apples from darkening and also saves using a lot of lemon juice. When all have been prepared, mix in a large skillet over medium heat. Cook/stir *3 tablespoons sugar* with *4 tablespoons butter or margarine* until melted.

Arrange enough apple slices to fill but not crowd the skillet.

Keep turning with 2 forks so the apples get glazed, but do not cook the apples until soft, just glaze them.

Put on a large plate until all are done.

If you have heatproof glass plates that you can serve on put the pancakes on them; otherwise, use a cookie sheet or whatever is convenient for you to use that is heatproof and arrange the apples on top of the pancakes. Sprinkle some of the sugar/cinnamon mixture on top. Preheat the broiler. When hot, place the cookie sheet with the pancakes on the second shelf from the heat and watch, don't go away, until the pancakes are hot and the apples are glazed, being careful they don't burn.

Serve hot and enjoy!

The Easiest Quickest Chocolate Soufflé Ever

it doesn't have to be chocolate either . . . it can be lemon, vanilla, strawberry or whatever you like . . . it takes only 20 minutes to bake and it comes out perfect every time

You need *one box* of your choice of regular *Pudding and Pie Filling* (3⅝ ounces) from Droste, Royal or Jell-O brand. For the chocolate flavor use the dark chocolate one.

Preheat oven 450°.

Grease with *margarine* a 1½ quart glass baking dish.

Sprinkle with *sugar*. Shake out excess.

Put 2 large bowls on your work surface.

Measure *¼ cup sugar;* set aside.

You need *4 large eggs.* Open 1 egg at a time; put the yolks in a saucer and the whites in one of the large bowls. Set aside.

Put the chocolate pudding into a medium saucepan.

Gradually stir in *1 cup skim or nonfat milk.* Add *1 tablespoon margarine.*

Over medium high heat or low heat (whichever suits you best), cook, stir, taking off and on heat as you stir, until this sauce gets thick and comes to a simmer. The trick is to cook, stir, taking off and on heat. Continue this, being careful not to let it burn. This takes about 2 or 3 minutes at the most. You can cook, stir on low heat, but it will take longer to get thick. Either way, when thick, cook 2 more minutes.

Put into the empty large bowl. Use a rubber spatula to get as much of the pudding as you can into the bowl. Wash and wipe the spatula.

Use a wooden spoon to stir, one at a time, the four yolks into the pudding. Set aside.

With an electric hand beater or a rotary beater start beating the egg whites until they foam. Add a *pinch of salt* and *¼ teaspoon cream of tartar.* Continue to beat until when you lift the beaters out, it holds a straight (not droopy) peak. Gradually add the ¼ cup sugar and continue to beat until you taste and feel no grains of sugar. This is called a meringue.

Quickly stir about ¼ of the meringue into the pudding to lighten it.

Quickly fold—don't mix—fold, the rest of the meringue into the batter, being careful to use an over and under motion. Immediately, so as not to deflate it, pour or spoon into the casserole, using the spatula to get it all out.

Bake in the 450° oven about 20 minutes.

Serve at once. Soufflés cannot wait.

This soufflé tastes good even when cold.

Delicious, isn't it?

A New Foolproof Chocolate Soufflé

it's easier to make than to read . . . that's because we give you step-by-step directions, so you absolutely, positively can't make a mistake . . . just have your admirers waiting, as no soufflé waits for anyone!

Heat oven 400°.

Grease with *margarine or butter* a 2 quart heatproof, glass baking casserole. (Pyrex is fine.) Sprinkle *sugar* over it and shake out excess.

Put these on your working surface: electric hand beater or electric mixer or a rotary beater, 2 large mixing bowls, a strainer over a medium saucepan, 2 deep saucers, a wooden spoon and a rubber spatula.

Measure *½ cup sugar*. Set aside.

Separate *4 large eggs*. Put the 4 yolks in one of the deep saucers and the 4 whites in one of the large bowls. Add *1 more white* to have 5 whites. Don't use the fifth yolk.

Into the strainer over the saucepan put *3 tablespoons flour, 4 tablespoons unsweetened cocoa* and *¼ cup dry nonfat milk*. With a spoon push through the strainer into the saucepan. Slowly, using the wooden spoon, stir in *1 cup cold tap water* and *1 teaspoon vanilla;* then stir in *¼ cup vegetable oil* (or 4 tablespoons) until smooth.

Cook, stir on medium high heat, taking off and on heat so it doesn't burn, until it gets thick and comes to a boil. The secret of fast cooking is our method of "cook, stir, taking off and on heat."

With the rubber spatula push this sauce (usually called a white sauce) into the large empty bowl. Wash the rubber spatula and wipe it.

Slowly stir one yolk in; then stir in one at a time the other 3 yolks. Set this aside.

With your beaters start beating the 5 whites until they foam. Add a *pinch of salt* and *¼ teaspoon cream of tartar.* Continue to beat until the whites hold a stiff, straight (not droopy) peak when you lift the beaters out. Slowly add, while continuing to beat, the *½ cup of sugar*. Continue to beat until when you taste this "meringue" you can feel no grains of sugar.

Add about ¼ of this meringue to the yolk mixture. Stir together to lighten this batter.

Quickly fold—don't mix—fold, the rest of the meringue into the batter, being careful to use an over and under motion. Immediately, so as not to deflate it, pour or spoon into the casserole, using the spatula to get it all out. About 1 inch from the edge of the casserole use a teaspoon to make a ring all around. This will make a "high hat" when it bakes.

Put immediately into the center of the oven. Close the door gently. Turn heat to 375°. Bake about 35 to 40 minutes. Test to see if done.

Serve at once.

If there is any left when cold, it's still light and delicious, so eat it.

Vanilla Soufflé
With A Strawberry Sauce

soufflés are easy to make so prove it to yourself by making this one

The Strawberry Sauce

Follow the directions on a *box of frozen, sliced sweetened strawberries* to defrost, so you have it ready when the soufflé comes out of the oven.

We like this sauce better than one made from fresh strawberries.

The Vanilla Soufflé

Grease a 2 quart glass, heatproof casserole (Pyrex is fine.) with *margarine or butter*. Sprinkle *sugar* over lightly. Shake out excess.

Put these on your work surface: 2 large bowls, electric hand beater or a rotary beater, a rubber spatula and a wooden spoon; also, *⅓ cup sugar, ¼ teaspoon cream of tartar, 1 cup nonfat milk* and *5 large eggs.*

Put one large bowl near 2 deep saucers. Open 1 egg; put the yolk in one saucer and the white in another; then put the white into one of the large bowls. Continue to do this with the other 3 eggs, being careful not to get any yolk in the whites. You will not use the 5th yolk, so put it in the refrigerator to use another time, but add the white to the rest of the whites. Set aside.

To make the white sauce put *3 tablespoons margarine or butter* into a saucepan and melt, don't burn. Take it off the heat and stir in *3 tablespoons flour*; then stir in the 1 cup nonfat milk. Put back on medium high heat. With a wooden spoon, cook, stir, taking off and on heat so it doesn't burn on the bottom, until it gets thick, takes about 3 minutes. Turn heat to low, cook, stir 2 minutes. You can cook this on low heat which takes about 10 minutes to cook. The secret of fast cooking is our method of "cook, stir, taking off and on heat."

When the sauce is thick, remove it from the heat and put it into the empty large bowl. Use the rubber spatula to get all of it out. Wash and dry the spatula, as you will need it later.

One at a time, using the wooden spoon, stir in the 4 egg yolks. Stir in *1 teaspoon vanilla.* Let stand.

With the electric hand beater or the rotary beater, beat the 5 whites until frothy. Add a *pinch of salt* and ¼ teaspoon cream of tartar. Continue to beat until the whites form a stiff, not droopy, peak when you lift the beaters out. Continue to beat while you gradually add the ⅓ cup of sugar. Beat until you taste it and do not taste any grains of sugar. This is a meringue.

Immediately stir ¼ of this meringue into the batter to lighten it.

Quickly fold—don't mix—fold, the rest of the meringue into the batter, being careful to use an over and under motion. Immediately, so as not to deflate it, pour or spoon into the casserole, using the spatula to get it all out. About 1 inch from the edge of the casserole use a teaspoon to make a ring all around. This will make a "high hat" when it bakes.

Put immediately in the 400° oven. Turn heat immediately to 375°. Bake about 30 minutes. Test to see if done.

Remove from oven and serve at once.

Pass the strawberry sauce.

Isn't it delicious? and easy?

Crepe Suzette

these pancakes are different than our American pancakes . . . they are used to stuff many delectable fillings to make Crepes Suzette, Blintzes, German Apple Pancakes, Cherry Pancakes, Chicken Pancakes

This makes about 18 thin pancakes. The pancakes should be very thin.

You need an 8 inch skillet. The Teflon lined ones are nice and so is a ¼ metal measuring cup or you can use a tablespoon. Spread 3 long sheets of wax paper on a surface near the stove.

Into a large bowl put *1 cup flour*. Add *¼ teaspoon salt* and a *pinch of sugar*.

Add 1 egg at a time, mixing each time well with a wooden spoon until you have added *4 large eggs* and there are no lumps.

Stir in *1 cup cold tap water* and *1 teaspoon oil*. Let stand 30 minutes or at least 15 minutes before baking them.

To bake—Heat on second highest heat an 8 inch Teflon lined skillet, preferably the one with rounded sides. Brush with oil.

Fill a ¼ metal measuring cup half full with batter to have ready, or you need 2 tablespoons batter for each crepe, and pour into the skillet, rotating very quickly so the batter spreads quickly, lifting the pan off the heat to rotate, and this makes a thin pancake. Cook until the bottom is lightly browned, turn and lightly brown the other side. Turn out on the wax paper to cool.

Continue to do this until all the crepes have been made. You can use at once, or store in the refrigerator or freeze and use as needed.

When ready to use make the sauce. See the sauce recipe.

Put only enough crepes into the large skillet that it will

hold without crowding. Heat. Spoon the sauce over the crepes, then fold the crepes into halves, continuing to spoon the sauce over, then fold into quarters. Continue to spoon the sauce over the crepes until hot. Serve on heated plates with some of the sauce spooned over them. Eat as soon as possible. These are truly a treat.

For a "Super" sauce. Before removing the crepes to the plates to serve, pour about ¼ cup brandy into the sauce, light a match carefully and let blaze for a spectacular finish.

Tip: You have to be most careful that the skillet doesn't spill or fall or that someone doesn't get burned. Most of the time, since the pancakes taste as good just pouring the sauce over, we omit the extra brandy—and that's what we do!

By the way, just in case someone with a pocket full of dollars or your favorite aunt left you a fortune buy a bottle of French Grand Marnier instead of our plain brandy. If you noticed though, we turned our plain brandy into something special by stirring it into orange marmalade.

The Sauce for Crepe Suzette—that's what makes these so special.

Put *1 cup thick orange marmalade* into a large skillet. (Crosse and Blackwell's *Sweet* Marmalade is fine or use your favorite marmalade.) Stir in *1 tablespoon grated orange rind, ¼ cup orange juice* and *1 tablespoon lemon juice.* Cook, stir about 5 minutes.

Stir in *¼ cup Brandy.* Cook stir about 2 minutes. Arrange the crepes in without crowding and fold each into fourths, spooning the sauce over as you fold them. Spoon and heat until hot. Serve with some of the sauce spooned over.

Blintzes

Or Cheese Stuffed Pancakes

made with our crepes they're the kind you'll always want to keep in your freezer!

You need 2 packages or 1 pound Farmer cheese or equivalent dry cottage cheese, an 8 inch skillet, preferably Teflon lined, and ¼ cup metal measuring cup or a tablespoon, 3 long sheets of wax paper.

Into a large bowl put *1 cup flour.* Add *¼ teaspoon salt* and a *pinch of sugar.*

Add 1 egg at a time mixing each time with a wooden spoon so there are no lumps until you have added *4 large eggs* and there are no lumps.

Stir in *1 cup cold tap water and 1 teaspoon oil.* Let stand 30 minutes. Yes, you can use at once.

To Bake—Heat on second highest heat an 8 inch skillet. Brush with oil. When hot, fill a ¼ cup measuring cup half full with the batter or pour 2 tablespoons batter into the hot skillet rotating very quickly so the batter spreads quickly over the skillet. You can lift the skillet off the heat as you do this. Cook just until the bottom is browned lightly. Touch the top and if it is dry, remove immediately and turn out onto the wax paper.

Continue until all the pancakes have been baked and are cold. Turn the pancakes brown side up.

Make the Cheese Filling:

Mix together the *2 packages (1 pound) Farmer cheese* with *1 egg yolk, 2 tablespoons melted butter or margarine, 2¼ teaspoons sugar* and *salt* if needed. (You can use strained cottage cheese—get as dry as possible—but this makes a "more or less runny filling" that is difficult to use.)

Place a tablespoon of the filling in the center of each pancake. Bring up the bottom part to cover the cheese, fold both sides to the middle. Then fold the top part to cover so the filling will not run out. Turn over folded side down. Continue until all are done.

You can cover these, refrigerate and use when ready or you can freeze them. If you freeze them, defrost them before frying.

To fry:

Heat a large skillet on medium high heat with ¼ inch *oil* until hot. Add *2 tablespoons butter or margarine.* Put in as many blintzes (without crowding) as the skillet will hold. Brown nicely on one side, turn, brown on the other side. These will be beautiful and crisp.

Remove to heated plates and serve.

Serve with the following sauces or preserves.

Sauces:

Blueberry Sauce

Into *1 can or jar Blueberry Pie Filling,* stir in *2 tablespoons lemon juice* and *1 tablespoon sugar.* Cook, stir until bubbly hot. Serve with the blintzes.

Black Cherry Sauce

Stir into *1 can (1 pound) large seeded black cherries, 1 teaspoon cornstarch, 1 tablespoon lemon juice* and *1 tablespoon sugar.* Cook, stir gently until it comes to a boil and thickens a little. Serve hot with the blintzes.

Black Cherry Sauce For A Special Occasion

Strain *1 can (1 pound) large seeded black cherries* to have *1 cup juice.* Stir in *2 tablespoons and 1½ teaspoons cornstarch* into a little of the juice so there are no lumps. Gradually stir in the rest of the juice, *1 tablespoon brandy, 1 tablespoon sugar.* Cook, stir until it thickens slightly and clears—about 3 minutes. Take off heat. Stir in *2 tablespoons more Brandy* and the cherries. Use.

Strawberry Preserves

These are wonderful over blintzes, especially if you have your own homemade ones. See our recipe index. They are special. They keep their beautiful red color and their delicious aroma because we keep them in our freezer.

Nonfat Whipped Cream

super whipped milk . . . as thick as whipped cream . . . has no preservatives, no additives . . . healthy and good tasting, too,

and no worries about calories . . . has protein, too . . .
what more could one want?

An electric mixer makes this a breeze. You can use electric hand beaters or a rotary beater or a wire whip. The wire whip takes forever, and the rotary beater is easier to use, but it takes time and muscle. The electric hand beaters are OK, but the standing electric mixer is the best.

This recipe makes 2 cups whipped cream (or rather, thick whipped milk).

Put *½ cup nonfat dry milk* into the small bowl of your electric mixer. (We like Alba nonfat dry milk best; you can use your favorite.)

Put *ice and water* into a bowl. When it gets "icy" cold, add *½ cup* of this iced water to the dry milk. (Tip: this very cold water makes the whipped cream thicker; we tested and found this out.)

Beat 10 minutes by the clock. The mixture will get thick as thick cream.

Gradually stir in *3 tablespoons sugar.*

Beat 3 to 5 minutes. Taste to be sure you feel no grains of sugar. Taste when you've beaten 3 minutes, as usually it's not grainy by then.

Gradually stir in *1 tablespoon oil,* takes about 1 minute.

Stir in *1 teaspoon vanilla,* takes about 1 minute.

You can use this immediately, or you can put it in the refrigerator up to ½ hour, and it will remain thick. We tested longer also, but it didn't work; it became liquidy.

We use this "super whipped milk" with strawberries on our Super Sponge Cake for a real treat. We also put this in our freezer for our Easy Do Vanilla Ice Cream.

Orange Gelatin Candy Squares

no artificial flavor or artificial color . . . everyone loves these

To *1 can (6 ounces) frozen orange juice* stir in *enough water to make 2 cups* orange juice.

Stir in *2 tablespoons sugar* and mix well.

Put *2 packages unflavored gelatin* into a medium bowl.

Stir in 1 cup orange juice. Stir until the gelatin is dissolved.

In a saucepan bring the other cup of orange juice to a boil.

Stir into the gelatin-orange mixture. Mix well.

Pour into an 8½" × 4½" glass pan.
Place in the refrigerator to congeal solid.
Cut into squares, and place in a bowl to serve. To keep, cover with Saran Wrap and place in refrigerator.
We used the unflavored gelatin because the flavored ones have artificial flavor and color at this time of our lives.

Grape Gelatin Candy Squares

a real treat . . . you hold it in your hand and eat

You need *2 cups of Welch's Grape Juice.* (The one that has no sugar added, no artificial colors or no artificial flavors added. Vitamin C is added.)
Put 1 cup of the grape juice into a saucepan. Bring to a boil.
In the meantime, put 1 cup grape juice into a measuring cup or bowl and stir in *2 packages Knox Unflavored Gelatin* until dissolved.
Stir the boiled grape juice into the gelatin grape juice until dissolved.
Very slowly, so as not to make bubbles, pour this into an 8½" × 4½" pan. Glass is fine.
Place in refrigerator immediately to congeal solid.
When congealed solid, cut into squares.
Place in a bowl ready to eat.
Cover with Saran Wrap. Put back in refrigerator to keep.
This is natural goodness and fun to eat.

Pineapple Gelatin Candy Squares

no artificial flavor or artificial color . . . teach the children to make these . . . they will gobble these up

In a large bowl stir *2 packages unflavored gelatin* into *1 cup canned pineapple juice* until the gelatin dissolves.
Bring *1 cup pineapple juice* to a boil.
Stir it into the gelatin mixture.
Pour into an 8½" × 4½" glass pan.
Place in the refrigerator to congeal solid.
When congealed, cut into squares and place in a bowl ready to eat. Cover with Saran Wrap. Keep in refrigerator.
We used the unflavored gelatin because the flavored has artificial flavor and color.

Raspberry Jell

full of flavor made the old Russian way but with good American style using frozen raspberries

Defrost *1 package (10 ounces) frozen raspberries.*

Mix together *2 tablespoons cold water* and *2 tablespoons cornstarch.*

Bring the raspberries to a boil.

Stir in the cornstarch slowly.

Turn heat to low.

Cook, stir slowly 2 minutes.

Pour or spoon into 3 small glass dishes.

Doesn't make much but what there is tastes real raspberry and good. Brings the good old summertime back.

Texas Peanut Brittle With Spanish Peanuts

Smear heavily 2 cookie sheets with *margarine.*

Measure *1½ cups raw peanuts* (Spanish preferable).

Measure separately *1½ teaspoons margarine or butter, ½ teaspoon salt* and *1 teaspoon soda.*

Put into a saucepan *1½ cups white sugar, ¼ cup water* and *½ cup white corn syrup.*

Bring to a boil. Let boil until when you hold up a spoonful, it spins a thread.

Add 1½ cups peanuts. Cook and stir until the peanuts turn a brownish gold color. Remove from heat.

Stir in the margarine or butter, salt and soda.

Pour onto cookie sheets to cool and get hard. Break into pieces.

Three Blueberry Sauces

Wild Blueberry Sauce

Put *1 can (21 ounces) Wyman's Wild Blueberry Pie Filling* into a saucepan with *3 tablespoons lemon juice* and *1 tablespoon plus 2 teaspoons sugar,* and *1 tablespoon water.*

Cook and stir just to heat.
Serve as you wish, hot or cold.

Another Blueberry Sauce

Put *1 can (15 ounces) blueberries* into a saucepan. Stir in *2 tablespoons lemon juice* and *3 tablespoons plus ½ teaspoon sugar.*

Mix together *1 tablespoon cornstarch* with *1 tablespoon water.*

Bring the blueberries to a boil. Stir in the cornstarch mixture. It will clear instantly. Cook, stir a minute.

Remove from heat. Use as needed.

A Third Blueberry Sauce

Put *1 can or jar Blueberry Pie Filling* into a saucepan.
Stir in *2 tablespoons lemon juice* and *1 tablespoon sugar.*
Cook and stir until bubbling hot. Serve as needed.

These three sauces can be used with stuffed blintzes or over plain cake, waffles or pancakes, or over ice cream. Makes a real treat.

Raspberry Sauce

with a lovely taste accented with brandy and a touch of lemon . . . wonderful over ice cream, custards or canned fruits, like pears

Mix *1 jar (12 ounces) raspberry preserves with seeds* with *¼ cup water.*

Cook, stir until it boils. Strain all the seeds out.

Stir into this clear sauce *3 tablespoons brandy* and *1 teaspoon lemon juice.*

This gives the raspberry flavor a little zing!

Keep in the refrigerator.

Vanilla Ice Cream Smooth As Silk

smooth as smooth can be . . . takes minutes to make and it's the healthiest ice cream you can make . . . the children will love to make this, too . . . it's that easy!

Put *1 cup nonfat dry milk* into the large bowl of your electric mixer. (We like Alba best.)

Put ice and water into a bowl and let melt and get icy cold.

Add *1 cup of this icy cold water* to the dry milk.

Turn the mixer to the highest speed.

Let mix 10 minutes. (You can do this with electric hand mixer, or work hard and use the rotary beater or a whisk.)

Gradually add *3 tablespoons sugar* and beat 2 or 3 minutes. Taste to be sure the sugar grains have dissolved.

Continue to beat gradually adding *1 tablespoon oil.*

Then add *1 teaspoon vanilla.*

Spoon into a plastic ice cream container or a bowl without a lid.

Place immediately in the freezer.

Let freeze, takes about 2 to 3 hours.

This is a smooth, delicious ice cream. It melts quickly, so don't let it stand, eat it.

PS: For the child who just doesn't like milk, he or she will gobble this ice cream up.

Low Calorie, Fine Tasting, Smooth Chocolate Ice Cream

Put *½ cup instant dry nonfat milk* into the small bowl of your electric mixer.

Strain *1½ tablespoons cocoa* over it and mix.

Put ice cubes into cold water. Let melt until icy cold.

Add *½ cup* of this *icy cold water* to the milk/cocoa mixture.

Beat in the electric mixer 10 minutes by the clock. It will not get thick.

Gradually add *4 tablespoons sugar.* Beat 3 to 5 minutes. Taste to be sure there are no grains of sugar.

Stir in *1 tablespoon oil,* takes about 1 or 2 minutes.

Stir in *1 teaspoon vanilla.*

Put in a bowl or plastic container without a lid. Place in the freezer. Freeze. This takes about 2 or 3 hours.

It will be smooth and very good, and it's low in calories, too, and—best of all—has no "saturated fat."

Pumpkin Ice Cream

something new, something good

Have ready a plastic ice cream container with lid to fit 3 cups of ice cream.

Mix together *¼ cup brown sugar, ¼ teaspoon salt, ½ teaspoon cinnamon, ¼ teaspoon ginger* and *¼ teaspoon nutmeg.*

Stir in *½ cup canned Libby's Pumpkin* until you feel no sugar grains.

Put *2 cups vanilla ice cream* quickly into a large bowl.

Work very quickly and fold, don't mix, with a large spoon the pumpkin mixture into the ice cream, so the ice cream doesn't melt.

Put immediately into the container. Put Saran Wrap right on top of the ice cream. Cover and place in freezer.

The trick is to work fast so the ice cream doesn't melt.

Nutty Spiced Pumpkin Brandied Raisin Ice Cream

it's something else!

Overnight steep *½ cup raisins in brandy to cover.*

Have ready a plastic ice cream container with lid to fit 3 cups ice cream.

Chop *¼ cup nuts.*

In a large bowl mix together *½ cup fresh or canned pumpkin, 1 tablespoon 10X confectioner's sugar, ¼ teaspoon cinnamon, ⅛ teaspoon nutmeg, ⅛ teaspoon ground cloves,* and *⅛ teaspoon ground ginger.*

Strain the raisins. (Save the brandy to steep more raisins as they can steep as long as a month in the refrigerator.)

Stir the strained raisins and the nuts into the pumpkin mixture.

Add *2 cups vanilla ice cream* and mix. Work fast so the ice cream doesn't melt. Immediately put into a plastic container.

Put Saran Wrap right on top of the ice cream. Cover with lid.

Place immediately in the freezer.

If the ice cream should melt, push the Saran Wrap right on top and place in freezer.

It will freeze and taste good.

Peanut Butter Ice Cream

easy to make

Have ready a plastic ice cream container with lid to fit 3 cups of ice cream.

Stir *¼ cup peanut butter* to soften.

Put *2 cups vanilla ice cream* into a large bowl.

Very quickly fold or mix the peanut butter into the ice cream.

Put immediately into the container. Put Saran Wrap right on top of the ice cream.

Cover and place in freezer.

The trick is to work fast so the ice cream doesn't melt.

Orange Sherbet

smooth and easy to make . . . I worked this recipe out after I came home from my trip to the Dordogne, a region in France where I ate my way around in the finest chateaus and inns and restaurants where they made the smoothest, most delectable sherbets . . . the secret, one chef told me, was making a "meringue" . . . I do—only I have a secret, too, and here it is

You need *4 egg whites, ¾ cup clear Karo Corn Syrup* (That's my secret, instead of standing over a stove making a tricky syrup.), and you need *1 can (6 ounces) frozen, concentrated orange juice,* defrosted. (That's my other secret.)

Make this in electric mixer, using highest speed and adding all ingredients without stopping.

Beat on highest speed the 4 egg whites until they are stiff and hold a straight peak when you lift the beaters out quickly.

Gradually stir in ¾ cup Karo syrup.

Then gradually stir in 1 can (6 ounces) defrosted, frozen concentrated orange juice.

Put into a bowl.

Place in the freezer.

Let stand in freezer about 7 hours.

This sherbet, unlike others, does not need to be mixed. Just let stay in the freezer until ready to use.

Can keep 3 days.

19. CAKES

When you MEASURE FLOUR, *spoon* it into the measuring cup and level it off. If you scoop it in, each time you might get a different amount.

A 1 Egg Vanilla Cake

a basic inexpensive cake that takes only minutes to mix and tastes as good as a much higher priced cake . . . it's even good enough to eat with strawberries when strawberries are in season

Heat oven 350°.

Separate *1 egg,* yolk in a cup, white in a small bowl.

Grease with *vegetable shortening or margarine* and *flour* an 8 inch round cake pan, preferably Teflon lined.

Put into a bowl *1 cup flour, 1 teaspoon wheat germ, 2 teaspoons baking powder, ¼ teaspoon salt, 2 tablespoons nonfat dry milk* and *½ cup sugar.* Mix with the pastry blender.

Mix the yolk with a fork. Stir in *¼ cup oil, ½ cup cold tap water* and *1 teaspoon vanilla.*

Add to the flour mixture. Mix until smooth with a wooden spoon.

With an electric hand beater or a rotary beater, beat the white until foamy. Add a small *pinch of salt* and *⅛ teaspoon cream of tartar*. Beat until a soft peak forms.

Add *2 tablespoons sugar* and beat until when you taste you can feel no grains of sugar. This is a meringue. Mix ⅓ of the meringue into the batter. Fold the rest of the meringue in.

Spoon into the cake pan. Bake in the 350° oven about 30 to 35 minutes until done.

Remove from the oven. Let stand 10 minutes.

Loosen the edges with a dull knife. Turn the cake out onto a rack. Turn face up. Let get cold.

FOR AN ORANGE CAKE—Follow this recipe and add *3 tablespoons grated orange rind* to the dry flour mixture. The rest of the recipe is the same.

A 2 Egg Vanilla Cake

a true Penny Pincher Cake and light and better than the usual cakes . . . it's a perfect cake to put whipped cream on and decorate with strawberries in season, but this changes it to a Special Occasion Cake

Heat oven 350°.

Grease with *vegetable shortening* and *flour* an 8 × 8 inch square cake pan. Shake out excess flour.

Separate *2 large eggs*. Put whites into a large bowl and yolks in a deep saucer.

Put into a large bowl *1 cup flour, 1½ teaspoons baking powder, ½ cup sugar, ½ teaspoon salt,* and *2 tablespoons dry nonfat milk*. Mix with a pastry blender.

With a fork, mix the 2 yolks. Stir in *¼ cup oil,* and *⅓ cup cold tap water* and *2 teaspoons vanilla*. Stir into the flour mixture. Mix until smooth.

With an electric hand beater or a rotary beater beat the 2 whites until foamy. Add *¼ teaspoon cream of tartar* and a *pinch of salt*. Beat until a soft peak forms when you lift the beaters out. Gradually add and continue to beat *¼ cup sugar*. Beat until you can feel no grains of sugar when you taste it. This is a meringue. Mix ⅓ of this into the batter. Fold the rest in.

Pour into the cake pan. Bake in 350° oven about 30 to 35 minutes. It's usually done in 30 minutes.

Put on a rack to cool. Let cool 5 minutes. Turn out onto a soft kitchen towel, then turn up onto a rack to cool.

Eat as is or you can frost. This cake is nice with strawberries or other berries or fruit in season.

Orange Cake

the touch of orange makes all the difference

Grease with *vegetable shortening* an 8 × 8 inch square cake pan. *Flour* pan and shake out excess.

Preheat the oven to 350°.

Separate *2 large eggs*. Put whites into a large bowl and yolks into a deep saucer. Grate *2 tablespoons orange rind,* measure *⅓ cup orange juice,* measure *¼ cup sugar*. Let stand.

Put into a large bowl *1 cup flour, 1½ teaspoons baking powder, ½ cup sugar, ½ teaspoon salt, 2 tablespoons dry nonfat milk,* the grated rind. Mix with a pastry blender.

With a fork, mix the 2 yolks. Stir in *¼ cup oil* and the ⅓ cup orange juice. Stir into the flour mixture. Mix until smooth.

With an electric hand beater or a rotary beater beat the 2 whites until foamy. Add a pinch of *salt* and *¼ teaspoon cream of tartar.* Beat until a soft peak forms when you lift the beaters out. Gradually add and continue to beat *¼ cup sugar.* Beat until you can feel no grains of sugar when you taste. This is a meringue. Mix ⅓ of this into the batter. Fold the rest in.

Pour into the cake pan. Bake in 350° oven about 30 to 35 minutes.

Put on a rack to cool 5 minutes. Loosen the edges with a spatula. Turn over onto a soft towel. Turn face up onto a rack to get cold.

Pineapple Cake

yes, an Upside-Down Cake

Heat oven 350°.

Melt *⅓ cup margarine* in an 8 × 8 inch square cake pan. Sprinkle *½ cup brown sugar* (packed) evenly over the margarine. Arrange *drained pineapple slices* on top (save the juice).

Separate *2 large eggs.* Put whites into a large bowl and yolks in a small bowl.

Put into a large bowl *1 cup flour, 1½ teaspoons baking powder, ½ cup sugar, ½ teaspoon salt* and *2 tablespoons dry nonfat milk.* Mix with a pastry blender.

With a fork, mix the 2 yolks. Stir in *¼ cup oil* and *⅓ cup of pineapple juice* and *2 teaspoons vanilla.* Stir into the flour mixture. Mix until smooth.

With an electric hand beater or a rotary beater beat the 2 whites until foamy. Add *¼ teaspoon cream of tartar* and a *pinch of salt.* Beat until a soft peak forms when you lift the beaters out. Gradually add and continue to beat *¼ cup sugar.* Beat until you can feel no grains of sugar when you taste it. This is a meringue. Mix ⅓ of this into the batter. Fold the rest in.

Pour over the pineapple slices in cake pan. Bake in 350° oven 40 to 45 minutes. Cool slightly and turn out onto cake rack.

Raisin Nut Cake

Heat oven 350°.

Grease with *vegetable shortening* and *flour* an 8 × 8 inch square cake pan. Shake out excess flour.

Separate *2 large eggs*. Put whites into a large bowl and yolks in a deep saucer.

Put into a large bowl *1 cup flour, 1½ teaspoons baking powder, ½ cup sugar, ½ teaspoon salt, 2 tablespoons dry nonfat milk, ½ cup chopped raisins* and *½ cup chopped nuts*. Mix with a pastry blender.

With a fork, mix the 2 yolks. Stir in *¼ cup oil, and ⅓ cup cold tap water* and *2 teaspoons vanilla*. Stir into the flour mixture. Mix until smooth.

With an electric beater or a rotary beater beat the 2 whites until foamy. Add *¼ teaspoon cream of tartar* and a pinch of *salt*. Beat until a soft peak forms when you lift the beaters out. Gradually add and continue to beat *¼ cup sugar*. Beat until you can feel no grains of sugar when you taste it. This is a meringue. Mix ⅓ of this into the batter. Fold the rest in.

Pour into the cake pan. Bake in 350° oven about 30 to 35 minutes. It's usually done in 30 minutes.

Put on a rack to cool. Let cool 5 minutes. Turn out onto a soft kitchen towel, then turn up onto a rack to cool.

Spice Cake

Heat oven 350°.

Grease with *vegetable shortening* and *flour* an 8 × 8 inch square cake pan. Shake out excess flour.

Separate *2 large eggs*. Put whites into a large bowl and yolks in a deep saucer.

Put into a large bowl *1 cup flour, 1½ teaspoons baking powder, ½ cup sugar, ½ teaspoon salt, 2 tablespoons dry nonfat milk, ½ teaspoon cinnamon, ¼ teaspoon nutmeg* and *⅛ teaspoon ground cloves*. Mix with a pastry blender.

With a fork, mix the 2 yolks. Stir in *¼ cup oil* and *⅓ cup cold tap water* and *2 teaspoons vanilla.* Stir into the flour mixture. Mix until smooth.

With an electric hand beater or a rotary beater beat the 2 whites until foamy. Add *¼ teaspoon cream of tartar* and a pinch of *salt.* Beat until a soft peak forms when you lift the beaters out. Gradually add and continue to beat *¼ cup sugar.* Beat until you can feel no grains of sugar when you taste it. This is a meringue. Mix ⅓ of this into the batter. Fold the rest in.

Pour into the cake pan. Bake in 350° oven about 30 to 35 minutes. It's usually done in 30 minutes.

Put on a rack to cool. Let cool 5 minutes. Turn out onto a soft kitchen towel, then turn up onto a rack to cool.

Vanilla Cake Marbled With Chocolate

you'll like this one!

Heat oven 350°.

Grease and flour an 8 inch round cake pan.

Mix together *2 tablespoons cocoa* with *3 tablespoons sugar.* Set aside.

Separate *1 egg,* put yolk in a cup and the white into a small bowl.

Put into a large bowl *1 cup flour, 1 teaspoon wheat germ, 2 teaspoons baking powder, ¼ teaspoon salt, 2 tablespoons nonfat dry milk, ½ cup sugar.*

With a pastry blender mix until combined.

Mix the yolk with a fork. Stir in *¼ cup oil, ½ cup cold tap water* and *1 teaspoon vanilla.*

Add to the flour mixture. Mix with a wooden spoon until smooth.

With an electric hand beater or a rotary beater beat the egg white until foamy. Add a pinch of salt and *⅛ teaspoon cream of tartar.* Beat until soft peak forms. Add *2 tablespoons sugar.* Beat until when you taste you can feel no grains of sugar.

Stir ¼ of this meringue into the batter. Fold the rest of the meringue in. Put ¼ of this batter into the cocoa mixture and mix. Spoon the rest of the batter into the cake pan. Drop the chocolate batter in 3 separate "blobs" on top. With a dull knife, swirl (don't mix) the chocolate around in the batter.

Some will be on top and make a design. Place in the 350° oven. Bake until done, takes about 30 to 35 minutes. Remove to a rack. Cool 10 minutes. Turn over onto the rack, then turn face up to get cold.

A One Bowl Delicious Chocolate Cake

this will become one of your favorite cakes . . . it sounds odd but it comes out light and fine

Grease an 8 × 8 inch or a round cake pan.
Heat oven 350°.
Put into a bowl *½ cup flour, 1½ teaspoons baking powder, ¼ teaspoon salt, ¾ cup sugar, 2 tablespoons dry nonfat milk, 3 tablespoons cocoa, ¼ cup oil, ¼ cup and 2 tablespoons cold tap water, 1 teaspoon vanilla* and *2 eggs.*
Mix on highest speed of electric mixer 2 minutes.
Pour into the greased cake pan.
Bake about 30 minutes.
This cake really doesn't need an icing but just in case, here's a chocolate icing:

Chocolate Icing

Mix together *1½ cups 10X sugar, 4 tablespoons cocoa, 1 tablespoon margarine, 4 tablespoons nonfat milk* and *½ teaspoon vanilla.*
If necessary, add—drop by drop—a little milk until you get the icing as you like it.
This is a flattish, tender, light cake, well worth making.

Easy To Make 2 Layer Vanilla Cake

we tested this using the conventional long way against our new "easy to make" cake and all agreed our method produced a cake just as good and ours rose even a little higher

Heat oven 350°.
Grease and flour 2 (9 inch) cake pans.

Put into the large bowl of your electric mixer, or use your electric hand mixer, *1½ cups sugar, 2 eggs, ¾ cup margarine, 2 teaspoons vanilla, 2½ cups flour, 3 teaspoons baking powder, ¾ teaspoon salt* and *1¼ cups nonfat dry milk.*

Mix on lowest speed to combine. Turn speed to highest speed; mix 2 minutes stirring with a rubber spatula all the while.

Spoon into the greased and floured cake pans.

Bake in 350° oven 30 to 35 minutes.

Remove from oven to a rack. Let stand about 5 minutes; then remove pans to a rack. Let cool.

You can ice this cake, or eat as is. It's good both ways.

Banana Spice Cake With Nuts

Grease and flour 2 nine-inch cake pans.

Heat oven to 350°.

Chop *½ cup nuts.*

Put into large bowl of electric mixer *2 bananas* cut into pieces. Turn to highest speed. Beat until bananas are mashed smooth.

Add *½ cup vegetable shortening, 1½ cups sugar, 2 cups flour, 1 teaspoon soda, 1 teaspoon baking powder, ½ teaspoon salt, 1 teaspoon cinnamon, ¼ teaspoon ginger, ¼ teaspoon cloves, ½ teaspoon nutmeg, 2 eggs, ¼ cup sour milk* (made by adding 1 teaspoon lemon juice to ¼ cup milk) and *1 teaspoon vanilla.*

Beat on highest speed 2 minutes.

With a spoon stir in ½ cup chopped nuts. Spoon into the cake.

Bake in 350° preheated oven 30 to 35 minutes.

Easiest Ever Chocolate Cake

a two layer chocolate cake so good you don't even need an icing

Grease and flour two 9-inch cake pans. Shake out excess flour.

Heat oven 350°.

Put into the large bowl of the electric mixer *1¾ cups sugar, 3 large eggs, 2¼ cups flour, ⅔ cup cocoa, 1 teaspoon soda, 1 teaspoon baking powder, ½ teaspoon salt, ¾ cup soft margarine, 1⅓ cups skim or nonfat milk* and *1 teaspoon vanilla.*

Mix on highest speed 2 minutes.

Spoon into the greased pans.

Bake in 350° oven 35 minutes

Remove to a rack. Let stand 5 minutes before removing from pan. Let cool on rack right side up.

You can eat as is; or make this chocolate icing:

Mix together until smooth *1 package (1 pound) 10X sugar* (confectioner's sugar), *⅔ cup cocoa, ½ cup margarine, 6 tablespoons milk* and *1 teaspoon vanilla.*

Frankly, the chocolate cake doesn't need the icing—Oh, well, for a party, O.K.

Chocolate Marble Cake

this cake not only tastes good but looks very pretty

Preheat oven 350°.

Grease with *vegetable shortening* and *flour* an 8 × 8 inch square cake pan or an 8 inch tube pan. Shake out excess flour.

Mix together *2 tablespoons cocoa* with *3 tablespoons sugar.* Set aside. Separate *2 large eggs.* Put the whites in a large bowl and the yolks in a small bowl.

Put into a large bowl *1 cup flour, ½ cup sugar, 1½ teaspoons baking powder, ½ teaspoon salt* and *2 tablespoons nonfat dry milk.*

Mix the 2 yolks with a fork. Stir in *¼ cup oil,* then stir in *⅓ cup cold tap water* and *1 teaspoon vanilla.* Add to dry mixture. Mix until smooth.

With an electric hand beater or a rotary beater beat the whites until foamy. Add *¼ teaspoon cream of tartar* and a *pinch of salt* and beat until soft peaks form. Gradually stir in *¼ cup sugar* and beat until you can feel no grains of sugar when you taste.

Stir ¼ of the meringue into the batter. Fold the rest of the meringue in, using an under and over motion.

Divide the batter into 3 portions.

Spoon one portion in a layer into the pan. Sprinkle ½ of the cocoa mixture over the batter. Spoon another layer of batter on top. Sprinkle the rest of the cocoa mixture on top. Spoon the rest of the batter over. Swirl lightly.

Bake in 350° oven about 30 to 35 minutes. Place on a rack to cool. When cold, loosen sides and turn right side up.

The Best Ever Chocolate Cake

enter it in a food contest and you'll surely win a prize

Heat oven 375°.

In a saucepan combine *1 cup water, 2 sticks margarine or 1 8-ounce tub of soft margarine* and *10 tablespoons cocoa.*

On medium heat bring to a simmer, stirring all the while.

When it "curdles" or slightly separates, remove from heat.

Measure *2 cups flour.* Sift the flour into a large bowl. *Remove 2 tablespoons.*

Add *2 cups sugar* and the chocolate mixture.

Mix by hand, or use an electric mixer and mix 2 minutes.

Dissolve *1 teaspoon soda* into *½ cup buttermilk.**

Stir *2 eggs* and the buttermilk-soda mixture into the flour-chocolate mixture. Beat 2 minutes.

Pour into 2 greased and floured 8-inch square baking pans.

Bake in 375° oven about 25 to 30 minutes.

Frost while still hot in pan.

*You can make a "homemade buttermilk," which is quite good. Stir in 1½ teaspoons lemon juice or vinegar into ½ cup milk.

Let stand 5 minutes. Use instead of the buttermilk.

Frosting

Sift *¾ box confectioner's sugar,* which is 3 cups.

Bring *1 stick margarine or ½ of an 8-ounce tub of soft margarine, or 4 ounces soft margarine, 7 tablespoons cocoa, ⅓ cup milk* (or coffee) to a boil.

Immediately stir in the 3 cups confectioner's sugar, *1 teaspoon vanilla* and *1 cup chopped pecans.*

Pour on cake and spread immediately, as it becomes thick and difficult to spread.

Vanilla Chiffon Cake

makes any meal special . . . it's so light

Have ready an 8 inch tube pan (ungreased) or an 8 inch square cake pan.

Heat oven 350°.

Separate *4 large eggs.* Put the 4 whites into a large bowl and *3 of the yolks* in a saucer. Do not use the fourth yolk.

Into a large bowl put *1 cup flour, ½ cup sugar, 1½ teaspoons baking powder, ½ teaspoon salt,* and *2 tablespoons nonfat dry milk.* Mix with a pastry blender.

Make a well in the center. Put in *¼ cup oil,* the 3 egg yolks, *⅓ cup cold tap water* and *2 teaspoons vanilla.* Mix with a spoon until the batter is smooth.

With an electric hand beater or a rotary beater beat the whites until foamy. Add a *pinch of salt* and *¼ teaspoon cream of tartar.* Beat until the whites hold a soft peak. Gradually add *¼ cup sugar* and beat until stiff and you taste no grains of sugar.

Quickly stir in ¼ of the meringue into the batter to lighten it. Quickly fold, don't stir, fold the rest of the whites into the batter.

Pour the batter into the baking pan. Use a rubber spatula to get all of the batter. Place in the 350° oven. Bake 30 to 35 minutes until done.

Place on a rack right side up to cool. Do not remove until cold.

Tip: This is a delicious cake to eat as is. Can be iced if you like. A lemon or chocolate sauce or ice cream are nice with it too.

Orange Chiffon Cake

Have ready an 8 inch tube pan (ungreased) or an 8 inch square cake pan.

Heat oven 350°.

Separate *4 large eggs.* Put the 4 whites into a large bowl and *3 of the yolks* in a saucer. Do not use the fourth yolk.

Into a large bowl put *1 cup flour, ½ cup sugar, 1½ teaspoons baking powder, ½ teaspoon salt, 3 tablespoons grated orange rind,* and *2 tablespoons nonfat dry milk.* Mix with a pastry blender.

Make a well in the center. Put in *¼ cup oil,* the 3 egg yolks, *⅓ cup cold tap water.* Mix with a spoon until the batter is smooth.

With an electric hand beater or a rotary beater beat the whites until foamy. Add a *pinch of salt* and *¼ teaspoon cream of tartar.* Beat until the whites hold a soft peak. Gradually add *¼ cup sugar* and beat until stiff and you taste no grains of sugar.

Quickly stir in ¼ of the meringue into the batter to lighten it. Quickly fold, don't stir, fold the rest of the whites into the batter.

Pour the batter into the baking pan. Use a rubber spatula to get all of the batter. Place in the 350° oven. Bake 30 to 35 minutes until done.

Place on a rack right side up to cool. Do not remove until cold.

FOR A LEMON CHIFFON CAKE you can substitute 1 teaspoon lemon juice and 2 tablespoons grated lemon rind for the orange rind.

Fantastic Party Chiffon Cake

you can bet there won't be a crumb left!

Preheat oven 325°.

You need a 10 inch ungreased tube pan preferably with legs.

Grate *3 tablespoons orange rind.* Let stand. Measure *½ cup sugar.* Let stand.

Separate *6 large eggs.* Put the whites in a large bowl. Let stand.

Put the yolks in a bowl. Stir in *½ cup oil, ⅔ cup and ¼ cup cold tap water* and *2 teaspoons vanilla.* Let stand.

Put into a large bowl *2 cups flour, ¾ cup sugar, 3 teaspoons baking powder, ¾ teaspoon salt, ¼ cup nonfat dry milk* and the grated orange rind. Mix with a pastry blender.

Make a well in the center of the flour mixture. Pour in the yolk mixture and mix until smooth.

With an electric hand beater or a rotary beater, mix the whites until foamy. Add a *pinch of salt* and *½ teaspoon cream of tartar.* Beat until soft peaks form when you lift the beaters out. Continue to beat and gradually add the ½ cup sugar and beat until you taste and can feel no grains of sugar. This is called a meringue.

Mix ¼ of the meringue into the batter to lighten it.

Fold, fold the rest of the meringue into the batter using an over and under motion so as not to deflate it.

Spoon into the tube pan. Bake in the 325° preheated oven. Bake 55 minutes, then turn the heat to 350° and bake 15 minutes until done. Test.

Remove from the oven. Invert pan. Let stand on legs so air can circulate around it and under it. If your tube pan has no "legs," put something in the hole of the pan to hold the cake up so the air can circulate under it.

Leave in the pan until cold. Do not try to remove it until it is cold.

When cold, carefully loosen the cake around the edges with a knife or a spatula—also around the center. Remove from the pan. Turn right side up.

This is a fantastic high-rise cake and everyone will admire you for making it.

Our Favorite Gingerbread

it's a fine tasting, tender cake

Grease two 8 × 8 inch baking pans.

Heat oven 350°.

Put into the large bowl of your electric mixer *3 eggs, 1 cup sugar, 1 cup molasses, ¾ cup oil, 1 teaspoon cloves, 1 teaspoon ginger, 1 teaspoon cinnamon, 2 teaspoons soda, 2 cups flour* and *1 cup and 2 tablespoons cold tap water.*

Beat on highest speed 2 minutes. Put into 2 greased 8 × 8 inch baking pans.

Bake in 350° oven 45 minutes.

Remove from oven. Let stand a few minutes.

Turn out on rack to cool right side up.

Fruit Cocktail Cake

something different for a change

Heat oven 350°.

Grease and flour two 8-inch cake pans.

In large bowl of electric mixer put *½ cup oil, 2 eggs, 1½*

cups sugar, 2 cups flour, 1 teaspoon soda, 2 teaspoons baking powder, ½ teaspoon salt, ½ cup chopped nuts and *1 can #303 Fruit Cocktail, including juice.*

Beat on highest speed of mixer 2 minutes.

Pour into the 2 greased and floured pans.

Bake in 350° oven 35 to 40 minutes.

Full Of Flavor Thrifty Pound Cake

it means what it says

Grease an 8-inch tube pan or a bundt pan. Sprinkle flour over. Shake out excess.

Heat oven 350°.

Mix together with a pastry blender *1¾ cups flour, 2 teaspoons wheat germ, 3 teaspoons baking powder, ¼ teaspoon salt, ¼ cup instant dry milk, 1¼ cups sugar* and *3 tablespoons grated orange rind.*

Mix *3 eggs* with a fork, stir in *½ cup oil;* then stir in *¾ cup cold tap water.*

Add the egg mixture to the flour mixture and beat 2 minutes.

Pour in the greased and floured pan.

Bake in preheated 350° oven about 1 hour. Test to see if done.

Icing

Mix together *¾ cup 10X Confectioner's Sugar* with *1 teaspoon grated lemon rind* and *¾ teaspoon lemon juice.*

This makes a thin icing that you spread on with a dull knife.

You can serve this cake without an icing, but we like it better with the icing.

High Rise Sponge Cake

makes 6 eggs rise like 12 . . . and light as a feather!

Sprinkle a 9 inch tube pan with *flour.* Shake out excess flour.

Heat oven 325°.

Separate *6 large eggs.* Put whites into the large bowl of electric mixer. Put yolks in a small bowl.

Measure *1 cup flour.*

Measure *1 cup sugar.*

Strain *¼ cup lemon juice.* Grate *1 tablespoon lemon rind.*

Beat the egg whites on highest speed until they foam. Add *¼ teaspoon cream of tartar* and continue beating until it forms a straight peak when you lift the beaters up.

Gradually beat in the *1 cup sugar.* Beat until when you taste the meringue, you cannot feel any grains of sugar.

Gradually beat in the yolks, one at a time.

Continue beating while you add the grated rind and the lemon juice.

Remove the bowl from the stand, and a little at a time, fold in the 1 cup flour.

When all have been folded in, spoon into the tube pan, or into two 9 inch cake pans.

Place in 325° oven. Bake 1 hour to 1 hour and 10 minutes, but don't overbake. Test to see when done. For the 9 inch cakes, bake 30 minutes.

Remove from the oven. Turn upside down on the tube pan's legs. Let cool until cold before removing. Cool the 9 inch cakes by putting on a rack right side up until cold.

Isn't it a lovely cake?

The "tube" sponge cake is delicious with a lemon sauce or a lemon icing.

One of the 9 inch layer cakes can be "iced" with whipped cream and topped with strawberries for a delicious strawberry cake, when strawberries are in season. The other could be topped with a lemon or chocolate sauce or a lemon or chocolate icing.

Butternut Cake

as rich tasting as it's full of Vitamin A—the vitamin that gives you, among other things, a healthy skin . . . nice to know, isn't it?

Slice, peel and cut into 1 inch cubes *enough (1 or 2) butternut squash to make 2 cups.*

Steam 6 minutes until soft, or cook in water, then drain.

Push through a strainer; or use a blender; or if you are

lucky enough to have a Cuisinart, use it. Don't be worried if you don't have a Cuisinart—you can live without it—to tell the truth, I hunted all over France in all kinds of stores and couldn't find one store that sold it. The French are fine cooks and true Penny Pinchers!

Heat oven 350°.

Grease and flour two 9-inch cake pans.

Put into the large bowl of electric mixer *1¾ cups brown sugar, 1 cup oil, 4 eggs, ½ teaspoon salt, 2 cups squash, 2 cups flour, 1 teaspoon soda, 2 teaspoons baking powder, 1 teaspoon cinnamon, 1 teaspoon nutmeg, ¼ teaspoon cloves* and *½ teaspoon ginger.*

Mix on highest speed 2 minutes.

Pour into the greased and floured cake pans.

Bake in 350° oven about 35 minutes.

Mini Orange Pumpkin Date Nut Loaf Cakes

3 mini loaves so good you'll want to gobble them up

Heat oven 375°.

Grease and flour 3 foil (6″ × 3½″) mini loaf pans.

Chop *1 cup dates* and *½ cup nuts.* Set aside and grate *3 tablespoons orange rind.*

With a pastry blender mix together *2 cups whole wheat flour, 1 teaspoon soda, 1½ teaspoons baking powder, ½ teaspoon salt, ½ cup nonfat dry milk* and 3 tablespoons grated orange rind.

Add 1 cup chopped dates, ½ cup chopped nuts. Mix with your clean hands or the pastry blender.

Mix *1 egg* with a fork. Stir in *¼ cup oil,* then *1 cup canned pumpkin, ¼ cup brown sugar* and lastly, *1 cup cold tap water.*

Pour into the flour mixture. Barely mix just to combine.

Spoon into the 3 mini loaf pans. Bake in 375° oven about 25 minutes.

Remove from the oven and turn out onto a rack to cool.

A slice of this for breakfast really makes it a treat and as a dessert with a cup of coffee or tea for dinner, it is not to be sneezed at!

Three Mini Peanut Butter Raisin Loaf Cakes

with a peanutty taste

Preheat oven 375°.

Grease and flour the bottoms of 3 (6 × 3½ inch) foil loaf pans.

Measure *½ cup peanut butter.*

Grate *enough orange rind to make 3 tablespoons.*

Put into a large bowl *2 cups flour, 2 teaspoons wheat germ, 1 teaspoon soda, 3 tablespoons nonfat dry milk, ¾ cup sugar, ½ teaspoon salt* and *½ cup raisins.*

Mix with a pastry blender.

Add ½ cup peanut butter. Mix with the pastry blender—not too much.

Mix *1 egg* with a fork. Stir in *¼ cup oil,* then stir in *¾ cup cold tap water.*

Pour into the flour mixture. Barely mix, just to combine.

Spoon into the 3 foil pans.

Bake in 375° oven about 40 minutes.

Remove from oven. Let stand a few minutes. Remove from pans to a rack to cool.

No matter how you want to, wait until cold before eating.

These freeze beautifully.

Three Spiced Pumpkin Mini Loaf Cakes

one of the nicest ways to eat pumpkin

Preheat oven 375°.

Grease 3 foil pans 6″ × 3½″.

Grate *2 tablespoons orange rind.*

Chop *½ cup nuts.*

With a pastry blender mix together in a large bowl *2 cups flour, ½ teaspoon cinnamon, ½ teaspoon nutmeg, ¼ teaspoon dried ginger, ½ teaspoon ground cloves, 2 teaspoons wheat germ, 1 teaspoon soda, ¼ teaspoon salt, ¾ cup sugar, 3 tablespoons instant dry milk, 2 tablespoons grated rind* and *½ cup chopped nuts.*

Beat *1 egg* with a fork. Stir in *¼ cup oil* and *¾ cup cold tap water* and *½ cup canned or fresh pumpkin.*

Pour into the flour mixture. Barely mix just to combine.
Spoon into the 3 foil pans.
Bake in the preheated 350° oven about 50 to 60 minutes until done.

Three Mini Nut Raisin Loaf Cakes

with a touch of orange rind, the flavor is enhanced and with less sugar, this isn't a real sweet cake but—is certainly lovely to end your dinner with along with that cup of coffee, tea or milk . . . or who could refuse a couple of thin slices for breakfast

Preheat oven 375°.
Smear 3 foil 6 × 3½ inches pans lightly with *oil*, then *flour*. Shake out excess flour.
Steam *1 cup raisins* and chop *½ cup nuts*. Grate *2 tablespoons orange rind.*
With a pastry blender, mix together in a large bowl *2 cups flour, 2 teaspoons wheat germ, 1 teaspoon soda, ½ teaspoon salt, ½ cup raisins, ½ cup chopped nuts, ¾ cup sugar* and *2 tablespoons grated orange rind.*
Mix *1 egg* with a fork well. Stir in *¼ cup oil,* then stir in *¾ cup cold tap water.*
Add to the flour mixture and mix just to combine.
Spoon into the 3 mini pans.
Place in the preheated 375° oven. Bake about 30 to 40 minutes.
Test to see if done.
Remove from the oven. Take out of loaf pans.
Cool on a rack.
This loaf goes nicely spread with some Philadelphia Cream Cheese, mixed with a little milk to lighten and make it spreadable.

Date, Nut Loaf Cakes

everyone likes to have a date with this date loaf

Preheat oven 375°.
Grease 3 (6 × 3½ inches) foil pans.

Grate *enough orange rind to make 3 tablespoons grated rind.*

Chop *½ cup walnuts.*

Chop *½ cup dates.*

Put into a large bowl *2 cups flour, 2 teaspoons wheat germ, ¾ cup sugar, 1 teaspoon soda, 3 tablespoons nonfat dry milk, ½ teaspoon salt.* Mix with a pastry blender. Add the chopped walnuts and the dates. Mix with the pastry blender.

Mix *1 egg* in a bowl. Stir in *¼ cup oil* and *½ cup cold tap water.* Add to the flour mixture. Mix just to combine.

Spoon into the loaf pans.

Bake in preheated 375° oven about 40 to 50 minutes. Test when done.

Remove to a rack. Let stand 5 minutes.

Remove from the rack. Let cool.

Six Zucchini Mini-Loaf Cakes

you want to fool someone? then make these cakes . . . no one will believe they are made with zucchini . . . they are true spice cakes

Grease and flour 6 mini foil pans.

Heat oven 375°.

We need a scant 1 pound *zucchini* washed and grated to make *2 cups.*

Chop *1 cup nuts* and measure *1 cup raisins.* Set aside.

With a pastry blender, mix together in the large bowl of your mixer *2 cups flour, 2 teaspoons wheat germ, 1½ teaspoons soda, 1 teaspoon baking powder, 1 teaspoon salt, 1 teaspoon cinnamon, 1 teaspoon nutmeg, ½ teaspoon ground cloves, 1¾ cups sugar.*

Put the mixer bowl on the electric stand or use your electric hand beaters or beat by hand when ready.

Add the zucchini to the dry ingredients, then add *¾ cup oil, 3 eggs, 1 teaspoon vanilla.* Mix slowly to start; then turn to highest speed and mix, using a rubber spatula to get the batter into the beaters, for 2 minutes.

Fold in the nuts and raisins.

Spoon into the greased mini foil pans. Place in the preheated 375° oven. Bake about 40 minutes.

Remove to a rack. Cool 3 minutes. Turn out onto the rack.

These freeze beautifully. Many people like these as is, and some like the slices spread with softened cream cheese.

Banana Tea Bread

this is good to make anytime, especially when you overbought on bananas and you're like I am—appalled at how quickly they ripened!

Heat oven 350°.
Grease an 8″ × 4″ loaf pan.
In a large bowl of your electric mixer, or use your electric hand mixer, or use a mixing spoon, put *1½ cups and 1 tablespoon flour, ¾ teaspoon soda, 1 teaspoon baking powder, ¼ teaspoon salt, ¼ teaspoon nutmeg, ⅓ cup margarine, ⅔ cup sugar, 2 eggs* and *3 small ripe bananas.* Mix 2 minutes.
Stir in *½ cup chopped nuts,* if you wish.
Pour batter into the greased 8″ × 4″ bread pan.
Bake in 350° oven about 50 minutes.
Remove from the pan to a rack to cool.
Slice thinnish when ready to eat, as all fruit breads taste better so.
Tip: If you have a husband and children like mine who like raisins, you'll add about ½ cup raisins.

Jelly Roll

always welcome and you can make different kinds by changing the fillings from apricot, plum, peach, strawberry preserves or jam or from fresh strawberries in whipped cream, which is superb but so rich!

Line a 15 × 10 inch cookie pan that has sides with wax paper.
Heat oven 375°.
Put a kitchen towel on a clean surface. Into a strainer put about *½ cup 10X sugar* and with a spoon push the sugar over the towel. This covers it easily and nicely and will keep the baked jelly roll from sticking, and you can easily roll it.
Separate *4 eggs,* yolks from the whites. If using an electric mixer, put the yolks in the large bowl and the whites in another large bowl.

To the yolks add *¾ cup sugar, ¾ cup flour, 1 teaspoon baking powder, ¼ teaspoon salt, 1 teaspoon vanilla* and *5 tablespoons cold tap water.*

Start at lowest speed and mix just until combined. Turn to highest speed and beat 1 minute.

Whip the whites with a rotary beater until stiff but not dry.

Mix 2 tablespoons of the egg whites into the batter.

Fold the rest of the egg whites into the batter.

Spoon evenly over the cookie sheet lined with wax paper.

Bake in 375° oven about 14 to 15 minutes. Remove from oven.

Turn over onto the towel sprinkled with 10X sugar.

Peel off the wax paper. Cool 5 minutes.

Roll up (the long side). Let stand until it cools. Unroll.

Spread about *¾ cup preserves* on, leaving an inch edge all around.

Roll up again. Let stand 10 minutes to keep its shape.

Refrigerate.

Cooked Dried Apricots

for Jelly Rolls and other baked pastries

Bring *1 pound dried apricots* and *2 cups water* to a boil.

Turn heat to low and simmer, stirring now and then so they don't stick, about 30 minutes.

Add *6 tablespoons or more sugar to taste.* Bring back to a boil. Correct sugar, if necessary. Boil 1 minute.

Stir and mash with a metal spoon, so that it is spreadable, or push through a sieve.

Cool.

This freezes beautifully. You can put it in sterilized glasses, cover with paraffin and a lid and keep on a shelf.

We once kept a jar in our large freezer 5 years, and it tasted as if we had just made it. Unbelievable!

Chocolate Cupcakes

Heat oven 375°.

Separate *2 eggs,* yolks from whites.

Put into the large bowl of the electric mixer *1½ cups flour, ½ cup cocoa, 2 teaspoons baking powder, ¼ teaspoon soda, ½ teaspoon salt, ½ cup soft margarine, 1¼ cups sugar, 1 teaspoon vanilla, ¾ cup nonfat milk* and the 2 egg yolks.

Mix on low speed until everything is moistened.

Turn the speed to #7 or "creaming butter and sugar." Mix 2 minutes, using a rubber spatula to help get the batter into the beaters.

With a rotary beater beat the whites until stiff. Fold into the batter.

Put 2 paper baking cups together for each cupcake. They bake better this way.

Spoon the batter ⅔ full into each baking cup.

Place in 375° oven. Bake 20 minutes. Test if done.

The cupcakes are light in color and deliciously light in texture.

Cool on a rack.

Tip: You can use the bottom paper or foil cup over again.

Vanilla Cupcakes

Heat oven 375°.

Put 2 paper baking cups together for each cupcake. This keeps the cakes from overbrowning on the bottom and also helps them to hold their shapes. Place the baking cups on a cookie sheet.

Separate *2 eggs,* yolks from whites.

Put into the large bowl of the electric mixer, or mix by hand, *2 cups flour, 3 teaspoons baking powder, ½ teaspoon salt, 1¼ cups sugar, ½ cup soft margarine, ¾ cup milk, 1½ teaspoons vanilla* and the *2 egg yolks.*

Mix on low speed until everything is moistened.

Turn the speed to highest speed. Beat 2 minutes.

With a rotary beater, beat the egg whites stiff.

Fold into the batter.

Spoon the batter ⅔ full into the baking cups on the cookie sheet.

Bake in 375° oven for 20 minutes.

These cupcakes are light in color and tender and light in texture.

Raisin Cupcakes

For a change add ½ cup or 1 cup raisins to the flour mixture.

For another change also add nuts to the flour mixture.

Silver Cupcakes

makes about 22 cupcakes

We use paper baking cups, 2 for each cupcake, and put them on a cookie sheet. We use 2 so the cupcakes don't burn on the bottom.

Heat oven 375°.

Put into the large bowl of your electric mixer, or use electric hand beaters, or mix by hand *2 cups flour, 3 teaspoons baking powder, ½ teaspoon salt, 1¼ cups sugar, ½ cup margarine, 1 cup nonfat milk, 2 teaspoons vanilla* and *⅓ teaspoon almond flavor.*

Mix 3 minutes on highest speed.

Beat *4 egg whites* with a rotary beater until the whites hold a straight peak when you lift the beaters out.

Mix 2 tablespoons of this beaten egg white into the batter.

Fold in the rest of the whites with an over and under motion.

Spoon into the paper baking cups on the cookie sheet.

Bake in 375° oven about 20 to 25 minutes.

Remove from oven to a rack. Let stand 5 minutes before removing the paper cups; otherwise you will tear the cakes.

Apple Brown Betty

or peach, apricot or rhubarb are all good . . . this is almost like scalloped fruit

Grease a 1½ quart baking dish with *oil.*

Preheat oven 350° or 400°. (You can bake this along with your main course, casserole dinner.)

Mix together *2 cups graham cracker crumbs* with *¼ cup oil.*

Mix together *½ cup brown sugar, ½ teaspoon cinnamon, ¼ teaspoon nutmeg* and *1 tablespoon grated orange rind.*

Peel and slice *enough apples to make 4 cups.*

Make a layer of ⅓ of the crumbs.

Make a layer of ½ of the sliced apples. Sprinkle with *lemon juice (about 1½ teaspoons)* and *¼ cup brown sugar.* Sprinkle *¼ to ½ cup raisins* on top.

Top with a layer of ⅓ of the crumbs.

Repeat the same, ending with the crumbs and pour *½ cup canned apple juice* over the top.

Cover. Place in 350° oven. Bake 30 minutes.

Remove cover. Bake 20 minutes until top is browned.

3 Icings For Cakes

Tip: Each icing makes enough for 1 cake or about 12 cupcakes.

Vanilla Icing

You need:
1 cup plus 2 tablespoons 10X confectioner's sugar
3 tablespoons soft margarine or butter
⅛ teaspoon salt
1 teaspoon vanilla
2 tablespoons milk

Put 1 cup 10 X confectioner's sugar into a bowl.

Stir in 3 tablespoons soft margarine or softened butter.

Add ⅛ teaspoon salt, 1 teaspoon vanilla and 2 tablespoons milk.

Mix well until it becomes creamy and smooth.

Spread on the cake or cupcakes.

Chocolate Icing

You need:
1 cup 10X sugar
3 tablespoons soft margarine
4 teaspoons unsweetened cocoa
⅛ teaspoon salt
1 teaspoon vanilla
2 tablespoons milk

Put into a bowl. Mix together until smooth and creamy.

Orange Icing

You need:
1½ cups 10X confectioner's sugar
¼ teaspoon salt
3 tablespoons soft margarine
2 tablespoons grated orange rind
2 tablespoons concentrated frozen orange juice
1 teaspoon milk, add more if needed

Mix together until smooth and creamy.

Creme De Cacao Icing

this is not a "Penny Pincher" recipe but it's good

Strain *1 box 10X confectioner's sugar* gradually into a bowl.

Strain *½ cup cocoa* into the sugar. Mix well.

Add *¾ cup soft margarine*. Stir well, *adding 8½ tablespoons Creme de Cacao* and *1 tablespoon nonfat milk*. Stir until smooth.

This is enough icing for a 2 layer, 9-inch cake to be iced.

No one ever refuses this.

Lemon Sauce

very good over plain cakes and apple dumplings and gingerbread and wherever you want a tasty lemon sauce

Mix together *1 cup sugar* with *2 tablespoons cornstarch.*

Stir in *1 cup water* and *½ cup strained lemon juice.*

Cook and stir slowly on medium high heat until it thickens and clears, takes about 10 minutes.

Cool.

Vanilla Sauce

for rice pudding and white cakes

In a saucepan mix together *¼ cup sugar, 3 tablespoons cornstarch,* and *¼ teaspoon salt.*

Stir in *2¼ cups milk.*

Cook and stir on medium high heat until it comes almost to a boil and starts to thicken, takes about 5 minutes.

Take off heat and stir slowly as it thickens.

Stir in slowly *3 tablespoons soft margarine.*

Stir in *2 teaspoons vanilla.*

The sauce is ready.

For a chocolate sauce recipe see Index under "M" Mixes, "Chocolate Sauce Mix."

Blueberry Sauce

To *1 can (15 ounces) Blueberries* add *2 tablespoons lemon juice* and *3 tablespoons and ½ teaspoon sugar.*

Mix together *1 tablespoon cornstarch* and *1 tablespoon water.*

Bring the blueberries to a boil. Stir in the cornstarch mixture. It will clear instantly. Remove from heat.

Serve with pancakes, blintzes or plain cakes.

Another Blueberry Sauce

made with wild blueberry pie filling

Mix *1 can Wyman's Wild Blueberry Pie Filling* (21 ounces) with *2 tablespoons and 1 teaspoon lemon juice* and *2 tablespoons sugar.*

To serve hot, cook, stir until hot; otherwise, serve cold.

Brandied Cherry Sauce

for blintzes, ice cream, cakes and anything else you can think of

Strain *1 can (1 pound) Dark Sweet Pitted Cherries.* You will have 1 cup juice. Set the cherries aside.

Into a saucepan measure *1 tablespoon cornstarch.* Stir a little of the cherry juice in. Mix until smooth. Gradually stir in the rest of the juice.

Stir in *2 tablespoons sugar.*

Place on medium high heat. Cook and stir until it thickens and clears, takes about 4 minutes.

Remove from heat.

Gently stir in the cherries and a *small pinch of salt.*

When ready to serve, stir in *2 tablespoons brandy.*

Serve over ice cream or cake or even over blintzes.

Tip: This is a wonderful sauce, because it can be made the day before and reheats beautifully; only do not add the 2 tablespoons brandy off heat until right before you will use the sauce.

Another Cherry Sauce

with a hint of lemon . . . makes a plain cake fancy

Strain *1 can (1 pound) Dark Sweet Pitted Cherries.* You will have 1 cup juice. Set the cherries aside.

Into a saucepan measure *1 tablespoon cornstarch.* Stir a little of the cherry juice in. Mix until smooth. Gradually stir in the rest of the juice.

Stir in *2 tablespoons sugar.*

Place on medium high heat. Cook and stir until it thickens and clears, takes about 4 minutes.

Remove from heat.

Stir in the cherries.

When ready to serve, stir in *1 tablespoon plus 2 teaspoons lemon juice* and *1 tablespoon brandy.*

Serve over cake or ice cream.

Tip: If you plan to make this sauce ahead, don't put in the lemon juice and brandy until you are ready to serve the sauce. Then stir them in after you have reheated the sauce.

20. COOKIES

Delicious Cookies—
Sliced And Spiced With
Lemon And Almonds

taste so good you'll always have some handy in the freezer, if they get to the freezer!

Heat oven 375°.

Grate *3 tablespoons lemon or orange rind.*

Put into a large bowl *3¼ cups flour, 2 teaspoons baking powder, 1 teaspoon soda, ½ teaspoon salt, ¼ teaspoon ground mace, ¼ teaspoon ground cardamom* and *1 cup sugar.*

Mix together with a pastry blender.

Add *¾ cup cold butter or margarine.* Cut in the butter or margarine with the pastry blender until it looks like coarse crumbs.

In a bowl mix *1 egg* with a fork. Stir in *¼ cup and 3 tablespoons plain yogurt, 1 teaspoon vanilla, ¼ teaspoon almond extract* and *2 tablespoons rum.*

Stir into the flour mixture.

Add *½ cup currants, ½ cup golden raisins, ½ cup almonds,* chopped or sliced, the 3 tablespoons grated lemon or orange rind. Mix with your hands. The dough will be sticky.

Sprinkle a *little flour* on a surface.

Put the dough on the flour. Flour your hands. Sprinkle a *little flour* over the dough.

With your hands shape the dough into a flat ball.

With a large sharp knife cut into 4 portions.

Shape, one at a time, into an even loaf.

Put on a Teflon cookie sheet. Place in 375° oven. Bake 25 minutes.

Brush with milk without moving the cookie sheet. Continue to bake 5 minutes more until the loaves are done. You bake altogether 30 minutes.

Remove to a rack to cool.

Slice in thin slices to serve.

These are not moist and the flavor is super.

They can be frozen and cut as you use them.

Crisp Orange Raisin Cookies

with peanut butter and cubed orange (candied or glazed orange rinds) this is delicious

Heat oven 375°.

You can use either one or two cookie sheets. The Teflon ones are best.

Into the large bowl of your electric mixer put *½ cup peanut butter, ½ cup "tub" margarine, 2 eggs, 1 teaspoon vanilla, 1½ cups flour, ½ teaspoon vanilla, ½ teaspoon baking powder, ¼ teaspoon salt, 1 tablespoon wheat germ, 2 tablespoons instant dry nonfat milk* and *¾ cup brown sugar,* packed down.

Mix on highest speed 2 minutes.

With a spoon, mix in *1 cup raisins* and *4 ounces orange peel, glazed and cubed* (the kind sold at supermarkets for fruit cakes).

Pinch off pieces of this dough about the size of walnuts, and make into balls. Arrange these balls 3 inches apart on the cookie sheet.

Cut a piece of Saran Wrap or wax paper 6″ × 4½″. Put on top of each ball, one at a time, and flatten with the palm of your hand, each into a circle about 3 inches in diameter. (This will keep your hand from getting sticky and works faster, too.)

Place in 375° oven. Bake about 12 minutes.

With a spatula remove to a rack to cool and get crisp.

Continue until all are done.

These freeze well but are fragile, so freeze them in a plastic container or cookie tin with lid.

Banana Peanut Butter Crisp Cookies

crisp cookies that are so easy to make . . . on a rainy day when the children make you want to climb the walls, let them make these

Heat oven 375°.

Into the large bowl of electric mixer put *½ cup peanut butter* with *½ cup "tub" margarine, 1 ripe, small banana* cut into pieces to make it easier to mash, *1 egg,* and *1 teaspoon vanilla.*

On highest speed mix until smooth.

Add to the bowl *1½ cups flour, ½ teaspoon soda, ½ teaspoon baking powder, ¼ teaspoon salt, 1 tablespoon wheat germ, 2 tablespoons nonfat milk,* and *¾ cup dark brown sugar,* packed down.

On highest speed mix 2 minutes.

Pinch off pieces of this dough about the size of walnuts and make into balls.

Arrange the balls 3 inches apart, preferably on a Teflon cookie sheet.

Cut a piece of Saran Wrap 6″ × 4½″. Put on top of each ball, one at a time, and flatten with the palm of your hand, each into a circle about 3 inches in diameter. Continue until all are done.

Place in 375° oven. Bake about 12 minutes.

With a spatula remove to a rack to cool. These will harden as they cool.

These freeze well.

To bake two cookie sheets at the same time, put one sheet on the second rack from the top and the other sheet second from the bottom.

Tip: We find that, unlike what people tell us, the heat does not brown the bottom of the cookies more on the bottom shelf than closer to the top, as heat rises to the top.

Crispy Thin Vanilla Drop Cookies

the easiest cookie to make and so good, tender, yet crispy

Heat oven 375°.

Put into the large bowl of electric mixer *¾ cup sugar, ½ cup margarine, 1 cup and 2 tablespoons flour,* a *pinch of salt, ¼ teaspoon soda, 1 teaspoon baking powder, 1 egg* and *1 teaspoon vanilla.*

Start first at low speed; then turn to highest speed. Mix 2 minutes.

Drop by tablespoonfuls, not too close as they spread as they bake, onto a Teflon cookie sheet.

Bake in preheated 375° oven about 8 to 10 minutes.

For 6 different kinds of cookies, add one of the following to the above recipe:

1. Raisin Cookies — ½ cup raisins
2. Nut Cookies — ½ cup chopped nuts
3. Raisin, Nut Cookies — ½ cup raisins, ¼ cup chopped nuts
4. Spice Cookies — ¼ teaspoon each cinnamon, nutmeg and cloves
5. Nutmeg Cookies — ½ teaspoon nutmeg
6. Chocolate Chip Cookies — ¼ cup chocolate morsels

Sherry Chocolate Chip Cookies

no one ever refuses these!

Heat oven 425°.

Mix together in an electric mixer on lowest speed or by hand: *2 cups flour, 3 teaspoons baking powder, ½ teaspoon salt, 1 cup and 2 tablespoons sugar, 6 tablespoons margarine* (or ¼ cup and 2 tablespoons), *¼ cup dry sherry, ¾ cup nonfat milk, 2 eggs* and *1 teaspoon vanilla.*

Turn to highest speed; mix 2 minutes.

Stir in *1 package (12 ounces) chocolate chip bits.*

Drop by tablespoons onto a preferably Teflon-lined cookie sheet.

Bake in 425° oven about 11 minutes.

Remove to a rack to cool.

Crisp Chocolate Chip Cookies

these are tender and crisp

Heat oven 375°.

Mix together, preferably with a pastry blender or a mixing spoon, *2¼ cups flour, 1 teaspoon soda* and *½ teaspoon salt.* Set aside.

Mix together until creamy *1 cup brown sugar, packed, 1 cup soft margarine or vegetable shortening, 1 teaspoon vanilla, ¼ teaspoon cold tap water* and *2 eggs.*

Add the flour mixture. Mix well.

Stir in *1 package (6 ounces) chocolate chip morsels.*
Drop by teaspoonfuls onto a Teflon-lined cookie sheet or greased cookie sheet.
Bake in 375° oven 10 to 12 minutes until light brown.
Remove from oven. Let stand a minute.
Remove the cookies to a rack to cool.

Chocolate Chip Cookies

these are soft cookies

Heat oven 375°.
With a pastry blender mix together *2¼ cups flour, 1 teaspoon soda, ½ teaspoon salt,* and *1 cup brown sugar, packed down.*
Add *1 cup margarine.* Blend with the pastry blender. It will look crumb-like.
Mix *2 eggs* with a fork. Stir in *1 teaspoon vanilla* and *¼ teaspoon tap water.*
Add to the flour mixture and mix together.
Add *1 cup (6 ounces) chocolate chips.*
Use a teaspoon or 2 teaspoons to drop the batter, a teaspoon at a time, onto a preferably Teflon-lined cookie sheet.
Bake in 375° oven about 10 to 12 minutes.
Remove to a rack to cool.
You can add *½ cup nuts* if you wish.

Oatmeal Raisin Cookies

Heat oven 375°.
Put into the large bowl of electric mixer: *½ cup brown sugar, packed, plus 2 tablespoons brown sugar, packed, 1 egg or ¼ cup Egg Beaters, ½ cup oil, ½ cup plus 1 tablespoon nonfat milk.*
Measure *1½ tablespoons wheat germ* in a cup. Fill the cup with *flour to make 1 cup.* Add to sugar mixture.
Add *½ teaspoon baking powder, ½ teaspoon cinnamon, ¼ teaspoon nutmeg, ¼ teaspoon cloves* and *¼ teaspoon salt.*
Mix 2 minutes on high speed or by hand.
Add *1 cup oatmeal, 1 cup raisins* and *½ cup chopped nuts* by hand. Mix.

Drop by spoonfuls onto a Teflon cookie sheet.
Place in 375° oven. Bake 11 to 14 minutes.
These cookies taste better when cold or even the next day.

Brandy Cookies

crisp, tender, lovely flavored, and the brandy accents the good taste

Heat oven 400°.
Mix together in an electric mixer on lowest speed or by hand: *2 cups flour, 3 teaspoons baking powder, ½ teaspoon salt, 1 cup and 2 tablespoons sugar, ½ teaspoon nutmeg, ¼ cup and 2 tablespoons soft margarine, ¼ cup brandy, ¾ cup nonfat milk, 2 eggs* and *1 teaspoon vanilla.*
Turn to highest speed; mix 2 minutes.
Add *1 cup raisins* and, if you wish, *½ cup chopped walnuts.*
Use a tablespoon to drop the cookie batter onto a preferably Teflon-lined cookie sheet.
Bake in 400° oven about 13 to 14 minutes.
Remove to a rack to cool.
Tip: If you don't have brandy, you can substitute orange juice or nonfat milk.

Butternut Spiced Drop Cookies

what could be better . . . full of "goodies"

Slice, peel and cut enough butternut squash (1 or 2) into 1 inch cubes to make 1½ cups squash.
Steam 6 minutes until soft, or cook in water and drain.
Push through a strainer, or use a blender, or if you are lucky to have a Cuisinart, use it.
Heat oven 400°.
Measure, then put into the large bowl of the electric mixer *1¾ cups brown sugar, 2 eggs, ¾ cup margarine, 1½ cups butternut squash, 2½ cups flour, ½ teaspoon salt, ½ teaspoon ginger, ½ teaspoon cloves, 2 teaspoons nutmeg* and *2 teaspoons cinnamon.*
Beat on highest speed of the electric mixer 2 minutes.
Drop by teaspoonfuls on well greased cookie sheet.
Bake 15 minutes in 400° oven.

Vanilla Nutmeg Cookies

simple and simply delicious!

Heat oven 400°.

Mix together in an electric mixer on lowest speed or by hand: *2 cups flour, 3 teaspoons baking powder, ½ teaspoon salt, 1 cup and 2 tablespoons sugar, ½ teaspoon nutmeg, ¼ cup and 2 tablespoons soft margarine, ¼ cup dry sherry, ¾ cup nonfat milk, 2 eggs* and *1 teaspoon vanilla.*

Turn to highest speed; mix 2 minutes.

Stir in *1 cup raisins.*

Drop the cookie batter by tablespoonfuls onto preferably Teflon-lined cookie sheets.

Bake in 400° oven about 13 to 14 minutes.

Remove to a rack to cool.

Tip: If you don't have sherry wine, substitute nonfat milk or water.

Persian Cookies

with the wonderful taste of the Far East

Heat oven 425°.

Mix together in an electric mixer on lowest speed or by hand: *2 cups flour, 3 teaspoons baking powder, ½ teaspoon salt, ½ teaspoon ground cardamom, ½ teaspoon ground mace, 1¼ cups sugar, 6 tablespoons margarine* (or ¼ cup plus 2 tablespoons), *¼ cup brandy, ¾ cup nonfat milk, 2 eggs* and *¼ teaspoon almond flavor.*

Turn to highest speed; mix 2 minutes.

Stir in *1 cup raisins* and *½ cup chopped almonds.*

Drop by tablespoonfuls onto a preferably Teflon-lined cookie sheet.

Bake in 425° oven about 11 minutes.

Crisp Peanut Butter Cookies

you can make half with raisins and the other half just plain cookies; or make all of them into crisp cookies

Heat oven 375.°

You need 1 or 2 cookie sheets. (Teflon lined are nice.)

Into the large bowl of your electric mixer put *½ cup*

peanut butter, ½ cup "tub" margarine, 2 eggs, 1 teaspoon vanilla, 1½ cups flour, ½ teaspoon soda, ½ teaspoon baking powder, ¼ teaspoon salt, 1 tablespoon wheat germ, 2 tablespoons instant dry milk and *¾ cup dark brown sugar* packed down.

On highest speed mix 2 minutes. Divide into half. Pinch off pieces of this dough about the size of a walnut and make into balls. Arrange about 3 inches apart on the cookie sheets.

Cut a piece of Saran Wrap 6 inches by 4½ inches. Put on top of a ball. With the palm of your hand, flatten into a circle about 3 inches in diameter. Continue until all are done.

Place in 375° oven about 12 minutes.

With a spatula remove to a rack to cool. These will harden as they cool.

To the other half mix in *½ cup raisins.*

Make into balls, and do as you did with the others.

Bake in 375° oven about 12 minutes.

Remove to a rack to cool and become crisp.

These freeze well, but use a plastic container or a can to freeze, because they will break in plastic bags.

If you wish, use 2 cookie sheets to bake, one on the second shelf from the top of the oven and the other one on the second shelf from the bottom of the oven.

Some stoves get too hot on the bottom. If your stove gets too hot on the bottom, put 2 sheets foil on the cookie sheet. We have found on the contrary that the heat rises to the top, and so we do not have this problem.

Orangy, Nutty Carrot Cookies

they're mighty good

Heat oven 375°.

Grate 1 cup carrots and 2 tablespoons orange rind.

Into a large bowl put *1 stick margarine, ¾ cup sugar, 1 egg, 1 cup grated carrots, 2 cups flour, ½ teaspoon salt, 2 teaspoons baking powder, 2 tablespoons grated orange rind* and *1 teaspoon vanilla.*

Mix on highest speed of electric mixer or by hand 2 minutes.

Add *½ cup nuts* and *½ cup raisins.*

Drop by tablespoons onto a Teflon cookie sheet.

Bake in 375° oven 14 to 15 minutes.

21. FRUIT DRINKS AND PRESERVES

Homemade Drinks

Orange Milk Shakes

Mix together in a large plastic pitcher *1 can (6 ounces) frozen orange juice, ¾ cup instant dry milk, 3 cups water, 1 cup crushed or cracked ice,* or use a blender if you have one.

Most refreshing!

Banana Orange Milk Shake

use a rotary beater; or a blender is most welcome

Mix together *1 large or 2 small bananas* cut into small pieces, *1 can (6 ounces) frozen orange juice, ¾ cup instant dry milk, 3 cups water* and *1 cup crushed or cracked ice.*

Extra nutritious and most refreshing!

Homemade Lemonade for One

Mix together until sugar is dissolved *3 tablespoons lemon juice* and *1½ to 2 tablespoons sugar* and *¾ cup water.*

Chill thoroughly.

Another Homemade Lemonade

Stir *3 tablespoons sugar syrup* with *3 tablespoons lemon juice* and *¾ cup water.*

Chill.

Lemonade for Six

Mix together *1 cup plus 2 tablespoons lemon juice, 1 cup sugar syrup* and *3½ cups water.*

Chill.

Strawberry Flip

it's a most refreshing, nutritious drink, and if you put a scoop of ice cream in, it becomes a "Strawberry Float"

In your electric blender put *10 ice cubes, 1 can frozen (6 ounces) concentrated orange juice, 1 eight-ounce strawberry yogurt* (We like Dannon best.), *3 tablespoons instant dry nonfat milk, 2 ripe bananas* cut into pieces and *6 tablespoons sugar.*

Turn the blender on and off until it becomes liquid.

Put into a large bowl.

Stir in *2¾ cups ice water.*

You can drink at once or refrigerate or freeze.

If you wish, for a special occasion, like a children's party, drop a scoop of ice cream in. That makes it a real party!

Some people in a hurry use this as a breakfast drink, as it's waiting to be used in the refrigerator. It is nutritious! The orange juice has Vitamin C; the dried milk has protein and calcium; the bananas have potassium; the yogurt has nonfat milk, which also has protein and calcium; and, all in all, it has good taste. The sugar? The sugar hasn't anything going for it, just sweetening.

Pineapple, Banana Shake

a most refreshing, nutritious drink

Put into a blender *10 ice cubes, 1 can (6 ounces) frozen orange juice concentrate, 1 can (8¼ ounces) crushed, unsweetened pineapple, 3 tablespoons instant nonfat dry milk, ½ cup sugar, 1 cup Dannon's Plain Yogurt,* and *2 ripe bananas,* cut up.

Turn the blender on and off until it becomes liquid.

Put into a large bowl.

Stir in *2¼ cups ice water.*

You can keep in the refrigerator or freeze.

This is not only a delicious drink, but also nutritious. The pineapple gives us carbohydrate, potassium and Vitamin A; the orange juice gives us Vitamins C and A; the yogurt gives us some protein and calcium; and the bananas give us potassium and Vitamin A.

Apricot Flip

you'll "flip" over this, especially as apricots are a lovely tasting Vitamin A fruit

Put into the electric blender *10 ice cubes, 1 cup (8 ounces) Dannon's Apricot Yogurt, 2 bananas,* cut up, *3 tablespoons dry nonfat milk, ½ cup plus 1 tablespoon apricot preserves, 1¼ teaspoons lemon juice* and *2 tablespoons sugar.*
Turn blender on and off until it becomes liquid.
Put into a large bowl. Stir in *2¼ cups ice water.*
You can drink at once; or you can refrigerate or freeze.
What does this "do" for you besides give you good taste? The yogurt gives you protein and calcium; the apricots give you Vitamin A; the nonfat milk gives you some protein and calcium; and the lemon juice gives you some Vitamin C.
OK? Now you know.

A Peach Fruit Drink

from the juice you get when you make our "Fresh Peach Square" recipe

To *½ cup strained juice* when you prepare the peaches for "Peach Squares," add *6 tablespoons water.*
Put in refrigerator, as this makes a refreshing drink. It's a "Penny Pincher" idea, a bonus from making the "Peach Squares."
To *1 cup strained juice* add *¾ cup water.*
Refrigerate.

How To Freeze
Fresh Peaches

you will enjoy these peaches all winter long because they will taste like fresh peaches

We use 1½ cup freezer jars.
We peel our peaches, as we like to use peaches that have flavor but are definitely not soft, and we find the peaches are prettier when you peel them.
Since the peaches are not soft, we cut the peaches in quar-

ters, if we can, or some slices the size of halves and other pieces are smaller.

Since our juice is clear, our peaches, which are a beautiful yellow with hearts of red, look lovely in their jars.

And now for the recipe:

Put about ⅓ *juice* into the jar. One at a time so the peaches don't discolor, peel and cut and put immediately into the jar *enough peaches to come almost to the top of the jar,* adding *juice as needed* but leaving about 1 inch "head room" for the juice to expand when frozen. Be sure the juice covers the peaches completely. Tip: If the peaches aren't completely covered with the juice, they will darken on top and look ugly.

Tip: To keep the peaches covered with the juice and to keep them from "popping" out of the juice, we hold them down by criss crossing with 2 Q tips. The jar helps the Q tips hold the peaches down. This sounds crazy, but it really works!

When all the jars are filled with peaches and juice, we label and put in the freezer.

Our peaches are never soft or squashy even if they are frozen. For years I didn't freeze peaches, because they used to come out soft like frozen strawberries do.

This recipe sounds complicated, but it's really very easy.

Juice For Freezing

Fresh Peaches

a very good tasting juice

In a pot stir together *4 cups water, ¾ cup clear lemon juice* (We use the frozen lemon juice that we defrost.), and *1¼ cups sugar.*

Cook, stir until it boils. Cool quickly by placing in jars or other containers. We cool our juice in the refrigerator. Of course, you can cool it right in your kitchen. It just takes longer. If you do, put the containers in a large bowl of cold water, changing the water often so the juice cools quickly.

We freeze this juice with our peaches in 1½ cup glass, freezer jars. You can freeze as you wish.

Now see how we prepare the peaches.

Beautiful Clear Grape Jelly

it tastes better than any grape jelly I've ever eaten

We use the concord grapes.

Do not remove the grapes from the stems! To remove stems is unnecessary work!

Wash in plenty of water *enough grapes on their stems to fill, after mashing, 3/4 full an 8 1/2 quart large pot.* To mash, use your hands in rubber gloves (keeps hands from staining).

When mashed, put lid on, bring to a boil. Boil 5 minutes.

Put in a large strainer over a bowl. Do not mash; let it strain so you will have beautiful clear jelly.

To *4 cups grape juice* add *3 cups sugar* and *2 tablespoons strained lemon juice*. Bring to a boil. Turn heat to second high heat. Boil about 18 minutes. Take off heat. Test by putting a spoonful in refrigerator 3 minutes.

The grape jelly should be jelled; if not, cook at 2 minute intervals, take off heat and test. Our jelly usually jells when cooked 18 minutes.

Take off any scum and pour the jelly immediately into small, screw top jars.

Let stand, uncovered, until cold. Put the screw top lid on and store in the freezer; or cover with paraffin and store in a cool place.

Ruby Red Clear Crab Apple Jelly

the most beautiful clear jelly!

Wash in three changes of water enough small red crab apples (which most people don't use, as they are small) with their stems attached to make 20 cups of crab apples. Put into a large kettle (about 8 1/2 quart size). Add 8 cups water. Do not cover. Bring to a rolling boil. Boil until the apples are soft, about 10 minutes. Remove from heat.

Put into a large strainer over a bowl about 4 cups apples and juice at one time. Be very careful not to push any of the apples through the strainer; only the juice should strain by itself into the bowl. This is what makes a clear jelly, so be careful. (Save the apples, though, to make apple sauce, if you wish.)

Wash the cooking kettle. Put *4 cups strained apple juice*

into the kettle, *4 cups sugar* and *¼ cup strained lemon juice.* Bring to a boil on high heat. Turn heat to second. Cook 13 minutes. Take off heat. Start testing.

Put a spoonful of jelly in a deep saucer and place in the refrigerator one minute. Tilt the saucer to see if a skin forms and the jelly is thick and not runny. If this happens, it is done and doesn't need any more cooking. If runny, put the kettle back on the stove; and when it starts to boil, let cook one minute; take off heat and test again. If necessary, test at one minute intervals up to five minutes until done.

When done, put into a large ceramic bowl. Quickly remove any scum. Immediately spoon or dip the jelly into jars. (This jelly jells quickly.) Cool. When cold, screw lids on. We freeze ours. Or you can melt paraffin, and carefully pour it over the jelly in the jars to seal them. When the paraffin gets hard, screw the lids on.

Apricot Preserves

if you have an apricot tree, then this is the answer

Wash the apricots. Cut in halves; remove seeds. Cut each into quarters. Measure *5 level cups.*

In a large kettle put *1 cup water* and *3½ cups sugar.* Mix with a wooden spoon.

On high heat bring to a rolling boil.

Add the *apricots.* Stir. Bring back to a boil.

Turn heat to second heat and stir now and then.

Cook 10 minutes. Take off heat and test.

To test put a spoonful into a deep saucer in the refrigerator. Let stand a couple of minutes. Tilt the saucer.

If it is ready, you can see a skin formed on top. If not, put the kettle back on the heat and bring to a boil again. Cook one or two minutes more and test again.

Remove from heat. Carefully pour into a large bowl.

Quickly remove any scum on top with a spoon. Immediately pour into jelly glasses.

Leave uncovered until cold. Close with a screw top lid and freeze.

This is the best way for best taste.

If you do not wish to freeze, you can cover the hot jars of preserves with melted paraffin. Let get cold; then cover with the lid and store in a cool place. Unlike strawberries, apricots do not lose their color when stored this way.

Peach Marmalade

yummy! yummy! yummy!

This recipe is for peaches you freeze when peaches are in season and there's so much to do we prepare the peaches for the marmalade and freeze them. In the winter when a hot kitchen is welcome, we cook our peach marmalade. Here's how we do it. We use Yorkhaven, Redhaven, Halehaven or Sunhaven.

Cut *enough peaches* in half, remove seeds, peel and cut into ½ inch pieces *to make 6 level cups.* Put into a plastic bag and freeze.

When ready to cook defrost the peaches. It takes about an hour or more. You can also defrost overnight in the refrigerator.

Cook, stir and bring to a rolling boil in a large pot *¾ cup water, 3 cups sugar,* and *¼ cup strained lemon juice.*

Add the defrosted peaches. Bring back to a rolling boil. Turn to second highest heat.

Cook 20 minutes, stirring now and then, but at the last few minutes cooking and stirring so it doesn't burn.

Test by taking off heat (but leave the heat on) and put a spoonful of peach preserves into a deep saucer; then put into the refrigerator about 3 to 5 minutes. Tilt the saucer; if the juice forms a skin and is thick, the preserves are ready. If not, put back on the heat, bring back to a rolling boil. Cook, stir 2 minutes and test again. Repeat this, if necessary. Ours usually is cooked thick in 20 minutes.

When the preserves are cooked, immediately pour into a large bowl. Since this is a marmalade, spoon into the freezer jars immediately. Let get cold before putting in freezer.

If you do not want to store these in the freezer, melt paraffin and pour on top to cover well. Let get hard; then put the top on and store in a cool place.

These peaches retain their golden color and their wonderful "Peachy" taste.

Fresh Peach Marmalade

These peaches are not ones you have frozen. These are fresh peaches and you prepare them the same way.

You cook them the same; only you have to cook them longer.

Be sure toward the last ten minutes to stand by and stir, as they will burn easily. You have to cook these about 31 minutes, and you get less marmalade than when you freeze them.

But these also have a delectable flavor.

Peach Preserves

when peaches hang ripe on the tree, it's time to make our Peach Preserves . . . won't it taste heavenly as a dessert some early winter night on those "Quickie Mix" biscuits you make so well?

Wash, peel, cut into small cubes *enough peaches to make 4 heaping cups.* (Here's a tip—cut into halves, quarters, eighths, and then into small pieces.) (Another tip: the peaches with red rose hearts make the most beautiful preserves. Any of the "haven" varieties—Redhaven, Hale-haven, Cresthaven, Richhaven—are good for adding the rosy, red color.)

Put into a large—preferably heavy—kettle *1 cup water, 3 cups sugar* and *6 tablespoons lemon juice.* Bring to a rolling boil, stirring now and then with a wooden spoon. This forms a syrup.

Add the peaches. Bring back to a rolling boil.

Turn heat to No. 2 heat or medium high heat. Cook, stirring now and then about 23 minutes. Test. *Take off heat.* Put a spoonful in a deep saucer and refrigerate. In 3 minutes test whether it is cooked enough by tilting the saucer to see whether a skin has formed; if not, cook 1 minute longer and test again.

When cooked, remove the preserves to a large bowl. Don't burn yourself.

With a metal spoon, skim off any scum you can. (Tip: tear off little pieces of a paper towel and blot any of the scum remaining on top.) This works very well, and the preserves look beautiful without any scum on top.

Let get cold. When cold, spoon into screw top jars. (We use the small freezer jars, because we freeze our preserves when cold.) They keep their fragrance and their wonderful taste best this way. Of course, you can seal with paraffin and store in a cool place.

Luscious Nectarine Preserves

nothing but nothing tastes as flavorful as these . . . if you are lucky enough to have a nectarine tree . . . well, you are lucky indeed!

You need enough nectarines to make 5 level cups.

Wash, drain and cut each nectarine in half. (Do not peel.) Remove the seed, then cut the halves into 4 strips. Tip: Then use sharp scissors to cut the strips into about ½ inch pieces. (The scissors is wonderful, because you can cut the skin without "mangling" it like a knife does, and the skin adheres to the nectarine pulp.)

Cook, stir, bring to a rolling boil in a large pot *1 cup water, 3 cups sugar* and *¼ cup lemon juice.*

Add *the nectarine pieces.* Cook, stir now and then and bring back to a boil. Turn heat to second high heat. Cook, stir now and then 15 minutes. Test by taking off heat, but let the heat stay on, and put a spoonful in a deep saucer in the refrigerator 3 to 5 minutes. Check whether you can see a skin formed on top by tilting the saucer. If not, bring back to a boil. Boil 2 minutes, cook, stir, and test. When ready, pour carefully so as not to burn yourself, into a large bowl.

With a metal spoon remove any scum from the top. Let the preserves get cold.

When cold, spoon into freezer jars. Freeze.

If you do not freeze, cover with melted paraffin well. Let get cold, and when hardened, keep in a cool place.

Strawberry Preserves

as easy to make as it's delicious to eat

Use a heavy kettle or pot to cook.

Wash *1 heaping quart (4 full cups) firm, not over ripe, fresh strawberries* in a large bowl full of cold water, changing the water 3 times, lifting the berries out with your hands so as not to crush them. Remove the stems.

Bring *1 cup water* with *4 cups sugar* to a rolling boil, stirring now and then so it doesn't stick, until it becomes a syrup.

Add strawberries to the boiling syrup, bring back to a boil. Cook on second high heat, don't let boil over, stir now and then, but don't crush the berries. Don't let burn.

Boil 12 minutes, remove from heat, and test by dropping a spoonful of jelly in a saucer and putting it in the refrigerator. After about 2 minutes, tilt the saucer to see whether it has formed a skin. If not, put back on heat, cook another minute, and test as before, taking off the heat while you test.

Continue this process until you can see a skin. It will depend on the strawberries how long it will take. Usually it takes from 12 to 14 minutes; don't overcook.

Remove preserves to a large bowl. With a metal spoon, remove the scum by pushing it to the center and scooping it out.

Set aside until cold before ladling into small screw-top jars.

This is a strawberry *preserve,* not a jelly or jam. It has body, but it is runny; and each strawberry is beautifully whole in the juice.

The best place to store the preserve is in your freezer. The color, the beautiful aroma and the exquisite taste will keep, even for two years or more.

22. TURKEY GIBLETS AND LIVERS

I couldn't finish this book without giving you some recipes that I have found both delicious and terrifically penny pinching.

Noodle Soup With Cut Up Turkey Hearts Or Gizzards

Clean, remove fat and cut up *1½ pounds turkey hearts or gizzards.* Put in large kettle with *8 cups water, 1 stalk celery leaves or stalk celery, 1 large onion* cut in half and *1 carrot* cut into thirds. Bring to a boil. Remove scum. Add *½ teaspoon salt.*

Bring back to a boil. Turn to low; simmer about 1¼ hours if using hearts or 1¾ hours for gizzards until done.

Bring back to a boil and add about *2 to 4 ounces either fine or medium noodles.* Bring back to a boil; turn heat down so that the soup boils gently until noodles are done as you like them according to directions on package. Add *salt to taste.*

You can cook the noodles along with the hearts for a meal in a soup plate. If you are planning to do this, then chop the onions, celery and carrots. Otherwise, before you add the noodles, strain the vegetables and/or the hearts to have just a plain noodle soup. The hearts can be used to make different dishes, such as a Turkey Pâté, which recipe we will give you, or a Shepherd's Pie; or use as a filling for our Half Moon recipe.

Turkey Rice Soup

To make a rice soup drop as much rice as you like to make a thin or thick soup into the broth while it is cooking, about 20 minutes for white rice or about 30 or more minutes for brown rice.

Old Fashioned Deep Dish Turkey Pie

Preheat oven 450°.

You need *2 cups cooked turkey hearts* cut into ½ inch cubes, *2 cups turkey heart broth, 3 cups potatoes* cut into 1 × 1½ inch cubes, *1 carrot minced to make about ¾ cup, 1 cup onions,* cubed, and *3 tablespoons parsley minced.*

Bring to a boil with water to cover the potatoes, onions and carrots. Cook 10 minutes.

Bring the 2 cups turkey broth to a boil with *1 teaspoon salt.* Mix *2 tablespoons cornstarch* with *2 tablespoons water.* Stir into the broth until it clears. Mix this broth with the cooked vegetables, the parsley and 2 cups cooked hearts. Pour into a two-quart casserole.

Make a *crust of your choice.* Place on top. Brush with *milk.* Make a small hole in the center with a sharp knife; make slits around it. Put foil around edges.

Place in 450° oven; bake 15 minutes. Remove foil. Bake 10 more minutes until done.

Serve at once.

Everything can be made ahead and baked right before dinner. This also freezes well.

Shepherd's Pie

You need 2 cups cooked turkey gizzards cut into cubes and add *2 cups turkey broth.*

Preheat oven 450°.

Bring to a boil with *water to cover ½ cup fresh,. minced carrots, 1 cup onions,* cubed, and *½ teaspoon salt.* Cook 5 minutes. Strain; save the water.

Add *enough water to this water to make 2 cups* and bring to a boil. Add *1½ cups frozen peas, 1 cup frozen lima beans, 1½ cups frozen corn* and *1½ teaspoons salt.* Cook 3 minutes. Cool.

Bring *2 cups turkey broth,* fresh, canned or bouillon broth, to a boil. Mix together *3 tablespoons cornstarch* with *3 tablespoons water.* Stir into the boiling turkey broth. Bring back to a boil and boil until it clears.

Pour this over the vegetables and the cooked gizzards. Add *3 tablespoons fresh parsley,* minced, *salt* and *pepper* to taste.

Pour into a 2 quart casserole.

Cook *enough potatoes to make 6 cups.* Shake the cooked potatoes over heat to dry. Push through a ricer into a large bowl.

Stir in about *½ cup and 1 tablespoon margarine.* Heat *½ cup nonfat milk.* Add only enough to make a light, fluffy whipped potato. Add *salt* and *pepper* to taste. Spoon, without crushing, on top of the casserole. Sprinkle a little *paprika* on top.

Bake in 450° oven until topping is browned and the vegetables are hot.

This freezes very well.

Stuffed Half Moon

this is beautiful to look at and very good to eat

Preheat oven 375°.

You need *2 cups cooked turkey gizzards or hearts.*

Hard cook *1 egg.* Let get cold.

Slice *2 medium large onions, enough to make 2 cups.* (When the onions are cooked, you should have 1 cup cooked onions.)

Heat a skillet with *¼ cup oil* and add the onions. Cook, stir about 2 minutes. Do not brown; do not burn. Put lid on, turn heat to simmer and simmer until soft and clear, takes about ½ to ¾ hour. Strain the onions. Save any oil or juice left in the skillet. Let onions get cold.

Grind into a large bowl alternately the gizzards or hearts, the hard cooked egg and the onions. Add *½ teaspoon ground allspice, ¼ cup mayonnaise, ½ teaspoon onion powder, 3 tablespoons minced parsley* and *as much of the juice from the onion as necessary to make this mixture spreadable.* Add *salt* and *pepper* to taste.

Set aside while you make the "Rich Baking Powder Dough."

Put into a large bowl *2 cups flour, 3 teaspoons wheat germ, 1 tablespoon baking powder, ½ teaspoon salt* and *1 tablespoon sugar.* Mix together with a pastry blender.

Add *½ cup vegetable shortening.* Mix with the pastry blender into fine crumbs.

Put *1 egg* in a medium bowl. Mix the egg with a fork. Stir in *¼ cup plus 3 tablespoons nonfat milk.*

With a fork, then with your clean hands, stir until the flour mixture forms a ball and cleans the bowl.

Throw the ball hard from one hand to the other over a clean surface 20 times.

On a lightly floured surface roll out into a rectangle about 10 or 12 inches by 16 inches. Brush either with *melted margarine, soft margarine or butter.* Spoon the mixture on top. Roll up.

Place on a baking sheet, seam side down. Shape into a half moon. Cut slits on the outside on a slant and spread apart a little so that it bakes well.

Brush with *egg wash.* Bake in preheated 375° oven about 35 to 40 minutes.

Serve hot.

This goes very nicely with a hot plate of vegetable soup to make a delicious, nutritious meal.

In our market these giblets are sold for around 50¢ per pound . . . a true penny pincher! Just to give you an idea what other dishes you can make from this beautiful penny pincher protein, you can use these to make Shepherd's Pie, Chicken and Dumplings and soups, such as lentil, lima bean and barley, bean soup and chicken corn soup. You can also make individual turkey pies, turnovers, and, of course, everyone likes giblet gravy.

You can also make croquettes from the ground gizzards or hearts. We have made a salad from this, and how about substituting this for the hamburger in your lasagna?

The Delectable Pâté

the French make delectable pâté out of goose livers . . . turkey livers not only look beautiful but they can be made into equally as delicious dishes as the French pâté . . . because many of us are penny pinchers, we have made ours into an old fashioned, country style pâté using turkey livers and onions . . . turkey livers are much easier to prepare than chicken livers, and more inexpensive, too . . . (unless there will be a rush on them in the supermarkets)

Hard cook *2 eggs.* Put under cold running water, peel and cool.

Slice *1 large onion.* Heat a skillet with *3 tablespoons oil* on medium heat. Cook, stir the onions about 2 minutes. Put lid on. Turn heat to low. Let cook until soft and clear, takes about 20 to 25 minutes or more.

Strain the onions but leave the oil and the juice in the skillet.

Add a *little oil as necessary* and heat until hot on medium heat. Cut *½ pound turkey livers* into strips and put in the heated skillet. Fry the strips of turkey livers until no red shows, but do not brown or let get mealy. Remove to a plate to cool and save the juice in the skillet.

Put into a grinder alternately the livers, the onions and the eggs. Put through twice. Mix together in a bowl. Add *salt* to taste and a *pinch of allspice*. Add enough of the onion juice to make it light and spreadable.

Store in refrigerator.

You can serve this with melba toast; or you can serve it on a plate and eat it with dark rye bread; you can serve on a lettuce leaf with sliced tomatoes on the side with some lovely fresh rye bread; or you can make sandwiches of it between thin slices of bread. Either way, it's delicious!

Another way to serve these turkey livers is to saute onions and serve with the sauteed turkey livers, but be sure to cut the livers into strips because they taste better this way. The Italians serve sauteed chicken livers and onions and sometimes chicken livers and mushrooms over rice or over spaghetti, and certainly we can do the same with the turkey livers.

On this happy note, we end "Penny Pincher 3."

Drawings by Gail MacMillan Leavitt

INDEX

C

D

E

F

G

H

I

J

K

L

M

N

O

P

Q

R

S

T

V

W

Y

ABOUT THE AUTHOR

SOPHIE LEAVITT used to spend most of her time on her husband's horse farm in Pennsylvania. She raised three children and wrote a gourmet cookbook. Then, ten years ago, her life changed. A maid in Palm Beach, Florida, where Mrs. Leavitt had gone for some winter golf, mentioned that she had been living, unhappily, on food that the government gives to the needy. "The government food is so bad," the maid said, "that some people just throw it away." Mrs. Leavitt was aghast. As a taxpayer, she was helping to pay for the wasted food. As a cook, she could not believe that food could be so bad that hungry people would refuse to eat it. She tested the food herself and found it wholesome. She tried serving it to the poor as they picked up their own food supplies and was met with hostile reactions. Mrs. Leavitt kept experimenting. She traveled and gave cooking demonstrations. To enlarge her audience, she persuaded the U.S. Department of Agriculture to distribute recordings of her talks to radio stations. Finally, she compiled *The Penny Pincher's Cookbook*. Sophie Leavitt has appeared on the *Phil Donahue Show* numerous times and has been a guest on the *Today* show. She also writes a weekly food column for the *Chicago Sun-Times*.